ESSAYS ON NEPAL

The author as Second-in-Command of the Gurkha Boys Company at
the Training Depot Brigade of Gurkhas, Sungei Patani, Malaya, in 1966.

SAM COWAN

ESSAYS ON NEPAL
PAST AND PRESENT

Cover design by **Norbo Lama** shows *(in the background)* rice terracing in the village of Takam in Myagdi District on the trail from Beni to Dhorpatan and Dhaulagiri base camp; and *(clockwise from top left)* Maharaja Chandra Shum Shere Rana at Oxford University in 1908; a religious ceremony in Saldang village in northern Dolpo; threshing barley in Nyamdo village in northern Mustang; and Maoist combatants on the march. All photos by Sam Cowan except the one from Oxford (© British Library Board (430/67(60))) and of the Maoists (© Dhurba Basnet).

In the essays, all photographs by or from Sam Cowan unless otherwise indicated.

© Sam Cowan, 2018

First published, 2018

ISBN: 978 9937 597 51 7

Layout: Chiran Ghimire

Himal Books
Himal Kitab Pvt Ltd
521 Narayan Gopal Sadak, Lazimpat
Kathmandu – 2
GPO Box 4249, Kathmandu, Nepal
Tel: 4422794
info@himalbooks.com • www.himalbooks.com

Printed in Nepal

Price: NRs 990/-

To Anne, for everything

Contents

Preview of Contents

Introduction

After retiring from the army at the end of 2002, I could express my views publicly and this book, apart from the first chapter, is made up of articles published from 2006. My early articles concentrated on the Maoist conflict, and my professional reasons for doing so should be clear. The article 'Raid into Tibet', published in May 2014, began a new phase in my writing. It was the first of my articles to be published in *The Record*, an online magazine which was founded and launched in May 2014 by Gyanu Adhikari and Kate Saunders. I am hugely grateful to them: Gyanu for his constant support and encouragement, and, Kate, for her brilliant editing. It was also the first article I wrote which drew heavily on contemporaneous evidence from British Foreign Office files in the National Archives at Kew, in London, which helped me to correct important detail in previously published accounts of this raid. The availability of *The Record* as an outlet for my writing, and a determination to make greater use of material in the Foreign Office files in the British Library and National Archives, to help shed illuminating light on key events in Nepal's history, encouraged me to be more ambitious in my literary output.

The articles appear in the order in which they were published. They are wide-ranging but reflect some common themes, as this preview of contents highlights.

I am grateful to Deepak Thapa for suggesting that the articles should be brought together into a book and to Tracy Ghale who has done all the hard work to make it happen. I am also grateful to Himal Books for publishing the book. I have added an updating addendum to a number of the articles. Otherwise they all appear in their original form, with the exception of the report on a 2011 Dolpo trek which I have shortened considerably, but have added some new material on cross border transactions which I hope will be of interest to readers.

Finally, I am most grateful to Aditya Adhikari, a friend who is the author of the acclaimed, *The Bullet and the Ballot Box: The Story of Nepal's*

Maoist Revolution, for writing such a generous and insightful Foreword based on a close reading of all the articles. He has correctly exposed my underlying motivation for writing them and, in his last sentence, has paid me a fine compliment: 'Those seeking a more just and inclusive Nepal will find a firm ally in the author of these essays.'

Maoists

The Maoist conflict figures prominently in four of the articles. Taken together, they aim to explain how the Nepal Army, heavily armed by the US, and with the UK in support, was fought to a strategic standstill by what, in conventional military terms, was a very poorly organized and equipped armed force.

Nepal's Two Wars (Chapter 2, pp. 27-36) was published in *Himal Southasian* in March 2006 as the conflict was reaching a critical final stage. The Maoists had publicly indicated that they lacked the military means to achieve their original aim of military victory. Those in authority in Kathmandu, however, were still indicating a firm commitment to seek a solution by force of arms. This essay explains the directly opposite military strategies pursued by the two sides and concludes that, 'neither will be able to deliver a decisive strategic result that will end in the capitulation of the other.' By the end of April 2006, the conflict had effectively ended through a political agreement, and Nepal had started a journey towards momentous political and constitutional change. Given the continued transformations in Nepal's politics since 2006, I have added an important addendum to this article.

Inside the People's Liberation Army: A Military Perspective (Chapter 6, pp. 54-88) was published in the autumn of 2010 in the *European Bulletin of Himalayan Research*. The detailed analysis in it is based mainly on a study of six Maoist-produced videos which cover three significant military actions in the last year of the conflict. Two of these actions resulted in defeats for the Maoists, one with very high casualties; the third was a major success for them. Both Commanders-in-Chief were directly responsible for the two major defeats. The action on the videos provides a reasonable means for assessing the PLA's fighting effectiveness: its strengths and weaknesses; the state of its training; and the quality of its people, particularly at the crucial leadership level of company, battalion and brigade, which has seldom been publicly exposed. Translations of the video extracts used are given, as is advice on how to view the original clips.

Maobadi (Chapter 7, pp. 89-91) is a Foreword I wrote to accompany Kevin Bubriski's book of photographs taken in two of the cantonments in which the Maoist fighters resided after the conflict ended. The photos provoke many questions. What motivated these young people to commit themselves so totally to the Maoist cause? How much dying and suffering did they see and contribute to? Four years after the conflict ended, do they still think that all the death, suffering and destruction was worth it? During the conflict, both sides committed appalling human rights abuses but in this essay I argue that it is the State and its security forces that must set a higher standard of behaviour based on operating within the law. If they descend to lawlessness, people inevitably conclude that for them, there is no difference between the army and those who are opposing the State by violent means. In such a situation, all legal and moral anchor points break away and the inevitable result is the widespread abuse of human rights that was seen during the conflict and, sadly, in the state of impunity which still prevails in Nepal today.

Letter to the Editor (Chapter 3, pp. 37-40) was written for publication to the editor of the *Nepali Times* about the death in Nepal Army custody of 15-year old Maina Sunar. I took such a step having read in the secret official Nepal Army Court of Inquiry report that, 'in the process of questioning by torture, in not being able to withstand the torture, her death occurred', and that this torture was closely supervised by at least four officers. In my letter, I appealed to the army chief to call in the civil police for a full and open investigation into the killing of Maina, with a view to having the alleged perpetrators appropriately charged under the criminal law, and tried before the civilian courts. Just as importantly, I also appealed to the new government to immediately honour its international obligations and declare torture to be a criminal offence under the law of Nepal. Both appeals fell on deaf ears. I have added an important updating addendum to the originally published letter.

British Gurkha Recruitment

Next, I have included two short articles on the British recruitment of Gurkhas which pack in a lot of history on the subject and dispel some myths.

Ochterlony's Men (Chapter 4, pp. 41-46) is a review of John Pemble's book, *Britain's Gurkha War: The Invasion of Nepal, 1814-16*, published in *Himal Southasian* in May 2009. It gives details on the origin and conduct of the Anglo-Nepal War and describes how Gurkha recruitment began, but it also addresses the question of what is in this recruitment for Nepal today, now that Gurkhas become British citizens during their service and settle down in UK on retirement?

Colonial Dogma (Chapter 8, pp. 92-94) is an opinion editorial, published in *The Kathmandu Post* in May 2012. Gurkha recruitment began during the Anglo-Nepal War but, up until 1885, recruiting from Nepal had to be done clandestinely because the Kathmandu authorities actively opposed it. The article explains how all this changed in 1885 when the British forced a newly appointed Nepalese ruler to do the recruiting for them. This coincided with a greatly increased demand for more Gurkha recruits, stimulated by the influences of a perceived growing Russian threat to India and a novel new conviction that only newly designated 'martial races', suitably led, could oppose them.

The Northern Borderland

I have long taken a close interest in Nepal's northern border. After I retired from the army, I finally had time to trek in many areas adjacent to it. My aim was to trek in all the Tibetan speaking areas along the border, from Humla in the far northwest to Taplejung in the far northeast. The principal interest was to see what changes were impacting on the life of the people who live in these remote areas, particularly the major shifts taking place in trans Himalayan trade. Historically, my interest also extended to notable locations along the border and to some key events which had taken place there. These six articles range widely over all the above.

Crossing the Larkya La (Chapter 5, pp. 47-53) is a report of a journey round the Manaslu circuit, one of Nepal's great trekking trails. The Laryka la is an historic trading pass which has been traversed for centuries as a means of bringing salt to the middle hills of Nepal and grain to those who lived on the Tibetan plateau. Cross border movement continues today but in a form which hardly merits the description of 'trade'. The report also summarises the extraordinary story of the people of Samdo, the last village before the frontier, who moved with all their possessions to Nepal from their village in Tibet, just across the border in the 1960s. They built Samdo from scratch and, after a long fight, were granted Nepali citizenship, partly by being able to produce two engraved copper plates from the 14th century that showed that the kings of Jumla had given them, in perpetuity, grazing rights in the area.

To the Northern Borderland (Chapter 9, pp. 95-107) is a shorter version of a published account of a 25-day trek in Dolpo in the late summer of 2011. It introduces readers to the extraordinary land of Dolpo, and highlights new challenges being faced by the people who live there. These challenges stem mainly from a changed basis of trans Himalayan trade: no longer, as was traditional, salt-for-grain but cash-for-Chinese-goods. The cash comes from the sale of yarsagunba, the so-called 'Himalayan viagra', most of which in this area is sold at good prices direct to Chinese middlemen. The Chinese goods come from large temporary markets which are established in Tibet during a 10-day period in August, a little way across the frontier. Economic change is invariably the harbinger of social change and this is well illustrated by what is happening in Dolpo. The sudden influx of large amounts of cash into what until very recently had been a mainly agro-pastoral community is having a profound impact on the life, culture, economy and environment of Dolpo.

All Change at Rasuwa Gadhi (Chapter 10, pp. 108-127) is an article published in the autumn of 2013 in *Himalaya, the Journal of the Association for Nepal and Himalayan Studies*. It was inspired by the great changes I saw at the Rasuwa Gadhi frontier crossing point between 2006 and 2013, the year in which the Chinese had completed a road from Rasuwa Gadhi into the Nepal road network at Syabrubesi. They were also on the verge of completing a large road bridge at the crossing to connect Kathmandu to Kyirong, a major town in Tibet. The railway from Lhasa and Shigatse is planned to reach Kyirong in 2020. The article summarises some of the history of this historic crossing, and contrasts it with the equally historic Kodari/Friendship bridge crossing. Written nearly two years before the great earthquake of April 2015, the comments on the geology surrounding both crossings are still pertinent, as is the scepticism expressed about Nepal becoming the transit bridge of choice for trade between China and India.

Raid into Tibet (Chapter 11, pp. 128-135) tells the story of the filming by three British citizens of an ambush of Chinese army trucks in Tibet in 1964 by Khampa fighters, armed by the United States Central Intelligence Agency (CIA) but based in Nepal, and their subsequent departure from Nepal. The raid was carried out without approval from the CIA or the Khampa command structure. The event put a recently arrived British Ambassador in a difficult predicament, seriously discomfited King Mahendra, and caused major problems for Panchayat ministers and officials. A close study of two 1964 British Foreign Office files, containing contemporaneous information on details of the raid, and its aftermath, enabled me to correct some previous inaccurate accounts of what happened after the threesome returned to Kathmandu.

The Indian Checkposts, Lipu lekh and Kalapani (Chapter 16, pp. 224-261) examines the political and security contexts that led to the deployment in 1952 of Indian soldiers and police officers in checkposts to cover the approaches to most of the high passes between Nepal and Tibet. It includes detail on the checkposts given in the accounts of early foreign travelers who encountered them in various remote places. Also examined in detail are the origins of the vexed disputes between Nepal and India over Lipu Lekh and Kalapani in the high territory of Nepal's far northwest. Nepal claims that the pass at Lipu Lekh should be the tri junction between Nepal, India and China. India rejects this claim; its de facto control of the pass goes back well into the British period. Kalapani is an area of contested territory on the east side of the upper reaches of the Mahakali river which is occupied by India. The dispute over it is linked to Lipu Lekh, not least in determining where the border should be drawn. The article examines the evidence of when the Indians first occupied Kalapani; who in Kathmandu knew about it, and when, and, on the evidence, why they kept silent?

The Curious Case of the Mustang Incident (Chapter 17, pp. 262-298) examines the circumstances under which, on June 28, 1960, Chinese troops fired on an unarmed party of Nepalese in the area of the Kora La in northern Mustang, killing one, wounding one, and capturing others. The group had been sent to the area to investigate a reported large-scale border incursion of Chinese soldiers. The Chinese subsequently apologised for the incident but maintained that the shooting had taken place inside Chinese territory. An analysis of the inconsistencies in the Chinese explanation and a study of the topography of the area show clearly that the shooting took place on the Nepal side of the traditional border. The article also addresses the significant diplomatic aftermath of this incident, based on a study of the letters exchanged between the two prime ministers, BP Koirala and Chou En-lai, and 100-pages of information in a 1960 British Foreign Office file, based on the ambassador's personal conversations with BP Koirala and other political leaders and senior bureaucrats.

History of Nepal

Falling under this heading are two long articles covering visits to the United Kingdom by Maharaja Chandra Shum Shere Rana in 1908 and King Mahendra in 1960. Descriptions of these visits are used as a basis to provide an overview of the modern history of Nepal from its formation under the King of Gorkha, Prithvi Narayan Shah, to the present day. Both Chandra Shum Shere and Mahendra visited the University of Oxford during their stays: the maharaja received an honorary doctorate, and the monarch, who had hoped to receive one, was disappointed when told beforehand that he was not going to be offered one. Foreign Office files in the British Library and National Archives, and the Oxford University Archives and the Bodleian Library Records, were drawn on heavily to write both articles.

The Maharaja and the Monarch. Part 1: The Maharaja (Chapter 13, pp. 148-169) traces Chandra Shum Shere's invitation to visit UK to the friendship he obsequiously cultivated with the Viceroy, Lord Curzon, and to his role in supporting the British invasion of Tibet in 1904. Chandra strongly urged on Curzon the necessity of taking punitive action against Tibet despite Nepal being bound by treaty to come to Tibet's aid in the case of any foreign invasion. He was also the source of much false information about the activities of Russians in Lhasa – information which Curzon needed to persuade a reluctant British government to give the green light for the invasion. Various aspects of the UK visit are described, including an audience with King Edward VII and the day spent at Oxford, with his large supporting suite of Rana relations, for the award of the doctorate. The Bodleian Library in Oxford holds the Chandra Shum Shere Collection of over 6,000 paper and palm leaf Sanskrit manuscripts. The concluding section of the article describes its provenance which, like the degree, was connected to Curzon's friendship with Chandra and their joint enterprise of deceit over the Tibet invasion.

The Maharaja and the Monarch. Part 2: The Monarch (Chapter 14, pp. 170-207) gives numerous details from King Mahendra's visit to UK, but it also describes: the downfall of the Rana regime and the restoration of the Shah monarchy; King Mahendra's succession to the throne and the first democratic elections held in 1959 which resulted in BP Koirala becoming prime minister; and the coup which Mahendra launched in December 1960, ending the short-lived democratic government of BP Koirala. The political brief for the visit from the

Foreign Office stated that, 'There is little doubt that this Government represents Nepal's best hope for the future.' The article argues that, with the clarity of hindsight, one can see that Mahendra's action in December 1960 started the long process that led to the end of the Shah monarchy in Nepal. His inability to see that preservation of the lineage lay in accommodating the monarchy to a constitutional position, which, for all its inadequacies, was sketched out in the 1959 Constitution, set the monarchy on a precipitous path.

The circumstances leading to the end of the monarchy are described in detail. A major theme throughout the article is the role that the army has played in different periods of the history of Nepal, and particularly over the last ten years which has resulted in it becoming the ultimate arbiter in Nepali politics. The article concludes by asserting that it is not possible to build a properly functioning democracy on such a basis.

The Sino-Indian War of November 1962

Prisoners of War (Chapter 12, pp. 136-147) starts by quoting a claim in a British diplomatic file that soldiers from Indian Army Gorkha regiments, taken as prisoners during the one-month long Sino-Indian war of 1962, had been singled out for special interrogation aimed at turning them into Chinese agents on their return to Nepal. The article examines this claim within the wider context of the total number of Indian Army soldiers taken prisoner, when they were released, and how they were treated. There is general agreement that Gorkhas were separated from other Indian POWs at a very early stage. They were treated differently, perhaps better, and subjected to a distinct line of interrogation, aimed mainly at persuading them to abandon, as the Chinese saw it, fighting as mercenaries for India. The files reveal a growing fear in London, verging on paranoia, that brainwashed Gorkha ex-POWs would soon be returning to Nepal with subversive intent, and that this would lead to regime change and the ending of Gorkha recruitment into the British Army. The article considers whether some of these Gorkha POWs could have returned to places like Rolpa and Rukum and planted the seed corn for the later Maoist insurgency. The article has an important Postscript, based on a secret file released following a Freedom of Information request and, rereading it again, I believe I have not done full justice to its significance.

The Earthquake of April 2015

Who will Guard the Guards Themselves (Chapter 15, pp. 208-223) examines how state mechanisms in Kathmandu measured up to coping with the destruction caused by the earthquake on April 25, 2015, with a particular focus on how civil-military relations stood up to the test. An excellent article in ekantipur on May 1, 2015, stated that, 'The absence of a powerful central disaster response mechanism adversely impacted the coordination of rescue and relief operations . . . Led by a joint-secretary, a Disaster Management Department under the Home Ministry is mandated to respond to natural disasters at the central level. . . . The joint-secretary-led department has been unable to provide instructions to the Nepal Police, the Armed Police Force, and the Nepal Army due to issues of protocol.' A simple analysis shows that the protocol problem boiled down to who the army was prepared to take orders from. Attitudes to foreign assistance from leading personalities are examined, as is the case of the refusal to allow the British Chinooks to enter Nepal. An example is given of how civil-military relations worked extremely well at the local level.

Corruption in Nepal

Corruption in the World of Football and the Fall of Ganesh Thapa (Chapter 18, pp. 299-340) is a story about the ugly venality of powerful men of many nationalities, but the focus is on Nepal: on the weakness of parliamentary authority, on the failure of the Commission for the Investigation of Abuse of Authority to do its job, on match-fixing involving the national team, and, crucially, on the shameless arrogance of those who consider themselves to be above the law because of money and connections. Above all, this essay is about how corruption occurs in Nepal and is covered up or is simply ignored, not in the abstract, but by focusing on the emblematic case of Ganesh Thapa who was president of the All Nepal Football Association for 20 years before FIFA banned him for 10 years from all football related activities on multiple charges relating to corruption.

Freedom of Information

A Secret Nepal File and the Battle for Information (Chapter 19, pp. 341-362) describes a protracted struggle with the Foreign and Commonwealth Office (FCO) to get redacted information released from a 1963 Nepal file. The file's title is, 'Conversation with Inspector General of Police about Intelligence Requirements and Counter Surveillance', but the redacted information related to Khampa fighters based in Mustang, a remote area of northern Nepal, with the aim of challenging Chinese control in Tibet. They were armed and supported by the CIA, and the article gives details on who they were and how they came to be based in Nepal. An appeal to the UK Information Commissioner resulted in most of the redactions being removed. His published Decision Notice laid out his reasons and criticised the FCO for their handling of the case.

Foreword

Sam Cowan first encountered Nepalis in the mid-1960s when he served with British Army Gurkhas in Malaya and Borneo. He visited Nepal for the first time in 1966, when he went on a six-week trek. His engagement with the country deepened as he rose through the ranks in the British Army. At the time of his retirement in 2002, Cowan was a four-star general and Chief of Defense Logistics for the British armed forces, as well as Colonel Commandant of the Brigade of Gurkhas (the titular head of British Gurkhas). After his retirement Cowan continued to trek across the Himalayas and has maintained a sustained intellectual commitment to Nepal and its people. Readers of this book will discover that he has been a perceptive and deeply invested eyewitness to the country over the past half-century.

All the essays, apart from the first one, were written after Cowan retired from service in 2002. They reveal his profound concern with the nature of political and military power in Nepal – how it operates, who benefits from it and who suffers. The essays cover a wide range of themes. Yet each is grounded in a crucial historical fact – Nepal originated as a military state based on land revenue extraction from a subjugated population. As Cowan demonstrates, this legacy continues to hamper Nepal's development despite the democratic movements of the past century and the abolition of the monarchy.

Cowan explores his subject with tenacity, seeking out sources that seem almost inaccessible and burrowing into painstakingly minute details. (The final chapter in this volume provides an account of his year-and-a-half-long struggle to retrieve certain documents concerning the Khampa rebellion from the British Foreign Office files). As a result, this book offers not just fresh interpretations but also original contributions to Nepali history.

The accounts of his treks reveal more than just his fascination with the landscape. The reader will come across surprising nuggets of local history and illuminating reflections on life in the Himalayas. For instance, the essay titled Crossing the Larkya La taught me something entirely new about Samdo, a village in the upper reaches of Gorkha district, which I once travelled through. The village, Cowan tells us, was established by migrants from Tibet who moved to Nepal 'lock, stock and barrel' in the 1960s. They were granted Nepali citizenship partly because they possessed engraved plates, given to their ancestors by the 14th century kings of Jumla, which allowed them grazing rights in what is now Nepali territory. Another essay on Dolpo explores the transformations that have occurred in the region as a result of the availability of cheap consumer goods from China and the increasing importance of yarsagumba as a source of income for the locals.

The first half of this volume also deals with the Maoist war. These essays are quite simply the most incisive and illuminating pieces of writing available on the military dimension of the conflict. With his wealth of military experience and knowledge, Cowan was among the first to recognize the critical weaknesses of the Royal Nepal Army (RNA). His 2006 essay Nepal's Two Wars remains essential reading for anyone interested in the topic. Cowan argues that the RNA's sole focus on destroying the Maoist party organization was misguided and doomed to failure, especially as it made no corresponding efforts to win people's support and prevent the rebels from expanding their alliances.

The 2010 essay Inside the People's Liberation Army: A Military Perspective explores the organization, strategy and psychology of the Maoist army. The piece offers a detailed analysis of three battles fought in the latter years of the conflict. Before this essay was published, few writers on Nepali politics had any real conception of how Maoist leaders planned attacks with a view towards achieving concrete political outcomes or how they rethought their strategy following military setbacks. Cowan made a seminal contribution by demonstrating the interrelationship between military and political developments. Particularly notable is his account of the battle of Khara. We learn that the failure of the PLA's 2005 attack at Khara directly led to Baburam Bhattarai's rehabilitation, following which the Maoists sought an agreement with Nepal's mainstream political parties. Cowan thus sheds significant light on a crucial but obscure period of the history of the Maoist party.

In later chapters, Cowan delves deeper into Nepal's past, excavating documents from British Foreign Office files in the British Library in

London and National Archives in Kew. The events that he uncovers lie at the fringes of the main currents of Nepali history. He recounts how Khampa rebels based in Nepal ambushed Chinese army trucks in Tibet in 1964; how the Chinese carried out a military incursion into Nepal in 1960, leaving one Nepali policeman dead; and how they treated Indian Army Gorkha soldiers captured during the 1962 Sino-Indian war. Cowan provides an extended analysis of how India came to occupy Kalapani, and how Indian checkpoints were established at 18 locations along Nepal's northern border between 1952 and 1969. Two long essays describe Prime Minister Chandra Shamsher's visit to the UK in 1908 and King Mahendra's in 1960.

These chapters are bound to delight any reader interested in Nepal's modern history. Rather than treating these events as mere curiosities, Cowan uses them to illuminate the broader historical setting in which they occur. The account of Chandra Shamsher's visit to the UK reveals Nepal's position vis-a-vis the British Raj in the twentieth century. We see the extent to which Chandra ingratiated himself with the British to receive honors, including an honory Doctorate of Law from the University of Oxford, and security guarantees. Mahendra, on the other hand, failed to receive equivalent honors from the British and harbored some resentment towards the Ranas, though he recognised that he needed their support to accomplish his goals. Cowan also dissects the king's ambition to gain a dominant position in Nepali politics. The shadow of the 1960 coup, which Mahendra carried out soon after returning from the UK, looms large. Cowan draws parallels between the 1960 coup and King Gyanendra's coup of 2005 and discusses how they retarded Nepal's democratic development.

A number of essays describe events from the 1950s and early 1960s and collectively shed light on the politics and personalities from this period. The themes that Cowan has chosen are likely to excite Nepali nationalists obsessed with the country's sovereignty and relations with India and China. They will find much of interest in this book, though they might be disappointed to see some of their key assumptions being dismantled. For example, Nepali nationalists have in recent years sought to establish that autocratic monarchs were better than democratically elected leaders at promoting Nepal's national interest. Contrary to their claim, Cowan shows how judiciously the Nepali Congress leader B.P. Koirala responded to the shooting of a Nepali policeman by the Chinese army in 1960. Koirala took a firm position on Nepal's behalf while also avoiding antagonizing the Chinese government. In contrast, King Mahendra deliberately ignored India's occupation of Kalapani to gain Delhi's support for his rule.

Other essays in the volume revolve around contemporary events. Cowan examines the role of the military in national politics and the government's continued inability to bring it under civilian supremacy. A long piece on the All Nepal Football Association (ANFA) meticulously exposes the corruption of ANFA's longtime president Ganesh Thapa and his deep ties with powerful figures in international football and Nepal's political elite. Cowan voices the outrage that many Nepalis feel at the abuse of power by the state elite. Those seeking a more just and inclusive Nepal will find a firm ally in the author of these essays.

Aditya Adhikari

Tumlingtar to Rumjatar

An unpublished report of a 2001 trek in East Nepal

Introduction

Why I have chosen to open with this unpublished trek report

I first visited Nepal in 1966, spending 6 weeks trekking in the east and west of the country. During that period, I was second-in-command of the Gurkha Boys Company at the Training Depot Brigade of Gurkhas at Sungei Patani in north west Malaya. At the time, the strength of the Brigade of Gurkhas was over 14,000. There were over 1200 adult recruits in training who did a one-year course (see photos below of their passing out parade). In a separate part of the depot there were 300 boys, aged between 12 and 15, divided into wings of 100, doing a three-year course which was mostly educational but with a lot of physical activity and some elementary military training in the syllabus. On completion of the three years, they joined the adult recruits for one year of military training.

The author about to greet the Inspecting Officer, Major General Pat Patterson, at the passing out parade of the recruits in 1966, at the Training Depot, Brigade of Gurkhas, at Sungei Patani, in Malaya. The depot was located at what had been a Japanese air force base during the Second World War.

The march past begins.

The author in the lead, stepping out at 140 paces to the minute!

Prior to being posted to Boys Company, I had served for a short time at the Regimental Headquarters of Queen's Gurkha Signals in Seremban in Malaya, done the Jungle Warfare School course at Johor Bahru and completed an operational tour in Borneo. I had also done a six-week language course at Sungei Patani. Even before visiting Nepal, I spent many hours during off-duty periods talking informally to soldiers, and later to boys at the depot, about life in the hills. During my time in Borneo I once had an intensive six-day teach-in on the subject when, because of bad weather, I was isolated on a high mountain ridge on the Indonesian border with little food and not much shelter, and with just Lance Corporal Nar Bahadur Rai for company. We had plenty of time for wide discussions on life in the hills and, as this trek report will highlight, there is a lot to be learnt about the Rai people of east Nepal! (We had been roped in from a helicopter through the jungle canopy to check the place. The remaining party of ten soldiers was to follow but immediately the helicopter departed, we were left in heavy rain and thick cloud which did not lift for another five days.)

This first trek gave me the opportunity to see life in the hills for myself and to talk to people of all ages about their daily lives and concerns. I met many Gurkha pensioners but I also visited the homes of parents of some of the boys from Boys Company to give them a recent photo of their sons. These visits inevitably started with a mother shedding tears over the photo but quickly turned into the most hospitable of welcomes. This exposure to a different culture, language, religion and ways of life, broadened my outlook on life and changed me as a person in many ways. Above all, it gave me an abiding love and respect for the hill people of Nepal who face a daily struggle for existence, with little help from anyone, not least their government. It also filled me with a desire to help them in any way I could.

Circumstances did not allow me to return to Nepal until 1989 but I soon made up for lost time. This account is of my twelfth trek since 1989, most of them done with my wife, Anne. Later when I retired, with time to spare, we could take more time to visit, for example, the remote Tibetan speaking lands on the northern border, and later chapters describe two of those treks. However, when I was serving, and particularly in the later years when I was filling important senior appointments, time was at a premium. Necessarily, therefore, because of my ambition to make the maximum use of the limited time available, these treks were more akin to forced marches than leisurely strolls, as this report will highlight.

In 1989, Queen's Gurkha Signals invited me to be the Colonel of the Regiment which I was proud to accept. This appointment carried with it the responsibility of being a trustee of the Gurkha Welfare Trust (GWT) which was set up to help Gurkha veterans, their widows and their wider communities through the provision of financial, medical and community aid in Nepal. This support is delivered through twenty-two Area Welfare Centres (AWCs) spread across traditional Gurkha recruiting areas. Each centre is run by an Area Welfare Officer (AWO) who is a retired senior Gurkha officer. The treks during my service were primarily designed to visit different AWCs to check how they were being run, to meet pensioners in their villages and to appreciate how life was changing in the hills.

In 1994, I was appointed as Colonel Commandant of the Brigade of Gurkhas, an appointment which also carried the responsibility of being Chairman of the GWT. I held these twin appointments until early 2003. During this period, I occupied successively the appointments of Inspector General of Army Training, Quartermaster General and, for the last four years, Chief of Defence Logistics. These were demanding appointments but discharging my responsibilities as Chairman of the GWT, and keeping my sanity, required me to block off two weeks and a few days each year, well in advance, for visits to Nepal. The visits during my years as Colonel Commandant, also included audiences with the reigning monarch to deliver a yearly report on the Brigade of Gurkhas. I had six official audiences with King Birendra and two with King Gyanendra. Each visit also involved official calls on the Chief of Staff of the Nepal Army.

This opening article describing a trek we did in the eastern hills in 2001 has been selected to convey my abiding affection and admiration for the people of the hills, and my keen interest in their life and culture. It is also intended to introduce readers to that world, the Nepal I first fell in love with in 1966. More prosaically, since there are several articles about the Maoist conflict in the book, I thought it would be helpful to give readers a view on how life was in the hills during a period of intense Maoist activity. At a much deeper level, it is also intended to draw attention to Nepal's rich ethnic and language diversity which should be one of it crowning glories. It is claimed to be but, sadly, it is a different story in practice; and from this neglect flows many of the country's enduring problems. I dictated most of the report, at various times on the trek, into a small hand-held tape recorder, so, generally, what is written are my contemporaneous views and impressions.

From Tumlingtar to Rumjatar: A Trek Through the Land of the Kulung Rai
(6 to 16 October 2001)

Kathmandu: 6 October 2001
I am starting this record in the garden of our Defence Attache's house in Kathmandu. Anne and I arrived from UK late yesterday afternoon and we head to the airport shortly to get the midday flight from

Kathmandu to Tumlingtar in east Nepal to start the trek. We will meet there the man who is to be our friend, mentor and companion over the next 10 days. Honorary Lieutenant Mohan Kumar Gurung who works at the Headquarters of the Gurkha Welfare Scheme at Pokhara and is responsible for co-ordination and supervision of all the Scheme's AWOs and AWCs in East Nepal. Our daughter, Caroline, is with us for the first time on a trek. She made her own way to Kathmandu to join us, and her presence has added an extra sense of anticipation.

The Trek will take us across many ridges and a fair chunk of east Nepal. The inspiration for the route is a description of part of it given in Harka Gurung's ever-informative and engaging, 'Vignettes of Nepal'. I have a copy of the relevant chapter in my pocket and will be sharing his insights. The first outsiders to visit the area was an American party under the leadership of Oscar Huston which made the first reconnaissance of the south side of Everest in November 1950. That party also included the British mountaineer H W Tilman who gave his own inimitable version of the journey in his excellent read 'Nepal Himalaya'. Tilman was the first European to be given permission to tackle some of the Himalayan peaks from the Nepal side. He was a character who had a way with words. A major part of the route is also well described in 'Trekking in Nepal' by Stephen Bezruchka, and I have a copy of the relevant pages with me. They all agree that it is an interesting route but, for the first five days at least, the terrain is rugged. We will need all of ten days to complete it which is why we must try to do at least four to five hours walking today after we reach Tumlingtar. Our porters should have arrived there last night and their instructions were to leave just a few men at the airstrip to carry our personal kit, with the remainder pushing on to establish the first night's camp site. It is a glorious day so all we need for a good start is for the plane to be reasonably on time.

First Night: By the Arun River
All went to plan. It was a four hour walk from Tumlingtar, following a path beside the Arun, one of the great rivers of Nepal, to get to this camping place. The Arun rises in Tibet and enters Nepal with great force through a narrow gorge at Kimathangka. We are camped beside the river just outside the small village of Kartike Ghat. Tomorrow's walk takes us up the west side of the Arun for the first couple of hours before we cut across to move westwards along the Irkhuwa Khola, one of its main tributaries. It promises to be another hot day's work before we

finally start climbing into cooler territory. For me, the highlight today was meeting the AWO from Khandbari whose territory we walked through today. I last met Captain Krishna Bahadur Limbu 36 years ago when he was a boy in Boys Company of the Training Depot Brigade of Gurkhas at Sungei Patani. I was then the Company 2 1/C and, after much chat this evening, we agreed that it was the happiest time in our Army service. It is a warm, sultry evening as I finish dictating this piece inside the tent at a quarter past nine, late by our standards on trek but it has been a good start.

Day Two Lunch: Above the Irkhuwa Khola

I am dictating this piece, while waiting for lunch, in the sunshine high above the Irkhuwa Khola surrounded by terraced fields of rice, maize and corn which run down to the river far below. After a cup of tea, the whole party was clear of the campsite by 06.20. After two hours of climbing we left the Arun behind to walk high above the Irkhuwa Khola to finish up at our present point. In the past, East Nepal was the domain of the Kiranti people composed of Mongoloid tribes. The Kiranti land was sub-divided into the Rai area of Khombuwan to the west and Limbuan (Land of the Limbus) to the east with the Arun River as the boundary. Limbuan was known as Pallo Kirant (Far Kirant) with the area to the west between the Arun River and the Dudh Kasi known as Majh Kirant (middle Kirant), the old heart land of Rai Kirant where the archaic Kiranti words of Khuwa or Kosi for streams are preserved in the forms of suffixes for river names (as distinct from the Nepali 'Khola'). (From Harka Gurung)

There were some significant battles in this area during the unification of Nepal (or conquering, depending on one's point of view) by the King of Gorkha's Army. In August 1774, the Gorkha commanders and Kirant tribal leaders entered into an agreement by which the latter recognized the King of Gorkha as their overlord while retaining their right of self-government for their districts, including their right to hold the land as 'Kipat', meaning, to hold as community land as distinct from in individual ownership. Since the Gorkha occupation in the last quarter of the 18th century, the Kiranti land has been receiving immigrants from many quarters. These were mainly Sherpas from the North, Lepchas from the East and large numbers of high caste Brahmins and Chhetris, along with Magars and Gurungs, from the south and west. On our travels so far, we have come through the low-lying and most productive land, occupied mainly by Chhetris and Brahmins. The Rai villages lie ahead in the higher hills.

The route we are following is an historic route into the Khumbu, home of Everest and many of the Sherpa people. It was used by Limbu and Rai people to transport grain to Namche Bazaar. From there it was carried by yaks into Tibet across the glacier pass called the Nangpa La and traded for salt from salt lakes deep in Tibet. As we have found over the last 24 hrs, the route is far from obvious so a guide is helpful and, even with one, some questioning of locals is required. In places, it is like a village track through the paddy fields – narrow and slippery. In these few weeks, before the great festival of Dasain, we have seen quite a few porters on the route. Most of them are either going or coming to the road-head at Hille, about five days walk from where we are now, carrying rice and other provisions for sale at various points up to the Khumbu area.

Second Night: Dhobhane

It is half past nine which is late by our standards for going to bed but it has been a long day. We are camped at the small hamlet of Dhobhane by the banks of the Irkhuwa Khola. We walked for over nine hours but the most tiring aspect was the concentration needed as we were constantly walking on narrow trails through the terraced hillsides of small paddy fields. In the last couple of hours, we kept crossing and re-crossing the river on bamboo bridges to get here. These bridges are rebuilt every year after the monsoon rains, often at different points, which adds to the uncertainty of the route.

It took time to sort out the camp site and we had a long chat after supper with Mohan Saheb and Captain Gajendra Bahadur Dewan, the AWO from Bhojpur who took over from Krishna Bahadur Saheb last night after we crossed the Arun. He will be with us for the next day and a half. We start to climb tomorrow and the message from Gajendra Saheb is that for the first 2 hours the track is even worse than anything we experienced today and that it gets steep towards the end of the day.

Day Three Lunch: Phedi

Lunch is being prepared in hazy sunshine just below the Rai village of Phedi (1676m) at the meeting of the Irkhuwa Khola and Sanu Khola. It is my 60th birthday and I am feeling it! We set off at 0630 hrs and the first hour was tiring as we moved along the side of the Irkhuwa

Daughter Caroline crossing one of many bamboo bridges during the early part of this trek.

Khola through some low-lying jungle. It was hot, humid and difficult. After about an hour and half the valley opened and we had a pleasant one hour walk up to lower Phedi which is a small collection of houses around a couple of tea shops set up for the passing trekking trade. We rested for a cup of tea for 20 minutes watching porters arriving from the high forest carrying bark for paper-making. There was a small building beside us where the work was done and a lady showed us the impressive product.

The one-hour walk which followed to get here involved more crossings of the Irkhuwa Khola by bamboo bridges. Tilman describes the Irkhuwa Khola as 'a cheerful flashing stream.' There are clearly plenty of fish in the river as there were endless parties of fishermen along the river yesterday using the ubiquitous bamboo in different ways to catch their prey. We say farewell to the Irkhuwa at this point as our route now lies up through Phedi to Salpa Bhanjyang (saddle) which we should reach at some stage tomorrow. There has been much conjecture about how far up we will get tonight since water for cooking is scarce as we move higher.

Third Night: Jaubari
The campsite is at the small hamlet of Jaubari. We stopped at half past three which is early by our standards, not just because of fatigue but because of the assessment that it was going to be extremely difficult to

reach the next place with water before dark. We are camped beside a small lodge which offers basic facilities to trekkers. The climb up from Phedi was steep and took about three hours. Half way up we entered the clouds which is not much good for photography so I concentrated on getting photos of faces of interesting people who I met on the way, always engaging them with chat first before getting their permission. Among them was a fine old lady who was climbing the hill with a load and spinning what I thought was wool at the same time. It turned out that the fibre was from the giant Himalayan nettle. This is harvested after the monsoon before the plant flowers and the outer barks are twisted in bundles and boiled in a water and ash mixture. The washed fibres are rubbed with clay to separate them and then dried before being stretched and spun using a hand spindle. The lady took great pride in telling me that everything she was wearing she made herself from the fibres.

After we moved past the last house of Phedi we entered a steep forest before reaching an area of cleared land where there were lots of people working from their goths (temporary high dwellings for those who look after animals). During the summer months, the goths would be three or four days walk away in great kharkas (clearings in the forest) right up on the edge of the Himalaya. I am finishing this dictation at half past nine in my tent, and the prospect is for a five hour climb up to Salpa Bhanjyang before a descent to tomorrow evening's planned location at Tiu.

Day Four Lunch: Below Salpa Bhanjyang

We are in a clearing on the ridge just short of the small hamlet called Gaurassie. We must be at about 9,000 ft and it took 3 hours of effort to get here. We saw very few people on the trail but twice a year huge crowds head in this direction to attend the fairs at Salpa Pokhari. This is a small lake above the pass. Harka Gurung records that pilgrims come from far and near to bathe in it and *dhamis* (shamans) congregate to propitiate their occult patrons. When he passed this way, the pilgrim crowd was multi-ethnic with a lot of Rais, Chhetris and Brahmins. He describes what he saw at the fair as 'a meeting of Hinduistic Khasa and tribal Kirant cultures in the context of a common hill ecology. Just as the Rai's exhibited a veneer of Hinduism, the dhamis were drawn from different castes'. The various trek guides describe the fair as one of the great events in east Nepal and all stress the amount of singing, drinking and dancing that goes on.

We have now moved into the heart of tribal Rai territory. One of

Lady in homemade clothes spun from the fibre of the giant Himalayan nettle.

the first sayings I ever came across in Nepali was ' Jati Rai, uti kura' – as many Rais as there are, that is as many languages they speak. (Upwards of 15) Elaborating on this point, Stephen Bezruchka states that, 'Rai was originally an honorific term bestowed by the Gorkha conqueror, designating village headmen who acted as intermediaries between local people and the government. Today it stands for several ethnic groups who speak a variety of interrelated dialects which are often unintelligable from one watershed village to the next. Among the sub groups of the Rai are Bantawa, Chamling, Dumi, Khaling, Kulung, Mewahang, Thulung, Yakka and Yamphu'.

We are now moving into Kulung territory, though a couple of days ago when I asked one old man whether he was a Rai with the intention of asking subsequently what type of Rai he was, he replied emphatically, waving his khukri above his head, 'I am a Kiranti!' Rais tend to occupy the higher land which restricts them to such crops as corn, millet, barley, wheat and potatoes which they grow on the higher, drier and steeper hillsides. Dor Bahadur Bista in his short but monumental book, *People of Nepal*, states that, 'Rais are renowned for their bravery, fearlessness and straightforwardness. They are also said to be proud and easily offended, and therefore have the makings of good friends or serious enemies'. They are also extremely tough and hardworking. On the trail we have passed some Rai porters carrying very large loads: they had been on the trail from the road-head at Hille for twelve days and will arrive at their own village in another two days. They were being paid the equivalent of 70p a day.

This afternoon we have a two hour climb to Salpa Bhanjyang and a three hour plus walk down to our overnight stop at the village of Tiu. The clouds are getting ever thicker and we are looking forward to our dhal bhat supplement this morning: sardines in tomato sauce!

Fourth Night: Tiu
After lunch today we climbed steadily and reached the pass at Salpa in just under two hours where we said goodbye to the AWO Bhojpur, Hon Captain Gajendra Bahadur Dewan who had been such an excellent companion for the past two and a half days. There to greet us was the Assistant AWO Diktel, SSgt Thakur Singh Gurung who is to be our guide and companion for the next three days. I asked him if there are any Maoists around. He told me that he is constantly meeting them but not in the last couple of days.

We were in cloud up until just before we reached the pass at Salpa. It is part of a ridge which is the watershed of the Dudh Kosi and the Arun River. We descended quickly through a dense and well preserved forest before crossing over the Lidung Khola which brought us to the first clearing of a single house at Wakka. Forty-five minutes later we arrived at some terracing of millet at the small Sherpa village of Sanan. We followed the ridge round to Tiu, another Sherpa hamlet, a drop of about 3,000 ft from the pass at Salpa, where we are spending the night in a couple of small fields beside the main path. It has been another long day.

Day Five Lunch: Beside the Hongku
We set off at 0615 hrs this morning and had a reasonably level walk for a couple of hours along the ridge through the small Sherpa settlements of Sorung and Konkhu before we came to the large Kulung Rai village of Gudel. We were in shade most of the way until we arrived just above

the village where we rested for 20 minutes to study the compact layout of the village and admire the view across the Hongu Khola to the village of Bung. This brought us to one of the seminal points of the trek where, much rehearsed in the days previously, and to the great amusement of the porters, Caroline and I declaimed loudly the lines which Tilman composed when faced with the same sight:

> For dreadfulness naught can excel
> The prospect of Bung from Gudel;
> And words die away on the tongue
> When we look back at Gudel from Bung.

I know from my reading (C.W. McDougal's *The Kulunge Rai*) that this is the heart of Kulung Rai territory; centred in just thirteen villages scattered along twelve miles of the gorge of the Hongku Khola.

The Kulunge are one of the northernmost of Rai tribes and among the most isolated. They claim descent from one of two brothers (Chhemsi son of Khap) who first settled at Chheskam (a village 3 miles further up the Hongu). They are divided into sub-tribes which in turn are divided into branches consisting of clans – and there is plenty of rivalry. McDougal sums up their character as 'strongly individualistic and egalitarian, and no great respecters of arbitrary authority' Good for them!

On the trail this morning we met ex-Lance Corporal Bhim Bahadur Rai 2/7 GR. He is a service pensioner who acts as an interpreter for the AWO in these parts because many of the old Second World War pensioners speak very little Nepali: only their own Kulung Rai language. He told me that he was happy with his lot. Further along we gave first aid to a man from Gudel who had just given himself a bad gash in the leg with his kukri when cutting up some wood. He looked as tough and cheerful as they come, dressed in traditional hill dress. He assured us that the cut was nothing and was very grateful for our help.

Just before we reached Gudel we passed above another Kulung village called Chuchulung where just two weeks before a landslide had killed the wife of one of our welfare pensioners and sadly just two days ago the pensioner, aged 75, had committed suicide by hanging – a sad story.

We took our time descending through Gudel as the path was steep with a vigorous small stream criss-crossing it. After clearing the village we descended through rice and millet terracing and the last half-hour down to the Hungu Khola was very steep. We are having lunch beside the bridge and the noise of the river is booming in our ears. We can see that the afternoon walk through Bung and beyond is going to take plenty of effort.

'The prospect of Bung from Gudel.'

Fifth Night: Kiraule
Our journey here started with an extended climb through the large and very spread out village of Bung – like Gudel across the river, a Kulung Rai village. There was rice terracing on the lower slopes and

Girl of Gudel.

on the way through the village we met ex-Rifleman Saptarman Rai of 2/7 GR. He is a service pensioner and is not in good health. We gave him some medicine and discussed the possibility of him being carried (in a hill ambulance – a specially cut down porter's basket) the four-day walk to the Area Welfare Centre at Diktel to have him assessed by a doctor.

We also saw a Kami (an iron worker caste) hard at work in his small forge making sickles. He told me that he was one of just two Kami in the village: he lived in the lower part and the other lived at the top of the village. There was a high school in the village and the children were very friendly. When I asked, they told me proudly that they spoke the Kulung Rai language in their homes.

We got clear of the village eventually and could look back at Gudel through the haze on the other side of the valley. The impression was that Tilman's last two lines had even more force than the first two lines, as the full extent of the traverse was even more striking from the Bung side.

Above the village we climbed through extensive dry crops. We met a marvellous old grandmother who proudly told us that she had 15 grandchildren. She was aged 80 and was on her way up to her goth to look after her two bulls which are tethered there. There were various other women, most with babies on their backs, all heading in the same direction. We eventually reached the area of the goths; they were extensive and there was evidence of a lot of activity with the animals. As we climbed higher, we came across a man clearing some dried terracing with a pair of oxen. The field had just been harvested of potatoes and this work was in preparation for the planting of winter wheat. His two young daughters were clearing the land behind the oxen with short-shafted hoes which they worked two-handed using quick, sharp vertical and horizontal movements to clear about two or three inches of the top soil. It looked hard work.

It was starting to cloud-in as we arrived at Kiraunle. This is a Sherpa settlement in this mainly Kulung Rai territory. It started to rain as we arrived at the campsite and morale was not exactly at its highest after another long day. We took shelter in a small hut which the porters clearly wanted to use as a kitchen. Outside the hut, they quickly made up an overhead cover with sticks and a tarpaulin so that they could get on with the job of preparing some tea and the evening meal.

Day Six Lunch: Najing

First light this morning revealed that, for the early part at any rate, a clear day was in prospect. We started to walk at 0630 hrs and quickly found that Kiraunle was a very extensive and extended settlement. When Harka Gurung passed this way 30 years ago he formed the view that Kiraunle was originally a monastic settlement because the Sherpa people here still shaved their head and abstained from smoking. At the edge of the settlement we walked passed Boksom Gompa. When Stephen Bezruchka was here he recorded that it was once a beautiful monastery but was now in disrepair. He also says that the distinctive ring of Juniper trees surrounding it were introduced from Darjeeling. There is a lodge beside the monastery and the owner informed us that the monastery is now active again with a head lama who lived in a house a short distance away and that there were other monks attached to the Gompa. He couldn't find the key but we had a look in through the windows. It was good to hear that attempts were been made to revive the establishment. It is certainly now not in disrepair but I could not help but feel that its great days might have passed.

After three hours walking we reached the saddle of the ridge at Sipki La (shown on some maps as Surki) at 10,120 ft or 3085 metres. The last half hour was steep but the first part of the descent was even steeper. Eventually we came down to easier walking through the forest and after another hour we arrived at this lunch spot, shown in some maps as Najing Dingma at 8,500 ft. There are a few lodges here for the passing trekking trade. After a glorious five hours of sunshine the weather has clouded in again but we can clearly see what lies ahead this afternoon. We must descend to 6,200 ft to cross the Inukhu Khola. We are told that the bridge across it is in a bad state and that the climb on the other side is exposed.

Sixth Night: Sibuje

It took us nearly two hours to make the descent from Najing to the Inukhu Khola through the small settlement of Gai Kharka. The glaciers which sustain the raging waters of the Inukhu can only be about 10 kms away from this point. The gorge is particularly steep and the fast rushing river has carved the rock below the bridge into a long chute. The water was a brilliant blue/green and was passing through at a terrific rate. The bridge condition was not as bad as we had been led to believe but there were still too many suspect planks for total comfort.

We were told about an unfortunate incident involving a man from Kiraule. While taking two goats across the bridge, a couple of days ago to sell them in Namche bazaar, five days walk away, the goats fell through a faulty plank. In trying to rescue them he slipped through the same gap but managed to hang on until someone rescued him. Sad, not so much for the death of the goats whose end was only brought forward a couple of days, but for the loss of what would have been a significant amount of money for the man.

However, we will always remember this bridge for the testing two hours we faced after we crossed it. It was the steepest, most extended climb that I have done in all my years of trekking in this land. We were on our hands and knees on some sections. Bezruchka' s description of it as extremely steep and exposed is accurate. We had another hour of climbing after we had cleared the worst of it and arrived here at Sibuje very tired. The clouds were gathering and it was getting cold as we arrived in the village but we managed to talk our way into a large Sherpa house to drink tea and warm ourselves by a fire while the porters put up the tents outside. It has been a tough three days but the remaining three and a half should be a less taxing, all being well.

How are we going to get up that? Contemplating the climb out of the steep valley of the Inukhu khola.

Day Seven Lunch: Above Khari Khola

We left at 0630 hrs this morning and a two hour walk took us up to the pass, the Satu La at 10,410 ft (on some maps Pangkongma La). On the way we had a good view of Mera Peak and as we started to descend we had an outstanding view of another peak called Dudhkhunda. A reasonably gentle descent brought us to the small and very pretty Sherpa village of Pangum which is the upper limit of cultivation in the Khari Khola valley. Another half hour brought us to this lunch spot where we have some great views stretching down into the valley below.

The small Sherpa hamlet of Pangum.

After lunch we descend to the village of Kharikhola to join the main trail from the road-head at Jiri up to Lukla, Namche bazaar and Everest base camp. We then head west to cross the Dudh Kosi and will therefore have negotiated the land between it and the Arun River. Harka Gurung, a geologist, points out that the three great ridges which we have crossed during the last three days all extend directly south from Himalayan peaks and we can bear witness to his description of it as 'a wild country of steep slopes and dense forests' but it has left us with a host of vivid memories.

When we reach Khari Khola we will be greeted by Lt Prem Kumar Tamang, the AWO from Rumjatar who will accompany us for the remainder of the trek. We will therefore be saying goodbye to SSgt Thakur Singh Gurung, the Assistant AWO at the Diktel AWC, who has been such a good guide and companion over the last three days. He has some landslide hardship cases to investigate on his way back to Diktel and we wished him well.

Seventh Night: Nuntala (also known as Manidingma)

We started our journey down towards Khari Khola in great heart before torrential rain hit us. Khari Khola is a big, prosperous looking village with large imposing houses well spread out across the hillside. We crossed the impressive, modern bridge over the Dudh Kosi at about a quarter to three and, after a cup of tea at a tea house just the other side of the bridge, we started the ascent to Nuntala. It was taxing enough. Every house in the village was covered with painted Maoist slogans. With the sky darkening, morale got a great boost when Prem Saheb told us that he had arranged for us to have exclusive use of a lodge owned by an ex-servicemen, Bhim Raj Rai.

Day Eight Lunch: Ringmo

The night at Bhim Raj's house went extremely well. We all had hot showers and a very relaxed evening in the main dining room before returning to our rooms for an excellent night's sleep.

There was a two hour climb to reach the pass, Traksindho La (10,075 ft). Just below it we passed the impressive Traksindho monastery. Judging from its excellent state, and the number of monks walking around, it was clearly thriving. We leave the main Jiri-Namche bazaar trail at this point. Our journey this afternoon to Salleri, the district headquarters of the area, should be a relatively sedate one

Eighth Night: Salleri

As expected, we had a pleasant 4 hour walk this afternoon in the sunshine. We were in a forest for the first part of the journey and then into open country for the last two hours. This is the Solu, occupied by Sherpa people within the last 200 years and what a good job they have made of it. The relatively gentle slopes are extensively cultivated, with potatoes a specialty. The hillsides are dotted with large, impressive houses which stand in their own ground, and the general prosperity is greatly helped by the large number of people from this area who work abroad and transmit money back to their families. We passed the small airstrip at Phaplu which provides a vital air link into this area. It is used by tourists who want to walk a little way into the Khumbu area rather than fly directly into Lukla.

It was getting cloudy as we approached Salleri but there was a small reception committee led by the imposing figure of ex-Riflemen Dendu Sherpa (2/10 GR Pipes and Drums) and Lance Corporal Bishnu Bhaktor Rai (ex-Queen's Gurkha Signals) who had walked a day's march to see me. They were assisted by some ex-servicemen's children who were boarders at the local high school. The reception took place in front of a house in Salleri which is used by the GWT as a patrol base to serve servicemen and welfare pensioners who live in this area. It is open for 4 days every 3 months. It was also to serve as our residence for the night, porters and all! Bishnu Bhaktor is a Kaling Rai who lives in a high village about 6 hours walk up the hill from the bridge over the Dudh Kosi which we crossed yesterday afternoon. We had an interesting chat about some of the pressures of living in his remote village at present, mainly generated by visiting Maoists.

Hot showers were provided by an ex-Nepalese policeman who ran a shop across the street and once everyone had been suitably refreshed we made our way for drinks to Dendu's large and imposing house. He told us that he had two sons in the United States, one who worked in the hotel business and one in the airline business. He also has another large house in his home village on the route that we will be taking tomorrow in which his daughter lives. He seems to own plenty of land around here and his hospitality consisted of platefuls of boiled potatoes recently harvested from his fields. Large quantities of tomato ketchup and salt were also provided and we did full justice to his offerings. He is quite a character. He served only 7 years before being sent off with a medical pension because of contracting TB which so many Gurkha soldiers fell victim to during the early fifties in Malaya. He was recruited in Darjeeling in 1948 and told us that he was supremely happy going around Malaya with the pipes and drums, performing in such exotic places as Penang and Singapore, while his colleagues were fighting the communist terrorists in the jungle! We managed a small dhal bhat before retiring for another early night.

Day Nine Lunch: Above the Sulu River
We set off at 0610 hrs this morning – our earliest departure yet, no doubt hastened by a combination of a fitful night's sleep caused by a barking dog, the amount of noise in the house, once the first person had stirred, and the pressure on the single loo from its 20 residents! It took about 40 minutes of walking before we finally got out of Salleri. It was a cold,

clear morning which promised the best day's weather yet. The head of the valley down which we walked is dominated by Dudhkhunda Himal and it provided a brilliant backdrop in the early light. This is a beautiful valley and the walk this morning enabled us to appreciate it to the full.

After crossing the bridge, we faced a stiff hour's walk to our present location. I think there is probably another 2 hours climbing this afternoon before we reach the main ridge above us. After that it should be reasonably level until we start to descend towards Rumjatar at some stage tomorrow morning. Anne and I last walked this way in the opposite direction about 6 years ago. We were in the clouds most of the way and hardly saw a thing but the weather has come right for us this time. With luck, we might even be able to appreciate a Himalayan sunset.

A word about our party which, for various reasons, is large. We have eight porters and Mohan Saheb has two. The number one porter is Kumar who is with us for the fourth time and has been doing his usual brilliant job. Most significantly, we also have four members of the army's special forces, including a Lieutenant, who are with us as close protection. They are here as at the strong insistence of the Chief of Army Staff. With very great reluctance, I accepted this imposed condition in the interests of preserving peace and harmony. Over the previous years of the Maoist insurgency we have done numerous treks visiting AWCs in the hills and have seen how AWOs go about their work without hindrance. Besides, a truce is presently being observed. The soldiers also have a couple of porters to carry their tentage which helps to swell the numbers. The team have fitted in reasonably well but their presence makes our party too large and conspicuous for comfort. Despite being dressed as trekkers, plenty of people on the trail have clearly recognized them as soldiers. For a start, you don't see a lot of people wearing earpieces in these parts!

This is not the place to give a full account of the Maoist insurgency which has so dominated Nepalese political and other life during the last 6 years. It started in a small way in the midwest region in 1996 when a splinter group of a breakaway group of the main communist party decided to resort to armed force to advance their aims. A combination of playing on genuine grievances and ineffective government action has led to a rapid expansion of Maoist influence across large swathes of Nepal. In recent years, it has been impossible to plan any trek without going into areas which, to put it mildly, are partly under their influence. This also means that our AWOs and their staff, must operate in these areas, Maoists notwithstanding. Apart from 'asking' for donations, (receipts always given!) the Maoists have generally left tourists alone, and indeed the slogans I have seen on this trek on various walls and villages proclaim that they welcome them. The attacks against the police have been so successful that apart from the district capital in Salleri, there is not a single policemen in any of the areas which we have walked through, and this state of affairs extends to most of the hill areas of Nepal. This has given the Maoists a free run and they have exploited this opportunity to the full. Up to now the Maoists have not targeted the army and, for complex reasons, the government has not committed the army to support the police against the Maoists.

It has therefore been particularly useful and informative to have with me the four AWOs from the areas we have been trekking through. In walking their territory to investigate hardship cases they often meet Maoist bands in full uniform and with arms. The Maoists have not interfered with the working of the GWT and at local level have professed that we are on the same side in helping the poor and disadvantaged. They also recognise the integrity of our work as one of their main areas of attack is the corruption which dominates both government and non-government activities across the country.

So far on this trek we have not met any Maoists, though we have become increasingly aware of extensive army deployments in the area which seem to be governed by our movements. Indeed, the thought has crossed my mind that, allied to concerns he might have about our safety, the army chief might be equally determined that we would not meet, or even see, a Maoist!

It has been encouraging to find evidence that the people themselves are now starting to resent the extortion and intimidation which is such an intrinsic part of the activity. It is not just the extortion of money but the insistence that the Maoist armed bands should be fed and housed as they roam around the country that is so resented.

There is a great opportunity here for the government. A programme of reform has been promised by the new Prime Minister, Mr Deuba, but he and his government must translate plans into action. It is worth stressing again that the Maoists exploit real grievances, most notably people's resentment at the blatant corruption which goes on at every level of public life in Nepal, and the fact that large numbers of them feel that the government is doing next to nothing for them. Five weeks ago, the Maoists unilaterally declared a truce and talks are currently taking place with the government. How these will turn out is anyone's guess but, frankly, the country is on a knife edge and some mighty effective action is going to be required to steer the country forward to a better future. I have dictated this passage surrounded by some of the most magnificent hill country in Nepal where the people are working from dawn to dusk to eke out a living in this harsh land. They deserve all the support they can get.

Ninth Night: On the Okhaldhunga Ridge

We had another sharp hour two hour climb after lunch to get on to the main part of the ridge which leads to Okhaldhunga and the following two hours also involved a steady climb to the present point. This makes the ground gained during this trek at over 29,000 ft and by the time we get down to Rumjatar tomorrow we will have descended some 22,000 ft. There have been some long days so little wonder that we are starting to feel tired. We did not get as far as we had hoped today but at least we are in a perfect position to get a good view of the Himalaya early tomorrow morning if conditions permit. The signs are good. The highest point around here is about 300 metres away and from there we could just see the tip of Everest through the clouds. It is a clear and very cold night and the Milky Way is at its most brilliant.

We have a tight programme tomorrow morning. It should take about 5 hrs to get to Rumjatar and there is a lot of sorting out to do at the AWC before we can catch the helicopter back to Kathmandu in the early afternoon. Tea has been ordered for 0500 hours in the hope that we can take full advantage of the sunrise and still be on the road before 0630. In the meantime, on this cold night we are at that stage of trying to decide just how much clothing to keep on before we get into the sleeping bag. The text books say that we should take everything off and let the sleeping bag cope but our technique is to slip into the bag with everything on and remove as required as the night progresses.

Day Ten: The walk to the finish at Rumjatar and meeting the Maoists

What was to prove an eventual last six hours started with tea at 0500 hours. It was a clear morning and from a small knoll near our campsite we had a great view of the Himalaya. Everest is a notoriously difficult peak to see because of the way it is set back from the main Himalayan range but we had a particularly good view from where we were standing and confirmation came when the sun illuminated its great black mass before all the others. Dudhkhunda Himal was straight in front of us and by 0610 everybody in the party had assembled at the viewpoint for the group photograph. By 0620 we were on our way but, for the next thirty minutes, as we descended slightly, the views of the Himalaya become more and more striking. Seeing them so clearly on our last morning was a great morale booster.

We moved along the ridge through the very small bazaars of Thare and Torke with views on either side across the great ridges of East Nepal. We also passed some Gurung shepherds with a large flock of sheep which they were taking down to the lower winter pastures. Mohan Saheb originally came from Rumjatar. His father was a shepherd and earlier in the trek he told us about how as a small boy he used to accompany him on the great annual circuit: from the summer pastures on the very edge of the Himalayan glaciers to the winter pastures far to the south.

Just before we started to make the sharp descent to Rumjatar at Ratale we brought some apples from a couple of local ladies who had set up a small stall on a Chautara (a resting place for porters and their loads). After about thirty minutes we stopped at another chautara to enjoy the apples and to drink some tea from a flask. We were relaxing in the sunshine and could see right across to the highest ridge that we crossed at Salpa Bhanjyang seven days previously. We were congratulating each other on our endurance and staying power but the mood changed when it gradually dawned on us that an armed Maoist group was heading slowly up the hill in our direction on the path which we were just about to take. Frankly, with a ceasefire operating, and our GWT Identify cards in our pockets, the only real concern at this point was that we had never satisfactorily resolved with the soldiers how precisely we were going to play just such an encounter. We decided to wait at the chautara with Anne, Caroline and myself put firmly to its furthest edge. The soldiers switched off their concealed radios, took out their earpieces and it was decided to leave this one to the man of the trek· Mohan Saheb!

The Maoists were out of sight to us as they moved up the hill and after a few minutes the first of them appeared in front of us moving slowly, silently and very deliberately. Two armed women in full combat kit moved about 20 yards ahead of the main group. There were 16 of them in all, including a very tall man, by Nepal standards, who was wearing full combat clothing, and carrying a pistol in a large brown leather holster. The leader was a small middle-aged man, wearing an ordinary pair of trousers and a rolled-up shirt. There were a couple of other shotguns being carried, and at the rear of the group were three women carrying .303 rifles held over their right shoulders with the barrels pointing horizontally back. These women were identically dressed in the same cotton pattern material in trousers and a long three-quarter-length coverall.

I think their initial inclination was to keep on moving up the hill. However, as they drew level, I heard the leader say, 'Ek chin, hernu paryo' (Just a moment, let's have a look). He came up the steps of the Chautara, and, after eyeing us up, looked straight at Mohan Saheb and said, 'they are not Americans, are they?' Mohan Saheb, rather too enthusiastically I thought, quickly assured him that we were British. He then had to answer a series of quick questions from the Maoist leader. Where have you come from? Where are you going to? What trekking agency do you belong to? What is its address? Are you flying from Rumjatar today? Have you already checked your flights? Where are you yourself from?

Mohan Saheb performed brilliantly. If we had been on our own, he would have told them that we were part of the Gurkha Welfare Scheme and had the identity cards to prove it. However, because of the presence of the soldiers, he decided rightly to play the trekking agency card and spontaneously created an agency called Snowland Travel with its address in Thamel in Kathmandu. The Maoist leader was clearly suspicious: things did not look quite right with these four strong young men with very large packs sitting amongst us when he would already have passed our porter party who had gone ahead. Just as one of the Maoists was starting to show an interest in the large pack of one of the soldiers, the leader indicated that he had no more questions, and we all rose as one to make our way down the hill. Round the next bend, I saw the officer in charge quickly set up an antenna to make a radio call, I suspect to inform his boss that, contrary to the plan, we had indeed met some Maoists.

Mohan Saheb later told me that he had just about run out of lies, and if the Maoist leader had asked him one more question he was going to tell him the truth. I am glad that we did not get to that complication. The critical moment was when the Maoist started to show an interest in what was in the soldier's pack. I knew that at the top of each was an Israeli Uzi submachine gun, and the soldier, rightly, would have used whatever force was necessary to stop any Maoist getting their hands on it. A potentially nasty incident was averted by the quick thinking of the soldier who, as soon he heard the word that we could go, immediately snatched his pack away from the prying hands of the Maoist, put it on his back and got on the move.

The Maoist group could have been on their way to some meeting to be held in a village that day. For the purposes of such meetings, the whole village is corralled and forced to listen to a series of speeches from the group members for some hours. On such occasions, there is also extended singing of Maoist songs. They could also have been on their way to extort money from an individual; in such cases, there is always a set pattern of a letter which sets out the actual amount to be paid, followed by one call to give a warning that by a specific date the amount must be paid or else.

It took us two hours to reach the beautiful village of Rumjatar, situated on a small plateau between the large ridge of Okhaldhunga to the West and another smaller ridge to the East. It was looking at its best in glorious sunshine as we walked between the orange orchards though, sadly for us this time, the fruit was four weeks off being ripe. This is a strong eastern Gurung community with a lot of ex-servicemen. We were given a very warm greeting by the local school children and the ex-servicemen. After a light lunch we moved to the small airstrip, said our goodbyes and within 40 minutes we were back in Kathmandu, in another world, having, as ever, learnt a lot and been given plenty to think about.

Finally, those who return to walk the trails of Nepal inevitably keep being asked the same question: why do we keep doing it? For me, Toru Nakano, a Japanese climber who was killed in the Karakorum in 1985, caught the mood in the afterword to his beautifully illustrated book, *Trekking in Nepal*:

> Nepal lures the trekker with its mysterious charm. While trekking I encountered many obstacles due to language and customs; indeed, my tranquil days could be counted on the fingers of one hand; I experienced a continuous series of problems and happenings. But now when I look back after being away for 6 months, I find myself longing for the scenery of Nepal. In my mind, I find myself planning 'to cross x pass' and 'to enter y valley'. I forget my troubles in Nepal and only remember it as a land of mystery.

Afternote

On the night of 23 November 2001, just four weeks after the completion of this trek, a large Maoist force unilaterally broke the truce by attacking the army barracks and arms depot in Ghorahi, in south west Nepal, killing fourteen soldiers and seven policemen, and seizing a huge number of arms and a lot of ammunition and explosives. Two nights later, they attacked Salleri and the control tower of Phaplu airport, killing thirty-four people, including eleven soldiers, and looting a lot of cash and gold from banks. The following day, on the 26 November, the government declared a State of Emergency across the country and deployed the army in the fight against the Maoists. The conflict effectively ended in April 2006 in ways and with consequences which will be described in some of the articles in this book.

Nepal's Two Wars

How the Maoist conflict ended in strategic stalemate

What is war? This short, profound question is posed by Clausewitz, the 19th century Prussian military philosopher, at the start of his monumental book, *On War*. Later, he concludes a brief analysis of warfare through the ages by saying that all warring parties 'conducted war in their own particular way, using different methods and pursuing different aims'.

Despite this conclusion, Clausewitz's great work is to some extent time-bound due to his obvious belief that Napoleon and revolutionary France had succeeded in bringing warfare to its ultimate level; they had 'liberated war, due to the people's new share in these great affairs of state'. Bringing in 'the people' was novel for his day, and prescient about the conditions of modern conflict. But the quote indicates his unquestioning acceptance of the prevailing concept of his day: that war is the exclusive province of states; that only the state has the legitimate right to use force; and that warfare consists of the uniformed soldiers of states clashing on a battlefield to determine whose interests should prevail. For Clausewitz, 'everything is governed by a supreme law, a decision by force of arms.'

Even in Europe, however, this concept only made sense as an explanation of war after the Treaty of Westphalia in 1648, which concluded the chaos of the Thirty Years' War. It is a concept that makes even less sense now. Today the armed forces of states are being challenged, in many cases successfully, by the fighters of non-state forces, who are bound by none of the norms of conventional war and who operate in a way that neutralises a large percentage of the expensive and sophisticated equipment and armaments of state forces. This may not be the 'people's war', as Nepal's Maoists designate their struggle, but it is certainly war about the people, amongst them, and against them. There is no specific battlefield; military engagements can take place anywhere. This new style of warfare also starkly reveals the limitation of military force to achieve desired political outcomes, even for the most powerful of states.

All of this is well exemplified by what is happening in Nepal. The Royal Nepal Army (RNA) and the Maoists' self-styled People's Liberation Army (PLA) are fighting two very different wars, where even such basic concepts as combat success and failure are at variance, as are their respective estimates of what constitutes military strength and weakness.

The RNA's war

The RNA is fighting a conventional war of attrition, in which the emphasis is on the control of key territory, and the engagement of the enemy to inflict casualties, thereby weakening his will to resist. Clausewitz would recognise the approach. For him, 'wearing down the enemy means using the duration of the war to bring about a gradual exhaustion of his physical and moral resistance' – an idea that well describes the RNA's current intent, though it is publicly expressed differently. In a February interview, King Gyanendra explained his views on the possibilities of winning the current war. 'It's not a question of winning or not winning,' the king said. 'It's a question of taming.' The government studiously ignored a recent four-month Maoist unilateral ceasefire; this, coupled with recent official statements that there will be no talks until the Maoists disarm, indicates that the government is firmly committed to seeking a solution by arms.

So can the RNA achieve this mission? Can it 'tame' the Maoists? More conventionally, can the RNA wear down insurgents to the point that their morale collapses, they hand over their weapons and abandon all military efforts to achieve their stated objectives? All recent counterinsurgency experience indicates that the way they are going about the task makes it almost certain that they cannot do so. Military textbooks state that the key to success is gaining the support of the people, and the way to do this is to treat the people with respect, give them security, and integrate military efforts with development projects, social programmes and reforms aimed at tackling the underlying sources of discontent.

Such an approach is rooted in the strategy recommended by Sun Tsu, who 2500 years ago drew on an existing corpus of Chinese war experience to write what is generally regarded as the other great book on war, *The Art of War*. 'What is of supreme importance in war is to attack the enemy's strategy,' he wrote, 'next best is to attack his alliances; next best is to attack his army.' In other words, if the enemy's strategy is to gain control over the people, denial of this must be the main thrust of any response. But the RNA's task in this battle for hearts and minds is the more difficult one, because ultimately the Maoists do not need the support of the people to stop effective governance in rural areas. All they need is for the people not actively to support the state. It is the state that needs the people's support, and numerous intelligence failures, manifest in the number of times the RNA has been surprised by large-scale Maoist attacks, indicate a deficiency in this key area.

There are various factors that contribute to this. For example, apart from the moral and legal imperatives, there is a human rights link to military effectiveness. The most committed Maoists – those seething with resentment against the state – can invariably relate stories of family members killed in cold blood by the army and police. Intimidation from the Maoists is also a factor, as is the RNA's inability to provide continuous security to villagers. Here the RNA is faced with the oldest tactical dilemma of all: how much effort should be applied to hitting the enemy, and how much to stopping him from landing his blows? Doubling in just the past five years, RNA strength is now nearing 100,000, but a very large proportion of this number is devoted to protecting major towns, the 75 far-flung district headquarters and other vital static locations, particularly the Kathmandu Valley. Even an additional doubling of troops to 200,000, as has been discussed, would not enable the army to provide a permanent presence across countryside that is ideal for guerrilla warfare, and such wide deployment would open up another range of targets for Maoist attacks. The recent rapid expansion in RNA strength also inevitably leaves a leadership vacuum at senior levels. The significant issue of how this huge expansion is being funded, as well as its impact on other parts of the Nepali economy, both merit separate study.

The RNA reaction to this challenge is to ignore the Maoist strategy, as well as much of what is found in military textbooks. Their concept of operations is based on the third-best of Sun Tsu's options. All effort is focused on attacking the PLA – including those perceived as giving them succour and support – to inflict the maximum number of casualties and thus wear them down until their morale collapses. But there is limited operational capacity to pursue this objective, and absolutely no guarantee that a greater capacity would greatly increase the chances of success. Periodic 'sweeps' do take place in areas designated as Maoist heartlands, with predictable results – the Maoists who appear to fade away, return when the soldiers leave a couple of weeks later. Undercover operations are also clearly being carried out by Special Forces and related units, with results manifest from time to time by the killing of alleged Maoists in isolated locations, usually publicly designated as 'encounters'. Many of these incidents have given rise to allegations of human rights abuse, which are invariably denied. The main RNA offensive capability – greatly feared by the Maoists when they concentrate in a particular area for any purpose – is the use of helicopters, from which mounted machine guns are fired or 81mm mortar bombs are thrown out, two techniques that have given rise to many civilian casualties.

To date, the RNA military effort has led to the death of many thousands of Maoists, as well as many more civilians. Whatever the numbers, there is little evidence of any collapse of Maoist motivation. To understand why it is holding up so well, it is necessary to examine what morale is and what contributes to it, both in general and in specific relation to the Maoists.

Maoist morale

British military doctrine usefully defines 'fighting power' or 'military effectiveness' as having two components. One is the physical component – the means to fight, consisting of manpower, equipment and logistics. The other is the moral component, the ability to get people to fight, and this is fundamentally about leadership and motivation. This neatly reflects Clausewitz's description of war as both a trial of strength and a clash of wills, 'two factors that can never be separated'. His emphasis on the crucial nature of the moral component, however, is clear: 'The physical factors seem little more that the wooden hilt, while the moral factors are the precious metal, the real weapon, the finely-honed blade.'

The simple point is that, in assessing military strength, full weight must be given to that which cannot be measured – the unquantifiable but eternal martial qualities of leadership, discipline, courage, tenacity, endurance, and willingness to sacrifice one's life. Without these, numbers and equipment mean little; and, whatever their other failings, Nepal's Maoists have shown that they are not short on the qualities or the motivation needed to fight.

To appreciate the basis of the high morale in this poorly armed force, it is necessary first to understand the war that the Maoists are fighting, which is guided by a fundamentally different concept of conflict, as set down in the writings of Mao Tse-Tung. Mao's basic ideas about tactics are well known: 'Ours are guerrilla tactics. Divide our forces to arouse the masses, concentrate our forces to deal with the enemy. The enemy advances, we retreat; the enemy camps, we harass; the enemy tires, we attack; the enemy retreats, we pursue.'

At the strategic level, Mao's concept of 'protracted war' is his most enduring legacy. He stressed that at all times the revolutionary army must stay unified with the people among which it fights. The people can thus supply the recruits, supplies and information that the army needs, and can be politicised at the same time. In this way, the cultural and political structure of society can be transformed step-by-step with military success. Revolution thus comes about not after and as a result of victory, but through the process of war itself. Hence, Mao's best-known slogan, with its very distinct but often-misunderstood meaning: 'Power flows out of the barrel of a gun.'

This is the strategy being followed by the Maoists in Nepal. For an armed force that probably has only between 4000 and 5000 effective personal weapons, including about 1500 fifty-year-old .303 rifles of limited utility, it has brought them remarkable success. Such a deficiency in the physical component of military effectiveness indicates that there must be a very strong moral component to compensate. The factors that contribute to this have been inadequately assessed in military terms.

One example of this is the little-understood sociology of the Nepali Maoist movement, aspects of which contribute powerfully to the qualities needed to get people to fight and to sustain their commitment whatever the hardship and danger. Marie Lecomte-Tilouine wrote in the February 2004 Anthropology Today: 'The movement offers to its members a new ideology which provides an understanding of reality for those who have not succeeded educationally or economically as much as they may have wished: in particular it offers them the possibility of fighting against their situation, and a new understanding of their oppression and exploitation. The Maoists have been able to develop a genuine mystique ... which combines violence and the bonds of brotherhood; this produces a very high degree of cohesion inside the movement and terror outside it.'

Call to sacrifice

Perhaps the most complex aspect of Maoist morale strength to grasp, particularly for Westerners, is the cult of sacrifice. Anne de Sales, in the European Bulletin of Human Research (EBHR, v24), discusses this aspect in a way that brilliantly conveys its strength and centrality as a motivating force for Maoist fighters. In 1997, writing about preparations for launching the 'people's war', Prachanda noted that, 'New definitions of life and death were brought forward. The physical death for the sake of people and revolution was accepted as the great revolutionary ideal for oneself as it gave true meaning to life.'

Revolutionary songs are an important part of Maoist culture, with cassettes and song-sheets widely distributed. The melodies are based on evocative Nepali folk songs and have an immediate appeal. The first part of the lyrics depicts the struggle for existence and the pain of exploitation and poverty, instantly relatable sentiments. During the second part, however, the tone changes, conveying the challenge: 'The night is gone: this is the morning of a new day. The bugle of freedom is blowing ... The oppressor can be crushed.' The message to the listener is that you are required to fight, shed your blood, sacrifice your life, 'so that the people can be made one, and triumph'.

Anne de Sales points out that this is not the conventional Hindu view of the sacrifice of a substitute for personal gain. Rather, this is 'the self-sacrifice of the martyr who gives his life so that he can benefit by living on, if only in the memory of the people of which he is part, and for whose better future he sheds his blood.' Given the high number of woman combatants, she and her can be freely substituted.

This belief of what 'death in action for the cause' means is clearly an extraordinarily powerful motivating force when facing extreme danger. It must be fully integrated with the other factors contributing to Maoist morale in any assessment of the likelihood of RNA success through its current approach of simply killing as many Maoists as possible. For the RNA, such a policy carries with it the clear danger of measuring operational success and campaign progress by that most misleading of yardsticks – the body count.

The attack on Beni

A brief look at the largest-ever Maoist military operation offers a good insight into their military capabilities. This was an attack on the evening of 20 March 2004 against the headquarters of Myagdi District, a western

Nepali town called Beni. The aim was to overrun all security forces in the town and hold it for the night. After an all-night battle, one RNA battalion continued to hold their barracks on the edge of town. But the Maoists captured the town itself before withdrawing the following morning, having destroyed all government buildings and taking with them some 40 prisoners, including the chief of police and the Chief District Officer. Weeks later, all were released to the International Committee of the Red Cross. While the operation was not a complete success tactically, it was a major psychological blow to both the government and the RNA, who, not for the last time, had been proclaiming that the Maoists were finished.

A Kathmandu-based Japanese journalist, Kiyoko Ogura, has published some exhaustive research on the attack in EBHR (v27). Altogether, 3800 fighters and 2000 unarmed Maoist volunteers marched for about twenty days to an assembly area around two days away by foot. While there, they were able to advance the attack by 48 hours due to worries that their intention had leaked to the RNA. Equally impressive was the security they imposed on such a large-scale operation and the total surprise they achieved. Their medical support and evacuation arrangements were detailed, and indeed textbook, in both planning and execution. The local people of Beni commented specifically on the very young age of the fighters, the bravery of the wounded, that one-third of the fighters were women, and their particular agility and commitment in the attack.

Since Beni, the Maoists have been sparing with such large-scale attacks against defended RNA positions. They have carried out some, however, including a large assault on 1 February 2006, the one-year anniversary of King Gyanendra's royal coup. During that attack, on the district headquarters of Palpa District, every government installation except the army barracks was destroyed, 130 prisoners from the local jail were set free, and millions of rupees were looted from the local banks. As at Beni, both the CDO and the chief of police were taken prisoner and later released. Again, it was clearly an impressively planned and well-conducted operation, having achieved total surprise despite the large numbers involved. The Maoists risk heavy casualties with such attacks, but they have an acute awareness of the psychological and political impacts of military action. In Palpa, they received an unexpected bonus when, a few hours later, in an address to the nation to mark the first anniversary of his takeover, King Gyanendra claimed that 'acts of terrorism are now limited to petty crimes'.

No military solution

Although in conventional military terms the Maoists appear a pathetic armed force, when the vital morale component of military strength is taken into account, they are by no means weak. They have a proven strategy, favourable terrain, immense dedication, and an absolute willingness to sacrifice their lives for the cause. All of this gives them the capacity to make large areas of Nepal ungovernable in any meaningful sense for many years.

Their critical deficiency is the inadequacy of their means to fight. However strong Maoist will and motivation might be, the vast superiority the RNA enjoy in weapons and equipment have forced the Maoists to acknowledge publicly that they cannot seize and hold anything in the face of RNA action. That the military path they had originally set to their objectives is doomed has been particularly acknowledged through statements in late 2005 and early 2006. It is also manifest in the 12-point agreement signed with the agitating political parties in November 2005, which signals their willingness to shift (given certain vague conditions) to a multiparty political track.

In this conflict of 'two wars' there is no possibility of a solution by arms. Each side can demonstrate that it is making progress according to its own criteria of success. By the same logic, however, notwithstanding tactical gains, neither will be able to deliver a decisive strategic result that will end in the capitulation of the other. Thus, there is strategic stalemate, in both the general and literal meanings of the term. Claims about the Maoists that 'their back is broken' are both misleading and meaningless. War is not metaphor. War is death, destruction, ruined lives, communities torn apart, children orphaned, women widowed and much, much more. All decisions and discussions about its utility should be guided solely by awareness of these harsh consequences, not by mind-sets inured from reality by soft words and platitudes.

The history of the last fifty years of counterinsurgency operations the world over is littered with optimistic predictions about imminent victory that have proved consistently and hopelessly illusory. Similarly, in Nepal before the end of the last ceasefire, there were claims that 'the RNA can finish them off in six months'. The country is now into its fifth or sixth such 'six-month' period; while the Maoists have been weakened, they are a very long way from being finished.

Unless there is a ceasefire and the start of a peace process to which both sides are committed – not just to the cessation of hostilities, but to finding, through negotiations and compromise, a political solution – Nepal faces the prospect of war without end. The key lesson from other conflicts is that the start of such a process, and indeed the precondition for any hope of success, is when both sides come to the conclusion and publicly acknowledge that they cannot achieve their aims by military means. The Maoists have already done so. Recent statements by officials, however, indicate that the government is still firmly committed to seeking a solution by force.

Finally, and most obviously, both of Nepal's wars are having a devastating impact on the lives of its rural people. Caught in the no-man's land of a nasty and brutish conflict, they yearn desperately for peace. This can only be achieved by following the well-established pattern of people sitting around a table and negotiating a political way out. In Nepal, as elsewhere, all will have to compromise. The only questions are: when and how many young Nepalis will die in the interim? Far too many have died already.

This article has been republished with permission from *Himal Southasian*, where it was published in Issue #287, 24 Feb 2006– 02 March 2006. http://old.himalmag.com/component/content/article/1657-nepals-two-wars.html

Addendum, December 2017

It is pertinent to say, as I allude to it in 'The Maharaja and the Monarch, Part II', that, in addition to my two official audiences with King Gyanendra, I also had a one-hour private conversation with him in Narayanhiti Palace in November 2002, just after he had taken his first step towards seizing absolute power, which would prove fatal for the monarchy. No one else was present. At the meeting, I elaborated on what is written in the final three sentences of the last paragraph above. I advised King Gyanenda that, self-evidently, since there were three parties in the conflict, himself, the Maoists and the political parties, it was imperative that he form an alliance with one of them, preferably, by a long way, the political parties, otherwise he would find himself isolated, as the other two parties would inevitably, at some stage, form their own alliance. In the end, with disastrous results for the monarchy, King Gyanendra decided to go it alone, relying on the assurances he was constantly receiving from the army, and no doubt his close advisers, that the Maoists could and would be defeated militarily, and taken out of the equation. This would obviate the need for him to do any deal with the political parties. Thus, the way would be clear for him to establish a version of his father's Panchayat system, under a constitution that would be granted to the people by him, their sovereign, as his father and brother had done in 1962 and 1990. As in those constitutions, ultimate power would have remained in the sovereign's hands. All of this was very clear from my conversation with King Gyanendra.

Letter to the Editor of
Nepali Times

Written for publication in Nepali Times *on the torture and death of 15-year old Maina Sunar in army custody*

Maina

Two weeks ago you bravely published a translation of the *Kantipur* article 'How Maina was killed'. Shocking though the detail was, I write to say that it did not prepare me for reading the horrendous full account in the army Court of Inquiry report. One sentence in it makes all clear-'*in the process of questioning by torture, in not being able to withstand the torture, her death occurred*'. In other words, the torture and the torturers killed Maina. It is surely a matter of extreme shame that the three officers who personally ordered and directed this killing were not appropriately charged, and continue to serve on in the army today, even in the same ranks.

All armies worthy of the name prize honour above all else, and I know the Nepal Army well enough to say that no one in its ranks would dispute that assertion.

The reason is both simple and profound. It is what makes soldiering, the profession of arms, an honourable one, to be followed with pride, and which separates it from barbarism. But, sadly, that is the only appropriate word I can find for the behaviour that led directly to the death of Maina.

As Nepal moves into a new era, the new COAS, General Katuwal, has rightly and publicly declared his commitment to ensuring that the army operates within the law of the land. That law requires the killing of civilians by soldiers to be dealt with by the civil courts. There could be no better signal that Nepal is indeed changing for the better in regard to the observance of human rights than for the COAS to call in the civil police for a full, open investigation into the killing of Maina with a view to having the alleged perpetrators appropriately charged under the criminal law, and tried before the civilian courts. I appeal to him to do so.

In the same spirit, I appeal to the new government, without further delay, to honour its international obligations and declare torture to be a criminal offence under the law of Nepal.

There can be no bringing back Maina but surely your readers would agree that the actions proposed above would be a worthy memorial to her young life, so tragically and brutally ended while she was still at school.

Sam Cowan

This letter has been republished with permission from *Nepali Times*. The original was published in Issue #316, 22-28 September, 2006. http://himalaya.socanth.cam.ac.uk/collections/journals/nepalitimes/pdf/ Nepali_Times_316.pdf

Addendum December 2017

Background

Based on an army press release, *The Kathmandu Post* reported on 27 September 2005, that:

> A General Military Court of the Royal Nepalese Army has slapped a six-month jail term on a colonel and two captains in connection with the killing of a teenage girl in army barracks in early February 2004 in Kavre district. The Military Court last week decided to jail Colonel Bobby Khatri and Captains Sunil Adhikari and Amit Pun who were working in Shanti Gate Barracks of the RNA at Dhulikhel, where 15-year-old Maina Sunuwar was killed allegedly after severe torture. According to informed sources, all the three have been freed since their judicial custody counted as jail terms, as per law...
>
> ...The court said in its verdict that the girl was found dead in bed, not during torture, but there were serious lapses on the part of the commanders after her death. Failure of the commanders to conduct post mortem, prepare first information report of the death and others have been pointed out as major lapses on the convicted officers' part.

In late August 2006, there was a leak of the army's Court of Inquiry report. Some details of this were published in *Kantipur* and a translation of that article was given in the *Nepali Times* on 1 Sep 2006. To quote from the opening paragraph:

> The board of the Court of Inquiry set up by the Military Court has concluded that the army killed young Maina Sunuwar of Kavre by subjecting her to severe torture, despite the availability of 'alternative measures of interrogation'. Maina was arrested on the morning of 17 February 2005 by a covert team despatched by the Birendra Peace Operations Training Centre, Panchkhal. She died while being tortured, but the army's story was that she was killed while trying to escape, in the Hokse area.

As indicated in my letter, I had access to a copy of this report which spelt out in detail the horrendous and sustained nature of the torture inflicted on 15-year-old Maina. The torture lasted one and half hours. First, her head was immersed in water 'for about one minute before removal' and this happened '6 or 7 times'. After this, an electric current, taken straight from a hot water heater, was applied to her wet soles and wet wrists. With blood coming from her wrists she fainted and was carried away to be given food. The evidence indicates that she never recovered consciousness. She was later found dead and Colonel Khatri ordered that bullets be fired into her dead body.

For several months after her death, much to the distress of her grieving mother, the army denied that they knew the whereabouts of Maina or that they had ever detained her.

Update

Despite my plea in the above letter, torture is still not a criminal offence under the law of Nepal. A new Penal Code, due to come into force in August 2018, does criminalise torture, but not retroactively. An Anti-Torture Bill has been pending in parliament for several years, and lapsed when parliament was dissolved in October 2017. It remains to be seen whether it will be reintroduced when the new government takes office.

My plea to General Katuwal also fell on deaf ears as the army refused to cooperate in any way with the police investigation. On 16 Apr 2017, after overcoming a protracted number of legal and political hurdles, the Kavre District Court sentenced Colonel Bobby Khatri and

Captains Sunil Adhikari and Amit Pun (all now retired and apparently out of the country) to life imprisonment for Maina's murder. The court recommended that the sentence be reduced to five years' imprisonment because of the political context at the time and the possibility that those convicted did not intend to kill her.

Five months later, in October 2017, in a totally unexpected move, the army filed a petition to the Supreme Court 'in the public interest', asking for the Kavre District Court judgement to be annulled on the basis that it flouts the universal principle against double jeopardy and that the district court lacked the jurisdiction to hand down such a verdict. At the time of writing, the case is pending in the court.

Ochterloney's Men

Review of Britain's Gurkha War: The Invasion of Nepal, 1814-16 *by John Pemble, Frontline Books, London, 2008*

Thucydides begins his monumental *History of the Peloponnesian War* by saying that whatever the publicly declared reasons and complaints, the truest explanation was that 'the growth of Athens's power and the fear this caused among the Spartans made war inevitable'. Written nearly 2500 years ago, it is a fair judgement against which to assess the causes of innumerable wars since, including the one that took place between Britain and the Gorkha state of Nepal between 1814 and 1816.

In the 60-year period after 1742, when Prithvi Narayan Shah became its king, Gorkha's growth as a military and political power was phenomenal. War with China in 1792 arrested its westward expansion; but within a few weeks of Bhim Sen Thapa seizing power in Kathmandu, in 1804, the drive westward from Garhwal resumed, with even greater energy and success. Only the failure, after a three-year siege, to take Sansar Chand's massive fortress of Kangra denied Gorkha the possibility of seizing Kashmir, the greatest prize for which it strove.

The formidably efficient Gorkha war machine, coupled with its insatiable desire for conquest, was powered by the desire for land revenue, particularly that from the fertile and productive Tarai lands over which many of the hill rajas had control. More revenue sustained a bigger army, which in turn needed more land and more conquests. These stark linkages stemmed primarily from the fact that Gorkha was a military state. The nobility made up the bulk of the army leadership, and it was their loyalty to Gorkha and to the throne that ensured the throne of the loyalty of the army. In the most literal sense, therefore, political power rested on the army, and its loyalty had to be constantly cultivated.

The East India Company, the agent of British power in India, was well aware of Gorkha's expansion from small impoverished hill state to potential rival as empire builder. The renewal of Gorkha's drive to the west in 1804 started to harden the attitude of the Company towards Gorkha as a potential impediment to its interests and profits. To quote Edward Thornton, in his 1843 The History of the British Empire in India, 'The Goorkhas thus acquired an extent of dominion and a degree of power which, combined with the disposition they had manifested, rendered them dangerous neighbours.' A decision was thus made that Gorkha needed to be put in its place, and that place was to be the hills. The plains were to be exclusively British. This would also have the advantage of permanently weakening Gorkha, by denying it the revenue from the Tarai that it needed not just for expansion but also to maintain itself as a unitary state. This intent was embodied in a unilaterally derived Principle of Limitation, which Gorkha was 'invited' to accept. It was, in effect, an ultimatum, and its rejection in word and deed inevitably led to war.

Securing the north

John Pemble's book is a well-written and well-researched comprehensive history of the conflict. It was first published in 1971 under the title The Invasion of Nepal: John Company at war (using the colloquial reference to the East India Company), and this is a more accurate description of what the book is about. With a devastating analysis of the East India Company's main military force, the Bengal Army, as an instrument for waging war, military-history buffs will also relish the vivid descriptions of the many actions of the war. Particularly memorable are the scathing characterisations of the senior British commanders, most of whom were ditherers and vacillators of a high order.

The Marquis of Hastings, the newly arrived governor-general of India, was a military man of some considerable experience. He personally drew up the invasion plan, and was confident that it would lead to a quick, perhaps even bloodless, victory. The two main objectives – Kathmandu and the army of Amar Singh Thapa in the far west – were each to be attacked with two cooperating columns of troops. Some of Hastings's confidence was based on a firm belief that it would be easier to attack a mountainous country than to defend it. This gross misperception was not his only error. Just as serious was his grave underestimation of the fighting capability of the enemy, as well as an overestimation of his own forces.

Not surprisingly, therefore, the war, which began in October 1814, started badly for the Company's forces. The impetuous Rollo Gillespie, the most experienced and famous of its commanders, was killed in the first main action. The commander of the force intended to capture Kathmandu deserted. Another was paralysed into inaction, and his successor also fell into the same torpor. Only Colonel David Ochterlony, the commander of the westernmost column, in Garhwal, showed the acumen and patience to work out what was required: tactics adjusted to the terrain and full exploitation of his powerful artillery. His brilliant generalship led to the surrender of Amar Singh Thapa and his much-depleted army at the Malaun fortress on 15 May 1815, thus effectively ending the war. After delays caused by reluctance to accept all British stipulations, and a second brief phase of hostilities, which threatened Kathmandu, the Treaty of Sagauli was ratified in March 1816. This confined Nepal between the Mechi and the Mahakali rivers. All the Tarai lands were also to be lost, though substantial tracts were eventually handed back by the British in order to achieve a secure border.

Pemble, a historian with the University of Bristol, is very fair in his judgements on the conflict. Fulsome tribute is paid to the fighting spirit of the Gorkhas. Particularly moving and memorable are his descriptions of the scene of slaughter found when the British entered the Nalapani fort, near modern-day Dehradun, where Bal Bahadur Kunwar's forces had bravely offered prolonged resistance to sustained British attacks; and the successive charges against the British guns before the Malaun fort (in present-day Himachal Pradesh), led by the aged but valiant Bhakti Thapa, in a vain attempt to save the day for Gorkha.

Two subsidiary chapters are also worth commenting on briefly. It is unfortunate that the section on the causes of the war perpetuates without question a singular British view. For Pemble, 'the war was made acceptable by the need to define and secure the northern boundary of the East India Company's possessions and to vindicate the Company's raison d'etre as a government by defending the subjects under its protection.' With regards to Hastings' motives, he does write that 'it would be wrong, probably, to discount entirely love of imperialism for its own sake'. But the probably here is revealing, as is the acknowledgment that Hastings was delighted when the Kathmandu court reacted to his ultimatum in the way that it did.

Second, a long chapter on Himalayan trade goes into impressive detail to prove that, by 1814, trans-Himalayan trade was commercially unimportant for the Company. But while Pemble makes a persuasive case, a great deal of this chapter is taken up explaining away the evidence that the main actors on the Company's side – starting with the governor-general himself – were motivated by a view quite to the contrary.

In contrast to the attention paid to Britain's 'fears' and 'necessity', there is scant mention of Gorkha's equivalent concerns. Although Pemble acknowledges that the Gorkha empire would have proved viable if the war with Britain had not intervened, and that 'its great strength was the army by which it had been won and by which it was held, for no rival among the Himalayan states had a force more efficient and more loyal,' nowhere does he analyse the basis of that loyalty or the dynamics that drove the army on to further conquests. In this, it should be pointed out that Pemble's research was done in the 1960s. Originally, he did not therefore have the benefit of reading Ludwig F Stiller's *The Rise of the House of Gorkha*, published in 1973, many of whose ideas were referred to earlier in this review. With its extensive references to Nepali sources, Stiller brought out, in convincing detail, the fact that the land-military nexus was fundamental to the successful growth of Gorkha.

In the event, despite the great cost and the loss of the lands west of the Mahakali River, Nepal emerged from the war still in possession of large tracts of Tarai lands. This gave it the capacity to remain a unitary state, something that might not have been possible if it had merely accepted the Principle of Limitation as a means of avoiding war. After the conflict, the army continued to be indulged and pampered. Indeed, it increased in size and, with the loss of revenue from conquered land, the ordinary peasant had to be squeezed – many to the point of impoverishment – to produce the money needed. Their unheard, anguished appeal for some relief was 'The Silent Cry' of Stiller's 1976 book. There is a contemporary echo here, as well. The Maoist conflict ended nearly three years ago, but an untouched and bloated Nepal security sector, plus the Maoist combatants in the UN supervised cantonments, still has to be paid for. About this, few in authority seem concerned, at least so long as ever-pliant donors continue to produce the funds required to preserve the status quo.

Serving the crown

One other significant outcome of the war is briefly but accurately covered. On 14 April, as part of the actions around Malaun, Lieutenant Peter Lawtie, Ochterlony's aide-de-camp and field engineer, led a volunteer body of deserters and prisoners from the Gorkha army into action against their former masters. They immediately impressed. Even before this first use, Ochterlony had adopted them as very much his own. After the conflict, he masterminded the recruitment of some 4700 men of Gorkha's western army into British service as an irregular corps. The best estimate (from A.P. Coleman, *A Special Corps*) is that about 1500 of these were Chhetri, Gurung and Magar soldiers from the Gorkha heartland. The rest were hillmen of Kumaon, Garhwal and Sirmur.

It is beyond the scope of this review to describe the endless twists and turns that have led to some 3400 citizens of Nepal serving under the rubric of the Brigade of Gurkhas in today's 100,000-strong British Army. But serve they do, and with great distinction, as a valued and integral part of the army. Their recent and current service in operational theatres, particularly Afghanistan, has added even greater lustre to their reputation as soldiers of the very highest quality. One of the original 40 demands of the Maoist rebels was that all recruitment of Nepalis into foreign armies must cease. But Maoist Prime Minister Pushpa Kamal Dahal (aka 'Prachanda') recently told some visiting British MPs that recruitment would in fact not be stopped. However, changes are taking place that could well revise Nepali attitudes in years to come. New terms and conditions of service introduced in 2007 put Gurkha soldiers on full British rates of pay and pensions, and gave them the right to settle in UK after discharge, a right that can lead to citizenship. This right was also extended to those who retired after 1997, the year of British withdrawal from Hong Kong. The courts are currently considering appeals to extend this right to an indeterminate number who retired before that year.

Since 2007, remittances to Nepal from serving Gurkhas have come down by 97 percent. This indicates that just about everyone now serving intends to settle in the UK. There is clearly no further need to buy land and a house for a future back in Nepal. Pensions will also be paid in UK. Thus, the direct value to Nepal of the UK's right to recruit Gurkhas will rapidly diminish to zero. Capital flight and loss of pension revenue are already underway. Since 2004, some 6000 former Gurkhas have been granted settlement in the UK, a figure that includes 3500 who retired before 1997 and have been granted the right under existing discretionary rules.

In the UK, the extensive and sympathetic coverage that has been given to Gurkha court cases seldom refer to Nepal or its interests. It is as if Gurkhas have mysteriously materialised from a Gurkhaland, somewhere. In Kathmandu, meanwhile, the media seldom mention the trend highlighted. Justification for the huge number of young Nepalis who leave each week to search for work overseas is accepted on the grounds that Nepal gains through remittances. Yet comment is scarce on the fact that this no longer pertains to British Gurkhas, who arguably constitute Nepal's most privileged and richly rewarded group of 'expatriate workers'. Allowing citizens of Nepal to be recruited into the British Army has traditionally been based on the principle of mutual benefit. Clearly, thought must now be given to finding new ways of making certain that this continues to be the case. It cannot become a one-way street.

All of this is a far cry from the days of Ochterlony and Lieutenant Lawtie. But they would be proud to know that the direct descendents of the Special Corps they formed remain special in every sense, and far exceed in bravery and loyalty even their lofty expectations. Long may it be so!

This article has been republished with permission from *Himal Southasian*. The original was published in May 2009 and can be found online at: http://old.himalmag.com/component/content/article/735--ochterlonys-men.html.

Crossing the Larkya La

A report of a trek on one of Nepal's great trekking trails which goes close to the border with China

The Lonely Planet guide *Trekking in the Nepal Himalaya* is unequivocal in saying that 'the Larkya La is one of the most dramatic pass crossings in the Himalaya'. In every sense, the pass is the high point of the Manaslu circuit. To get into position to tackle it entails following the Buri Gandaki to its origin in the Himalayan glaciers. The trail, starting from Arughat or Gorkha, is rated as arduous but the rewards of experiencing Nepal's rich cultural diversity at first hand are hugely satisfying.

The first six days leads through one of the longest of the Himalayan gorges and a series of small hamlets mainly inhabited by Gurungs. One emerges north of the main Himalayan range with the trail still following the Buri Gandaki as it turns from flowing north-south to west-east. At this point one enters the region of Kutang inhabited by people of mixed Ghale and Tibetan origin who speak their own distinctive language and practice an amalgam of shamanistic and Buddhist ritual. For complex reasons, people who live north of Kutang regard it as a land of sorcerers and poisoners, and are always extremely nervous about travelling through it. I must in fairness record that I suffered no ill effects from drinking many cups of teas in the teahouses along this part of the trail! I also found the people charming, helpful and very good-humoured.

After 8 days the trail emerges from dense forests and deep valleys into the region of Nubri, a land of entirely Tibetan culture dominated by bright chortens, snapping prayer flags, small gompas, long mani walls, yak caravans, spectacular Himalayan peaks and very tough people. Sama, the largest village, is a fascinating place to spend a necessary acclimatisation day. This applies with equal force to Samdo, the last village before the pass, built from scratch by people from the village of Ru, just a few miles away across the nearby border with Tibet, when

Entrance to the village of Sama from the south.

they moved lock, stock and barrel to Nepal in the 1960s. They claimed and were granted Nepali citizenship, partly by being able to produce two engraved copper plates from the 14th century that showed that the kings of Jumla had given them in perpetuity grazing rights in the area.

Because they live close to the border, the people of Nubri can apply for special permits which enables them to go into Tibet when they please except, of course, when the passes are closed by snow or when the Chinese close the border, usually on a whim. Large numbers take advantage of these permits. They need to do so to generate income from cross border trading to survive. This trans-Himalayan trade has been going on for thousands of years, and because they have the yaks and the physiology to cope with the high altitude, the people who live in areas such as Nubri have always been key middlemen. With roads opening up on both sides of the border, the nature of the trade has changed dramatically but somehow these people have adapted and are still driving their yaks across the passes as their ancestors have done before them. It is a living that is as vital as ever to their existence but also one which gets more and more precarious by the year. On a single day I saw 14 caravans, each of about 12 yaks coming back from Tibet, and earlier that morning I saw a similar number heading in the other direction.

Eventually, on about Day 12 on the Manaslu trail, one sets off from the last camp, about a four hour walk up from Samdo, to cross the Larkya La.

Yaks leaving Sama to cross the frontier to the roadhead market. They will return after 5 or 6 days carrying goods purchased from across the frontier.

At 5200m it is not one of the highest of the trekking passes but it carries its own challenges and dangers, not least because of the need to commit to a 10-hour day, including 4 or 5 hours at altitude on rough and exposed terrain. The pass is also notorious for sudden storms developing quickly. Snow the day before our crossing had wiped out the trails but on the day the weather was glorious. The pass is not sharp edged. It is one of those where the trail just seems to go on and on. I could see the prayer flags for a long time before I got to them. As I ground it out, large Himalayan peaks started to appear to the left and right and, from the top, I was completely surrounded and indeed emotionally over whelmed by them. A long 1700-metre descent leads to the campsite at Bhimtang, a sublime high Alpine valley, which itself is surrounded by Himalayan peaks.

Bhimtang is of great historical interest because in the days when the salt-for-grain trade was at its height this was where Tibetans brought their yaks and dzos with the salt. From here it was carried on the backs of people to the middle hills. The Marsyangdi Khola trail was notoriously treacherous and was not made suitable for animal transport until the trail was improved 30 years ago to facilitate trekkers going to Manang.

From Samdo, to the left (west) the trail to the Larkya la, to the right (north) to the Gya la and frontier. The clear area of ground at the junction of the two trails, directly over the top of the prayer flag post, is the site of the historic trading post of Babu (Larkya bazaar). An Indian 'pundit' (surveyor/British spy) in 1861 recorded: 'Babu is a large mart for the exchange of goods; Bhotiyas from all parts frequent it. Salt, wool, felt, and borax are brought here from Tibet prior to being carried into Nepal and adjacent territories, while tobacco, rice, grain, cloth, copper-plates, &c., are brought from Nepal, prior to being carried into Tibet.'

On the Larkya la, looking west, just before the start of a long, steep descent to the overnight camp at Bimthang.

From Bimthang, looking north, the trail to the Larkya pass goes up to the head of the valley and then swings high to the right. Trade in salt-for grain gradually shifted here from Babu. David Snellgrove passed through the area in September 1956 and recorded in 'Himalayan Pilgrimage': 'Bimthang is a small trading mart occupied only during the summer months like Babu across the pass eastwards. From Tibet, via Babu come yak-loads of salt and wool, and from the Nepalese side, rice and other food grains, cotton cloth, cigarettes, matches, and other useful oddments.'

Tilman, who visited the place in 1950, describes (in *Nepal Himalaya*) a great hive of activity with, during the short season, more than 3000 animal loads being traded.

For good measure, the spectacle of great peaks continues most of the next day, as one drops down from Bhimtang to follow the valley of the Dudh khola which, after two further days, meets the Annapurna Circuit trail at Dharapani on the banks of the Marsyangdi khola. Here the trekker must decide whether to turn left to the road head two and half days away or take his courage in his hand and turn right to enjoy the delights of Manang, the Thorung La, Mukhinath, Jomsom and beyond. For the record, your correspondent did turn right. Despite all the trekkers on the Annapurna circuit, the walk up to Manang was well worth the extra effort. Indeed walking the high route from Upper Pisang to Braga through the fascinating villages of Ghyaru and Ngawal in glorious weather with the Annapurna peaks in full view is now very high on my list of great days of trekking.

The village of Manang, however, was my limit of exploitation. I had previously been up to Mukhinath from the Mustang side and had assessed that 21 days on the trail would be more than enough. So, early on the morning of 31 Oct 2010, I left the airport lodge at Hongde (readers should disregard the notion of all places they have ever known with the same or approximate name) to walk the 15 minutes to the airstrip. In contrast to the brilliant weather of the previous 8 days, the sky was overcast and the Himal was shrouded in clouds with snow falling up high. I was concerned at the prospect of the weather closing in but on reaching the strip a young, very cheery young man shouted from the tower that the Pilatus Porter aircraft I had chartered was just about to leave Pokhara where it and the crew had spent the night to get into position to pick my party up. We had dismissed the camping crew and taken to lodges from Dharapani so we were now down to me, Kit Spencer, the sirdar and one porter.

The young man in the tower explained that Hongde was Nepal's highest working airport. It emerged that the working was extremely rare. No flight had landed or taken off for 4 months until two days previously when a Pilatus Porter had done so to test the strip to see if it was safe to fly us out after some recent work aimed at extending the length of the strip. Fifteen minutes later we saw the aircraft with its lights on approaching very slowly. It landed and pulled up in about 75 metres. I was reassured to see from its gleaming paintwork that it was a relatively new aircraft. Some goods were unloaded for the people of the small village of Hongde and to feed the passing trekking trade. After boarding, the pilot took the aircraft to the end of the strip, turned up the engine revs until the whole plane shook, released the brakes and in less that a 100 metres we were airborne. Forty minutes later we were in the very different world of Kathmandu. At 08.30 we were demanding breakfast in the Summit Hotel. It was a huge and very rapid cultural jump, and a memorable way to finish a great trek

So, how do I rate the crossing of the Larkya La? Quite simply, *dramatic* in no way overstates it. The whole experience was sharpened by my knowledge of its historic importance to trans Himalayan trade and of the tens of thousands of Tibetans and Nepalis who had risked their lives over centuries to bring salt to the middle hills of Nepal and grain to those who lived on the Tibetan plateau. The fact that the trade still continues today, albeit in a much modified form, simply added to the rich emotional experience of tackling one of Nepal's great trekking trails; and, yes, of crossing the Larkya La!

For a slideshow of photos of this trek go to: http://www.youtube.com/ watch?v=aWnvdIexbFQ

This article has been republished with permission from *The Kukri, The Journal of the Brigade of Gurkhas*, No. 61, 2009/2010. The original can be found online at: http://www.gurkhabde.com/wp-content/ uploads/2015/01/Kukri_2009_2010.pdf

Addendum, December 2017

Information on the extraordinary story of the people of Samdo comes from the excellent book, *Where Rivers Meet: A Tibetan Refugee Community's Struggle to Survive in the High Moutnains of Nepal* (2008), by Clint Rogers, published by Mandala Book Point. This book also gives many valuable insights into the changing pattern of trans-Himalayan trade.

Inside the People's Liberation Army: A Military Perspective

A detailed analysis of three major battles of the Maoist war which had significant political consequences

Introduction

Much has been written about the Maoist conflict in Nepal, which lasted from 1996 to 2006,[1] but little that gives objective insight into the basis of the military effectiveness of the armed wing of the Maoists, the People's Liberation Army (PLA).[2]

This analysis is based mainly on a study of six Maoist-produced videos which cover an ambush that went badly wrong at Ganeshpur on 28 February 2005 and two significant battles that took place at Khara (on 7 April 2005) and Pili (on 4 August 2005). Ganeshpur is notable for the loss of an elite group of PLA fighters, including a particularly popular PLA commander, in a botched military action, and the

1   This article owes its provenance in part to a joint research programme funded by Agence National de la Recherche and coordinated by Marie Lecomte-Tilouine, People's War in Nepal: An anthropological and historical analysis. The results of the programme will be published in a book, with a DVD included, under the same name. The present article will be a chapter in the book and I am most grateful to Marie Lecomte-Tilouine for agreeing to its early publication. Relevant video clips can be viewed at <http://bit.ly/EBHRvideo1>, <http://bit.ly/EBHRvideo2> and <http://bit.ly/EBHRvideo3>.

2   A notable exception is Kiyoko Ogura's painstakingly researched and very graphic account of the PLA attack on Beni, the District Headquarters of Myagdi District, on 20 March 2004 (Ogura 2004). I am most grateful to her and to my friend Anne de Sales for the support and encouragement they have given me in preparing this article. Their respective singular and illuminating insights have been invaluable to me, although the views and judgments expressed are of course mine alone. I am also most grateful to David Gellner for his sustained encouragement and for some expert proof reading.

consequent impact on morale. The Khara and Pili battles are notable for their significant political consequences, as well as for the fact that the two commanders-in-chief were personally involved in the instigation of deeply flawed plans that led to humiliating disaster and significant loss of life. Both sides, therefore, have a continuing strong vested interest in drawing a veil over what happened in these battles and why. The period covers the culmination of the feud between the top two Maoists, Prachanda, the party chairman, and Baburam Bhattarai, his recognised number two, which came close to splitting the party. It also covers their subsequent reconciliation and the start of 'the Delhi process' which led to the first formal political deal between the Maoists and the political parties. All these developments are seen impacting on the military actions covered by the videos. The analysis is also based on discussions with senior military sources from both sides which confirm and in some cases amplify what is seen and heard on the videos.[3] I have also applied my own experience as a professional soldier for forty years and a knowledge of Nepal gained over many visits and extensive trekking since 1965.

The videos I have studied first became available to selected journalists in late 2006. They were shot by Maoist journalists attached to the PLA's western division, using small hand-held cameras. It would appear, not least from the candour of what is said in them, that initially they were intended primarily for internal use for analysing military actions, and very possibly also for recording for posterity the contribution of the PLA to the Maoist struggle.

The videos provide a singular insight into the military capability and internal dynamics of the PLA. No commentary is provided: the people seen on the videos, from senior commanders down to the most junior ranks, speak for themselves, often in the most candid and critical terms. A feature of them is the use of revolutionary songs as background music. These songs are an important part of Maoist culture, recorded on cassettes, written in song sheets and distributed widely: the melodies are based on the evocative folk songs of Nepal and have an immediate appeal.[4] Some are lyrical ballads and some, as on these videos, are much more martial.

---

3   I am very grateful to Hikmat Khadka for translating what is spoken in the extracts of the videos referred to in this analysis. The sound is of variable quality so there is room for doubt on some minor detail, but I am confident that the general sense of what is spoken is accurately conveyed.

4   See Stirr (forthcoming), de Sales (2003), Lecomte-Tilouine (2006), Mottin (2010).

Two particular songs are frequently used. The first is 'Lamo Bato' ('Long Road'). The chorus refrain is 'A long track of a thousand miles begins with a single step' and typical verses are:

He who loves the people wins,
He who loots the people loses.

He who can win over death drives the world,
He who can enjoy gunpowder can exist in every fierce battle.
Bodies fall before the bullets, but confidence never does,
Physical remains degrade after death, but ideology never does.

The second song is 'Hami Rato Manche' ('We the Red People'). The constantly repeated chorus is 'We the red people, the people of People's Liberation' and typical verses are:

We can swallow fire, we can dry the ocean,
We are the people who were created from the martyrs' blood,
We are the people who go on destroying the enemies' forts.

We are the people who go on hunting for the people's enemies,
Making earth and sky tremble, causing wind and storm to blow,
Chewing up the hearts of feudalists and imperialists

These brief extracts illustrate a strong ideological drive centred on notions of sacrifice, violence and contempt for death. I leave the interpretation of such songs within a Hindu cultural context to anthropologists, but it is my contention that what is seen and heard on the videos show that the PLA combatants were not simply blinded by ideology or driven by it. As with soldiers everywhere, they were vulnerable to demoralisation, appreciated the practical and tactical importance of sound plans and knew that success in combat depended ultimately on martial qualities such as strong discipline and brave leadership.

In sum, the action on the videos provides a reasonable means for assessing the PLA's fighting effectiveness: its strengths and weaknesses; the state of its training; and the quality of its people, particularly at the crucial leadership level of company, battalion and brigade, which has seldom been publicly exposed. Although there are few images of actual fighting, not least because most attacks took place at night and the obvious danger to the journalists, the videos also provide an opportunity to judge the quality of the PLA's battle procedures, a military term of art covering all the complex processes necessary to launch a force into action in good order at the right time and place. These range from the giving of orders, to logistic support, to the movement, usually over many days, to (using conventional military parlance) an Assembly Area near the objective, and the subsequent insertion and correct positioning of assault formations in a Forming Up Point (FUP) prior to crossing the Start Line at H Hour, the time given for an attack to begin.

The strategic context and Maoist strategy

The PLA and its opponents, the Royal Nepal Army (RNA), fought two very different wars. Essentially the RNA fought a conventional war of attrition in which the emphasis was on the control of key territory such as urban centres and district headquarters, and on inflicting casualties through military engagements with the aim of weakening the Maoist will to fight, through a gradual exhaustion of physical and moral resistance. The PLA fought the war guided by a fundamentally different concept of conflict, as set down in the writings of Mao Zedong which in turn reflect many of the ideas of Sun Tzu who, 2500 years ago, drew on an existing corpus of Chinese ideas and practices in formalising his theory of war. Sun Tzu focuses on the need to manipulate the enemy to create the opportunities for easy victories and on lulling the enemy into untenable positions with prospects of gain, then attacking when they are exhausted. He stresses that avoiding a strong force is not cowardice but indicates wisdom because it is self-defeating to fight when and where it is not advantageous (see Keegan (1993: 202) and Sawyer (1993: 155)). This emphasis is reflected in a number of Mao's best-known military maxims: the enemy advances, we retreat; the enemy camps, we harass; the enemy tires, we attack; the enemy retreats, we pursue.[5]

---

5   Mao's prolific writings are summarised in various compilations of what is generally known as 'the little red book'. His ideas, including the link with Sun Tzu, are well analysed in Griffith (1961), which includes a translation of Mao's 1937 essay *Yu Chin Chan* ('Guerrilla Warfare'). Griffith writes: 'Guerrilla tactical doctrine may be summarised in four Chinese characters 'Sheng Tung, Chi Hsi' which mean 'Uproar (in the) East; Strike (in the) West'. Here we find expressed the all-important principles of distraction on the one hand and concentration on the other; to fix the enemy's attention and to strike where and when he least anticipates the blow. Guerrillas are masters of simulation and dissimulation; they create pretenses and simultaneously

At the strategic level, Mao's concept of 'protracted people's war' is his most enduring legacy. He stressed that at all times the revolutionary army must stay unified with the people among which it fights. The people can thus supply the recruits, supplies and information that the army needs, and can be politicised at the same time. In this way, the cultural and political structure of society can be transformed step-by-step with military success. Revolution thus comes about not after and as a result of victory, but through the process of war itself. Hence, Mao's best known slogan: 'Power flows out of the barrel of a gun (Keegan and Wheatcroft 1976: 209). Intrinsic to Mao's ideas about protracted war is the need to establish base areas and liberated zones and also the need to move through the stages of strategic defence, strategic equilibrium and strategic offence.

So, in Mao's terms where had the conflict in Nepal progressed to in early 2005? The period of Strategic Defence in the People's War was deemed to have ended with the completion of the Sixth Plan in February 2001. In a document presented to the Central Committee in February 2004, Prachanda claimed that the stage of Strategic Balance or Equilibrium was reached with the attack on the RNA base at Ghorahi in Dang in November 2001. The Maoists announced the launch of their Strategic Offensive on 31 August 2004 but declared a preliminary sub-phase of Strategic Counter Offensive (see Ogura 2008).

A framework for an assessment of fighting effectiveness
The above sets the context for analysing the performance of the PLA in the three military operations selected but, before doing so, it is useful to have a framework for assessing the effectiveness of any military force. British military doctrine[6] usefully defines 'fighting power' or 'military effectiveness' as having three distinctive but related components: the physical, the moral and the conceptual:

a. The physical component is the means to fight. This requires that people be recruited and trained; and that weapons be acquired and distributed for them to fight with.

---

disguise or conceal their true semblance. Their tactical concepts, dynamic and flexible, are not cut to any particular pattern. But Mao's first law of war, to preserve oneself and destroy the enemy, is always governing' (Griffith 1961: 26).

6 *Design for Military Operations - British Military Doctrine,* Chapter 4, Military Effectiveness. http://nssc.ge/cms/site_images/British_Military_Doctrine.pdf

b. The moral component concerns the ability to get people to fight. Those recruited have to be infused with the warrior spirit and mentally prepared for fighting through discipline and by convincing them of the merit of the cause for which they are being asked to risk their lives. Getting people to fight also involves the key area of motivation. This follows from high morale, but also depends crucially on maintaining a strong sense of purpose, a key task of commanders at all levels. A vital element of the moral component is leadership – the projection of personality and character to get soldiers to do what is required of them, whatever the difficulty and danger. Skill in the techniques of leadership is the foremost quality in the art of command and contributes very largely to success at all levels of war.

c. The conceptual component can be described at one level as the thought process behind the ability to fight. It is often based on 'military doctrine', not in the sense of providing rigid rules to follow but in establishing a common understanding of the approach to war that can be followed by all commanders from top to bottom. In short: this is how we fight. This component also emphasises the importance of effective command and the centrality of psychological factors in war, whatever its level of intensity, reflecting Clausewitz's view that 'all military action is intertwined with psychological forces and effects' (von Clausewitz 1984: 136).[7] In other words, war in all its manifestations is as much a mental as a physical struggle, and is fought as much with brains as with force. This struggle of opposing minds lies at the heart of strategy, the art of which is not to apply force on force but to employ strength against weakness; what Sun Tzu memorably described as achieving a situation where one is 'throwing rocks at eggs' (Sawyer 1984: 187). To achieve the concentration and surprise necessary to do this, a successful commander must read his opponent's mind while disguising his own intentions. He must also minimise the potentially destructive effects of Friction, a term Clausewitz used to describe the host of factors that work against the successful implementation of any military plan. In this specific context, Clausewitz said, 'everything in war is very

---

7   See also, of many examples, on page 137 – 'Military action is never directed against material force alone: it is always aimed simultaneously at the moral forces which give it life, and the two cannot be separated.'

simple but the simplest thing is difficult' (von Clausewitz 1984: 119). Size is a critical factor: the larger the force the more difficult it is to control, particularly when things go wrong. Hence the importance of experienced, strong willed commanders, a well-practised chain of command, the proper delegation of authority and responsibility, and reliable channels of communications.

In assessing the military strength and effectiveness of any force, full weight must be given to all these factors.

Ganeshpur

In late February 2005, the PLA's western division was deployed in the Tarai to carry out an attack on Gulariya, the district headquarters of Bardiya district, about three miles from the Indian border. This plan was aborted because of fears that it had been compromised but, rather than withdrawing immediately to the relative security of the hills, a decision was made to mount an ambush in the Ganeshpur area on the main road connecting Gulariya with Nepalganj, the headquarters of Banke District, about 25 miles to the west. The ambush was carried out on 28 February 2005. While withdrawing, the ambushing force was surrounded by forces of the RNA and suffered heavy losses. The 37 PLA fighters killed in this action included Jit, the Brigade Commander of Second Brigade, an elite PLA formation designated as 'the mobile brigade'. A further sixteen PLA people in a blocking position were also killed.

'Jit' was Prembahadur Roka from Dhyar village, near Ragda in Jajarkot. He was a legendary fighter of renowned bravery who had taken part in many Maoist attacks since the start of the People's War, including the major assaults at Dunai in September 2000, Holeri in July 2001 and Mangalsen in February 2002. He was also a key commander in the successful attack on a RNA Ranger battalion in the forest area of Pandaun in Kailali in December 2004. Just two weeks before his death he had led the attack on the prison at Dhangadi in Kailali which had released 150 prisoners, over half of them Maoists.

The statement issued after the action by Prabhakar, the commander of the Western Division, pulled no punches. It showed in stark terms how scarred the Maoists were by the mauling they received:

> We consider this incident very serious. The human and logistical losses have seriously affected the Western Division..... having given

serious thought to our shortcomings in our analysis and synthesis of the comprehensive situation of that particular battle, we have to embrace the fact that we must advance through many sacrifices to turn the negative to positive.[8]

As divisional commander, Prabhakar must have authorised Second Brigade to carry out the ambush but Vividh, the vice divisional commander, was jointly responsible with Jit for the ill-conceived and badly executed plan which had such disastrous consequences.

Video Clip 1 is a short extract of a starkly realistic and insightful appraisal of what went wrong from a wounded combatant. In essence, he says that they were committed to the plan, and had the spirit to carry it out, but failed to understand that the enemy could discover what they were going to do. They also failed to observe his movements. They were still on the last plan. The plan was weak by being over-focused on attack. There was no plan for all-round defence when the enemy attacked them. Later in the video he says that the loss of their group leader left them devastated and that even when they broke clear there was no one to direct them.

Given all he has been through, his stoical and very articulate comments are impressive, and reflect well on his training as a PLA fighter. He concludes his analysis by saying:

> Although we may be wounded or suffering due to physical pain, we hold a spirit to give all our blood and sacrifice our lives for the Party. In that spirit of sacrifice, we are proud of the (wounded) situation we are in.

However, the body language of those around him indicates a degree of demoralisation, and this is more manifest in Video Clip 2. What is seen and heard vividly demonstrates that, whatever might be claimed in Maoist poems and songs, the PLA, like other military forces, was not immune from the fact that casualties can hit morale hard, particularly the loss of popular and well respected leaders, and particularly their loss in ill-considered and badly executed actions. It is the job of commanders to deal with the consequential damage to morale.

---

8 'Indian Army Intervenes against the Nepal People's War' by Li Onesto, 30 Jan 2005 (Countercurrents.org).

On the videos Vividh is shown addressing two different groups of clearly demoralised fighters. To the first group, shown on the clip, he says that only Jit has been lost and that the party has many more commanders. He appeals to those listening to come forward bravely and aspire to be commanders. His acknowledgement of the impact of Jit's death, and his effort to use his reputation and sacrifice to inspire those he is addressing, are common features of both talks. To the second group, not shown in the video extract, he says;

> Together we must move forward, and we must become Jit. The common goal of every member, commander and commissar of this brigade has to be: 'I want to become Jit.' How to become Jit? This is the main issue. This is a beautiful and selfless goal, one that is filled with courage and wisdom. You and I must fulfil that goal.

Aside from ideological references, most military commanders would be very satisfied to give talks of such quality to soldiers who are in the state we see them in. The body language of many of those listening is not very responsive or encouraging but, given the searing experience they have been through, that is what one would expect. They all know the commitment expected of them when they became soldiers in the PLA: in Vividh's words, at that point they signed their own death certificates.

Despite the imagery, it is a moot point how much this obligation, with its stress on the merits and value of sacrifice, differs from that of professional soldiers down through the ages. One distinguished soldier and academic memorably described the obligation as 'an unwritten contract with unlimited liability' (Hackett 1983), and the universality of remembrance rituals and the names and tributes on war memorials in every town and village in the western world attest to the near universal recognition of the value and honour placed on sacrifice.

At the practical level, Vividh assures his listeners that 'a careful and detailed analysis' of the action will be carried out. This echoes Prabhakar's reference to 'an analysis and synthesis' to identify 'shortcomings'. Nothing is known of the extent of this investigation or if anyone was held personally to account for the disaster. What is known is that just 39 days after the Ganeshpur action, despite Prabhakar stating that 'the human and logistical losses have seriously affected the Western Division', the division was part of a large force that attacked the RNA base at Khara, on the border between Rukum and Rolpa. Some elements of the division did not take part in this attack, including Vividh, the vice divisional commander. The reason for his absence, with others, can only be speculated on, but the setback at Ganeshpur must have had some impact on the morale of those from the western division, particularly from Second Brigade, who did take part in the Khara attack.

Assessment of the Ganeshpur action

The action shows the massive advantage the RNA had in tactical mobility over the PLA in the flat lands and good roads of the Tarai, and the effective use it could make of these. It also showed the tactical and operational naivety of senior PLA commanders, amounting to recklessness, in not appreciating the dangerous position their force was in, and not just because of much inferior tactical mobility. The RNA knew exactly what the Maoists were going to do, yet all too obviously the Maoist commanders had no awareness of RNA movement and positions. The inevitable result of this massive disparity in mobility and intelligence was the human and logistical losses referred to by Prabhakar in his statement. Jit and other key fighters were among the human losses, but equally significant would have been the psychological damage to confidence and morale which are key ingredients of effectiveness in any fighting force.

Background to Khara

The PLA first attacked the RNA base at Khara in May 2002. It was repulsed, with over 150 Maoists killed. It is hard to understand why the Maoist high command thought that it could succeed with another attack just two years later, knowing that the RNA had greatly strengthened the Khara fortifications. The video footage (Video Clip 3) shows the base to be well sited on high ground, thus requiring any attacking force to fight uphill through minefields and elaborate barbed-wire obstacles, all capable of being covered by machine-gun fire. The fortifications also included a layout of well-prepared trenches and bunkers. One infantry company and one engineer company, about 250 men, occupied the base.

A conventional military assessment would have indicated that an attacking force would need a strong opening bombardment of artillery and mortars, perhaps supported by air strikes, to weaken the defences before assault forces could be launched with any chance of success. Even with such preparation, however, the attacking force itself would still need strong superiority of firepower to succeed. The Maoists enjoyed none of these advantages, and the lessons of previous failed attacks should have been clear to them. In November 2002, they had failed to overcome the strongly prepared RNA positions at Khalanga in Jumla District, a setback that the Maoists subsequently acknowledged to have been a turning point in the war, and one that required a serious downscaling in their aspirations for overall military victory (see Ananta 2008). In March 2004, the PLA likewise failed to overrun the RNA defences at Beni in west Nepal, and Khara was a much tougher objective.

Information on Khara is very difficult to come by. The battle has now been written out of Maoist history, and no member of the party is prepared to talk about it to anyone. So why did this attack go ahead? Why the sensitivity and the collective amnesia about it? The answers are rooted in the bitter dispute between Prachanda and Bhattarai, which came close to splitting the CPN (Maoist) in late 2004 and early 2005. Much is known about this feud because, as part of the reconciliation deal, all their acrimonious exchanges were published at the time on the Maoist website.

The dispute came to a head in January 2005, when a politburo meeting demoted Bhattarai, his wife Hisila Yami, herself a prominent Maoist activist, and a few other key supporters, to the level of ordinary party membership. They also had restraints placed on their movement and outside communications. This dispute had a long history and many facets, but from early 2004 one key issue had begun to dominate. For some time the Maoist leadership had known that there was no solely military way forward towards seizing state power. As indicated by Ananta (2008) this truth had most likely dawned on some leaders as early as the setback at Khalanga in Jumla two years earlier. All eventually came to agree that an alliance was needed, but the two sides remained divided over whether it was to be with Nepal's political parties, facilitated by India, or with then King Gyanendra and his army. Baburam Bhattarai crystallised the division starkly when he characterised his opponents as 'those who consider feudal despotism as more progressive than capitalistic democracy.'[9]

We now know that in late 2004 Prachanda was involved in direct talks with personal representatives of Gyanendra. There was the prospect of an imminent meeting between the two and it is alleged that the carrot

---

9   Letter from Baburam Bhattarai dated 23 November 2004, published in *Samay* magazine on 6 January 2005.

being dangled before Prachanda was the prime ministership. Then came the body blow of 1 February 2005, when Gyanendra launched his coup and seized absolute power. Journalist Bharat Dahal, in an August 2007 article in *Nepal* magazine (Dahal 2007) asserted that this action led directly to the decision to launch the Khara attack:

> The timing of action against Baburam coincided with the time when Gyanendra seized power. To Prachanda, all the doors to the palace, India and Baburam were closed. He prepared a draft of the attack on Khara in order to prove his 'brilliance'. The Party's huge armed forces were mobilised for the attack, but the plan failed miserably.

This allegation could hardly be more damning – that Prachanda chose to attack the strongly held Khara position to show that, despite what Baburam Bhattarai and his supporters were saying and the hard lessons from past battles against well defended positions, there was a military way forward to seizing state power. The evidence from the videos shows the allegation to be soundly based.

The Khara battle: The start of conventional warfare

Prachanda committed both the PLA's western and central divisions to the Khara attack. Video Clip 4 shows some of the PLA crossing the Bheri river and marching through the hills on the way to the assembly area for the attack. The considerable logistic challenge of moving and feeding thousands of people across long distances in the terrain shown is not dwelt on in the videos. The two songs used as background on this clip are 'Lamo Bato' and 'Hami Rato Manche'.

In a briefing to troops on the march, Prabhakar, the commander of the Western Division, links the need for the battle directly to Gyanendra's seizure of power, and spells out its extraordinarily ambitious aim, which is to open the door to final victory (Video Clip 5). He also gives a clear exposition of the reasons for moving from combatant warfare, and from the stage of strategic balance, to one of strategic counter attack: the alternative was 'to allow our base areas to be demolished and all the people there to be massacred and destroyed'. He says that revolutionary transformation of the party was needed to escalate the war and that the party is now moving forward by being integrated and centralised – a reference, surely, to Baburam Bhattarai's demotion.

All brigade commanders and commissars interviewed before

the battle make it clear that this battle marks the move away from mobile/ combatant/guerrilla warfare to *morchabaddha yuddha* or conventional warfare; in sum, a test of strength between Prachanda's and Gyanendra's armies. All are fully confident about victory in the battle, and about its aftermath. All echo the theme of *digbijaya abhiyan* – a campaign of conquest.

The first question asked of Jiwan, the Third Brigade commander, (Video Clip 6) is very significant in pointing to Prachanda's direct and personal involvement in making the plan and defining its aim: 'In the words of Chairman Prachanda, you are in a campaign which leads up to the campaign of conquest. How have you taken this moment?' His reply is a clear confirmation of the assumption in the question. He is in no doubt either about the expected domino effect that will follow success. He says that now: 'We will launch attack after attack. We will achieve success after success. We will destroy the enemies' forts, and now we will probably advance by sweeping away the enemy.'

The same optimism radiates from Bikalpa (Video Clip 7), the Eighth Brigade vice commander, and this answer again points to Prachanda as the prime mover behind the plan to attack Khara: 'Our Chairman has a dream, which is very much linked to reality. That dream relates to victory, we have a dream to advance through Digbijaya Abhiyan.....We have an aspiration to open that door to conquest.'

Confidence in the plan and the chances of victory are vital prerequisites to success in war. One can only speculate about how it was that battle-hardened Maoist military commanders got themselves into such a delusional state of mind, but it is clear that Prachanda personally convinced them of the need for the battle, that it could and must be won, and that success would open the way to final victory.

The final orders for the attack were given round a large model built to represent Khara's features and defences. Impressive as it is, it is one-dimensional and the earlier video views of the actual Khara position show how inadequately the model represents the difficulties of attacking it. Pasang, the Central Division commander, was given overall command for the operation. His orders start with a ritual-like greeting to those present, reminding them that they have taken 'an oath of your own deaths'. He goes on in more matter-of-fact language to echo imagery from the writings of Mao about becoming 'a real new person in history'. In Video Clip 8 he produces further evidence about the provenance of the imagery of 'opening the door to conquest' and the higher purpose of the decision to attack Khara:'Let us take our revolution to that level, and let us really open the door to revolution, or in the words of the Chairman, let us 'open the door to conquest'. It is with that commitment that we have fixed this target'. The clip also shows Pasang moving on to use the model to point out ground of tactical significance. His remarks sound more like general exhortation than detailed orders, though clearly the video gives only a short version of what he must have covered.

In the video, Pasang and Prabhakar are shown sitting side by side. The body language between the two is not good, particularly that of Prabhakar when Pasang is speaking. Prabhakar's own contribution (Video Clip 9) is muted, to say the least. He opens with a rather off hand remark and gesture towards Pasang: 'We also took some help. Comrade Pasang even attended a class and returned with some training' before making some vague remarks about the history of the conflict up to this point. A later interview with Bikalpa hints strongly at major differences of opinion between the two divisions over the plan for the attack: differences that were apparently never resolved. To preserve the vital principle of unity of command, general military custom would have required the brigades of Prabhakar's division to be put under Pasang's command, with Prabhakar having no place in the command chain. In military operations, there must never be any doubt about exactly who is in charge; there can only be one overall commander and one aim, in order to ensure absolute unity and focus of effort. Any other arrangement risks confusion and disaster, which is exactly what happened to the Maoists at Khara.

Video Clip 10 shows elements of the lead assault groups moving from the Assembly Area towards the FUP on the afternoon prior to the attack. What is striking is the scarcity of rifles. In conventional military terms, those shown would be classed as engineer assault troops who will lead the attack to cut through the wire or to dig under it. Shots from this and other videos suggest that quite a few women were employed for this most hazardous of military tasks. Those seen with back packs will be carrying the ubiquitous Maoist socket bombs and others will be carrying pliers for wire cutting. The clip is also interesting for the confirmation it gives of how the PLA conducted such attacks. One survivor of a successful Maoist attack on a fortified Armed Police Force and RNA camp at Gam in Rolpa district in March 2002 describes it clearly and accurately:

> We were sleeping peacefully. We were in a very small number and
> proved no match against thousands of Maoists, most carrying grenades
> and armed to the teeth. They were Terai-based people, Tharus and
> Kham Magars. These terrorists came in three groups. At first, there
> were those who hurled grenades and at their back, there were those
> who held guns in their hands. And after those gunmen, there were
> those who were trained in carrying the dead and the wounded. Among
> them were also groups of medics (Ghale and Dangi 2002).

The evidence from the videos confirms this description. No actual
fighting is shown but there is a short sequence (Video Clip 11), which
conveys the message that the attack started in darkness. An M-17
helicopter gunship is shown hovering over the position and there is
a short sequence which shows some PLA dead and wounded near the
objective itself, with one of the latter being treated for a serious wound.
The clip is enough to convey just a little of the harsh reality of a battle
of this intensity.

The PLA did well to achieve total surprise. During the previous three
days the RNA had received reports of large columns of Maoist forces
moving across Rolpa and Pyuthan, but the exact location of the attack
was known only after it began. The attack was intense and came from all
directions. The reserve water tank of the position, which was raised above
ground, was hit at the start of the attack, draining away all the drinking
water. The M-17 helicopters giving fire support to the defenders during
the night gave a big boost to the morale of the defenders. Although the
attackers were able to close up to the wire perimeter and dig in round
the position in places, by dawn only one section of about ten people had
managed to fight their way inside the camp perimeter; but only to a
distance of 15 metres, and all of them were killed on the spot. No further
penetration was achieved.

The RNA claimed that in follow-up operations it captured documents
that showed that Pasang's plan covered the contingency of renewing
the attack the following night from the PLA's dug-in positions around
the perimeter, and there is evidence in the video that this was the
case. The attack did pause at dawn and there was a subsequent loss of
momentum. During the morning an M-17 helicopter can be seen landing
about twenty men from a Ranger battalion as reinforcements (Video
Clip 12). Their arrival gave a great boost to the morale of the surrounded
defenders. Clearly it would have had the reverse effect on the morale

of the attackers who had fought all night at such a high cost to achieve so little. It is significant that the video shows the time of this event as the point when the attack was called off. Some fifty PLA bodies were recovered from around the perimeter, but casualties must have been much higher. Some reports speak of over 200 PLA killed, with many others seriously wounded.

The attackers fought long and bravely against determined RNA resistance, but they lacked the firepower to achieve success against such a strongly entrenched and defended position. Other significant factors also worked against success. After the battle, two separate interviews with Bikalpa point to deep-rooted weaknesses within the PLA's chain of command that prevented all possibility of victory.

In the first of these (Video Clip 13) Bikalpa indicates the depth of the difference between the two divisions over the plan for the attack. He says that at a meeting Prachanda 'had made the spirit of the plan very clear to all comrades' but that there was 'a huge debate, a very long debate' between the two divisions over the tactics to be used in this first battle of conventional warfare. He alleges that Pasang's division did want the battle to be conducted over two nights, as the RNA claim the captured documents show, but that Prabhakar's division argued that the battle should start in mid-afternoon, and that they should fight through the night and take the position by noon of the next day.

Irrespective of the merits of these two plans, Bikalpa's second after-battle interview, given to some Maoist journalists, (Video Clip 14) points to even starker reasons why the attack was doomed to fail; namely, glaring weaknesses in the PLA's command and control arrangements during the battle, and confusion over the respective roles of the two divisions. He says that the western division's main role was 'to provide support'. He complains that the battle ended before some of the people under his command had been committed to the attack, generating real anger and even the threat of disobedience. This suggests that a large part of the western division were never committed to the battle. But his main criticism is more noteworthy:

> There were many problems when we went to the battle. There were many weaknesses. As we analyse things, we had to bear consequences because of certain shortcomings. Things did not happen the way we had imagined they would because there was mischief and betrayal. Many things ended up deceiving us. Whose weakness was it the

most? In clear and straightforward terms, it was the commander's weakness. It was the main commander's weakness and also ours.

An assessment of Khara

Bikalpa's criticism of Pasang is unfair and misplaced. The fact that it comes from a brigade commander in Prabhakar's division, and was filmed by a journalist attached to that division, simply confirms the suspicions expressed earlier, regarding rivalries and lack of unity of command. Pasang would seem to have done well to finish the attack when he did: throwing in more troops would simply have added to the casualties. This analysis shows that as well as lacking the firepower necessary to be successful at Khara, the PLA's senior commanders lacked the training, experience and the means of communication to ensure that up to 4000 people spread across six brigades and two divisions could be used in a properly coordinated way that made certain that their combined potential was applied effectively to the point of attack. In sum, it was not simply a case that the plan was weak, or that any of the commanders or combatants were weak. The fundamental weakness stemmed from the assessment that the PLA was in a fit state, in terms of training, equipment, experience and command arrangements, to move from mobile or guerrilla warfare to conventional warfare, and carry out a complex deliberate attack on a position as strongly defended as Khara. The responsibility for this flawed judgement ultimately has to rest with Prachanda, the PLA's Commander-in-Chief.

The final verdict on Khara is the simple, stark assessment of Ramesh Koirala, the Eighth Brigade Vice Commissar (Video Clip 15) 'the truth is: we lost. In the words of our Chairman, we weren't able to open the door of victory. It remains closed and padlocked. We couldn't unlock that padlock.'

For Prachanda, the defeat must have come as a crushing personal blow. His much-proclaimed dream of 'conquest' was shattered. There was only one direction in which he could now turn. Within four weeks of the Khara attack, Baburam Bhattarai, still reduced to a position of ordinary party member, was in Delhi with one of Prachanda's right-hand men, K B Mahara, to start the process that ultimately led to the agreement with the Nepal political parties in November 2005.

The Khara defeat left the Maoists' military reputation bruised and battered but within a few months, 'the feudal autocrat' in Kathmandu would order a deployment of his army that would give the PLA the chance to regain its lost prestige and to acquire over 200 modern weapons and large amounts of ammunition and explosives.

The background to Pili

On 24 July 2005, a mix of pioneer and combat engineers, supported by an infantry company, began to deploy to build a camp on the steep-sided banks of the Tila River, a major tributary of the Karnali in the mid-western Kalikot District. The purpose was to establish a base from which to resume the building of the Surkhet to Jumla road. The decision was taken at the direct behest of Gyanendra. By this time his credibility as an effective ruler was sinking by the day as the Maoist insurgency spread and strengthened, and as most development activities stalled. To boost his public reputation, he decided that decisive action was needed and in early July 2005, at the height of the monsoon, he ordered his army chief immediately to resume the building of the Jumla road.

The likely consequences of obeying this command should have been spelled out to Gyanendra. Instead, the order was merely passed on, and the soldiers were dispatched to build a camp in what the RNA official spokesman, Brigadier General Deepak Gurung, later described with excessive candour as 'a strategically unfavourable place'.[10] A second report quoted him as saying that 'the temporary security base at Pili was not an ideal location. The decision to set up the base there was a technical one, not a tactical one. We didn't expect our workforce to bear such an attack.'[11] It was a massive dereliction of duty not to have done so, not least in its disregard of one of the most important dictums of war: never underestimate your enemy. Grainy, long range video footage of the camp (Video Clip 16) shows that the camp was built into the side of the hill with the dominating ground on the ridge above left unoccupied, leaving it hopelessly vulnerable to any attack which came from that direction.

The Maoists heard about the RNA deployment on 2 August, ten days after the first soldiers arrived at Pili. Prabhakar was with the Second Brigade at Dashera village in Jajarkot, 70 km southeast of Pili. Vividh, the vice-divisional commander, was with the Third and Eighth Brigades in Turmakhand village in Accham District, 70 km directly west of Pili

---

10 'Defective weapons blamed for Pili disaster Kalikot debacle: a Post report'. *The Kathmandu Post,* 13 August 2005.

11 'Video footage shows gory images of slain soldiers, 'Maoists violated int'l humanitarian law': RNA' (nepalnews.com report 12 August 2005.)

but on the other side of the Karnali river, preparing to carry out an attack on Martadi, the headquarters of Bajura District. As soon as the PLA commanders heard about the Pili camp they decided that it would be an easy target and should be attacked as soon as possible.

Initially, Prachanda was reluctant to give his approval. At the time, CPN (Maoist) representatives were already in Delhi in consultation with the political parties, and a ceasefire was imminent. Prachanda clearly could not risk going into these negotiations on the back of a reversal on the scale of the failed Khara attack. His commanders assured him that success was guaranteed. The key commanders involved agreed that their forces should set off immediately with the aim of concentrating the division's three brigades at Raut hamlet, near Pakha village, just one hour east of Pili, during the early afternoon of 7 August.

PLA preparations

Before each major attack, the PLA held a 'coaching' day (the English term is used) to finalise preparations and to enable commanders to brief subordinates. Video Clip 17 shows such a briefing of company and battalion commanders of Second Brigade by Prakanda, the Regional Bureau-in-Charge. Prabhakar has spoken before him, telling those assembled that they have good intelligence about the Pili camp, that it is still being constructed, and that the fortifications are 'not something which had been constructed after years of hard work' and that 'the bunkers are made of wet mud, not cement.' He stresses that, since the work is still going on, they have no clear idea of the defensive layout they will find when they get there; flexibility and improvisation will therefore be needed. Prakanda's essential message is right on the mark: 'In war, whichever side makes mistakes faces defeat. Our enemy has just made a big mistake, and we must move quickly to take advantage of it.'

Over 150 kms away on the same day, Vividh held his coaching day for the commanders of Third and Eighth Brigades in Badi Malika secondary school in Raskot Siuna village in Kalikot district. In his 20-minute speech he, like Prabhakar, stresses the uncertainty surrounding the defensive layout they will find when they get to the objective but expresses confidence that its incomplete state gives the PLA an excellent chance of victory. He gives no orders but discusses general tactics that might be used in the attack. He also gives clear indications that the party leadership is nervous about the attack, ordering them, 'you are to return if you are not confident of success in what you are aiming'. Vividh says that the PLA has gone to attack too many places recently and has returned without fighting for various reasons, including nervousness among the top party leadership that 'we must not lose on any account'. His main message is that this time 'we must fight and win, whatever the difficulties'.

In Video Clip 18 Vividh makes a highly practical point on sacrifice which is perhaps not sufficiently stressed by academic commentators on Nepal's Maoists:

> The main thing is that we go forward at once. And although sacrifice is the main thing when we do this, we must not take the issues of arms, technology and the modalities of attack lightly. The history of the proletariat group has been such that it has captured the world through sacrifice of life. So if our sacrifice is in accordance with the right modalities, rules and procedures, such a sacrifice can be accepted more easily. But if there are flaws in our styles, procedures and processes, the sacrifice occurring under such pretext becomes a difficult one to accept.

This shows not a thoughtless and blind ideological approach to sacrifice but a highly practical consideration of what is required to make death in combat both worthy and acceptable.

Perhaps the most interesting parts of the Pili videos are the contributions that Vividh invites from the floor. Eleven unnamed commanders speak, probably of battalion and company level. These are the people at the heart of Maoist military success. It is a safe bet that they would not be in this room unless they had proved themselves in many actions, leading from the front in the style required by all successful military organisations. It is impossible to over-stress the importance of such leadership in war. None of the speakers dwell on ideology. All are clearly highly experienced battlefield commanders. They speak incisively, candidly and critically, often about lessons from past battles that have not been learnt or put into practice. Video Clip 19 shows just four of them.

The first speaker essentially says that attacks are failing because of a gap between the understanding of the plan beforehand and its practical application during implementation. Only by closing this gap will success come, he stresses. The second speaker makes this point even more starkly. He refers to Khara to highlight that if everyone has a different understanding of the plan beforehand, there will never be consistency in implementation. He underlines his case by asking a highly pertinent rhetorical question: before Khara everyone got the same coaching so why was there such variation in implementation? What is decided before the battle is not being implemented, he says.

The third speaker is emboldened enough to cast doubt over the move to *morchabaddha yuddha* or conventional warfare. He does not mention the phrase but his line is clear enough. After moving to the unique stage of strategic counter attack the desired results are not being achieved: 'Therefore, let's accept that we have not won. So if we are to return from this point, I would say that the party centre must reconsider the war-graph of the force's counter-attack strategy. They should look back and trace any mistakes.'

The fourth speaker's contribution is typical of many in highlighting practical lessons gleaned from previous attacks. His main point is that the PLA has limited arms technology so it is important to make the best use of what they do have. He highlights weaknesses such as wasting ammunition and throwing grenades to land outside wire perimeters rather than inside, and advocates the use of picking up and using discarded enemy arms and grenades as they fight through positions.

The approach march and battle

Getting to the objective on time required the three brigades to do a five-day forced march with little food or rest on two different routes. The videos show that both routes were very tough going at the height of the monsoon, and with a series of 4000-metre ridges to be traversed. Second Brigade travelled in an almost straight line from Jajarkot. Third and Eighth Brigades first had to head northeast in order to cross the Karnali at the Jharkot bridge in Ramkot, well to the north of Manma, the district headquarters. They then came south over Chuli Himalaya to meet up with the Second Brigade at Raut village.

Video Clip 20 shows: the nature of the terrain over which Prabhakar and Second Brigade marched from Jajarkot; a short briefing which took place at midday on the day of the attack, in which speed and urgency is stressed; and the descent to cross the Tila river and the approach march to the objective along the north bank of the river. A helicopter is seen landing 300 metres outside the perimeter of the RNA camp just as the Maoists are moving into position to start the attack. There are also some long distance views of the camp.

The quality of the video drops dramatically at the start of the attack because of fading light and loss of lens focus, but the very short Video Clip 21 is worth particular mention because of what it conveys in such a short time. Shot just after the helicopter landed, it shows elements of Eighth Brigade preparing to take their place in the assault. At the beginning, the light of battle can be seen in the eyes of the two young women being loaded up with the packs carrying the socket bombs. The scene then shifts to show very young and thin people on the trail waiting their turn to be committed, wearing little so that they do not get their clothes caught on the wire as they dig under it or cut it. At the end, two young girls are seen with wire cutters, with two lads behind them holding digging tools to burrow under the wire. This clip again indicates that quite a few women were employed for this most hazardous of military tasks: breaching defences. As fighters, they would probably have had the highest casualty rate of all. In most armies many of them would have their chests covered in medals, including those for the most conspicuous bravery.

Prabhakar and Vividh met as arranged at 1 pm at Raut hamlet near Pakha village and agreed that H hour should be 6pm that evening. The PLA plan was basic in the extreme. Each brigade was simply given an arc of responsibility so as to encircle the camp and ordered to breach the fence perimeter and make the best progress it could into the RNA camp. Attacking from all directions was a sure recipe for a fair measure of chaos and confusion, as well as increasing the risk of inflicting casualties on one's own forces. The very loose nature of the plan and the other factors mentioned would have put a very strong premium on dash, initiative, bravery and strong leadership at platoon and company level.

The attack achieved total surprise: this in itself is a massive indictment of the RNA's security precautions. The landing of the helicopter distracted the defenders as they went to unload it. The Maoist commanders decided to take advantage of this opportunity, and the attack began at 5:45 pm, though probably by fire only at this stage since the main attack formations were not yet in a position to physically attack the perimeter of the camp itself. The video shows that Second Brigade was about an hour behind the other brigades in getting into position.

The Maoists quickly captured a number of unarmed RNA soldiers who had been unloading the helicopter, including, they claim, the commanding officer of the battalion, who had come to the helipad. The commander managed to escape during the subsequent confusion, and turned up two days later at Manma, along with 114 other men from the battalion who had also somehow managed to escape from the camp. Some evidence of their rapid exit and bedraggled state comes from an article by Tularam Pandey, the first journalist to arrive in the camp, just six days after the attack. He describes a scene of utter devastation. Along the trail from Manma to Pili, he records, 'there were torn pieces of uniform, abandoned boots, caps and cartridges of bullets'. He also quoted villagers as recalling how the soldiers who escaped were 'hungry and naked', and that they gave the soldiers 'food, clothes, shoes'.[12]

The RNA later announced that 227 soldiers had been in the camp at the time of the attack. There were probably a few more, since we know that 58 were killed, 60 were taken prisoner and 115 turned up at Manma. This means that about 120 soldiers stood their ground to resist the Maoists. The RNA drew a veil over who bravely stood and fought, and who did not. Bad weather prevented any air support from MI-17 helicopters. More than 3000 Maoists took part in the attack, so it was not surprising that RNA resistance effectively ceased after about two hours of actual fighting. The outnumbered RNA men, taken by surprise in a badly sited and unprepared camp, did well to hold out for so long. The turning point in the battle came when a seven-man section, which was part of the force that attacked from the unoccupied higher ground, overran the one General Purpose Machine Gun (GPMG) and killed its crew. This had kept the Maoists pinned down for some time. Five of the section were killed and the other two seriously wounded. After that it became, in military parlance, a case of mopping-up other isolated elements, no doubt in an environment of considerable chaos, which probably accounts for different claims for the length of the battle.

The Maoists were ravenous and totally exhausted, so their first action after the battle was to cook a meal from captured RNA rations. Most slept near the camp, though some remained busy destroying and salvaging RNA kit and equipment during the night, an activity that might again have misled some villagers about the actual duration of the attack. The first Maoists began withdrawing at six the next morning. By midday they had all left, having stripped the camp of all that was useful to them, and taking along sixty RNA prisoners. Over 70,000 rounds of ammunition of different calibre were captured, and among

---

12 'Reporter's diary from Pili' by Tularam Pandey, *Kantipur*, 22 August 2005, as reproduced in *Nepali Times*, No. 262, 26 August 2005.

the Maoist weapon haul were: one 81mm mortar with 150 bombs, one GPMG, twenty Light Machine Guns, seventy INSAS rifles, and eighty SLR rifles. Video Clip 22 shows the weapons on display at a western division gathering that took place at Bhadam in Jajarkot five weeks later. The first RNA troops arrived at Pili from Manma at 11:00 am on 9 August, a full day after the Maoist withdrawal. Twenty-six Maoists were killed in the attack. The RNA prisoners were released to the Red Cross on 14 September.

The RNA at the time, and later, claim that the defenders held out for longer than is described here, but just 26 PLA killed in an attack of this scale does not indicate prolonged and over-resolute resistance from what was a very well armed force. Maoist journalists writing for *Janadesh*, the Maoist news outlet, with memories of Khara to expunge, also had an obvious interest in exaggerating the length of RNA resistance and the strength of the defences. They wrote what I believe to be elaborate, largely fictitious descriptions of the attack, including claiming that the PLA had to endure attacks from MI-17 helicopters. However, given the direct personal connection of Gyanendra and his army chief, General Pyar Jung Thapa, to the debacle, it was the RNA who had the greater interest in distracting people from asking questions about who was responsible. It quickly became apparent that there was to be no question of acknowledging mistakes or of paying proper tribute to the soldiers who fought bravely under such disadvantageous conditions. Instead, their sacrifice was derided and disparaged in an attempt to cover up for gross incompetence and grave dereliction of duty on the part of the top brass. Not even the dead bodies of the soldiers were to be exempt from being put on display in a public relations exercise designed to achieve this nefarious purpose.[13]

An assessment of Pili

What cannot be disputed is that Pili was a total rout and a serious humiliation for the RNA. It was an object lesson in the disastrous consequences of underestimating one's enemy. The outcome was a major boost to the prestige of the PLA and its military prowess, at a politically critical time for the Maoists. The PLA commanders and their soldiers deserve great credit for concentrating so quickly to carry out this attack despite the arduous terrain and difficult conditions they had

---

13 See nepalnews.com report referred to at Footnote 11. Also Cowan (2008).

to overcome. Their dash and skill achieved a situation of advantage akin to Sun Tzu's ideal of applying strength against weakness, in contrast to what had been attempted at Khara. The weakness that was exploited stemmed partly from poor tactical decisions by local commanders in how they laid out the camp, but mainly from the incompetence and appallingly bad judgement of senior RNA commanders who allowed their soldiers to be deployed in such an exposed position without adequate protection.

The video covering the action amply demonstrates the particular strengths of the PLA. The combatants are shown to have levels of toughness, resilience and commitment that one looks for in the best of military organisations. Most striking are the personal qualities shown by the company and battalion commanders who spoke at Vividh's coaching. Very few people from this group have ever uttered a word in public but their quality as soldiers and leaders shines through, as does their clear aptitude and very obvious enthusiasm for soldiering. As explained, the nature of the Pili battle would have put a premium on brave and innovative leadership at platoon and company level, and it is clear that those seen on the video measured up fully to what was required.

Overall assessment

So what is the overall assessment of the PLA when measured against the three components of fighting power listed earlier? On the physical component, the videos confirm that although the PLA was not short of manpower and could improvise logistic support to enable large numbers of combatants to move quickly across long distances in tough terrain, it was woefully weak in firepower. Large numbers of combatants did not have rifles, and machine guns and mortars were in scarce supply. Socket bombs and other home-made explosive devices could only compensate for this deficiency to some limited degree. This was one prime reason for the defeat at Khara, and would have been a lasting impediment to a successful escalation of their military effort to the level of conventional warfare.

The PLA also shows up moderately in the area of the conceptual component. Senior commanders were highly motivated and committed, and many of them had years of experience of fighting at company level, but understandably they lacked training and experience to command and manoeuvre brigades in a large contact battle. The communication means at their disposal was also inadequate for this purpose and Khara showed the inevitable outcome when unity of command is lacking and when there are no properly understood and well-practised procedures for the delegation of authority and responsibility. The escalation to *morchabaddha yuddha* ruthlessly exposed these weaknesses and was a grave error, as the young commander in the schoolroom pointed out.

On the moral component, the videos clearly show that the PLA scores impressively high against all the criteria listed: mentally prepared for fighting; belief in a cause; highly motivated; a strong sense of purpose; brave and talented leadership; and a willingness to put one's life on the line, whatever the danger. These very great strengths helped to compensate for many of the other weakness identified. However, Ganeshpur showed that the PLA was not immune from the fact that severe setbacks and casualties can hit morale hard, particularly when those concerned can see that their commanders failed them. The crushing defeat at Khara also showed the grievous error of elevating this component as being supreme above all other considerations. Before World War I, the French and British generals committed the same mistake but, like the PLA at Khara, they learned the hard way, and at great human cost, that offensive spirit and high morale can only carry an attack so far when faced with the physical realities of barbed wire, well-prepared entrenchments, machine-gun fire and determined defenders.

On balance, as a guerrilla army using the tactics and strategy of the form of warfare set down by Mao, the PLA performed highly effectively. It lacked the capacity to move successfully to the level of conventional war, but there can be little doubt about the significance of its central achievement in fighting an army armed to the teeth by India and the US to a strategic stalemate (see Cowan 2006). In doing so it played a pivotal role in ushering in the momentous political changes seen in Nepal over the last 4 years.

Nearly four years after the signing of the Comprehensive Peace Agreement that brought the conflict to a close, the PLA combatants who achieved this impressive feat of arms still languish in UN supervised cantonments despite the agreement providing for a special committee to supervise, rehabilitate and integrate them. Would they make good soldiers in a conventional army? There was a clear ideological dimension to their training and culture but, on the evidence of the videos, the PLA knew that, at root, military success is fundamentally based on the unquantifiable but eternal martial qualities of leadership, discipline, courage, tenacity, willingness to endure hardship and danger, and ultimately to risk and if necessary sacrifice one's life.

Bringing the combatants together with elements of the present Nepal Army to form a new army in Nepal would take time and considerable effort but with the right military and political will, and with the right investment in suitable confidence building measures, and as part of a total reform of the Nepal Security Sector, I am certain that it could be done, following patterns adopted in other parts of the world. All the provisos listed are important but the process will remain stalled until some political will emerges to make it happen. This seems further away than ever, as therefore does the prospect of consolidating peace and democracy in anything that remotely could be described as a New Nepal.

Appendix: Extracts from video clips cited

Video Clip 1 (Wounded combatant) 00.55
'Comrades, on the question of the implementation of our plan in particular, our spirit was at its own height. For our part, we were committed to implementing the plan made by the Party. We had the kind of spirit that would have been necessary in order to implement that plan and to attack the enemy, in one way or another, as a tiger would do. And we maintained that spirit. However, we did not realise that the enemy could possibly discover our plan, or (let us say that) we failed to understand the enemy. We observed the enemy's movement only from one side; and, like our Party, we failed to observe their all-round movement. Neither could we make the Party's plan an objective one accordingly. We did not watch the movement from the Gulariya side but followed the (same/previous) plan. While we even chased the enemy coming from the Gulariya side, we failed to look in all directions. Let us say that there was a planner's weakness in this. Anyway, such a situation arose.'

Video Clip 2 (Vividh to demoralised combatants) 01.10
'Comrades, at times of loss, incompleteness and inadequacy, we must find adequateness and wholeness. Only then can we go forward. We must bear this in mind. Therefore, we must not forget this, and we are together in this. Only Jeetji has been knocked down. Our Party still

has many more commanders. Those who cannot become commanders shall not become commanders now. The coming steps shall determine this. Please be prepared. We shall recruit people from here itself. Come forward bravely, and together we shall proceed. We shall sit with all comrades for a careful and detailed analysis.'

Video Clip 3 (Scenes of Khara objective) 00.18

Video Clip 4 (PLA approach march: crossing Bheri; through the hills) 00.51

Video Clip 5 (Prabhakar's orders on march) 01.59
'Gyanendra Shahi's (sic) coup is not his success; it is the success of the People's War. This dramatic change in circumstances has posed a question for us. Should we let the battle we have fought so far collapse? Should we return to combatant warfare? Or should we move forward? Should we demolish our base areas and let all the people there be massacred and destroyed, or should two to four hundred of us die in order to open the door of final victory? The question lies here.

From the point of class struggle, we have entered the plan of counterattack. From the subjective and two-line point of view, we have arrived at a new height of the Party's rectification. These two things – counterattack and rectification – the question of strategic counterattack and revolutionary transformation is linked to the entire life of the People's War.

Revolutionary transformation was necessary in order for us to enter the stage of strategic counterattack. A leap was necessary. Our styles, our organization, our mobilisation, our interim operation, all these had to be developed in a new manner. For our counterattack, it was necessary to redefine in a new way our political and military mobilisation. The Central Committee of the Party did so. We are in a situation where the Party is moving forward by still being integrated and centralised.'

Video Clip 6 (Third Brigade Commander Jiwan interview) 01.27
Question: Comrade Jiwan, you are the Commander of the PLA's Lisne Gam Third Brigade. In the words of Chairman Prachanda, you are in a campaign which leads up to the campaign for Digbijaya (conquering). How have you taken this moment?
Jiwan: The Party Headquarters has ordered the move to conventional

warfare to begin the Digbijaya Abhiyan (campaign of conquest). To transform our phase of strategic counterattack and mobile warfare into conventional warfare. I have taken this opportunity to be part of the PLA, fighting, clashing and winning, as a good opportunity. It may be that history will give us several other opportunities. We feel that this is an important opportunity for us to fight for the liberation of the country and its people, or our proletarian class.

Question: In one word, what would you say about the differences there will be between the last battle and this one?

Jiwan: In one word, I would say that during the last battle, after launching one attack we took plenty of rest (as we could afford it). Now, what order we will receive after the attack is not rigid. We will launch attacks after attacks. We will achieve success after success. We will destroy the enemies' forts, and now we will probably advance by sweeping away the enemy.

Video Clip 7 (Eight Brigade Vice-Commander Bikalpa interview) 00.58
Question: Comrade, what are your thoughts? How do you think this conventional warfare battle will go? What do you hope?

Bikalpa: Our Chairman has a dream, which is very much linked to reality. And that dream relates to conquest. We have a dream to advance through the *digbijaya abhiyan* (campaign of conquest), as the first morning after the success of our preliminary battle of conventional warfare dawns. We have an aspiration to open that door to conquest. At the moment, I am dreaming that I am with many people, many red combatants; together, we are marching to our victory campaign, firing our machine guns, chasing the enemies, capturing them; we are advancing and they are running away.

Video Clip 8 (Pasang's orders) 00.39
'We should become that new person, and we should make a commitment to become that person. It is necessary for us to make a promise and a commitment from a certain height so that we can prove ourselves a new person in history. Let us take our revolution to that level, and let us really open the door to revolution, or in the words of the Chairman, let us open the door to conquering. It is with that commitment that we have *fixed this target.*

This portion has been cleared (left empty) because if the enemy escapes from here, let them. We will ambush here to give them an exit from here, in one place.'

Video Clip 9 (Prabhakar's orders) 00.30
'We began to implement... In the first phase, we obviously used whatever strength and capabilities we had. We also took some help. Comrade Pasang even attended a class and returned with (some) training. And we did those exercises. We obviously had slogans relating to raising the development of the combatant warfare to a new height.'

Video Clip 10 (Move to the Forming Up Point for attack) 01.08

Video Clip 11 (Night scene) 00.52

Video Clip 12 (Helicopter arrival) 00.36

Video Clip 13 (Bikalpa second interview) 01.31
'Since there weren't many plans, we thought of going to one main point. The plan was thought out but stopped. Like we stopped at Bhalubang and came here. When that happened, it affected us to an extent. Then we had a meeting. Our Chairman Comrade made the spirit of our plan clear to all comrades.

We all had an opportunity to put forward our views, and we focused on what kind of plan to make. All the comrades from our Division suggested that we must plan things from a new angle. This was about the preparation of a long war through conventional battles. In the plan they submitted, it was proposed that the war should both begin and end at night. They were proposing to move the force to the day shift and fight for two days but only during night time. But we were emphasising that the battle should start during the day instead of at night and that we should also capture during the day. We would begin by at least 3 or 4, and by 12 on the next day, we would capture. That's how a plan to fight a long battle was being formed. There was also a huge debate on that topic. A very long one ... (speech incomplete)'

Video Clip 14 (Bikalpa third interview) 01.59
'There had been an agreement on how we were going to advance and what tactics were to be used. As this was the first battle of conventional warfare, it was a transitional plan. Therefore, we should not call it an absolute conventional battle. Let's say that there was a firm coordination that we would rise above a dynamic combatant battle.

There were many problems when we went to the battle. There were many weaknesses. As we analyse things, we had to bear consequences because of certain shortcomings. Things didn't happen the way we'd imagined they would because there was mischief and betrayal. Many things ended up deceiving us. Whose weakness was it the most? Our main role here was to provide assistance. As we've mentioned before, this is not the weakness of the combatants. In clear and straight-forward terms, it was the commander's weakness. It was the main commander's weakness and also ours.

The combatants were raising their fists and shedding tears, refusing to withdraw. Yet they had to. Those combatants do not have any weakness. This is what we'd stated, and this is also the truth. We are not exaggerating, for this is the reality and the science.

The entire force was ready to fight. But they did not have an opportunity. Our Company 21 did not get to fight. In fact, our Division's Company 21 was left untouched. But they withdrew. Why did they withdraw? Because they were withdrawn by the commander! The plan was withdrawn. Whose fault is it? It is the commander's. Again, there were certainly little weaknesses on our part, in the process of withdrawing.'

Video Clip 15 (Eight Brigade Commissar Ramesh Koirala) 00.17
'Having said that, the truth is we have lost. In the words of our Chairman, we weren't able to open the door of victory. It remains closed and padlocked. We couldn't unlock that padlock.'

Video Clip 16 (View of Pili camp) 00.34

Video Clip 17 (Prakanda's briefing) 00.51
'A discussion also took place between us. How do you think defeat happens? Whichever army makes a mistake faces defeat. Whoever makes mistakes or wherever mistakes occur, that leads to defeat. If you look at it closely, our enemy has made a grave mistake. However, there is also a military plan in there. They have an alternative plan, and a political plan is also in place. They have made a mistake. How quickly will our commander comrades and our army be able to spot this mistake and the position of the enemy? If we can go forward and do something by immediately taking an initiative and converting it into a scientific plan we can certainly take control...'

Video Clip 18 (Vividh Briefing extract) 00.56

'The main thing is that we go forward at once. And although sacrifice is the main thing when we do this, we must not take the issues of arms, technology and the modalities of attack lightly. The history of the proletariat group has been such that it has captured the world through sacrifice of life. So if our sacrifice is in accordance with the right modalities, rules and procedures, such a sacrifice can be accepted more easily. But if there are flaws in our styles, procedures and processes, the sacrifice occurring under such pretext becomes a difficult one to accept.'

Video Clip 19 (Four combatants speak at briefing) 28.1 MB 03.01

Speaker 1: 'The problem until now is the consistency in our understanding. Consistency in understanding means consistency in implementation. When there is consistency in implementation, or in understanding, we can win, as that guarantees our victory. We are attempting to focus our entire Division here at this point in time, and this is necessary, too. If the total force of our Division, especially ranging from the command force to other ranks, can maintain consistency in executing and understanding the plan, we can win there.'

Speaker 2: 'If every member has an incorrect understanding of every organisational plan, there is no question of consistency in implementation. There will obviously be variation in that case. We see a similar situation in Khara now. We believe everyone received coaching together at the same place. Why was there a variation? Commanders, commissars and VC comrades received coaching from the company VC. When we are at the implementation stage, the technique is put to test. The force technique on which we decided prior to the war is not being implemented.'

Speaker 3: 'It is certain that we have not been able to achieve the desired success after entering this unique stage of strategic counter-attack and conducting various activities. I think we are faced with challenges at the moment. The revolutionary party and the revolutionary people's power as well as communities are giving us a challenge. And we have not been able to fulfil our objectives. Therefore, let's accept that we have not won. So if we are to return from this point, I would say that the party centre must reconsider the war-graph of the force's counter-attack strategy. They should look back and trace any mistakes.'

Speaker 4: 'Therefore, in order to make every unit offensive (as in original use), we must keep them fresh and clear from every angle. On the other hand, our arms technology is limited. Therefore, we must pay attention to the issue of defeating the enemy and the proper use of the arms we have.

We have a problem with our arms. We have been carelessly firing more bullets and haven't been able to save them as necessary. If we look at what happened in the Kusum attack, when we entered their inner bunker and fortification, we threw away a lot of their ammunition. We succeeded in throwing them out of the barbed wire. We threw several M-36s and hand grenades out of the barbed wire. But there is no blade in our pockets and our guns are empty. We have run out of grenades, so we will order those from outside. What went wrong? Maybe we were not able to use our discretion. We could not use their arms, although we certainly used them at Gam. If we remain alert and use their weapons to attack them, get in close and at high speed, we can surely win this battle. For this to happen, we must move forward with seriousness, and if we do that I feel that we could win and that victory will be ours.'

Video Clip 20 (Second Brigade approach march to Pili, briefing before attack, march along Tila river, helicopter landing) 02.15

Video Clip 21 (Preparations for attack) 00.23

Video Clip 22 (The Pili weapons haul) 00.43

References

Ananta, Barshaman Pun 2008. 'The development of tactical line; history of Party and PLA.' *Red Star* 1(4), February 16-29.

von Clausewitz, C. 1984. *On War*. Translated by M.E. Howard and P. Paret. Princeton: Princeton University Press.

Cowan, S. 2006. 'Nepal's two wars'. *Himal Southasian*, (March): 32-5.

Cowan, S. 2008. 'The lost battles of Khara and Pili'. *Himal Southasian* (September): 25-30.

Dahal, B. 2007. 'Tripakshiya bhumaribhitra maobadi' (Maoists in the tripartite whirlpool). *Nepal*, 5 August.

de Sales, A. 2003. 'Remarks on revolutionary songs and iconography'. *European Bulletin of Himalayan Research* 24: 5-24.

Ghale, K. and K.R. Dangi 2002. 'A tale of Tuesday night horror in Gam'. *The Kathmandu Post*, 12 May.

Griffith, S. B. 1961. *Mao Tse Tung on Guerrilla Warfare*. New York: Praeger.

Hackett, J. 1983. *The Profession of Arms*. London: Sidgwick and Jackson.

Keegan, J. and A. Wheatcroft 1976. *Who's Who in Military History from 1453 to the present day*. New York: William Morrow and Co.

Keegan, J. 1993. *A History of Warfare*. London: Hutchinson 1993.

Lecomte-Tilouine, M. 2006. 'Kill one he becomes one hundred: martyrdom as generative sacrifice in the Nepal People's War'. *Social Analysis* 50(1) (special issue on 'Noble Death', edited by Michael Roberts): 51-72.

Mottin, M. 2010. 'Catchy melodies and clenched fists: performance as politics in Maoist cultural programs'. In *The Maoist Insurgency in Nepal: Revolution in the twenty-first century*, edited by Mahendra Lawoti and Anup K. Pahari. London and NewYork: Routledge, pp. 52-73

Ogura, K. 2004. 'Realities and images of Nepal's Maoists after the attack on Beni'. *European Bulletin of Himalayan Research* 27: 67-125.

Ogura, K. 2008. *Seeking State Power: The Communist Party of Nepal (Maoist)*. (Berghof Transitions Series No. 3). Berlin: Berghof Research Center for Constructive Conflict Management.

Sawyer, R. (tr.) 1984. *Art of War*, by Sun Tzu. Boulder: Westview Press.

Sawyer, R. (tr.) 1993. *The Seven Great Military Classics of Ancient China*. Boulder: Westview Press).

Stirr, A. 2013. 'Tears for the revolution: Nepali musical nationalism, emotion and the Maoist movement'. In *People's War in Nepal: An anthropological and historical analysis*, edited by Marie Lecomte-Tilouine.

This article has been republished with permission from *European Bulletin of Himalayan Research* 37:82-116 (2010). The original can be found online at: http://himalaya.socanth.cam.ac.uk/collections/journals/ebhr/pdf/EBHR_37_04.pdf

A later version of this article appeared as a chapter in a book edited by Marie Lecomte-Tilouine, *Revolution in Nepal. An Anthropological and Historical Approach to the People's War*. The videos quoted, neatly listed and named, with English sub titles, can be found at 'Chapter 9', under Sam Cowan, at this link: https://www.vjf.cnrs.fr/himalaya/RevolutionNepal/

Addendum December 2017

In the absence of any political will, there has been no meaningful reform of Nepal's Security Sector. A Seven-Point Agreement was eventually signed in November 2011 which outlined three options for the ex-combatants still left in the cantonments: integration into the Nepal Army, rehabilitation or voluntary retirement. The agreement also specified that up to 6,500 Maoist combatants would be integrated into the Nepal Army. The final tally of ex-combatants who opted for the army was 1,422 (104 of whom were women), while 15,630 opted for integration back into society. They were given a one-time cash payment that ranged from NPR 500,000–800,000 (approximately USD $5,000–8,000), depending on rank. The cantonments were finally closed in 2012. According to an agreement of 13 March 2013, the officer ranks in the Nepal Army allocated to ex-combatants, were: Colonel (1 position); Lieutenant Colonels (2); Majors (13); Captains (30) and Lieutenants (24). The Army was permitted to recruit an extra 3000 plus soldiers as part of this process. A significant number of senior posts were also added. An editorial in *The Kathmandu Post* of May 9, 2012, ('Right Sizing') stated, 'Nepal has no need for a military that includes over 95,000 personnel. This huge body poses a tremendous drain on the state exchequer, something which countries as poor as Nepal can ill afford. It is essential that the political parties decide in the near future to significantly cut down the size of this institution.' No such action has been taken.

Two of the PLA leaders featured in this article have made successful transitions to political life. 'Pasang', Nanda Kishore Pun, is the current Vice-President of Nepal and 'Prabhakar', Janardan Sharma, is a former Home Minister and Minister for Energy, and remains an influential Maoist political leader.

Maobadi: Photographs

Foreword to Maobadi *by Kevin Bubriski, Himal Books, Lalitpur, Nepal, 2011*

The strikingly evocative photographs in this book are bound to raise many questions in the minds of readers. What motivated these people to commit themselves so totally to the Maoist cause? How much fighting did they personally do during the long 10 years of conflict? How much dying and suffering did they see and contribute to? Four years after it ended, do they still think that all the death, suffering and destruction was worth it? Only the individuals concerned can properly answer such questions but three other pertinent questions are open to reasoned analysis. How effective were they as an armed force? What does the future hold for them? Would they make good soldiers in a conventional army?

In their smart new combat clothing the combatants look the part but such outward manifestations are notoriously poor indicators of military prowess. An objective analysis of the Maoist conflict in Nepal shows that it ended in a situation of strategic stalemate, largely because both sides fought two very different wars. The Royal Nepal Army (RNA) fought a conventional war of attrition to defend key territory and to impose maximum casualties on the Maoists with the aim of inducing a collapse in their morale. The Maoists, following the tactical and strategic dictums of Mao Tse-Tung, fought primarily for control of the people. When they stuck to Mao's basic guerrilla tactics of avoiding head-on battles they were very successful. However, through the hard lessons of tactical defeats, invariably when they over-reached their capability, they came to appreciate that an enduring deficiency in weapons meant that they could never seize or hold anything in the face of RNA action or reaction. In war that is fought among the people and waged primarily to gain their support, the task of the state's security forces is the more difficult one because ultimately the insurgents do not need the support of the people to stop effective governance in rural areas. All they need is for the people not actively to support the state. Much more than the insurgents, therefore, it is the state that needs the people's support. This is why, apart from the moral and legal imperatives, there is a human rights link to military effectiveness in such conflicts. In Nepal both sides committed appalling human rights abuses but it is the State and its security forces that have to set a higher standard of behaviour based on operating within the law. If they descend to lawlessness, people inevitably come to the conclusion that for them there is no difference between the army and those who are opposing the State by violent means. In such a situation all legal and moral anchor points break away and the inevitable result is the widespread abuse of human rights that was seen during the conflict and in the state of impunity which still prevails in Nepal today

In this conflict of 'two wars' there was no possibility of a solution by arms. Each side could demonstrate that it was making progress according to its own criteria of success but neither was ever able to deliver a decisive strategic blow that would end in the capitulation of the other. The history of the last sixty years of counterinsurgency operations the world over is littered with optimistic predictions about imminent victory that have proved consistently and hopelessly illusory, and Nepal was no exception. At various stages, public pronouncements were made in Kathmandu that 'the back of the Maoists had been broken'; and that 'the RNA would finish them off in another six months'. Many 'six-month' periods passed but, when the final peace accord was eventually signed, the Maoists were demonstrably a long way from being finished.

It is not surprising, therefore, that the Comprehensive Peace Agreement, reflecting the ground reality of strategic stalemate, speaks of 'armies of both sides', and that the Agreement on Monitoring of the Management of Arms and Armies treats the two armies together in such key areas as UN monitoring, while at the same time making specific provisions which reflect the continuing role of the army of the state.

As I write, over four years after the signing of the peace agreement that brought the conflict to a close, the Maoist combatants still languish in cantonments despite the agreement providing for a special committee to supervise, rehabilitate and integrate them. There have been various false dawns but no resolution of the issue has been achieved. All parties share the blame for this state of affairs. The Maoist leadership complicated the issue by bringing into the cantonments thousands who were not entitled to be there. When in government they failed to address the future of their own combatants or to develop a plan that could win broader political support for democratic control of the Nepal Army, which is a related and essential element of the peace agreement. Other political parties have shown little urgency to address the two issues and the Nepal Army has been, to say the least, uncooperative on both points.

There was and remains a clear ideological dimension to the training and culture of the combatants but a study of military actions during the conflict shows that the Maoists knew that, at root, military success is fundamentally based on the unquantifiable but eternal martial qualities of leadership, discipline, courage, willingness to endure hardship and danger, and ultimately to risk and if necessary sacrifice one's life. Time and again, in success and failure, the combatants displayed in abundance just such qualities. Bringing some of them together with elements of the present Nepal Army to form a new army in Nepal would take time and considerable effort but, with the right military and political will, and with the right investment in suitable confidence building measures, and as part of a total reform of the bloated Nepal Security Sector, I am certain that it could be done, following patterns adopted in other parts of the world. All the provisos listed are important but the process will remain stalled until some strong political will emerges to make it happen.

Sam Cowan
Oxford 27 Dec 2010

Note: For a short explanation on what eventually happened to these Maoist combatants, see the Addendum in the previous chapter.

Colonial Dogma

An op-ed published in The Kathmandu Post, *giving a brief but candid review of the history of Gurkha recruitment to serve the British Crown*

The NA's web site has a page headed 'State of Inclusiveness' which asserts that 'in Nepal different castes and ethnic groups have different motivation for their employment'. The context makes clear that this is a basis for explaining why so few Madeshis either join, or are interested in joining, the NA. There is a Nepali historical context for believing that certain groups are suited to fighting and others are not but the belief has strong echoes of the influential idea of 'martial races' which emerged in late British colonial history, and had a direct impact on Nepal. The background should therefore be of interest.

The main agent for the military conquest of large areas of India by the British East India Company was the Bengal Army of the Company. This was recruited from a very narrow social base; for example, by the early 19th century, three quarters of the Bengal Native Infantry were high caste men from Awadh, mainly Brahmans. The Bengal Army formed the bulk of the force which invaded Nepal in 1814, and destroyed the Sikh state in the wars of 1845 and 1849.

The revolt against British rule in 1857 was led by the Bengal Army but it is worth noting that even after this great trauma, which resulted in the abolition of the East India Company, the British decided that, although the reorganised Indian Army (as it was now called) would have a wider social base, it would still have to be based mainly on Bengali recruits.

It was not until the 1870s that this policy started to be turned on its head when the formidably powerful and persuasive Lord (as he later became) Roberts first started to enunciate his martial race theory. By the mid-1890s, to quote one authority, (Onassi: *The Sepoy and the Raj*) this theory had become not just a colonial policy but a colonial obsession.

Roberts was fanatic in his belief that the Russians were bound to attack India and that a European Army could never be defeated by soldiers reared in the plains: only 'highlanders' would have the necessary genes and breeding (through blood and climatic environment) to do so. Bengalis were to be discarded as fast as possible and more men of 'the right stamp' recruited to replace them

Sikhs were declared as honorary highlanders. Of course, part of the theory heavily stressed that these 'highlanders' would have to be led by British officers if they were to do the job expected of them. This all played into the parallel theory which gathered increasing momentum among the British governing classes in India during the later 19th century that Bengalis and other high caste Hindus were effeminate: that they lacked the necessary masculine character and qualities to fight.

After their success in the Afghanistan campaign of 1878-80, Gurkhas moved to the top of Robert's shopping list of men who had the right qualities to fight the Russians. In 1885, as C-in-C, he approved the doubling of Gurkha strength by recruiting five more Gurkha battalions. Bir Shumsher had just emerged at this time as the Maharajah after the assassination of Ranaudip Singh. He craved recognition by the British who had control over Jung Bahadur's surviving sons and relatives. He gained the legitimacy he sought after agreeing not just to cooperate with the clandestine system of regimental recruitment which has been in place up to that stage but actively to procure for the British the new recruits needed.

A measure of coercion and bribery had to be resorted to as the new demands exceeded the number of men willing to serve, particularly as the requirement stipulated that 75% of the recruits must be Gurungs or Magars, along with an admonition against sending recruits of 'objectionable castes'. This new emphasis narrowed considerably the base from which Gurkhas had previously been recruited. For example, in 1830 the records for two battalions show that nine per cent were Brahmans and up to seven per cent low caste.

By the late 1890s, this new martial races theory was codified in a series of Recruiting Handbooks which stressed and highlighted ethnic differences. This was a huge ethnographic undertaking; for example, the handbook on Gurkhas issued in 1897 listed over 370 clans and sub clans of Magars and about 190 of Gurungs. The handbook described these groups as 'the beau ideal' of what a Gurkha should be.

Men from Doti had previously been recruited in some numbers but were gradually re-categorised as non-martial. Chhetris continued to be recruited but when the first batch of recruits supplied by the durbar, consisting mostly of this caste, reached the depot, the recruiting officer wrote a letter of complaint to the British Residency ending with: 'in fact the fewer Chhetris the better'. This was because, in the spirit of the times, they were seen as being 'more liable to Brahmanical prejudices'.

Recruiting policy for Gurkhas has changed substantially over the years to widen the recruiting base considerably; and during the two World Wars instructions in the handbooks were widely discarded. The continuing outstanding record of Gurkha battalions needs no elaboration here but, as a general theory, the concept of martial races as laid down by Roberts and many of his followers is now widely discredited. Endless conflicts throughout history, and particularly insurgencies over the last 60 years, have shown that if you give someone a cause, the right motivation, the right training and, above all, the right leadership, they can fight.

Very recent Nepali history underscores that. Arguably, the Maoists helped to destroy two great myths that held the Nepali state together in its old form during their 10-year war. One was that as long as the king and the army stood together, nothing could defeat their hold on ultimate power in Nepal. The other was that people like Madeshis, Dalits and Tharus could not fight. The statistics from the cantonments show that there was no shortage of such groups in the PLA ranks, and that, in terms of ethnic and caste composition, the organisation was one of the most inclusive entities ever to exist in Nepal. This was one of its greatest strengths and a major contributor to its success when it operated as a guerrilla army despite being so poorly armed.

The NA has made clear its commitment to making itself more representative of Nepali society as a whole but holding strong to the belief, in a fast changing world, that in Nepal different castes and ethnic groups have different motivation for their employment is going to make it a hard objective to achieve. An inspection at Tribhuvan International Airport of the thousand-plus youths who leave for the Gulf every day would make that very clear.

This article has been republished with permission from *The Kathmandu Post*. The original published on 26 November, 2012 can be found online at: http:// kathmandupost.ekantipur.com/news/2012-11-26/colonial-dogma.html

Note: A week after this article appeared, the Nepal Army removed from its website the words quoted in the opening sentence. I am unaware of any subsequent policy change.

To the Northern Borderland

*A report of a trek in Dolpo in the late summer of 2011,
highlighting the totally changed basis of trans-Himalayan
trade and the new challenges for local people which stem
from it*

The village of Saldang, looking south along the valley of Nangkong.

Introduction

Anne and I trekked in Dolpo in the autumn of 2002 and 2009. We
returned in the late summer of 2011 to do a 25 day-trek which took us on
a circuit, Jomsom-Chharka-Tingkhu-Shimen-Saldang-Tarap-Chharka-
Jomsom. Summer is a special time to visit Dolpo. Masses of wild flowers
are in bloom, the barley is ripening in cleverly irrigated fields round

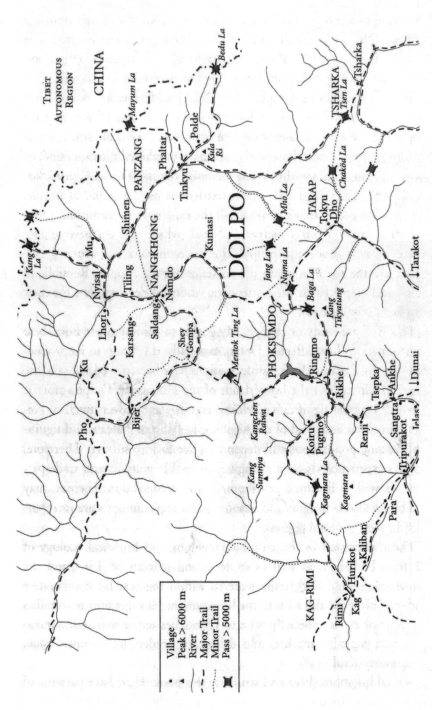

Map from 'High Frontiers: Dolpo and the Changing World of Himalayan Pastoralists' by Kenneth Bauer. Used with kind permission of the author.

the villages, the women and the elder children are in the high summer pastures supervising the yak breeding and making cheese, and large numbers of yaks are on the trails, going to, or returning from, Tibet over the high passes to the north. Anne wrote a full account of the trek for the Journal of the Britain-Nepal Society Journal. It is available on *Digital Himalaya*, under 'Journals of Himalayan Studies', 'Britain-Nepal Society Journal', 'Number 37, 2013.'

I also wrote an account which appeared in the 2012 Issue of *The Kukri*, the annual magazine of the Gurkha Brigade Association. This is a shorter version of that article, which focuses on introducing readers to the extraordinary land of Dolpo, and to highlighting new challenges being faced by the people who live there, mainly brought about by a new basis of trans Himalayan trade. This section has been updated on some key detail.

The land and people of Dolpo

There are at least 14 areas across Nepal's northern border where Tibetan language and culture dominate. Dolpo is one of the most remote of these regions, to the west of Mustang and to the east of Mugu. It falls in trans Himalaya, and is separated from the Tibetan plateau by another mountain chain known as the Tibetan Marginal Mountains which rise to 6000 metres. Various high passes cut through them to lead down to the Tibetan plateau. Older people in Dolpo can remember seven such passes in regular use for trans Himalayan movement. Now the number is reduced to two main ones, the Kung la and the Maryum la. There is another pass north of the small hamlet of Mu which is occasionally used for the delivery of subsidised rice, which originates in Nepal but is delivered across the Tibetan plateau to a road-head close to this pass. A lorry load of rice needs 70 yaks to take the load to villages across the border.

During the winter, snow on the passes to the south can isolate northern Dolpo from the rest of Nepal. The Himalayan mountain chain, including Dhaulagiri at 8,172 metres, acts as a barrier to the annual monsoon. This results in a semi-arid climate, with annual precipitations of less than 500 millimetres (20 ins). This puts a premium on water management to ensure the success of the annual crop of barley which provides sufficient food for 4 to 5 months.

The region is historically divided into the four main valleys of Chharka, Panzang, Nangkhong and Tarap, where most of Dolpo's villages are located. Chharka is an isolated and iconic village which stands fortress-like high above the Barbung khola which runs south into the Bheri river. The Tarap valley is very much the cross-roads of northern Dolpo. The valleys of Nangkhong and Panzang drain westward into the Karnali River via the Mugu Karnali.

There is an airstrip at Juphal, a three-hour walk from the District headquarters, Dunai. Early morning flights to Juphal leave from Nepalganj when the weather conditions at Juphal permit. By land, there are trails into Dolpo, in order of least difficulty, from Jumla in the west, Jomsom in the east and from Beni via Dhorpatan in the south. If Juphal is not operating, people also take road transport to Rari in Rukum. From there it takes 5/7 days to get to Dunai.

In anthropological terms, most of the people of Dolpo, the Dolpopa, are impressively resourceful agro-pastoralists. They keep substantial numbers of yaks and large herds of goat and sheep, which provide for many of their needs. Each year, using skilful irrigation techniques, they can grow enough barley or buckwheat to provide food for 4 to 5 months. However, life would still be impossible for them if they did not make money through trading to buy other essential needs. They are the archetypal trans-Himalayan traders who have the personal physiology and own the yaks to act as the middlemen in getting goods from both Tibet and Nepal across the high Himalayan passes.

For the Dolpopa, this trade was traditionally based on bartering grain-for-salt. Very little grows on the Tibetan plateau but there are huge salt lakes there from the time when the whole area was under the Tethys sea before the Indian plate hit the Eurasian plate to cause the rise of the Himalayas. In Nepal, there are no salt deposits but the middle hills, through clever irrigation, can provide a twice-a-year harvest of grain. Now the Chinese have built extensive networks of roads across Tibet so grain can be delivered easily enough to all remote areas. On the Nepal side, Indian salt (which is naturally iodised unlike the Tibetan variety from the dried-up lakes) is brought into the remote areas through a network of roads which, though nowhere near as extensive as the Chinese-built ones in Tibet, has greatly reduced the time needed to travel to obtain it. Thus, the traditional trade of salt-for-grain has reduced to a trickle. It has been mainly replaced by cash for Chinese goods.

Ripening barley and houses in Chharka. It had been an overcast day but, late in the afternoon, with storm clouds threatening, a short shaft of sunshine enabled the photo to be taken.

Changes in trans-Himalayan trade

This scale of the change was brought home to us on the two-day journey from Chharka to Tingkhu in 2011. We arrived at Chharka on Aug 30, and found the village empty apart from old people and very young children. The women were in the high summer pastures and all the men were away on their annual trading trip to Tibet. We were told that we would meet them returning home with their 500 yaks over the next 2 days as we headed north. The next day just before reaching the large meadow that is traditionally used as an overnight stop on the trail from Chharka to Tingkhu, we crossed a wide and fast flowing river in a thunderstorm. With an hour of daylight left, a weak sun appeared along with the first of the returning Chharka yaks to share the camp site with us. Our guide told us that the headman of Chharka was with the group so I went to have a chat with him. Like all his companions, he had been drinking heavily on the trail so there was not much chance of having an extended discussion about the challenges of life in Dolpo today! The yaks were loaded with every conceivable type of Chinese product so I simply asked him what they had traded in return. He raised a closed fist holding lots of cash, waved it around, and shouted *paisa!* So much for the salt-for-grain trade that has traditionally helped to shape and sustain life in these high trans Himalaya regions. It was clear that profound changes are now underway.

The weather was again mixed the following day: sunshine in the morning, cloudy later, and rain as we reached Tingkhu in the late afternoon – a typical Dolpo summer day! We passed the rest of the Chharka yaks in groups of about 20 during the day, and there were indeed over 500 of them. Sadly, the trail they had travelled was littered with discarded Chinese beer cans, whisky bottles and packets of foodstuff.

Meeting the returning Chharka yaks loaded with goods purchased from the Maryum market.

Where had all these heavily loaded Chharka yaks come from? Each year, for about 10 days in early August, though the dates can vary, two large temporary markets are established at road heads in Tibet, just a few hours walk north of the Kung la and Maryum la passes. The dates for the markets are fixed one year ahead. and are widely disseminated. Each market is supplied by about one hundred lorries. The markets are mainly in the hands of local Tibetans but Khampa traders from Lhasa are also present. There is competition and tension between the two groups, not least because the Khampa prices on goods are usually lower. Khampas originate from the region of Kham in eastern Tibet. In old Tibet, they had a fearsome reputation as brigands. They were also the people who most fiercely resisted the Chinese invasions. Historically, they have also been highly successful traders, with a reputation for ruthlessness; and the expansion of extensive road networks across the Tibetan plateau opened many new opportunities for them.

A busy day on the Maryum la. The frontier marker, Pillar Number 15, is just beyond the crest line. It is about a 5- to 6-hour walk with yaks to arrive at the Maryum market.

Dolpo friend of author

Goods for sale at the Maryum market.

Dolpo friend of author

The markets are under the general supervision of the Chinese police but prices are in the hands of the traders. The police issue a permit (10 yuan/person in 2011) at the entry to the market area. They are checked again when each group of Dolpopa leave to start their return journey. Photography is strictly forbidden. It is big business. For the Maryum market, people come from the eastern villages of upper Dolpo, such as Tarap, Tingkhu, Polde, Shimen, and also from Chharka and the villages in the Barbung and Tichurong areas. Large numbers also come from villages south of Dunai. They use mules which means that they can buy and shift goods from the markets at a much faster rate than villagers who rely on yaks. The Kaytoe market, established just over the Kung la pass, caters for villages such as Bhijer, Phoksundo, Namdo, Karang and Saldang in upper Dolpo and from Kaigaun, Rimi, Pahada, Octahorta, and other villages in lower Dolpo.

Yaks at the Maryum market.

Bags of subsidized rice at Dimolung, half way between the Maryum la and the main market venue. The rice is usually delivered and stacked under plastic tents in July and picked up in August-September after the *yarsagumba* harvest. Sometimes, as is suggested in this photo, it coincides with the annual Maryum market. The large tents are temporary shops and restaurants put up by local Tibetan traders.

Getting the cash to go on a spending spree

The story starts with a caterpillar-fungus fusion that occurs when parasitic mushroom spores (*Ophiocordyceps sinensis*) infect and mummify a ghost moth larva living in the soil. A spindly fungus later sprouts from the dead caterpillar host's head. Two to six centimetres long, the fungus shoots above the soil to act as a finger-shaped indicator for harvesters to find. This is *yarsagumba*, summer grass, winter worm, popularly known as the Himalayan viagra. It had long been used in Tibetan medicine as a tonic or energy giver, and for other medical ailments. Up until 2001 it was protected in Nepal as an endangered species. Villagers were forbidden to trade in it. They could only sell it at the District office for some trivial amount. The bureaucrats in the District office could then sell it on at a fat profit into the Chinese market through their connections in Kathmandu. No doubt hoping to expand this lucrative source of income, the law was changed in 2001 to allow unrestricted harvesting but sales across the border into Tibet were still forbidden; all still had to be sold at the District headquarters under the same arrangements as before.

This plan fell apart in 2002 when the Maoists expanded their military activities into Dolpo. All elements of the Nepali government in the area were withdrawn to the District headquarters, as we personally witnessed during our 2002 trek, and the Maoists immediately liberalised the *yarsagumba* trade to the great financial benefit of both themselves and the local villagers. Their message was a simple one: sell as much as you like to Chinese middlemen, but pay us a 20% tax and keep the rest as income. They also encouraged villagers from the south to take part in the harvest and taxed them for entering the previously restricted areas. In 2003, 20000 people from the lower southern areas arrived in Dolpo, 5000 of them to Tarap valley alone. *Yarsagumba* was a major earner for the Maoists during the war, and the Dolpo villagers had never been richer. After the Maoist conflict ended, the greatly enhanced scale of harvesting continued, large numbers of people kept coming from the south, and the arrangement of selling direct to traders from Tibet continued.

The harvesting starts each spring just after the snow melts at about the 16,000 feet plus level. Only the very old and very young are left in the villages during the harvesting which can last for up to two months. Otherwise every person is in temporary camps set up near the harvesting areas in some very cold and exposed places. With bitterly cold nights, each year produces stories of inadequately clothed outsiders dying through altitude sickness and hypothermia. The camps in turn are serviced by a

Yarsagumba.

large subsidiary industry taking beer and food up to them. Descriptions given to us of what went on in and around the camps suggested a state of affairs akin to what life must have been like in the American Wild West.

Disputes occur between locals and outsiders for various reasons. The latter cause disproportionate damage around their campsites and on the fragile rangelands which the Dolpopa later use as summer pastures. Another cause of friction stems from the fact that most of northern Dolpo falls within Shey Phoksundo National Park. Everyone must pay a fee to the District authorities to harvest *yarsagumba* in the Park, and in the buffer zone surrounding it. The Dolpopa pay a reduced fee but they firmly believe that Park rules should entitle them to collect an additional fee from outsiders who harvest in the Buffer Zone where they live and graze their animals. However, their fundamental complaint is that there is zero transparency on what happens to any of the collected fees.

The above photo shows a piece of *yarsagumba*. The fat piece is the dead caterpillar that has been progressively killed by the grass which grows through it and emerges through its head as a fungus. Only the fungus appears above ground and it is difficult to distinguish it from grass among the snowmelt. The sharp eyes of young children are particularly good at doing so. The work is done on hands and knees. Once identified, the dead caterpillar piece must be dug up carefully as only the combined whole piece has any value. The harvesting starts at dawn. At the end of each arduous day one person might have collected 80 to 100 pieces and another 5, or maybe none.

The ordinary Dolpo villager sells his *yarsagumba* either to middlemen in Dolpo or to Khampas across the border. Selling direct across the border is attractive because of the higher prices offered, and the avoidance of any Nepalese sales tax. For high quality *yarsagumba*, middlemen might pay approximately NRs 500 while Khampas would pay NRs 1000 across the border. However, prices can fluctuate widely within a matter of a few days. On quality, the bigger the better, and a golden-brown colour is also preferred.

Prominent among the middlemen are people from the three Kaike-speaking villages in the Tichurong area, a day's walk east of Dunai. They have a long history of being successful traders, and, reportedly, one of the biggest middlemen, who has made a fortune by selling *yarsagumba* in Hong Kong, comes from one these villages. Other middlemen are locals from upper Dolpo. Sometimes they go to the camps to buy the *yarsagumba*, but mostly they employ people to bring it to them. These middlemen sell large quantities across the border to Khampa friends or business partners. Some sell to Khampas who have advanced capital to them to make the purchases. Some Khampas come into Dolpo to do business and are prepared to pay a hefty bribe to the temporary police posted in Tingkhu or Tarap to cover the harvesting season. No tax is paid in Nepal on these cross-border sales, nor do the Chinese levy any tax.

The challenge of change

Economic change is invariably the harbinger of social change and this is well illustrated by what is happening in Dolpo. The sudden influx of large amounts of money into what until very recently had been a mainly agro-pastoral community is having a profound impact on the life, culture, economy and environment of Dolpo. Material wealth is now starting to be prized above all else. With cash as king, there is a lot more envy, and alcohol abuse, already a problem, is becoming even more prevalent with the import of cheap and very nasty Chinese whisky. At a much lower level of concern, though still indicative, we saw how small children are becoming addicted to cheap Chinese sweets and confectionary, and to

Chinese cola, great quantities of which are brought back by the yak caravans.

Just after we had completed this 2011 trek, my friend, Ken Bauer, (author of *High Frontier, Dolpo and the Changing World of Himalayan Pastoralists*) who has experience of living through a Dolpo winter, and has also carried out extensive research among the nomads of Tibet, emailed me as follows:

'Thank you for sharing the information on yarsagumba. It is astounding how that one commodity has changed rural life across the Tibetan world. The Tibetan nomads whom I have been interviewing about resettlement in Qinghai rely entirely on it for their income – not a sound economic strategy as history has shown us repeatedly. At least the folks in Dolpo will still have their land and animals if the golden goose stops laying that egg; Tibet's nomads, on the other hand, could be left without animals, motorcycles they can't fuel, and skills they can't use in the cities while they wait for their children to get educated and somehow pull them out of the morass of welfare dependence. I hope that at least some of the Dolpopa are investing the money for the long-term.'

It is easy to share the hope expressed but it will need education and a big change of culture to get the people of Dolpo to take the longer-term view necessary to protect their way of life while best managing the traumatic change they are living through. There is no easy way out. Money from trade has always been vital to sustaining life in these high, marginal lands. With the virtual ending of the traditional trade of salt-for-grain, the income from the sale of *yarsagumba* is vital to sustaining life on a year-round basis in places like Dolpo. What clearly should be guarded against are changes that would destroy the social and cultural foundations that are equally important to sustaining life in such a harsh and unforgiving land, not to mention the need to maintain the capability to sustain life should the *yarsagumba* harvest fail, either temporarily or permanently.

Summation

Despite some tough days, our 2011 journey was a wonderfully rewarding experience. We were always conscious of being privileged to see at first hand an amazing way of life in a land that was overwhelming in its grandeur and awesomeness. For a long time after our return to UK, we were still up there in spirit with the Dolpopa, beyond the Himalaya, on the fringes of central Asia, meeting the yak caravans, getting over another big pass, astounded by yet another spectacular view! The vivid memories will remain with us for a long time, as will our hopes that the Dolpopa can successfully manage the period of traumatic change they are living through. They are an extremely tough and resourceful people, who have adapted to great changes in the past while still managing to preserve their distinctive culture and way of life. This could be their toughest challenge yet but there are good grounds for believing that they can do so again. We will long remain with them in spirit!

Addendum

A recently published and very interesting book by the anthropologist, James F. Fisher (*Trans-Himalaya Traders Transformed*), gives important up-to-date information about how life has changed in a Tichurong village over the 44 years since he first did his fieldwork in it. The main agent of change has been *yarsagumba*. He states that in 2011, the year he returned to the village, the average family could fairly easily gather one kilogram of *yarsagumba* during the harvesting season. In 2011, that would have been worth Rs 400,000, roughly $4000, depending on the quality and the exchange rate. On quality, the bigger the better, and a gold brown colour is best. Prices can fluctuate widely and wildly, but Fisher gives the following sample prices for one kilogram of *yarsagumba* sold in Kathmandu: low quality, $15,500; average quality, $23,340; best quality, $32,158. Sold internationally, the price per kilogram increases by approximately $2000.

The biggest middleman in the *yarsagumba* business in Dolpo is Dhan Bahadur Budha, known by everyone as, 'Dhanu'. He is a Tichurong man and represents Dolpo in the national parliament. He started his political life standing for a right wing conservative party but only achieved electoral success after switching to become a candidate for the Unified Marxist-Leninist Party of Nepal, a party whose political outlook and way of operating belies its revolutionary-suggestive name. Fisher describes how Dhanu buys between 200 to 300 kilograms of *yarsa* each year and sells it in Hong Kong and Singapore to yield an approximate profit of equivalent to $155,000. Only alluded to in Fisher's book, but Dhanu uses his political connections to thrive in many business areas far beyond being an international trader in *yarsagumba*.

All Change at Rasuwa Gadhi

A history of one of the two historic border trading points between Kathmandu and Tibet, now transformed as the main road crossing between Nepal and China

From time immemorial, pilgrims, traders, artisans, and religious teachers going to Lhasa from Kathmandu had to decide between two main routes. One roughly followed the line of the present road to Kodari, crossed the border where Friendship Bridge is built and followed a steep trail to Kuti (Tib. Nyalam). Loads were carried by porters up to this point but pack animals were used for the rest of the journey. The alternative route went north on the route that vehicles now use to get trekkers through Betrawati and Dhunche to Syabrubesi, the start point for the popular Langtang treks. From there it was a twenty-kilometre trail following the Bhote kosi to cross the border at Rasuwa Gadhi. It was a further twenty kilometres, following the river trail, to reach Kyirong in Tibet. Besides being a staging post for mule caravans, Kyirong, like Kuti, was also a busy trading post where Nepalese traders from the border areas brought rice to barter for Tibetan salt.

The detail and hazards of both routes can be read in the accounts of the journeys made by the Lhasa-based Newar merchants of Kathmandu known as the Lhasa traders (Tuladhar 2004). They spent long periods in Lhasa but merchandise had to be regularly transported to maintain the stock in the trading houses located round the Barkhor in Lhasa, and the decision on what route to take must often have been an agonizing one. The Kathmandu to Kyirong journey was completed in nine stages on trails that are described as long, narrow and hard. The Kathmandu to Kuti journey was done in ten days and, if anything, the accounts suggest the trail was even more hazardous. Kathmandu Newars also permanently resided in Kuti and Kyirong to aid the transshipment of goods and to carry out major trading on their own account. Jest records that as late as 1959 there were forty five Newar households in Kyirong and forty in Kuti (Jest 1993).

The two routes were used for the invasion of Tibet in 1788 and 1791 by the forces of the recently formed Gorkha state under the direction of Bahadur Shah, which led to the plundering of Tashilhunpo monastery in Shigatse. The routes were also used by the Manchu armies when they launched their powerful counter offensive in 1792. When Jung Bahadur Rana launched his unprovoked war against Tibet in 1855, he divided his attacking forces between both routes, and built a fort at Rasuwa Gadhi as part of the preparation for the invasion.

In 1961 when the Chinese proposed the building of a road to connect Lhasa to Kathmandu, both the Kyirong and Kuti routes were given serious consideration. How one came to be selected rather than the other is an interesting tale well told by Rose (1971). On 25 September 1961, King Mahendra set off on a 17-day state visit to China and Outer Mongolia. He had a well-earned reputation for skill in handling pressures from India and China, and turning them to his and Nepal's advantage. It is clear that throughout the visit he was on maximum alert to resist Chinese blandishments to say anything that would offend India. The stated purpose behind the visit to Peking was the signing of a boundary agreement but, totally unexpectedly, on the last day of the visit, an agreement to construct the road was signed. Though not discussed during the visit, the Chinese presented a draft road agreement to Mahendra on the day before his departure and to quote directly from Rose, 'in such terms as to imply that implementation of the treaty depended upon a favorable response to the road question. Having been badly outmaneuvered for once, the King was in no position to resist the pressure' (1971: 238-239).

Dr. Tulsi Giri, who was accompanying Mahendra, signed the agreement for Nepal, but this did not deflect Indian anger towards Mahendra. The Chinese were insistent on immediate implementation. Survey teams did their work in early 1962 and proposed two routes, one through Rasuwa Gadhi and the other through Kodari, with a strong preference for the former as it was shorter and traversed easier terrain. Possibly hoping to postpone the construction for as long as possible, Mahendra insisted on the Kodari route. Within a remarkably short time, work started and the road was completed in 1966.

A visit in March 2013 confirmed that the section of the road (now called the Araniko highway) from Kathmandu to Bahrabise is reasonably well maintained but the 26 kilometres up the steep sided gorge from Bahrabise to the border is in a bad state. It is essentially a compacted and rutted dirt track susceptible in a number of places to major landslides, a situation made worse by unrestricted stone quarrying above the road at various points. The Chinese have recently started work on a dry port on the Nepal side to ease the congestion caused by the present archaic system for the transshipment of goods from Khasa (Tib. Zhangmu) on their side through the Tatopani custom offices on the Nepal side. They have black topped the road to the border, cutting the journey time from Kuti to about an hour. Little wonder they are showing signs of frustration and despair about the state of the road on the Nepal side, a point well illustrated by what the Chinese ambassador was quoted as saying on 23 December 2012 when he laid the foundation stone for the new dry port. 'As we are constructing a dry port on the Nepal-Tibet border we must repair the Araniko highway. Come up with a proposal. China is ready to help repair it' (Dangal 2012). Local traders are also quoted in the article as blaming the government for doing nothing to improve the road. Why Nepal is apparently dragging its feet can only be a matter of conjecture, but three days after the ambassador expressed his frustration on the issue, he attended a ceremony in Kathmandu at which a certificate was handed over to mark the completion of the Rasuwa Gadhi to Syabrubesi road, thus connecting Kyirong to Kathmandu exactly fifty years after China first proposed doing so. At a meeting held two days earlier, China had expressed interest in upgrading Nepal-China transit points and constructing other necessary physical infrastructures to facilitate trade with Nepal (Bhandary 2012).

I first visited Rasuwa Gadhi in March 2006. Before doing so, I had read accounts by two of the first outsiders to visit the place: Tillman in 1949 (Tilman 1952) and Forbes in 1956 (Forbes 1962). In his inimitable way, Tilman describes his walk to the border through the Tibetan speaking village of Timure with 'its row of five noble and ancient chortens' where 'some land-hungry heathen had planted and fenced his maize so that the south-bound traveller must pass them, willy-nilly, on the unlucky side.' At Rasuwa Gadhi, 'lying in the narrowest and deepest part of the gorge,' he found a few soldiers on the Nepal side but on the Tibetan side, apart from a stone slab inscribed with Chinese characters, 'there was nothing, not even an empty sentry box, to denote one had crossed a frontier.' He pitched his tent 'within a substantial stone fort, its walls embrasured for cannon and loopholed for rifles, and squeezed between the Trisuli river and one rock wall of the gorge' (1952: 53-54).

Forbes also commented on the Timure chortens and on the fact that there were some friendly Indian policemen manning a signal station in the village. Presumably this was one of seventeen such stations established across Nepal's northern border by secret protocol in 1950. They stayed until Mahendra requested their removal in 1969. Forbes also found little sign of activity on the Tibetan side of the frontier but he did photograph the inscription on the stone slab and later had it translated. It was erected on November 26, 1792 and refers to the demarcation of the frontier after 'the victory over the Gorkhas accomplished by General Fu, the Great General for the Pacification of the West'. Forbes also gives a translation by Sir Charles Bell of the inscription on a famous pillar in Lhasa which describes in great detail and colorful language the victories by the Manchu armies 'in the land of thieves' where they 'traversed the mountains, so difficult to pass through, as though they were moving over a level plain and crossed rivers with great waves and narrow gorges as though they were small streams' (1962: 126-130).

In 2006 I found that apart from a new footbridge, a two-storey building on the Tibet side and two small huts on the Nepal side, very little had changed since Tilman and Forbes had visited. It was delightfully tranquil. The chortens in Timure were still as impressive as ever and the walls of Jung Bahadur's fort were well preserved. A prominent notice in Nepali and English close to the fort helpfully summed up the historic importance of the place:

> Rasuwa Fort was a major gateway for the traders of Nepal and Tibet since the ancient time. It had remained a major passway and center for them up to the middle age (17th Century). The fort was built on the bank where two rivers, the Lingde River in the north and Kerung in the west, merge to form Bhotekoshi. It is said that, at the time of the war between Nepal and Tibet, during period of Bahadur Shah, the Chinese army marched across this passway to support the Tibetan army and pushed the Nepali army to Betrawati. Later at the time of the war between Nepal and Tibet, during period of Junga Bahadur Rana, the Nepali army reached Kerung and Digarwa across this pathway. Rasuwa Fort was built during this war period in 1912 Bikram era. (Notice on Rasuwa Fort in 2006)

The river junction at Rasuwa Gadhi in 2006. From the right, the Lende Khola joins the Bhote Kosi which flows down the valley from Kyirong, A footbridge leads to the buildings across the frontier.

The river junction in 2013. Behind the temporary military-style bridge are the concrete supports for the new fly-over bridge. The five-storey structure was built recently and extensive building work is still going on.

Just one historical detail is wrong. 'The Chinese army' in 1792 did not simply 'march across this passway.' Rasuwa Gadhi was the scene of a ferocious three day battle which yielded a victory that was much acclaimed in Chinese sources as an outstanding feat of arms. It was the first battle on Nepal territory of the powerful Manchu counter offensive launched in response to the invasion of 1791. The Gorkhas had sensibly destroyed the bridge over the Lende River and the setting in the steep and narrow gorge greatly favored defenders, leaving attacking forces with little scope to maneuver. The Manchu forces were commanded by two very gifted and highly experienced commanders, Generals Fukangan and Hailancha. The three regiments commanded by Fukangan managed to throw a bridge across the river and seized the checkpoint while two regiments under Hailancha secretly crossed the river upstream on rafts, skirted the mountains and managed to emerge above the enemy camp to combine with Fukanga's regiments to rout the Gorkha forces (Boulnois 1989).

I returned to Rasuwa Gadhi in March 2013. The new road from Syabrubesi is very impressive. It was built entirely by Chinese labor using their own trucks and road building equipment. It is not yet black topped, but the strong foundations are in place to make that a straightforward task. The nine concrete bridges are clearly built to carry the heaviest loads and the safety barriers stand out as unusual compared with other roads in Nepal where such considerations are given a low priority.

The road runs by the river just below the village of Timure. The chortens are therefore untouched but the village is becoming a sprawl so characteristic of other areas of Nepal where new roads are being established. Well before the road was completed, press reports carried stories of locals seeing short term advantages such as shortening the time to get to Syabrubesi but expressing concern about the long term consequences: 'All the land is being bought up by people from Trisuli and further south. Soon, the whole village will be owned by them, and we'll have to resort to collecting firewood and fodder for money. The poor will just get poorer' (Sthapit 2011). There was also a large police presence in the village and endless checkpoints along the road. The charming hamlet of Gadhi, just 500m from the border, was unchanged, saved by having no space to build anything.

Inevitably the area around Rasuwa Gadhi had changed dramatically and the contrast between the two sides of the frontier was stark. On one side a new large and very impressive five-storey building: on the other, one new bungalow-style building and a ramshackle collection of huts. Most of the outer walls of the fort still stood but the definition of the fort away from the river had been lost. The Chinese have built a temporary military-style bridge to facilitate the vehicles and equipment necessary to build the road. Part of the walls of the fort near the river had been demolished to accommodate the road that runs over this bridge but this could be restored when the main flyover-style bridge is completed. The anchored retaining wall on the Chinese side and two large concrete central supports for this are already in place and, depending on how and where the anchored retaining wall on the Nepali side is built, it is possible that the bridge will go over the walls of the fort and therefore leave one of its most striking features untouched. However, on 10 July 2013 an article in *Republica*, five months after my visit, reported that four metres of the fort's wall had already fallen down and cracks had developed along the length of the wall due to the use of heavy equipment and rampant extraction of gravel and soil for the ongoing construction of the bridge (Poudel 2013). The report also asserted that the local administration was trying 'to fudge the issue' and that the Department of Archeology had initially objected to the bridge but gave conditional approval to construct it at least a foot above the fort, and in such a manner that it would not have any impact on the structure. It is hard to see such understandable concerns carrying much weight in the final analysis given the very high political profile of the project.

I searched but could not find the board which gave the history of the place. Perhaps a new one is being made. If so, I hope it is based, like its predecessor, on simple historical fact uninfluenced by contemporary political sensitivities.

There is no doubting China's commitment to making this second road crossing with Nepal a significant one in further boosting Chinese exports to Nepal. The railway from Lhasa to Shigatse will be completed this year and the next extension will be to Kyirong, where China is already spending large sums of money to turn it into a major business hub by upgrading its infrastructure (Basnet 2013). As it is, the trade imbalance is already starkly unequal. According to statistics compiled by the Trade and Export Promotion Centre, Nepal exported goods worth 1.21 billion Rupees to China and imported goods worth 30.59 billion Rupees from China in the first five months of the current fiscal year (*Republica* 2013).

The figure for imports is almost certainly a gross underestimate because, as with most imports into Nepal, there is massive under-invoicing of goods entering Nepal at the Khasa/Tatopani border crossing with the connivance of officials on both sides. Significant imports from China, as with all countries except India, must be paid for through a dollar denominated Letter of Credit. However, to avoid customs duties, VAT and allied taxes, imports are invoiced at lower value and the balance is paid through informal channels, based entirely on trust, known as *hundi* (*Kathmandu Post* 2013). This is done, in a highly complex operation, mainly using remittance money converted into US dollars being channeled through Hong Kong from where it finds its way to the Chinese traders who have exported the goods to Nepal in the first place.[1]

A formidable civil engineering challenge stands in the way of maximizing the use of the new road. The first five kilometres out of Syabrubesi has recently been black topped but the remaining ten kilometres to Dhunche, through the villages of Mulkharka, Ramche and Gadkhola, traverses one of the most landslide-prone areas in Nepal. Each monsoon season, the Kathmandu media regularly reports the cutting off of the existing road for days and sometimes weeks on end. Crossing the area in a vehicle at any time is slow and tortuous. Numerous geological reports spell out why this is so. The area is very close to the Main Central Thrust (MCT) of the Himalaya. This is the weak junction where the Indian plate slid under the Asian plate causing the Indian plate to shatter and crush. To quote one report, 'it is one of the most tectonically significant structures in the Himalayan orogen. Detailed geologic mapping and structural analysis of the MCT in the Langtang National Park region of central Nepal reveals that this segment of the fault zone experienced multiple episodes of south-directed movement, under both brittle and ductile conditions, during the Tertiary period' (MacFarlane et al. 1992). To see what this means in practice today, go on YouTube[2] to see any of the many video clips that numerous trekkers have uploaded to share the excitement of crossing the land-slide affected areas. Road repair and road building, and the continual vibration of the land caused by heavy traffic movement, as well as monsoon rainfall, add to the general instability of the soil in the area.

---

1   Personal information in this paragraph from a senior banker in Kathmandu March 2013.

2   See, for example, covering just one section of the many landslide-prone parts of the road: 'Landslide when Trekking in Langtang Valley Trekking', https://www.youtube.com/watch?v=fiDDPU9pyNc.

No doubt, with massive Chinese investment some improvement could be achieved, but it raises the question of why China is currently spending so much on improving Nepal's infrastructure. Numerous politicians, bureaucrats and commentators in Kathmandu are constantly stressing the advantages which will open to Nepal if it can become the transit bridge of choice for trade between China and India. In my view, realizing such a prospect is a very long way off. Nepal would need to make massive improvements in its internal road transport network and in its merchandise and service handling capabilities to compete with the quantity and relative ease with which transshipments currently take place through the port of Calcutta. The reason for the ramping up of investment is based more on China's priorities than Nepal's. China wants to weaken India's dominance in Nepali affairs and to strengthen its own influence but it recognizes that the weight of history, culture, religion and language works against achieving this objective. It sees making Nepal, including ordinary consumers, increasingly dependent on its goods and investment as the surest way to give it greater strategic weight to press its concerns on the Government of Nepal on all issues, and particularly on Tibetan affairs.[3] The new road from Kyirong through the historic crossing point of Rasuwa Gadhi will certainly play its part in that; and China clearly wants quick action. A high priced delegation arrived in Kathmandu on 31 March 2013 with the declared aim of seeking ways of expanding cooperation with Nepal. On the agenda was a request to the Nepal government 'to speed up infrastructure construction at the Nepal-China border in Kerung-Rasuwa' (Ekantipur 2013).

What all this portends for Nepal was made clear in an article in the *Nepali Times* of 31 May 2013 which claimed that: 'Chinese exports to Nepal have exploded in the past ten years. Affordable Chinese apparel have transformed the way Nepalis dress, and Chinese electronic goods and vehicles have flooded the market' (Kumar 2013). The same article noted that China is also upgrading the border facilities at Rasuwa Gadhi, 'anticipating that most trade will move there once the highway on the Nepali side is complete and the Chinese railway network arrives in Kerung via Xigatse.' All too clearly, there is much more of this 'flooding the market' to come. The same issue carried an interview with Wu Chuntai, China's ambassador to Nepal, under a heading of a quote from

---

3   Insight shared by trusted contact who has interacted with senior Chinese officials. Kathmandu, March 2013.

him that: 'It is a win-win-win situation.' However, his answer to the question of what prospects he saw for balancing Nepal-China trade is notably thin on substantive detail (Interview 2013).

References

Basnet, Purna. 2013. 'China Rail to Reach Shigatse This Year'. *Republica*, March 12, 2013. http://www.myrepublica.com/portal/index.php? action=news_details&news_ id=51351.

Bhandary, Sharach Chandra. 2013. 'Syafrubesi-Rasuwa Road Opens: Traders Expect Rise in Trade with China'. *Republica*, December 27, 2012. http://www.myrepublica.com/portal/ index.php?action=news_ details&news_id=47215.

Boulnois, L. 1989. 'Chinese Maps and Prints on the Tibet-Gorkha War of 1788-92'. *Kailash* 15 (1-2): 83-112.

Dangal, Dhruba. 2012. 'China Ready to Repair Araniko Highway'. *Republica*, December 24, 2012. http://www. myrepublica.com/portal/index. php?action=news_ details&news_id=46966.

Ekantipur. 2013. 'TAR for Expanding Cooperation with Nepal'. *Ekantipur*, April 1, 2013. http://ekantipur. com/2013/04/01/top-story/tar-for-expanding-coopera-tion-with-nepal/369295.html.

Forbes, Duncan. 1962. *The Heart of Nepal*. London: Robert Hale.

Jest, Corneille. 1993. 'The Newar Merchant Community in Tibet: An Interface of Newar and Tibetan Cultures'. In *Nepal: Past and Present*, edited by Gerard Toffin, 160-163. New Delhi: Sterling Publishers Private Limited.

Kathmandu Post. 2012. 'Hundi Flourishing: Govt Helpless'. February 7, 2012. http://www.ekantipur. com/2012/02/07/business/hundi -flourishing-govt-helpless/348525.

Kumare, Ramesh. 2013. 'Hands across the Himalaya'. *Nepali Times* (658). May 31, 2013. http://nepalitimes.com/article/ nation/Hands,441.

MacFarlane, A. M., K.V. Hodges, and D. Lux. 1992. 'A Structural Analysis of the Main Central Thrust Zone, Langtang National Park, Central Nepal Himalaya'. *Geological Society of America Bulletin* 104 (11): 1389-1402.

Nepali Times. 'It is a Win-Win-Win Situation: China's Ambassador to Nepal'. *Nepali Times* (658). May 31, 2013. http:// nepalitimes.com/article/ interview/It,440.

Poudel, Nirajan. 2013. 'Rasuwa Gadhi Walls Falling Apart'. *Republica*, July 10, 2013. http://nepalitimes.com/article/ nation/Hands,441#. UajLn8u9KK0.

Republica. 'Govt Apathy Widens Trade Deficit with China'. January 19, 2013. http://www.myrepublica.com/ portal/index.php?action=news_details&news_id=48560.

Rose, Leo E. 1971. *Nepal: Strategy for Survival*. Berkeley: University of California Press.

Sthapit, Prasiit. 'The New Silk Road'. *Nepali Times*, November 4, 2011. http://nepalitimes.com/news.php?id=18684.

Tilman, H.W. 1952. *Nepal Himalaya*. Cambridge, England: University Press.

Tuldahar, Kamal. 2004. *Caravan to Lhasa: Newar Merchants of Kathmandu in Traditional Tibet*. Kathmandu: Tuldahar Family.

This article has been republished with permission from *Himalaya*, the Journal of the Association for Nepal and Himalayan Studies. The original can be found online at:
http://digitalcommons.macalester.edu/himalaya/vol33/iss1/14

Photo Essay which can be viewed at this link
https://himalayajournal.org/photo-gallery/sam-cowan-change-rasuwa-garhi/

Addendum July 2018

On 1 Dec 2014, the Sino-Nepal border at Rasuwa Gadhi was officially opened for commercial business with appropriate ceremony. I am reliably informed that the notice board giving the history of the crossing had been restored with the wording I recorded in 2006. Sadly, five months after opening, the area was hit by the 7.8-magnitude earthquake of April 25, 2015. The new, large and imposing buildings on the Chinese side survived largely unscathed but the small and mainly temporary buildings on the Nepali side were completely buried under deep rubble caused by a large landslide. An estimated 35 Nepali and Chinese workers lost their lives. Roads approaching the crossing from both sides were also badly damaged. A large Chinese relief effort was quickly and impressively deployed to clear the immediate area and the approach roads, including on the Nepal side. The bridge suffered significant damage but a temporary repair enabled traffic to start moving across the border again five months later. A new road to Syabrubesi is currently being built on the opposite side of the valley to the current road. This will obviate the need to cross the long landslide prone section north of Dhunche. It should be open for traffic in March 2019.

Galen Murton

New crossing ready for business, at least the Chinese are!

Galen Murton

Bridge open for business again. A military bridge built over the previous structure.

Start of the road to the frontier from Syabrubesi.

However, to reach the frontier, all vehicles must still travel on the Chinese-built road, up the steep-sided valley from Syabrubesi to Rasuwa Gadhi.An article, published in *The Record*, on July 8, 2018, 'All rubble on the road to China', highlights in graphic detail the slow progress being made to repair the earthquake damage on this road despite its new strategic importance.This short extract conveys the sense perfectly, 'Rasuwagadhi offers a stark picture of the difference between reality on the ground and rhetoric of successive governments, including that of the current Prime Minister KP Oli, who has promised greater connectivity with China for years. Despite being touted as a new trade route and a potential rail route connecting Nepal with China, construction of roads and other infrastructure on the Nepali side of the border is happening at a snail's pace.'[4] Three weeks after publication of this article, on July 26, 2018, a major landslide at Timure, just 4 kms from the border, cut the road and killed nine people and buried several buildings. The road was opened two days later but the next day all cross-border traffic was halted after rain-triggered floods damaged a bridge on the road, just 500 metres from the border.On July 30, 2018, an article in the Kathmandu

---

4   https://www.recordnepal.com/wire/nepal-new-trade-route-with-china-via-rasuwagadhi/

Balram Ghimire

Landslide damage at Timure, July 26, 2018.

Post ('Timure bridge to be repaired urgently') gave this detail on the damage:[5]

> According to Deputy Director of the Department of Roads, General Mukti Gautam, floods have severely impacted the base pillar, the reason why the bridge is out of service. The department has taken measures to make it functional temporarily by inducting big boulders to support the base. Works for permanent reinforcement will take at least two months to begin, according to Gautam. 'Water level needs to be low for us to begin permanent maintenance work,' he said, adding that this would happen only after a couple of months
>
> More than 300 containers and hundreds of light vehicles have been stranded due to the halt in vehicular movement, authorities said. According to the Department of Customs, the government is losing revenue worth around Rs10 million daily as overland cargo movement between the two nations has come to a standstill.

This whole area was badly hit by the earthquake. Many buildings in the nearby village of Timure collapsed and all houses in the small hamlet of

---

5   https://www.kantipurdaily.com/news/2018/07/26/153256918266988971.html

Photo of the bridge that was damaged, looking south, taken in Feb 2013. The frontier is about 500 yards behind from where I took the photo.

Ghatti Khola, visible in the photo, were destroyed. It seems reasonable to assume that the earthquake weakened the structure of the bridge to some extent, leaving it vulnerable to the damage caused by flood-water rushing down the stream on the left and undermining the foundations on the southern side. Reliable friends identified cracks in the supports of the bridge in Dec 2016.

The area round the Khasa/Kodari crossing, and the approach roads to it from both sides, also suffered extensive earthquake damage. Over three years later, cross-border trade and movement have not resumed; nor does there seem any immediate prospect of such a resumption. The bridge suffered damage, the extent of which is unclear, and the large town of Khasa above the crossing, the point of transhipment of goods on the Chinese side, moved 1.5 metres down the steep slope on which it was built. The inhabitants, both Han Chinese and ethnic Tibetans, were evacuated and relocated to Shigatse, 475 kms away, to live in a new and semi-permanent enclave known as Khasa Mall.

An even greater catastrophic event, known as the Bhote Koshi flood, hit the area on the evening of 5/6 July 2016. A report in the *Himalayan Times*, dated, July 10, 2016, 'Bhote Koshi flood adds to the woes of Tatopani earthquake victims,' gives a clear description:

The deadly earthquake of last year had devastated Liping and Tatopani

Friendship Bridge before the earthquake. The photo was taken in Feb 2013 from Kodari on the Nepal side with the Chinese town of Khasa in the background.

Bazaar of Sindhupalchowk. Before these places could recover, flood in the Bhote Koshi River has left these towns so battered that reconstruction seems impossible.

The flood in the Bhote Koshi River triggered by heavy rain across the border in China from last Tuesday night has wreaked havoc in Tatopani and Liping bazaars. Before these places could recover, flood in the Bhote Koshi River has left these towns so battered that reconstruction seems impossible. Of the 200 houses in Tatopani and Liping bazaars, the Bhote Koshi flood has washed away 67 houses till today noon, police said.[6]

More photos of the extensive damage appeared in an article in *Republica* on 13 Jul 2016, 'Liping Bazar turns lifeless again'. This article states that, 'the flood washed away over two dozen houses in Liping alone. Dozens of other houses are under risk due to serious damage to the soil. The popular bus park at the center of the bazar is no longer

6   https://thehimalayantimes.com/nepal/bhote-koshi-flood-add-woes-tatopani-quake-victims/

Anish Tiwari

The above photo shows some of the catastrophic damage caused on the Nepal side of Friendship Bridge by the flood which hit the area on the evening of 5/6 July 2016. Most houses on one side of the road finished up in the river and the the width of road was reduced to a few metres in places. No geological training is needed to see that within a very few years the entire slope, above and below the road, is likely to disappear into the river.

intact.' The article also reports that the flood and landslides destroyed settlements on the Chinese side of the border. A local man is quoted as saying that Chinese officials had told him that, 'the road has been swept away and parts of it have fallen into the river. Buildings, parking and shelters for waiting passengers have disappeared.' The photos in the article[7] also show extensive damage to buildings on the Chinese side of the bridge.

A further article in *Republica*, dated July 13, 2016, 'After Bhotekoshi',[8] explains the likely cause:

> Though the exact cause of the flood is yet to be established, the huge volume of water and debris brought down suddenly by the river points to the likelihood that a landslide dam upstream may have breached. Satellite images have indicated heavy rainfall in the upstream areas, which could have triggered a landslide in an area rendered geologically weak following the earthquakes. Information

7   http://myrepublica.nagariknetwork.com/news/1921/
8   http://myrepublica.nagariknetwork.com/news/1910/

passed on by the Institute of Mountain Hazards and Environment, Chinese Academy of Sciences, suggests that a heavy rainfall of about 85 mm in 24 hours caused a landslide in the area near bridge No. 707 in the Zhangzhangbo valley blocking the river· and accumulating water behind it. The subsequent outburst of the landslide dam caused the flood.

Subina Shrestha's excellent report on Al Jazeera on Oct 1, 2017[9], vividly brings to life all the above. Comparing the images on this clip to the photos taken 15 months previously, which appeared in the articles quoted above, it is clear that the Chinese have not done anything yet to start repairing damage on their side of the bridge.

In sum, the prospect for this crossing resuming its dominant role as an international crossing between Nepal and China looks bleak even though, on 15 March 2018, China and Nepal signed an agreement which included a Chinese pledge to help with 'Post-disaster Recovery for Tatopani Frontier Inspection Station Project'. In reporting this news, an article in *Republica*, 'China to reopen Tatopani border point', quoted the Chinese ambassador as saying that China had been making positive efforts to reopen the Tatopani transit point but, 'unfortunately, given the frequent occurrence of geographical disasters, facilities and roads surrounding Zhangmu port are further deteriorated. But the Chinese government will carry out positive work of disaster treatment and road repair on the Chinese side of the port.'[10]

This commitment from China, though sounding somewhat limited in scope, will be warmly welcomed but the geological challenges remain very great. As the photograph shows, the catastrophic event which hit the area near the bridge on the evening of 5/6 July 2016 caused immense damage and must have weakened an already very fragile steep slope above the road. The 40kms section of the road from Balephi to the border follows an alignment that crosses a series of old landslides. New landslides are common, causing blockages and a need for year-round repair.

This extract from a 2009 PhD thesis[11], referring to the last 15 kms of the route, gives a graphic description of the geology of the area:

9   https://www.youtube.com/watch?v=zC3Psp-1ewo
10 http://myrepublica.nagariknetwork.com/news/38084/
11 'Landscape, Livelihoods and Risk: Community Vulnerability to Landslides in Nepal'. Katie Oven, http://etheses.dur.ac.uk/183/

Two photos showing the bad state of the road north of Bahrabesi in February 2013.

The roadside settlements of Chaku, Larcha and Kodari are located along a stretch of highway deemed to be particularly problematic due to landsliding, characterised by large, deep seated failures, with active gully erosion above and below the road, combined with high rates of river incision. While the level of landslide hazard can be seen to vary along the highway, in a number of areas the hazard is acute, with the occurrence of landslides characterised by high movement velocities and long run-out distances, often from a distal source area. These events sourced higher in the catchment, are commonly not anticipated. rarely directly witnessed, and hence have often catastrophic impacts down slope.

This was written before the earthquake. These slopes are now much more unstable, and will be for years to come.

In conclusion, even before the earthquake, there were signs that the Chinese were going to give top priority to the new Rasuwa road crossing. One assumes this was partly driven by the planned arrival of the railway in Kyirong in 2020, but the major geological challenges surrounding the Friendship Bridge crossing must also have been a factor. The Rasuwa route was, of course, the one the Chinese first proposed to King Mahendra in 1961. We must wait and see.

Raid into Tibet

*The story of the unauthorised filming by three British citizens
of an ambush of Chinese army trucks in Tibet in 1964 by
Khampa fighters, armed by the CIA but based in Nepal*

A recent study of two Foreign Office files in the UK National Archives
(371/176118 and 371/176120) shed interesting light on events in
Kathmandu in July 1964 which put Antony Duff, the recently arrived
British ambassador, in a predicament, seriously discomfited the
monarch, and caused major problems for Panchayat ministers and
officials.

The man at the centre of the events was a dedicated supporter of the
Tibetan cause called George Patterson. He was a former missionary in
Kham and spoke the Kham dialect fluently. He arrived in Kathmandu in
March 1964 and was later joined by Adrian Cowell, a gifted documentary
film maker, and Chris Menges, an experienced television cameraman.
Their ambitious mission was to make contact with Khampa fighters in
Mustang and film them carrying out a raid so that the world could see
that Tibetans were still actively fighting the Chinese.

The buildup in late 1960 of Khampas in Mustang and their later
dominance in the area was a badly kept secret. An article in The New York
Times on March 3, 1962 quoted a Nepali foreign ministry spokesman
as saying that unidentified aircraft had been dropping arms to about
4,000 Khampas in Mustang. The same article said that official Indian
sources were expressing strong concern that the buildup of Tibetans on
Nepal's northern border could lead to China sending troops into Nepal.
There were 2,000 Khampas in Mustang and the first two air drops to
them, organized by the United States Central Intelligence Agency, had
taken place in April 1961 and December 1961. In each case, two Hercules
aircraft had delivered the weapons to a drop zone 10 kilometres inside
Tibet, just across the border from Mustang. The weapons dropped were
mainly of Second World War vintage.

The CIA's intention from the outset was for the Khampas to establish positions along the roads within Tibet, but despite sustained pressure (which increased considerably after a third and final air drop into Mustang in May 1965) such a move never took place. Setting up bases in Tibet would have led to heavy casualties on the scale of those suffered by Khampas who parachuted into Tibet between 1957 and 1962 after the People's Liberation Army had fully mobilized to meet the threat. Of the 49 men inserted, 37 were killed, most of them in pitched battles against the PLA. Lightly equipped guerrilla forces simply cannot stand and fight conventionally equipped armies supported by artillery and fighter ground attack aircraft.

The same heavy attrition occurred when the CIA shifted their point of effort in early 1964 to infiltrating small groups of Khampas into Tibet on intelligence missions. Four members of one of these groups were arrested in Kathmandu in June 1964 following a brawl. One of Duff's dispatches gives the detail of this arrest as told to him by the Inspector General of Police, P.S. Lama. Lama told Duff that the Khampas were trained abroad and were on their way to the border. He also gave Duff a list of sophisticated surveillance and communication equipment taken from the Tibetans which, they said, had been given to them in Kathmandu by Hugh McDevitt who was employed as the manager of Air Ventures, which operated two helicopters for the United States Agency for International Development.

All of this indicates that from an early stage the Nepali authorities knew what was going on in Mustang and who was backing the Khampas there with money and material. There was therefore no chance that the Nepali authorities would allow Patterson anywhere near Mustang but they underestimated the man's guile and determination.

In his book, *A Fool at Forty*, Patterson describes the web of deceit he spun in Kathmandu to cause maximum confusion about his real aim beneath the cover of making 'a TV film about Nepal.' King Mahendra was travelling in the Far West, but Patterson saw most of the key people: Tulsi Giri, the Chairman of the Council of Ministers; Prakash Thakur, the Chief of Protocol; Mr. Banskota, the Director of Publicity; and General Padma Bahadur Khatri, the Foreign Secretary. He also had a two-hour meeting with Mahendra's brother, Prince Basundhara.

Patterson clearly pulled the wool over all their eyes as he quickly got permission to start filming in and around Kathmandu. His application to go to Mustang was refused but on a visit to a Tibetan camp near Trisuli,

Patterson was informed about a small Khampa group in Tsum. After some delay he obtained a permit for 'a trek to Pokhara.' He had a further slice of luck when three separately nominated liaison officers all found some excuse not to go. At the last minute, a young college student was nominated and accepted. Soon after getting the permit, the group headed to Arughat at which point they left the trail to Pokhara by turning north up the Buri Gandaki. After passing the police check post and Indian wireless station at Setibas (one of 17 established along the northern border by secret protocol in 1950 and withdrawn in 1969), they left the line of the river to head north east up the long, steep trail to Tsum.

George Patterson, 1950.

Contact was quickly made with the small Khampa group of 15 men. They had been dispatched from their main base in Mustang two years earlier to establish an outpost in this distant location. They had one Bren Gun and eight rifles between them, and no means of communication. Tendar, their commander, had led reconnaissance sorties across the high snow passes that marked the border to monitor traffic on the Dzonkha-Kyrong road, but with supplies from Mustang having to come on a long and tortuous trail across the Thorung La and Laryka La passes, little offensive action had taken place.

At the time there was also apparently a lull in cross border raids from the main Khampa group in Mustang. A July 1964 dispatch from Duff reported a meeting he had with Michael Peissel who 'recently had spent two months in Mustang getting material for a book.' Peissel gave him a detailed account of where the Khampa camps were located and told him that there had been no raiding across the border since early 1963 'after the Dalai Lama had sent word that the raiding was to stop and the Tibetans were to settle down peacefully where they were and cultivate the land.' CIA sources also report this lull but give different reasons for it.

Patterson lost no time in putting his proposition to Tendar. With no means of checking with his superiors in Mustang, Tendar had his doubts. To decide the issue, he went to the gompa to cast the dice. The result was a clear indication to carry out the raid. On June 7, 1964, Tendar, with his eight lightly armed men, the three foreigners, and three

Khampa-provided porters, crossed the high snow passes that marked the border. Two days later at about two in the afternoon, having been in the ambush position since before dawn, they attacked four unescorted PLA vehicles traveling on the Dzonka-Kyrong road. Three vehicles were damaged and eight PLA soldiers killed. Patterson subsequently gave a detailed account of the raid to Charles Wylie, the defense attaché in the UK embassy, and listed all the weapons carried. All except one were of the type dropped by the CIA. The exception was 'one British rifle marked LSA & Co Ltd, 1919, which the Khampas claimed had been officially supplied to Tibet.' (In 1947, acting on a request for military aid, Britain supplied a substantial amount of arms and ammunition to the Tibetan government.)

Kelvin Kent

In his book, Patterson's detailed description of the raid closely follows the account he gave to Wylie, including how they left the student minder behind under the pretext that they were going to film refugees. The ambush was successfully filmed and the team returned to Kathmandu on June 27, 1964. Various lurid accounts have appeared of what happened next, including stories about the team being pursued to the border by the police and the Khampas misinterpreting a CIA order to retrieve the footage as a directive to kill them. Duff's dispatches are clear and generally tie in with what Patterson says.

British Ambassador, Antony Duff, 1964.

On the morning after they returned, Cowell dispatched the footage of the raid on the first plane out which happened to be going to East Pakistan. A few days later, the three of them went to see Duff to confess all, mainly on the grounds, Patterson says, that they thought it was the proper thing to do. (Duff had entertained him to dinner prior to his departure but he had said nothing about his true intentions.) Cowell and Menges were dubious, but Patterson agreed that Duff could pass the information to Mahendra at an audience already fixed for the evening of Friday, July 3, 1964. Duff waited until the Friday morning to alert London to what had happened. One of his two telegrams that day stated that he was going to inform the US ambassador. It would be reasonable to assume that this is when the CIA would have been first alerted. At this stage the UK was still accepting categorical denials from the US that it was involved in supporting the Khampas. Subsequently the CIA blamed Baba Yeshi, the Mustang commander, for ordering the ambush to get publicity. He was reprimanded and the flow of funds to Mustang was stopped for six months. Tendar was recalled to Mustang and reassigned to administrative duties.

Mahendra's first reaction was to tell Duff that the film would be 'a big headache for us and for you.' In a later audience, Mahendra told him that the Khampas constituted one of his major problems though many considered that he was at best ambivalent on the subject. However, such apparent sympathy clearly counted for nothing given what Patterson was now about to expose to the world. Immediately after meeting Duff, Mahendra summoned the foreign minister, Kirti Nidhi Bista. He lost no time in transferring the monarch's ire to his subordinates at a meeting he called on Saturday morning. Duff reported that 'the main brunt fell on Padam Bahadur Khatri who took it especially hard because he would much sooner not have known anything about it all.'

That same morning, as previously planned, Cowell and Menges left Kathmandu to drive overland to India via Rauxal, accompanied by their student liaison officer. Patterson stayed on in Kathmandu because his wife, a surgeon, had arrived in his absence to help in the United Mission Hospital, bringing with her their three small children. Cowell and Menges were detained overnight at the border but left the next morning for Calcutta. Some innocuous film footage and audio tapes were confiscated. These were later returned to them; the tapes through the UK embassy in Kathmandu and the film from the Nepali embassy in London. Duff reported that the palace had given the order to release them without informing the foreign secretary. Two days later he thought they were still under arrest and being brought to Kathmandu to face disciplinary action

A week later Duff reported: 'Judging by conversations with the King and the Foreign Minister at a reception, I have acquired no merit at all for telling the Nepalese about the sortie over the border into Tibet. The Foreign Minister indeed muttered something about it being sometimes better to conceal things for a while.'

At the same reception Mahendra said that the film ought to be stopped. Duff told him this was not possible. Patterson and Cowell had told Duff that they would wait for three months before showing the material. In the event, the finished film, called Raid into Tibet, was not shown on British television until May 9, 1966. It was widely acclaimed but, contrary to many reports, there is no record of it winning the Prix Italia. (Cowell did win it in 1971 for his documentary about a remote Amazonian tribe: The Tribe that Hides from Man.)

Patterson was clearly not prepared to sit on his story for 18 months. In March 1965 he wrote a lengthy propagandist-style article on the raid in The Reporter, an American biweekly news magazine published in New York. It described the ambush in graphic detail and made it clear that the action had been filmed for television. Large extracts immediately appeared in the Hindustan Times, under the heading: 'Nepal-based Khampas harass Chinese.' The files show that the articles caused concern among British officials, which suggests that perhaps ATV, the independent company who finally transmitted it in the UK, had been persuaded to delay showing the film. An earlier note in the files indicates a determination to do this if pressure on Patterson failed.

Tibet Film Archive

Screenshot of King Mahendra, from the film, inspecting the Chinese-built road after it was open to jeep traffic. He told the British ambassador that the film would be 'a big headache for us and for you'.

Throughout the furor in Kathmandu over the filming of the raid, Duff had argued that some control over the film's final content might be achieved by taking a conciliatory approach with Patterson. Only

Mahendra and the palace were receptive: Padam Bahadur Khatri and his cohorts wanted some measure of retribution. This manifested itself at the airport two weeks later when, without producing any authority, the police prevented Patterson from leaving on his booked flight. When Duff complained, no one in Kathmandu could or would identify who had given the order. Three days later Patterson was allowed to leave having signed a five-line note saying essentially that he was sorry for any inconvenience caused by visiting Setibas, which was not listed on his permit, and that he had not visited Mustang.

'Why that curious little statement should have satisfied anyone is merely one of the many mysteries about Nepalese behaviour throughout this affair.' That comment from Duff's final dispatch on the event seems an apt way to end this tale as it also neatly conveys the opaqueness of government during the Panchayat days, which so confused outsiders and so suited the monarch.

In addition to the UK archive material, and Patterson's book, other information about Tendar and the Khampas in Mustang comes from the well-sourced book, *The CIA's Secret War in Tibet* by Conboy and Morrison.

An abridged version of this article first appeared in *The Nepali Times* on January 3, 2014. This article has been republished with permission from *The Record*. The original can be found online at:
https://www.recordnepal.com/wire/raid-tibet

Addendum December 2017

As indicated in the introduction to the Preview of Contents, this was an important article for me. It was the first to be published in the newly launched online magazine, *The Record*, and was also the first article I wrote which drew heavily on contemporaneous evidence from British Foreign Office files in the National Archives. An example of the value of these is given by the corrections I have made to the endlessly repeated lurid accounts of what happened to Patterson, Cowell and Menges after they returned to Kathmandu. These include stories about the threesome being pursued to the Indian border by the police, and the Khampas misinterpreting a CIA order to retrieve the film footage as a directive to kill them. The dispatches from the British ambassador, based on first-hand knowledge of what was happening in Kathmandu, including conversations with the threesome, make clear that such accounts are totally wrong.

As mentioned in the essay, there has also been much speculation on the reason for the apparently long delay in showing the footage shot in Tibet but, in a telephone conversation with Chris Menges after the publication of this essay, he explained that whatever the Foreign Office files or others might say, there was no suppression. The reason for delay, he explained, was much more mundane. After Nepal and India, he and Cowell went directly to Hong Kong, Thailand and Burma to shoot footage for other documentaries. Only when they eventually returned to UK, could they finally edit the Tibet film along with the other material. *Raid into Tibet* was shown as a two-part series, under the name of Rebel. The second part was, *The Unknown War*, based on a seven-month stay with the fighters of the Shan state challenging the authority of the Burmese military rulers. Also produced from this Burmese visit and stays in Hong Kong and Thailand was, *The Opium Wars*. These documentaries were all shown on ATV in 1966, along with three other Adrian Cowell documentaries on Buddhism in Tibet, Thailand and Japan.

Prisoners of War

An examination of the different way the Chinese treated Indian Army Gorkha Prisoners of War following the Sino-Indian War of 1962, what they were trying to achieve and whether it subsequently changed the behaviour or beliefs of those concerned

The one-month-long Sino-Indian War ended on November 21, 1962 when China declared a ceasefire and simultaneously announced that it would withdraw from all the areas it had occupied. This article examines claims in a British diplomatic file (371/170851) that soldiers from Indian Army Gorkha regiments in Chinese hands were singled out for special interrogation aimed at turning them into Chinese agents on their return to Nepal. On the National Archives website, under Nepal, this file is listed as: 'Political relations: People's Republic of China: border incidents 1963.' Given the title, I was searching for information on Khampas, and I was surprised to find diplomatic correspondence dealing with the claim mentioned. However, before assessing its validity, it is worth addressing the wider questions of the numbers of Indian Army soldiers taken prisoner, when they were released, and how they were treated.

Beyond total figures, it is difficult to find a consolidated breakdown by unit or ethnic origin of Indian Army soldiers who were killed, captured, or declared missing. Getting a breakdown by time and location is equally difficult. On June 10, 1963, after China declared that all prisoners had been released, J.A.G. Banks, the British High Commissioner in Delhi, was tasked with getting information on Indian Army Gorkha ex-Prisoners of War (POWs). This request reflected a growing fear in London, verging on paranoia judging from the number of references to it in diplomatic files, that brainwashed Gorkha ex-POWs would soon be returning to Nepal with subversive intent and that this would lead to regime change and the ending of Gorkha recruitment into the British Army. Equal fears were expressed that the Kathmandu authorities were being slow to react to this new threat. These concerns explain what seems at this distance of time to be the disproportionate amount of interest the United Kingdom had in Gorkha POWs as reflected in diplomatic traffic between London, Kathmandu, Delhi, and Peking.

On June 27, 1963, Banks reported back that he could get little information. He reported that, 'There is a certain amount of covering up when people were questioned about the subject. Indian Army Headquarters have from the start been vague about the number of prisoners and missing sustained by individual units.' He also commented that the Indian media had been relatively muted about insisting that every prisoner be accounted for: 'But in defence of the Indians' behaviour one must bear in mind that the return of the prisoners is part of the unilateral Chinese cease-fire, and withdrawal proposals, and the Indians have, therefore, no agreement under which to demand the return of the prisoners; indeed the more fuss the government makes about them the more they emphasise their own dependence on the wishes of the Chinese.' I can add at this point that I was unable to find a definitive number for Gorkha POWs beyond some press reports speaking of around 700.

During my research I found further references to Indian Army POWs in a number of files in the National Archives. One dispatch (from 371/170709) dated February 21, 1963, from the embassy in Peking, gave interesting details that are worth setting down for the record. It was written by a mid-ranking diplomat, who in 1984, as Sir Richard Evans, returned as ambassador and conducted the final negotiations that led to Hong Kong being handed back to China in 1997. He was a distinguished Sinologist, who in retirement wrote a much-acclaimed book on Deng Xiaoping, Deng Xiaoping and the Making of Modern China. The dispatch was based on identical official figures given in the People's Daily of February 11, 1963 and in the English language weekly the Peking Review on February 15, 1963.

The Chinese declared that 3,940 Indian Army soldiers had been captured. (In 1965, the Indian Defence Ministry released casualty figures of 1,383 killed, 1,696 missing and 3,968 captured. The difference of 28 in those captured is not significant and could reasonably be accounted for by the two sides counting some figures in different ways – for example, over the number of those who died from wounds in captivity. In addition, there are reports that 15 fit soldiers were released in December

1962 when the Chinese used them to return captured weapons.) Of the 3,940, 716 sick and wounded were released to the Indian Red Cross. Of these, 105 captured before November 16, 1962 were released at Jang on December 31, 1962. Another 611 captured after November 16, 1962 were released at Bomdila, Mechukha, Walong, Dirang Dzong, and Jang between December 5 and 31, 1962. A further 10 who were seriously wounded or sick died despite treatment. Their names and causes of death were sent to the Indian Red Cross.

The names of the 611 released were given to the Indian Red Cross at the time they were released. The names of the other 105 released were included among six lists mailed by the Chinese Red Cross to the Indian Red Cross between December 16, 1962 and February 10, 1963. (The final list of 820 names was handed over on February 10, 1963.) The names on these six lists can be split into two groups: 1,131 were captured before November 16, 1962, and 2,188 were captured after November 16, 1962. The first group included a brigadier general, 9 field grade officers, and 12 company grade officers. The second group included 17 field grade officers and 20 company grade officers.

Evans concluded his dispatch by saying that the figures broadly corresponded with those seen in reports from Delhi about the total number of missing officers and men, and that the breakdown showed that the fighting was much heavier on the eastern sector than on the western, and also that the Indian Army suffered its heaviest losses during the second phase of the Chinese offensive, beginning on November 16, 1962.

A further dispatch from Peking, dated April 3, 1963, carried news that both surprised and astonished the world, including India. A statement by the Chinese Ministry of Defense published in that day's *People's Daily* announced the decision to release and repatriate all captured Indian military personnel, who now numbered 3,213. This was to start on April 10, 1963 with the release of 144 POWs. Another batch of 469 was to follow soon after. The releases started smoothly but on April 19 the Chinese government introduced a complication when it informed India that, 'at the request of some of their number, 27 captured senior officers, including Brigadier Dalvi, are to be taken on a conducted tour of China, including Peking, and will thereafter be released at Shumchun on the Hong Kong border.'

Following strong Indian objections, the idea of the Hong Kong handover was dropped but the tour did go ahead. On March 29, 1963, the group were driven to Lhasa to start their long tour of China which ended when they were handed over to India at Kunming on May 4. A description of the tour is given by one of the group in a 2002 interview of retired Major General KK Tewari by Claude Arpi. He was a lieutenant colonel in 1962 in the post of the Divisional Commander Signals. In the interview Tewari comments instructively on the situation he observed on the Namka Chu during the build-up to the Chinese attack, including during Lieutenant General BM Kaul's chaotic and ill-fated short visit, and on the morning of the attack when he was taken prisoner. (His insightful observations on his time in captivity are well worth a read.[1])

In mid-May, toward the later stages of the release process, various press reports originating in Delhi stated that no Gorkha POWs had yet been released. The reason for this is suggested in one of J.A.G. Banks' dispatches dated April 8, 1963. He reported that the Nepal desk officer in External Affairs had told him that 'the Chinese Government had been in correspondence with the Nepalese Government, suggesting that as the Indian Gorkhas that they had captured were Nepalese subjects, the Chinese Government would be willing to release them direct to Nepal. The Nepalese Government had replied to the Chinese that it was far from true to say that all Gorkhas lived in Nepal and they were not interested in taking up the Chinese offer.'

How far the Chinese pushed this offer is not clear but the very late release of the Gorkha prisoners suggests that they did have some hope that their suggestion would be accepted. At a press conference on June 15, Nehru finally confirmed that the Chinese had returned all the Gorkha POWs to India. The Indian military attaché in Kathmandu also passed this information to the British ambassador. I found no evidence to support a contrary view. Only the Indian authorities know the full truth. They hold the consolidated list of prisoners by name, rank, and number, passed from the Chinese Red Cross to the Indian Red Cross. Similarly only they can pronounce authoritatively on the number of Gorkhas held captive and the number designated as killed or missing.

The British files do refer to a letter dated February 1, 1963, which referred to an unconfirmed report by a Brigadier Smyth, which said that brainwashed Gorkhas had been returned direct to Nepal and were actively preaching communism in the hills. Given the date of the report, such an early return in January would not make sense for prisoners captured in November. In addition, all the northern passes would have been shut and

---

1   http://www.rediff.com/news/2002/nov/06chin.htm

would have remained so until late April at the earliest. Further research indicated that the informant was Brigadier Sir John Smyth VC MP. At this stage he was making regular and passionate speeches in Parliament opposing proposed cuts in British Army Gurkha numbers. In a debate on March 4, 1963 he claimed, 'There is more than a possibility that China will enlist the soldiers we do not want. Certainly, they are making every effort to do so.' This claim attracted some attention in Kathmandu and Delhi but was quickly and rightly dismissed as ludicrous.

After the confirmed return of all the POWs to India, media attention turned to how they had been treated and in particular to the subject of brainwashing. All the POWs had to go through a debriefing process, which also checked their physical and mental state. All media reports on the subject carried the same stories. This strongly suggests official briefings as the source, and much of the detail was later confirmed in diplomatic dispatches. Physically, most of the prisoners were in reasonable shape. Gorkhas were separated from other Indian POWs at a very early stage. They were treated differently, perhaps better, and subjected to a different line of interrogation. The Chinese effort with the Indian POWs was directed mainly at weakening their fighting spirit by trying to drive a wedge between officers and men. Contrasts were drawn between the gap in privileges in the Indian Army compared with the claimed equality between ranks in the PLA. With Gorkhas, the aim was to persuade them to abandon fighting as mercenaries for India.

Throughout the conflict and afterwards, the Chinese consistently claimed that the POWs had been treated with respect, and the injured particularly so. In 2008, Chinese sources uploaded to the Internet a documentary film called *The Crushing Moment: China-India 1962 War* (Part I2 and Part II3), which repeated these claims. Indian sources called the documentary propaganda but acknowledged that the black and white film did show authentic footage from the 1962 war. The film shows Chinese nurses feeding soup to injured Indian soldiers and doctors treating the wounded and the captured.

What was the official Indian view? A press cutting of a report in *The Times* of London from June 27, 1964 gave details of an official statement from the Indian government, dated the previous day, accusing China of

---

2   http://bit.ly/2L8xtIU

3   https://www.youtube.com/watch?v=XstW0q0efY4

having used subversion and persuasion, pressure and punishment, to break down the loyalty of Indian POWs. The most serious charge listed was that Brigadier John Dalvi was kept in solitary confinement in a small, cold room and that he was made to listen to Radio Peking broadcasts and not allowed to hear anything else, not even music. Another accusation listed was that with the exception of Chinese communist literature no other reading matter was provided.

Alleged violations of the Geneva Convention listed included an accusation that the Chinese falsely obtained background information on prisoners by issuing forms said to have been required by the Indian government. Another allegation was that the Chinese went out of their way to humiliate and degrade officers by making them remove their badges of rank and forbidding the men to salute their officers and give them respect. It was also claimed that no batmen were provided and officers had to do all their own work.

Unpleasant and inconvenient as some of these impositions would have been, apart from the treatment of John Dalvi, they hardly qualify as serious breaches of the Geneva Convention. A more balanced view emerged in the interviews of ex-POWs carried by many newspapers during the media coverage to mark the fiftieth anniversary of the war in 2012. *The Tribune* on November 18, 2012 recorded a Garhwal Rifles veteran as saying that the Chinese treated prisoners with the utmost care and that they were not harassed and received food on time. A number of prisoners reported that they were harangued from time to time about how the Chinese government and its policies were better than India's, but they let it all pass over their head.

One of the longest and most informative interviews was with a retired brigadier who was taken prisoner as a second lieutenant. It appeared on *Rediff.com* on October 18, 2014. He reported that the Chinese made repeated attempts to get them to admit that India had been the aggressor. Asked if he was fed properly he said, 'The Chinese were not well off themselves. I could see this. We had to eat rice and radish for breakfast, lunch and dinner. We had to survive with this.' He did however say that the Chinese gave them warm clothing. On Gorkhas he asserted that, 'The 1/9 Gorkhas were kept separately, they wanted to show that Chinese and Gorkhas are related, they were given a better deal.' KK Tewari in his 2002 interview also states that the Gorkhas were kept separate and that 'they were given special privileges, for obvious political reasons.'

Further detailed insight on the treatment of Gorkha POWs is given in a dispatch dated June 21, 1963 from Guy Clarke, the British ambassador in Kathmandu, sent in response to persistent enquires from London about the mental state of returning ex-POWs. The dispatch opened by stating that that the first report received was an alarming one from an officer who had met an ex-prisoner on a train who could not converse coherently and that 'he was in a state of mental incapacity due to injections given to prevent him from recalling details of his internment.'

Since then, Clarke said, an account of an entirely different kind has been given by a returning ex-POW who was interviewed at the British Gurkha depot in Paklihawa. The dispatch records that he said the prisoners were very well treated and were given everything they asked for within the resources of their Chinese guards. They were given three injections at ten-day intervals, which were ostensibly to improve their health. They demurred at first, but agreed to the injections after the Chinese officers had received injections in front of them. The ex-prisoner said that though there had been rumors of men going mad or dying, he himself remained fit and had been passed fit at an Army medical inspection on his return to India.

On brainwashing, Clarke reported that the ex-prisoner said that they had a short pep talk most days on the virtues of communism and on the foolishness of fighting for the Indian capitalists. They were told that the Chinese and Nepalese were brothers and that before long India, Pakistan, Nepal, and other small countries would become part of communist China. In addition to the daily pep talks, each prisoner had three private interviews of three hours each, of which the object seemed to be to obtain information about the conditions of service and welfare in the Indian Army. The ex-prisoner stated that he and his companions had treated all this as a joke and had no intention of being influenced against their Indian officers by what they had been told.

This one account can hardly be taken as representative of the state of mind of all returning Gorkha ex-POWs. Humiliating defeat, particularly when committed to battle poorly clothed and inadequately equipped, followed by incarceration, is not normally conducive to maintaining high morale. For various reasons, memories of battles and their aftermath can quickly get distorted, which is why in most regimental histories everyone is invariably portrayed as standing firm and resolutely doing their duty. In reality, this is not always the case. For many reasons, most notably the quality of junior leadership shown, performance can vary. Only those who were there know the truth and for many reasons might never speak it. Similarly, soldiers will react differently to how they are treated in captivity, to what their guards say, and how they say it. Such factors as the number of casualties taken by their platoon or company, and how they saw their officers perform, are among many variables that will impact the mind of captives in different ways. Depending on the state of organization and leadership within the prison camp, the morale of most POWs will recover quickly but others inevitably will remain depressed and vulnerable.

A professional assessment of the chances of the Chinese having some success with their approach with Gorkha POWs is given in a document written by a senior FO official at the time. He says that he discussed indoctrination with a member of 'the Foreign Services' who had direct personal experience of the subject. His judgment was that, 'Four and a half months is time enough for the Chinese to carry out some fairly effective indoctrination, at least of a negative sort, if not enough to produce full-scale political converts.' In fact, as I have outlined, some Gorkha POWs were in Chinese hands for six months.

In sum, it is hardly controversial to say that we cannot be sure exactly how the Chinese treatment of Gorkha ex-POWs might have influenced their behavior, either immediately, or perhaps more particularly, many years later. Some of those who were held captive in this war would later have returned on pension to a Nepal that was still an autocratic state. If they lived in places like Rolpa and Rukum they would have found a society that was still verging on feudal. They would also have found that the traditional power of the local Thakuri rulers, and their supporters, was being strongly challenged by their kinsfolk who had been fired up by revolutionary communist ideas throughout the 1950s.

These districts are chosen deliberately. Mohan Bikram Singh formed the communist party of Pyuthan in 1953. He set up and ran three-month long training courses for a large numbers of cadres. By 1954, organized large scale demonstrations were taking place for peasants' rights. As Anne de Sales has shown in her article *The Biography of a Magar Communist*, in neighboring Rolpa, revolutionary ideas also took root in the 1950s, and spread more quickly after Mohan Bikram Singh spent a few days in Thabang in the spring of 1956 after his release from prison in Salyan. The formidable Barman Budha became an influential communist leader. He started the first school in Thabang in 1959 and employed an ex-Indian Gorkha soldier who lived in Thabang to teach in the school.

In the first general election in 1959, all the voters of Thabang voted for a communist candidate.

In her article 'Maoists, People and the State as seen from Rolpa and Rukum', Kiyoko Ogura highlights the fact that, inspired by Mohan Bikram Singh, there was another movement in Rukum even before the people of Thabang had become communist. Kami Budha Magar was the first communist in Rukum. He was an ex-Indian Army soldier and one of the activists who had rebelled with K.I. Singh in Bhairahawa against the Delhi agreement in 1951. After K.I. Singh escaped to China, Kami Budha returned to Rukum and formed an alternative government. To avoid arrest by the administrator in Salyan, Kami Budha went to Humla in north-western Nepal, where he and his group captured the government office and stayed for some time. But he was arrested and taken to Jumla where he was killed by the police in 1955.

Thabang, often mentioned as the epicentre of the Maoist revolt, had a history of army recruitment going back to the pre-1947 Indian Army. Based on field research carried out in 1977, Augusta Molnar recorded in her book The Kham Magar Women of Thabang that 31 percent of households in the village had one member currently serving in the Indian Army and 10 percent were drawing a pension from a current or deceased member. Rolpa and Rukum were among the traditional recruiting areas for the 8th Gorkha Rifles, and the first battalion of the regiment had taken part in the heroic defense of the airstrip at Chushul in Ladakh in the 1962 war, during which it took very heavy casualties, including an unknown number taken prisoner. The second battalion was committed to operations in the northeast at the later stages of the war.

So it is possible that there could be some link between returning ex-POWs and the spreading of revolutionary zeal in places like Rukum and Rolpa, but the profusion of evidence now available about the provenance of the ideas that led to the Maoist conflict indicates that it was unlikely to have been significant. No doubt highly motivated new cadres would have been welcome, but in 1963 there were already many people in these areas who were committed to revolutionary change and, as later events were to show, were well capable of leading it. However, this research suggests that to some extent it still remains an open question. The part played by ex-Indian Army Gorkhas, whether they were ex-POWs or not, in promoting and enabling revolutionary change in Nepal starting in the 1950s, is a field ripe for study. Perhaps this article will inspire someone to do it. I also hope that it might give rise to new evidence that will throw some fresh light on the question, based not on speculation but grounded on fact.

Postscript

While doing research for this article, I discovered that one document in File 371/170851 was missing despite the National Archives declaring that it had been reunited with the parent file on January 1, 2014 after 50 years of closure. I soon discovered that the document was still retained by the Foreign Office. I submitted a request under the Freedom of Information Act (FOIA). After the usual delay, it was released with some lines redacted in the middle of the sixth paragraph. The justification given was that under two parts of Section 27 of the FOIA release, the redacted information would be prejudicial to the UK's relations with China and Nepal.

It was a secret document, dated February 11, 1963, giving a summary of conversations which Guy Clarke, the British ambassador, had just had with Dr. Giri, the then Chairman of the Council of Ministers who had recently returned from a visit to China, and, separately, with the Inspector General of Police, PS Lama. Paragraph 6 of Clarke's letter states,

> The realistic appreciation revealed by Dr Giri in this conversation of the menace of the Chinese presence on Nepal's northern frontier, was further reflected in a conversation I had recently with the Inspector General of Police in the course of which he told me something of the steps he is taking to keep track of Chinese intelligence activities in Nepal. He showed me a map in his office in which he had marked, among many other things, motorable roads and airfields constructed by the Chinese in the Tibetan areas adjacent to the Nepalese frontier.

The next lines in Paragraph 6 are redacted but information in two other open dispatches in the same file gives a good indication of what is redacted. One written on March 13, 1963 stated, 'The Nepalese are as you are well aware from paragraph 6 of my secret letter of February 11, alive to the danger of infiltration of Chinese agents from across the northern border and are doing their best to keep track of them...' Another written on August 20, 1963 stated, 'In my secret letter of February 11, I described in paragraph 6 an account given to me by the Inspector General of Police of the measures which he was taking to keep track of subversive agents in the northern frontier regions. This account included the story of an agent who was followed from Namche Bazar in Solu Khumbu until he was finally arrested in Kathmandu.'

The unredacted part of Paragraph 6 continues:

> Finally Lama said that he had personally been left in no doubt about the nature of Chinese intelligence sensitivities in Nepal by the fact that when, on one occasion, he had accepted an invitation to dinner from the Chinese Military Attaché, he had found himself the only guest and had been obliged to spend two hours alone with his host and an interpreter, during which time the Military Attaché had made various offers of aid for the police force and for the Inspector General's personal use. The Inspector General said that he had related this experience to the King, who had instructed him to accept nothing from the Chinese.

Clarke's final paragraph in the letter states, 'These two conversations indicate to me that, whatever their public position may be, the Nepalese government are in no danger of accepting Chinese protestations of friendship at face value, and are well aware of the potential menace from their northern neighbour both to the political independence of Nepal as a sovereign state, and also, through internal subversive activities, to the stability of the present regime.'

In sum, the loudly proclaimed British fears in 1963 about Nepal not being alert to the dangers posed by Chinese subversion were seriously misplaced. It is possible to take the view that Giri and Lama were telling the British ambassador what he wanted to hear, but, in its detail, Lama's testimony in particular suggests that they were speaking the truth. At this time and later, Lama passed to the British highly secret details of United States Central Intelligence Agency support to the Khampa guerrillas, which proved to be totally accurate.

What did this mean for India? After Mahendra's coup in January 1961, armed opposition to his autocratic rule, encouraged covertly by India, steadily built up through 1962 to a point that had the regime seriously rattled. After the November 1962 war, Indian opposition to Mahendra weakened rapidly and he was able to embark on his much acclaimed strategy of playing China off against India, which essentially consisted of worrying India that he was getting closer and closer to China. If India had known the extent of Nepal's concerns about Chinese actions and intentions, its relations with Nepal in the post war period could, to put it mildly, have taken a much less accommodating line.

This article has been republished with permission from *The Record*. The original can be found online at: https://www.recordnepal.com/ wire/prisoners-war/

Addendum May 2018

Following a Freedom of Information request, the Closed Extract from the Foreign Office file, 371/170851/1, which is the subject of the above postscript, was released to me on 29 Oct 2014. The Extract was designated as FN 103110/5 and the subject heading was, Sino-Nepalese Relations. About 10 lines were redacted but, as indicated in the Postscript, most of the content of these redacted lines can be deduced from information in two other open dispatches in the same file,

A quick check today on the National Archives Discovery webpage, under the main file heading of 371/170851/1, indicates that 'Closed extract: Jacket FN 103110/5' remains closed and that its opening date is 01 January 2024.

Thus, we have a situation analogous to that described in the last chapter of this book. My Freedom of Information Request was not a personal plea for me to have a private look at what is in the closed extract. It was a formal request for the file to be made public by releasing it to the National Archives. Three years on, there appears to be no excuse for the FCO not doing so.

The Maharaja

A detailed account of the visit of Maharaja Chandra Shum Shere Rana to Britain in 1908, including the background to it, and its significant consequences

© British Library Board (430/77(86))

'The Viceroy's Big Tiger.' Centre, holding hat and looking down at his tiger, Lord Curzon.

This is the first of two articles covering the visits to the United Kingdom of Maharaja Chandra Shum Shere Rana in 1908 and King Mahendra in 1960. Chandra's visit was a private one but he arrived on an official invitation and was treated as a state guest with all his expenses covered. Details of his visit are given in three thick files in the India Office archives in the British Library in London. King Mahendra paid a state visit to Britain in

1960, at the conclusion of which he stayed for a further two weeks on an official visit. Details of his visit are given in some 50 files in the National Archives at Kew. Both men visited Oxford and material in the University Archives and in the records of the Bodleian Library reveals interesting details not previously publicly exposed. (Note: Chandra's full name is transliterated in varying ways, but he signed himself as Chandra Shum Shere.)

This first article deals with Chandra's visit. He and his party left Kathmandu on April 6, 1908 and arrived in England on May 8, 1908, staying for over ten weeks. He was in the seventh year of his 29 years as an absolute ruler. The Rana usurpation of the power of the Shah kings started in September 15, 1846, when Jung Bahadur Kunwar (later to change his name to Rana), Chandra's uncle, massacred his rivals and quickly moved to establish the political system that bore his adopted name. To quote from Joshi and Rose in Democratic Innovations in Nepal, '(T)he Rana political system was undisguised military despotism over the King and the people of Nepal. Government functioned as an instrument to carry out the personal wishes and interests of the ruling Rana Prime Minister. Its main domestic preoccupation was the exploitation of the country's resources to enhance the personal wealth of the Rana ruler and his family.' Throughout his 29 years of rule, Chandra did nothing to weaken the family's absolute grip on absolute power. Indeed, even by Rana standards, his rule was notably repressive.

Control of the military was one of the keys to Rana family survival, as was support and friendship from the British. No Rana ruler worked more assiduously or more obsequiously to maintain and strengthen British support than Chandra, and this is well exemplified by his tireless cultivation of friendship with the then Viceroy of India, Lord Curzon. Chandra first met Curzon when he hosted him on a hunting trip in the Terai from March 29 to April 17, 1901. How this came about is a story in itself. In a letter to Kathmandu dated January 2, 1901, Curzon effectively invited himself to a hunting trip in Nepal. Maharaja Bir Shamshere reluctantly extended an invitation but said that for health reasons he would be unable to host him. On March 4, 1901, Bir Shumshere died under what some have described as mysterious circumstances. Dev Shumshere, his successor, also refused to go to the Terai to host Curzon but agreed to a request from his younger half brother, Chandra, to be allowed to do so. To quote from Leo Rose in *Nepal: Strategy for Survival*, 'What these two brilliant and ambitious men discussed in their meetings in the Terai can only be conjectured but it seems improbable that Nepali internal politics and the situation in Tibet were ignored.' On June 27, 1901, Chandra seized power from Dev and there is strong evidence that, at the very least, he gained British acquiescence before doing so. The British recognized his legitimacy immediately and privately commented that they gave him credit for avoiding the usual bloodshed. His contact with Curzon would clearly have helped.

Throughout the time that Chandra hosted Curzon, the notable photographic duo of Herzog and Higgins of Mhow were in attendance to record every detail, as they invariably were on Curzon's trips. An album of 121 photographs was produced which shows all aspects of life during the three weeks: from relaxing in three very comfortable looking camps, to moving on the trail on the backs of some of the 200 elephants provided, encircling the prey, closing the ring, the moment of the kill, and the aftermath. Given the primitive cameras in use, it must have been a hazardous business. The album is now part of the Curzon Collection in the British Library. The prints are mounted with handwritten captions with the title stamped in gold on the front cover: 'H.E. the Viceroy's Shooting Tour, Nepal, Tarai, April 1901.' The first photograph is a three-quarter length standing portrait, in formal dress, of 'Maharaja Chandra Shumsher, Prime Minister of Nepal, 1901.' The second is a full length standing portrait, again in formal dress, of 'Maharaja Dib Shumsher, Prime Minister of Nepal, Deposed.' It would have taken more than three months to produce the album so the use of these two photographs, separately sourced, was a neat way of getting round the problem that the man who hosted the viceroy had deposed the maharaja who had endorsed the invitation to him.

In various articles dating back to 1994, Pratyoush Onta describes an album with an identical title stamped on the front cover, which he said could be found in the Kaiser Library in Kathmandu. This album was possibly a gift from Curzon to Chandra. An album with the identical title was sold at Sotheby's in London in October 2014 for £2,750. It was submitted to the sale by a noted dealer and collector, Sven Gahlin. The provenance of this album was not given in the sales catalogue. A recent exhaustive search of the Kaiser Library failed to locate the album that Onta described and examined in the 1990s.

What is curious about the album from the Curzon Collection is that, apart from the one formal portrait, there is not a single photograph that shows Chandra. As host, he must have been in the area even if, for reasons of caste, he would have occupied a different camp. Whatever the explanation for this, the prints show that Chandra ensured that his guests enjoyed the full range of 'sport.' Curzon personally shot a leopard, a rhinoceros, and at least three tigers. The photograph above (430/77(86)) catches the essence well. The caption is apt: 'The Viceroy's Big Tiger.' Two Nepal Army colonels are in the photo: on the left, Colonel Jit Bahadur, and on the right, Colonel Hurck Jung who was 'in charge of the shoot.' Five of the ten members of his staff who accompanied the viceroy are also included: from the left, Colonel E. H. Fenn, Colonel C. Gordon, Captain the Honorable G. B. Portman, the viceroy, Brigadier-General E. Baring (military secretary) and Colonel T. C. Pears, the British Resident in Kathmandu. Curzon had a reputation for being fastidious about his dress, and even in the middle of a three-week hunting trip in the Terai he is immaculately dressed with matching jacket and trousers. A proper analysis of the detail and characters in this photo would merit a separate article, but, for the present, it is enough to say that it captures something of the character of Curzon – and of an imperial age which he so powerfully personified.

Chandra was given the ideal opportunity to ingratiate himself further with Curzon during the build-up to the dispatch of the British Expeditionary Force to Tibet in late 1903. Curzon was determined to launch this force but the home government was hostile to his proposal. After the searing experience of the Boer War, the British public had no wish to get involved in a war in a remote corner of Asia; nor was the government in London prepared to risk a European war with Russia over the issue, or complicate further its difficult relations with China.

Curzon dedicated his formidable will to changing this mood by, in the first instance, building up the immediacy of the threat posed to British interests in Tibet by alleged Russian activities. The archive evidence strongly supports the contention of Leo Rose in Nepal: Strategy for Survival that 'Chandra became one of the more assiduous abettors of British-Russian rivalry,' and that he 'urged on the Viceroy the feasibility and necessity of punitive action against Tibet.' At a long meeting between the two men in December 1902, after Chandra arrived in India to attend the Delhi Durbar held on January 1, 1903, Chandra assured Curzon that he would disregard Nepal's obligation under the 1856 Treaty with Tibet that required Nepal to come to Tibet's aid in the case of a foreign invasion. The relevant text said: 'Tibet being the country of monasteries, hermits, and celibates, devoted to religion, the Gurkha

Government have agreed henceforth to afford help and protection to it as far as they can, if any foreign country attacks it.' Chandra went further in assuring Curzon that any British military operation in Tibet would have Nepal's active support – but at a price. The verbatim account of the conversation records him as saying, 'If we have to do anything jointly, against Tibet I hope that we shall be allowed to take a proportion of the country for us to remunerate the present tribute paid by them to us and to compensate for the loss that we may suffer in our commerce.' The account records that at this point Curzon 'laughed softly' before asking and getting a categorical assurance that Nepal would back whatever action Britain took.

Chandra also started to feed in from the Nepal legation in Lhasa an endless series of stories about Russian influence in Lhasa. The wildest rumors were passed on as established fact: Russia and Tibet had signed a new treaty; Lhasa was teeming with Russians; Russia had supplied large numbers of weapons to Tibet; Russia was building an arms factory in Lhasa. All of this turned out in the end to be bunkum but it served Curzon's purpose. All such stories were passed to London and played their part in the home government reluctantly giving permission for a limited incursion.

As the 'incursion' was underway, by the deliberate disregarding of orders and the creation of further bogus intelligence, Curzon managed to persuade the government to expand it into a full-scale expedition to Lhasa, which would result in the imposition of terms on Tibet advantageous to Britain. What Patrick French in his book, Younghusband: The Last Great Imperial Adventurer, called Curzon's finest piece of casuistry relates to a dispatch that he sent to London, which claimed that an attack on the frontier by Tibetan troops on Nepali yaks was 'an overt act of hostility.' French rightly remarks, 'The fact that the Viceroy of India was sending telegrams about the fate of frontier livestock to the Secretary of State (and hence the Cabinet) shows the flimsiness of the justifications he was putting forward for invading Tibet. To describe yak-rustling as an overt 'act of hostility' by a foreign power is plainly absurd. It shows the way Curzon was willing to use almost any excuse to obtain sanction for a further advance into Tibet . . . ' Again Chandra played a helpful role in falsely presenting himself to the Tibetan authorities as an impartial mediator, even as a peacemaker, while mostly acting at Curzon's behest and in Britain's interests.

The whole misadventure is best summed up by Peter Fleming in his book, *Bayonets to Lhasa*. '(I)ts main purposes were rooted in fallacy,' he writes. 'By the time they were largely fulfilled they had been forgotten. Its achievements were largely disavowed and its staunch commander censured.' The last reference is to Younghusband, who was effectively in charge of the Expeditionary Force under the guise of heading the Tibet Frontier Commission, also known as 'the Mission.' However, all concerned knew that at every stage Younghusband acted with Curzon's full knowledge and authority. Among the units in the Force were a mountain artillery battery and six companies of the 8th Gurkha Rifles. In the support echelons were 3,000 ponies, 5,000 yaks and buffaloes, 5,000 bullocks, 7,000 mules, and six camels to carry the officers' cigars. Most of these animals died during the journey, as did many of their coerced owners. Over 10,000 coolies accompanied the invasion, mainly to carry the personal equipment of officers in boxes, trunks, cases, and containers. Younghusband needed 29 containers to carry his kit and extensive wardrobe, which included 12 coats of various types, 67 shirts, 18 pairs of boots and shoes, and a bath.

Chandra had offered the loan of ten regiments of the Nepal Army for the expedition, but this offer was politely declined. The offer of 3,000 yaks was accepted. Fleming records that '(t)he Nepalese yaks whose adventures while in transit had helped in a small way to launch the campaign, were completely wiped out; the thirty one who on paper survived were in fact slaughtered and eaten.' Rose in Nepal: Strategy for Survival quotes documents that record an eyewitness assessment that the Nepali porters 'were practically an impressed gang' who proved to be 'discontented and refractory' and were kept under control only with great difficulty.

The British government quickly repudiated some of the main terms imposed on the Tibetans as being unduly harsh and amounting to annexation. As a consequence of the invasion, the Chinese increased their influence in Lhasa but there was little gain for Britain, and even less for Nepal. Trade from Kathmandu through Kuti and Kryong diminished as a result of the British being able to increase the volume of trade through Sikkim and the Chumbi valley route to Gyantse. Chandra, however, gained personally through his now proven reliability as a staunch supporter of British policy. This was recognized by his appointment as Grand Commander of the Star of India in 1905. Henceforth he would be Sir Chandra. This, one British report said, met Chandra's highest ambitions as it strengthened his position at home by showing that he could go one better than his predecessors. It also led to him achieving one of his other great ambitions: to emulate his uncle Jung Bahadur by getting an official invitation to visit Britain. Curzon resigned as viceroy in November 1905. His reputation had been damaged by the Tibet adventure though the main reason for his resignation was disagreement with Kitchener over the control and administration of the Indian Army. Chandra, however, as we shall see, benefitted directly from his friendship with Curzon during his 1908 visit, as subsequently did the University of Oxford.

'Visit to Europe of Chandra Shumsher JBR, Vol. I'/Madan Puraskar Pustakalaya (MPP) Photo Collection)

Chandra Shum Shere Rana and his military suite in London. Seated, from left: Singha (Chandra's son), Kaiser (son), Major Manners-Smith, Juddha (half brother), Chandra, Rudra (nephew), Mohan (son), Baber (son), Hiranya (nephew).

How to designate Chandra during his British visit had been decided prior to his attendance at the 1903 Delhi Durbar. Chandra was not prepared to be regarded as equivalent to a mere Indian feudatory prince, and the British were equally adamant that he would not be given the title of ambassador, as this would concede that Nepal had an independent status. After prolonged correspondence, Chandra himself proposed a compromise in a personal letter he sent to the viceroy's staff:

> I have decided not to make mention of the word Ambassador, Envoy or Representative. In the Kharita from the King to the Viceroy my designation should be Maharaja Prime Minister and Marshal of Nepal, and representative of His Sovereign the Maharajadhiraj.

(Kharita is an official letter, usually from a paramount power, enclosed in a richly embroidered bag or silver casket, and written in Persian. Dhiraj is a shortened form of the Sanskrit word adhiraj, meaning 'sovereign ruler.' When Jung Bahadur in 1856 declared himself to be Maharaja of Lamjung and Kaski, he elevated the Shah king to the position of Maharajadhiraj.)

Early in the planning for the 1908 visit, the British Resident sent a long list to London of what Chandra had personally asked to be included in the program. It was clearly based on a close study of Jung Bahadur's 1850 program: Chandra wanted to do everything his uncle had done, and more. Nothing was missed out including, 'a Naval gun salute west of Aden.' Additionally, in the Resident's words, 'Sir Chandra wishes to be accorded precedence, honours and salutes as conceded to Jung Bahadur in 1850.'

Chandra set off for England with 19 servants and a personal suite of 22. (The names of those in the suite are listed at the end of this article.) Inevitably, senior Ranas figured prominently: General Juddha (half brother, age 33), General Rudra (nephew, age 29), General Mohan (son, age 23), Lieutenant General Baber (son, age 20), Lieutenant General Kaiser (son, age 16), Major General Singha (son, age 15). Only in regimes of 'undisguised military despotism' will one find teenagers shamelessly promoted to the most senior ranks. For the more privileged, such elevation came at birth. A large number of the descendants of those named have had successful military careers in post-Rana Nepal, though less rapidly promoted. Descendants of non-Rana members of the entourage have also done well through different political dispensations. Chandra's private secretary, Sardar Marich Man Singh, is the great-grandfather of the present deputy prime minister, Prakash Man Singh. Pundit Kashinath's family of Acharya Dixits are also well known. Two British officers were 'in attendance' throughout the visit: the British Resident in Nepal, Major Manners-Smith, and a young officer from the Fourth Gurkha Rifles, Lieutenant MacLeud Wylie, 'who Chandra remembered as a child when his father was Resident.'

Chandra and his party were received at Dover on May 8, 1908 by Sir Curzon Wyllie, the Political Aide de Camp to the Secretary of State for India (Lord Morley at the time). They traveled by special train to Victoria. The whole party was accommodated in Mortimer House, a large residence in Halkin Street, Belgravia. Photos of it had been sent in advance to Kathmandu. Prior to the visit, it had been redecorated at a cost of £3,500, and 17 British servants, including a house manager, had been hired for 13 weeks at a cost of £546. Many assurances were sought and given that these servants would be boarded out and that no female servants would be employed. The house is now called Forbes House and the 47-year lease on it was recently sold for £40 million. Twenty-two boxes of provisions also arrived with the party containing large amounts of spices, pulses, rice, and ghee. Chandra was persuaded not to bring his own cows. He was told that three would be hired with men to look after them. He was also informed that slaughtering of sheep in the grounds of Mortimer House would not be permitted.

'Visit to Europe of Chandra Shumsher JBR, Vol. I'/Madan Puraskar Pustakalaya (MPP) Photo Collection)

(Mortimer House, where Chandra and his entourage were hosted in London. In 'Visit to Europe of Chandra Shumsher JBR, Vol. I'/Madan Puraskar Pustakalaya (MPP) Photo Collection)

On May 11, 1908, three days after their arrival, Chandra and 14 of his suite attended a reception at Buckingham Palace to be individually presented to King Edward VII. Chandra was first to be presented and Lord Morley was privy to their conversation as was a secretary to record what was said. In welcoming Chandra, the king said that he still remembered 'the shooting' he had with Chandra's uncle in his country. This was a reference to his 1876 visit to the Terai when he was Prince of Wales. The next part of the conversation is worth setting down as recorded:

Maharaja: It is so kind of Your Majesty to still remember. (*After a pause*) On behalf of His Highness the Maharaja-dhiraj, my country and myself, I beg to pay Your Most Gracious Majesty our most humble and profound respects. (*The King Emperor bowed*) I am deeply thankful that the high honour and proud privilege of being in the august presence of the incarnate might and majesty of the British Empire have been vouchsafed to me. One of my long cherished desires was to be able to express personally our hearty and loyal devotion to Your Majesty's august person and throne, and I am happy that it has been so happily fulfilled today. I regard it as the happiest moment of my life.

King Emperor: Thank you. (*Turning to Lord Morley*) Is that not so Morley, that the Maharaja speaks English very well? (*Turning again towards the Maharaja*) Will you introduce your suite?

Maharaja: Your Majesty, before doing so I solemnly assure Your Majesty that this is my sword and all that it commands are ever at Your Majesty's services when required.

King Emperor: Thank you.

The two men met formally again only on the day before Chandra's departure from England, but throughout the visit, perhaps impressed with the declaration of near-fealty, the king took a number of personal actions that must have impressed and pleased Chandra. He approved a royal carriage for Chandra to use in London during his stay. The king invited him and two of his sons to ride in the procession on the King's Birthday Parade held annually at Horse Guards Parade in the center of London. Chandra and some of his suite were also invited to join him in the Royal Box at the Olympic Games on Monday, July 13, 1908. They also viewed the Royal Tournament from the Royal Box. An expensive box was hired for the suite to attend a gala performance at the Royal Opera House Covent Garden in honor of a visit by the President of the French Republic.

Outside these high profile public events, Chandra and his suite also visited such places as Edinburgh, Eton College, Windsor, Portsmouth dockyard, the Channel Fleet at Dover, the Vickers and Maxim firearms factories, and Woolwich Arsenal. A number of military reviews were included in the program and a day was spent on board one of the

The civilian members of Chandra's suite seated in front of his 19 servants.

recently built Dreadnaught battleships. In sum, Chandra was given plenty of opportunity to see at first hand the military basis of Britain's imperial power.

As the visits were going on, two problems emerged for the India Office officials to sort out. The first was straightforward. The British and Foreign Bible Society sent a letter to Sir Curzon Wyllie which stated that it was their long established custom to present distinguished visitors from abroad with a copy of one of the Society's editions in their own tongue, and asked that a deputation be allowed to meet Chandra for this purpose. When consulted, the reply from Mortimer House was clear: 'the Maharaja does not at all like the idea of receiving a deputation and would be very glad if they would be asked to abandon their proposal.'

The second problem took more time and effort to resolve. On June 22, 1908, exactly six weeks after Chandra and his suite had been presented to King Edward VII, a parcel arrived in the Indian Office. The official who received it forwarded it to the Palace using the following words, 'At the 11th hour this Kharita, or letter, in Persian, enclosed inside a silk bag, (with a translation in English inside the silver box) has been brought to me by Lieutenant MacLeud Wylie from Mortimer House. It is as well that His Majesty should be informed of the contents of the Kharita.'

The kharita from King Prithvi Bir was dated April 3, 1908. It must have been brought to London by Chandra who would also have carefully vetted its contents. It would clearly have been appropriate for Chandra to have handed it to King Edward VII when he was presented to him on May 11, 1908, but it does not take much imagination to understand why he decided to withhold it. The Indian Office official's letter stated, 'The truth is that although the Prime Minister, in whose hands all governing powers are rested, professes the greatest outward show of deference to the Maharaja Dhiraj, he is not inclined to make more of the Kharita than is absolutely necessary for official purposes.' The main 'official purpose' required was to draft a reply, and much consideration was given to it, not so much to the content but to what the king should write in his own handwriting in the address and in signing off the letter. Eventually, after much consultation, 'My friend' was used in the address and the letter finished with, 'I am Your Highnesses Sincere Friend.'

In the convention of the times, grandiloquent language is used throughout King Prithvi's kharita, but two extracts seem of enduring historical interest. The first comes from the opening substantive paragraph, which leads to the request to grant Chandra an audience:

(E)ncouraged by the exalted benignity, august consideration and chivalrous magnanimity of Your Majesty, convinced of the continuance of the kindness and good-will of the mighty British Government as indispensible for the well being and security of this poor hilly country, deeply conscious of the vast power and endless resources of the said Government, sincerely grateful for those favours which are the visible sign of Your Majesty's gracious kindness and condescension, and profoundly thankful to Your Majesty's Government in India for respecting and preserving intact the autonomy of this solitary and remote land of the Gurkhas who are ever ready to defend the fair name and the just and honourable cause of England with their heart's best blood, I beg most respectfully to send Major General Sir Chandra . . .

The second extract comes from near the end:

With a sincere and loyal heart I beg to entertain the hope that Your Majesty will ever be graciously pleased to continue to allow Nepal a place of security under Your Majesty's most exalted benignity as hithertofore . . .

Attached to the translation of the kharita in the files is a handwritten note from an official, which, following on from the above extracts, sets down clearly how Britain saw Nepal's position at this time. While acknowledging the prime minister as the de facto ruler of the Nepal state, he wrote, 'The precise nature of the protectorate of the British

Crown over Nepal has never been clearly defined, but the State is recognised as falling under our exclusive political influence and control, and the Maharaja Dhiraj is regarded as a Native Prince or Chief under the suzerainty of H.M. exercised through the Governor General of India.'

© British Library Board (430/67(60))

'Group Portrait, Encaenia at Oxford June 24, 1908.' Seated, from left: Sir Robert Hart; Sir Earnest Satow; Sir William Anson, MP; Chandra; Curzon; Dr. H.T. Warren, Vice-Chancellor; Mr. C. M. Parker; Dr. F. Raymond. Standing, from left: Mohan, Juddha, Rudra, unknown, Baber, Kaiser, unknown, Hiranya, Jaya Prithvi Bahadur Singh, unknown.

With the exception of his trip to Oxford for the conferment of an honorary degree, the details of Chandra's many visits are extensively covered in the three Indian Office files. The single reference to Oxford is in a letter, dated March 24, 1908, from Manners-Smith in Kathmandu to Sir Curzon Wyllie, which said, 'I have been counting on Lord Curzon to arrange a visit to Oxford which Sir Chandra would like to see as, of course, he knows Sir Chandra well.' Curzon Wyllie was an old Indian hand who would have known Curzon well, so he must have alerted him to Chandra's request privately. Files in the University Archives say very little about how Chandra came to be proposed for an honorary degree, but there are enough pointers to indicate Curzon's hand at work, not least in the speed at which the proposal went through the formal process of approvals.

Curzon had been elected as Chancellor in 1907. As befitted his character, he was very active in the appointment. His entry in the Dictionary of National Biography states that 'he threw himself so energetically into the cause of university reform that critics complained he was ruling Oxford like an Indian province.' Despite the late indication from Chandra that he wished to visit Oxford, acting quickly and decisively to honor his friend with the conferment of an honorary degree would have been the sort of challenge that appealed to Curzon. A lot had to be done in a short time, including getting Chandra to accept the honor officially, before his name could be formally published. The *Oxford University Gazette* published on May 26, 1908 listed those who would be proposed for honorary degrees at the annual ceremony of Encaenia to be held on June 24, 1908. Chandra's name was not on the list but a note stated that 'the list is incomplete pending the replies of other persons to the letters of invitation.'

At the time, the executive body of the University was called the Hebdomadal Council. There is a single reference in its record that states that on Monday, June 1, 1908, 'a letter was read from the India Office as to an hon. degree.' The record states that names were proposed for honorary degrees but there is no mention as to why they were proposed or who proposed them. Given the length of time to exchange letters between London and Kathmandu in 1908, it is obvious that the letter of invitation to Chandra must have been dispatched some weeks before the meeting on June 1. Chandra's letter of acceptance must have arrived just before that meeting as the Gazette published on June 2, under the heading 'Encaenia,' had Chandra's name at the top of a list of five men who were to be proposed for 'conferment of a Doctor of Civil Law honoris causa at a Convocation to be held in the Sheldonian Theatre on Wednesday, June 24, 1908, at noon.' A prominent notice published in the Gazette, dated June 16, stated that Lord Curzon 'has intimated his intention to be present at Encaenia and to confer the Honorary Degrees in person.'

Encaenia is the ceremonial high point of the Oxford academic year. It is the ceremony at which the university awards honorary degrees to distinguished men and (nowadays) women and commemorates its benefactors. The day starts with those involved assembling in the Hall of Magdalen College 'to partake of Lord Crewe's benefaction to the University,' consisting of peaches, strawberries, and champagne. They then walk in procession in full academic regalia to the Sheldonian Theatre on Broad Street. This was completed in 1668 after a design by Christopher Wren based on a first century Roman theater. Once the proceedings have been opened by the Chancellor, each honorand is introduced by the Public Orator with a speech in Latin and admitted to his or her new degree by the Chancellor.

Encaenia nowadays is a very solemn occasion, but it was not so in 1908 judging from the full-page report in the weekly *The Oxford Times* published on June 26, 1908. The Sheldonian was not full; the report indicated that there was a feeling of anticlimax compared with the previous year which was Curzon's first Encaenia as Chancellor. That was a very large scale affair with 35 honorands, including such notables as Mark Twain (under his proper name of Samuel Langhorne Clemens), Rudyard Kipling, and General William Booth, the founder of the Salvation Army, each of whom were greeted by prolonged cheering from the undergraduates. Before the 1908 event, the organist tried to keep things cheerful by playing such tunes as Auld Lang Syne and Rule Brittania, which the undergraduates enthusiastically sang. *The Oxford Times* reports that there was 'a round of cheers as the Maharajah's suite, a body of swarthy-visaged men arrayed in military uniform of olive-green bedizened with much gold braid and trimmings entered the building and were escorted to seats to what are known as 'Musical Honours', the undergraduates bursting out spontaneously with 'For they are jolly good fellows."

There were more cheers and ironic cries as the Chancellor's procession entered. The most notable honorand in 1908 was Mr. David Lloyd George, the Chancellor of the Exchequer, and later Britain's prime minister during the last three years of the First World War. When he was introduced, there was much cheering and shouted questions about women's voting rights, pensions eligibility, and the cost of beer. The report states that in the ensuing laughter, Mr. Lloyd George heartily joined. Also loudly cheered was Sir Robert Hart, the Inspector General of Chinese Customs and Posts, 'who had devoted 50 years of labour to improving the administration of the revenue of the Chinese Empire.' There was no reported hilarity when Chandra was introduced by the Public Orator as, 'a statesman who had guided the foreign policy of his country and added to the strength of its military position.' Reference was also made to the fact that he was a student of the University of Calcutta when Curzon was Chancellor, and that the king had already received him with a welcome due to a friend and an ally, 'and the University would now willingly add its meed of recognition.' Honorary Doctorates of Civil Law were also conferred on Sir Earnest Satow, a brilliant linguist and late Minister in Peking and C. M. Parker, an Honorary Fellow of University College. An Honorary Doctor of Science was conferred on Dr. Fulgence Raymond, a distinguished French professor of neurology.

After the conferring of degrees, the Public Orator (in 1908, the Rector of Lincoln College) delivered in Latin the Creweian Address (the same Lord Crewe of 'the benefaction') reviewing the year and commemorating the benefactors, 'which was attentively and sympathetically listened to, some of his humourous and cynical remarks being greeted with laughter.' All of this would have passed over the heads of the visitors but with his love of ceremonies, titles, and awards, Chandra would have relished it. One photograph from the day, shown above, in the Curzon Collection in the British Library, strikingly conveys his favored status as Curzon's special guest: Chandra is seated not only on Curzon's right, but Curzon's chair is also slightly turned toward Chandra. The photo is from an album of miscellaneous portraits of Curzon before and after his viceroyalty, with the caption, 'Group Portrait, Encaenia at Oxford June 24, 1908' (Photo 430/67(60)). Standing along the back are the military members of his suite who accompanied Chandra on the day, and whom the undergraduates had welcomed with 'musical honours' when they first appeared in the Sheldonian. Like his knighthood, his honorary doctorate from one of the world's great universities had again shown that Chandra could go one better than his predecessors. This was always a powerful driving force in his life.

A week later, on the evening of June 30, 1908, Chandra attended a debate on India in the House of Lords to hear Curzon make a rousing speech that was much acclaimed in the press. One report read, 'With his tall, commanding presence, his ringing voice, and air of authority, Lord Curzon dominated the House. No word of his was missed.' The reports noted the packed House and stated, 'Among the interested listeners was the dusky Prime Minister of Nepal, who gave a touch of colour to the diplomatic gallery with his scarlet cap.'

There was soon to be more satisfaction for Chandra in his quest to go one better. He and his party were due to leave England on July 21, 1908, but the king requested that the departure should be delayed a day so that, at a special audience arranged for the purpose, he could personally appoint him as a Knight Grand Cross of the Order of the Bath (GCB). A note in the files says that Chandra was 'the first Indian personage' to be so appointed by the King-Emperor personally. As an additional personal honor, the king ordered that the star of the Order should be set in diamonds. There is a letter from the Palace to the Treasury indicating that the cost was £480 and requesting that it be paid for out of public funds and only from the Privy Purse if necessary. There is no indication as to how the matter was resolved.

Chandra arrived back in Kathmandu on August 27, 1908. Three days later, a Grand Kharita Durbar was held to welcome him home. A separate Secret folder in the British Library gives details of its elaborate arrangements and a full translation of the speeches made. The Ranas were specialists in the organization of such events. They were clearly meant to impress the population with a display of military power, as well as gratify the egos of the large extended Rana families who could dress up in their elaborate military finery. Troops lined the route from Singha Durbar to Gaddi Durbar. Twenty minutes was allowed for the procession to cover the distance.

The ceremony started with Chandra handing over the Kharita from King Edward VII to the Maharajadhiraj, who gave it to Chandra's brother Bhim, as Commander-in-Chief, who opened it and handed it to Sirdar Marich Man Singh to read out a translation. Bhim then read an address 'on behalf of himself and the Bharadars present' which listed all Chandra's achievements in running the country and spoke of how he had improved relations with the mighty British Government. Mention was made of Chandra meeting the King-Emperor and being awarded the GCB. Chandra, in reply, also spoke of the award of the GCB and how well he had been received in England, particularly by the King-Emperor, and how deeply impressed he had been with the vastness of England's power and resources. 'We could see but part of the invincible navy and powerful army of England and her extensive armouries, and could see how easily she wields her sway over a fifth part of the globe,' he said. He concluded by saying that the visit had drawn the two countries still closer, adding, 'I feel perfectly assured that there is not the least desire anywhere to impair our autonomy or interfere with the administration of this government.'

Chandra's insatiable desire for yet more honors quickly manifested itself. On September 25, 1908, the Officiating Resident in Kathmandu, Lieutenant Colonel Macdonald, wrote to the India Office recommending that Chandra be given a personal salute and that his brother Bhim be appointed a Knight Commander of the Star of India. One official observed, 'the PM is anxious to have all the honours Sir Jang had, and he now has all with the exception of this salute.' Other comments in the file make clear Britain's hard-nosed approach to awarding such honors to foreign dignitaries. At this time officials were trying to get Chandra to agree to Britain negotiating a new treaty with Tibet that would recognize Britain as the sole power to negotiate on Nepal's behalf with both Tibet and China. In return, Britain would guarantee Nepal's territorial integrity. However, Chandra, to use the wording from the file, 'was not inclined to nibble.' The recorded decision was to stall the recommendation until he did. To quote directly again: 'We must not overdo it with the Nepalese . . . if we go on giving Nepal things without getting something in return, we may easily induce the Gurkhas to think themselves of supreme importance to us. And the Gurkha character is such that it does not want much inducement to think this.' However colonial this sounds now, we can be sure that Chandra knew the rules of the game and was adept at playing them to his advantage. Over the coming years he would complete the full set of British honors with appointments as a Knight Grand Cross of the Royal Victorian Order in 1911, and as a Knight Grand Cross of the Order of St Michael and St George in 1919.

There is one last twist. The Bodleian Library in Oxford is the repository of the largest known collection of Sanskrit manuscripts outside the Indian subcontinent, the majority of which are in the Chandra Shum Shere Collection. This is a huge and uniquely valuable collection of over 6,000 paper and palm leaf manuscripts. Contrary to what might be assumed, the gift of this collection is not directly connected to the award of the honorary degree, but, like the degree, it is very much connected to Curzon's friendship with Chandra. Telling the story of how the gift came about is an apt way to finish this article.

On October 7, 1908, Professor A. A. Macdonell, the Boden Professor of Sanskrit at Oxford wrote to the Bodleian librarian, E.W.B. Nicholson, telling him that on a 1907 visit to India, he had bought 100 Sanskrit documents from a Brahmin pundit in Banaras, and that this collector was willing to sell his whole collection consisting of more that 6,000 items for 10,000 rupees, 'that is, £666. 6. 8d. (666 pounds, 6 shillings, and 8 pence.)' He stressed that this was an opportunity that was never likely to recur and that the manuscripts should be acquired if money could be found. Attached to the letter was one dated September 27, 1908 from his Indian collaborator Haraprasad Shastri, principal of the Sanskrit College Calcutta, confirming that the offer was still open but that a decision had to be made quickly. A study of the files in the Bodleian records shows that the University acted with uncharacteristic speed through the agency of its chancellor. Only he could have contacted Chandra and engaged him in the venture.

The Vice-Chancellor wrote to Nicholson on October 9, 1908 urging him to call a meeting of the curators of the Bodleian urgently. The meeting took place on October 13, 1908 with the committee deciding what the Vice-Chancellor urged them to do: to express a strong opinion that the manuscripts should be purchased if the funds could be made available. On October 14, 1908, the Vice-Chancellor wrote to Nicholson asking him for the letters from Macdonell and Haraprasad to send to the chancellor. He told him to take copies, and it is these copies that are now in the records. Presumably Curzon sent the original letters with one of his own to Chandra.

The Vice-Chancellor informed a meeting of the curators on October 24, 1908 that 'the Chancellor approved their decision and would probably be able to obtain the necessary funds.'

There is a long gap in the records but Chandra clearly engaged Haraprasad as his agent as the next relevant letter on the files is from Haraprasad to Nicholson, dated September 9, 1909. This said that, at the request of Professor Macdonell, he had already dispatched six notebooks containing a list of 6,330 manuscripts, and that the manuscripts should arrive in Oxford in about eight weeks. He also indicated that they had been 'purchased by me at the cost of the Maharaja of Nepal for the Bodlian (sic) library from a vendor at Benares.' This letter explains that there are 633 bundles in 27 boxes and that there are 10 manuscripts in each bundle. ('The 28th contains a number of unspecified manuscripts in Old Kashmire and Old Dravidi scripts.')

There is also a letter to Nicholson, dated September 8, 1909, from the Secretary of the 'School Book and Useful Literature Society' saying that he was instructed by Haraprasad Shastri, 'who is acting on behalf of HH The Maharaja of Nepal, to ship to you about 6000 Oriental Manuscripts.' This letter also gave details of how the 28 tin boxes had been packaged, that the keys for them had already been sent by registered post and that the ship would sail on September 8, 1909. He also said, 'I am instructed to pay all expenses including freight London to Oxford and I have instructed my agent accordingly.' This is the first indication that Chandra's generosity extended to covering all aspects of the movement costs.

Initially the University spent £1,000 getting the manuscripts bound into some 2,150 volumes. In researching this article I was privileged to examine, under supervision, two items from the collection. First, circa 425, a work on divination composed in the twelfth century, which is one of seven manuscripts in the collection of the Narapatijayacaryā. This one was copied in 1620 and is the earliest known manuscript of the work in Europe. Second, circa 403, the main part of which contains Bhāskara's Siddhāntaśiromaṇi. He was a twelfth-century astronomer and mathematician. The item includes 17 extra folios that were not originally part of the manuscript, and one of them (159v) has a diagram illustrating the computation of the diameter of the earth's shadow at the moon's distance, written in Bengali script. The cataloguing of the complete collection is still work in progress.

Appreciation for the gift was expressed in three notable ways. A letter of thanks on behalf of the University, printed in gold by the Clarendon Press, was conveyed to Chandra. The librarian also wrote and received a warm, neatly typed reply, signed by Chandra, saying that he was delighted to hear that the books had arrived in good condition and that people thought so highly of them. Finally, a most impressive address, 'from the Chancellor, Masters and Scholars of the University of Oxford,' measuring over one metre in length and 50 centimetres across, beautifully and elaborately printed with the University seal attached, was dispatched to Chandra. A copy is kept in the University Archives.

The thirty lines of text of the Address starts by expressing profound appreciation for 'a magnificent gift which has added to the treasures of the Bodleian library.' The last paragraph of the address reads, 'The

A copy of the address sent to Chandra for his help in obtaining the Sanskrit manuscripts.

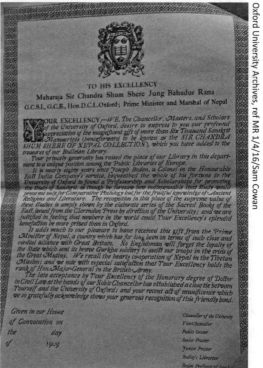

Oxford University Archives, ref MR 1/4/16/Sam Cowan

late acceptance by Your Excellency of the Honorary degree of our noble Chancellor has established a close tie between Yourself and the University of Oxford and your recent act of munificence which we so gratefully acknowledge shows your generous recognition of this friendly bond.'

The penultimate paragraph speaks of 'Nepal as a country which has for long been on terms of such close and cordial alliance with Great Britain.' Two examples are quoted. The first is, 'No Englishman will forget the loyalty of the State which sent its brave Gurkha soldiery to assist our troops in the crisis of the Great Mutiny.' The second example quoted provides an apt ending to this article. It touches on one of its main themes, the enduring friendship between two powerful and driven men, which had its origin in a joint enterprise of deceit. In the case of Chandra, the deceit was of a friendly state, in the case of Curzon, of his own government. The relevant sentence states, 'We recall the hearty cooperation of Nepal in the Tibetan Mission.'

The 'Mission' was the nadir of British imperial adventurism. Its purposes were indeed based on fallacies and its achievements quickly and largely disavowed. The military actions during the invasion were pathetically one-sided. British modern rifles and Maxim machine guns were pitted against antiquated Tibetan muskets, resulting in what was described by horrified British eyewitnesses at the time as 'bloody butchery' and 'cavalier slaughter.' There was much wanton destruction and pillaging and, as recent research has shown, looting of sacred objects took place on a grand scale. For little gain, thousands of Tibetans were killed and events set in motion that ultimately led to a very different future for Tibet and its people. Such was 'the Mission,' which Chandra ensured was launched with Nepal's 'hearty cooperation,' and directly led to the other outcomes outlined in this article.

I am most grateful to the staffs of the Oxford University Archives and the Bodleian Library Records for giving me access to some of the material I have drawn on in writing this article and for their most helpful guidance in finding it. I am also grateful to the Oxford University Archives for permission to use my photograph of the 'The Address,' the British Library for permitting me to use the two photographs from the Curzon Collection, and Madan Puraskar Pustakalaya for use of the photographs in its collection.

Chandra's suite, as listed in the British Foreign Office files:

Visit to England of the Prime Minister of Nepal, 1908

Names of His Excellency and Suite

MAJOR-GENERAL MAHARAJA SIR CHANDRA SHUM SHERE JUNG, BAHADUR RANA, G.C.S.I., PRIME MINISTER OF NEPAL.

Commanding-General Judha Shum Shere Jung, Bahadur Rana. (Half Brother)

Commanding-General Rudra Shurn Shere Jung, Bahadur Rana. (Nephew)

General Mohan Shum Shere Jung, Bahadur Rana. (Son)

Lieutenant-General Baber Shum Shere Jung, Bahadur Rana. (Son)

Lieutenant-General Kaiser Shum Shere Jung, Bahadur Rana. (Son)

Major-General Singha Shum Shere Jung, Bahadur Rana. (Son)

Major-General Hiranya Shum Shere Jung, Bahadur Rana. (Nephew)

Colonel Raja Jai Prithvi Bahadur Sing. (Son-in-law)

Colonel Kishore Nar Sing Rana.

Brigadier-Colonel Dilli Shamsher Thapa.

Colonel Dal Bahadur Basniat.

Lieutenant-Colonel Bishnu Kumar Panday.

Lieutenant-Colonel Chandra Jung Thapa.

Sirdar Marichi Man Singh (Private Secretary).

Sirdar Shum Shere Man (Assistant Private Secretary).

Major Ganga Bahadur Basniat.

Captain Narnarain Sahi.

Suba Gobinda Prashad.

Ratna Das Baidya.

Batu Krishna Moitra.

Pundit Kashi Nath.

Nineteen servants.

British Officers in Attendance

Major J. Manners Smith, V.C., C.I.E. (British Resident in Nepal).

Lieutenant Macleod Wylie, 4th Gurkha Rifles.

Subadar-Major Amar Sing Thapa, 2nd Battalion, 5th Gurkha Rifles.

Two orderlies of 4th and 5th Gurkha Rifles.

This article has been republished with permission from *The Record*. The original can be found online at: http://www.recordnepal.com/wire/maharaja-and-monarch/

The Monarch

King Mahendra's visit to Britain in 1960 is described in detail along with an overview of the history of Nepal from the days of Rana autocracy to the downfall of the Shah monarchy

This is the second of two articles covering the visits to the United Kingdom of Maharaja Chandra Shum Shere Rana in 1908 and King Mahendra in 1960. Although he was treated as a state guest, Chandra's visit was a private one. A government official met him on arrival and

A screenshot showing the reception at Victoria Station

he and his suite were accommodated in a large London house hired for the purpose. King Mahendra's arrival on a four-day state visit on October 17, 1960 was a much more regal affair. Traveling by air from Paris, he was met en route by six Gloster Javelin aircraft from the Fighter Command of the Royal Air Force, and greeted at Gatwick airport by the Duke of Kent on behalf of Queen Elizabeth II. On arrival by special train at Victoria Station, he was met by the Queen, escorted by Prince Philip, with other members of the royal family in attendance. The Queen personally requested that the Prime Minister, Mr. Harold Macmillan, should attend. Mr. R. A. Butler, the home secretary was also present.

There was a carriage procession to Buckingham Palace where King Mahendra and Queen Ratna with their small suite were accommodated for the duration of the state visit. Later that afternoon they visited Westminster Abbey to place a wreath on the grave of the Unknown Warrior.

A screenshot showing King Mahendra inspecting Gurkha soldiers prior to placing a wreath on the grave of the Unknown Warrior in Westminter Abbey.

The host nation spared no effort to ensure that King Mahendra and Queen Ratna were lavishly entertained and suitably impressed. A state banquet was held in their honor at Buckingham Palace on the first evening and on the third evening they were the guests of the government at a gala performance of Bellini's opera, *La sonnambula*, at the Royal Opera House, Covent Garden.

Crown Prince Birendra had started his studies at Eton College in

A screenshot of King Mahendra and the Lord Mayor at the Guildhall, after arriving for lunch in a carriage procession with Queen Ratna.

A screenshot showing King Mahendra reviewing soldiers of the Brigade of Gurkhas with Queen Elizabeth in the gardens of Buckingham Palace.

A screenshot showing King Mahendra, the Crown Prince, and Prince Dhirendra during a visit to an aircraft factory.

September 1959 and was given leave of absence for the state visit and part of the official visit. Prince Dhirendra and Princess Shanti were also in the party.

At the conclusion of the state visit, King Mahendra and his party stayed for a further two weeks on an official visit as guests of the government. For the majority of this period, the party had the use of the Royal Train which, when needed, also provided luxurious dining and sleeping accommodation. During this part of the visit, the party visited educational establishments and industrial plants. A number of days were spent in Scotland being hosted by the local aristocracy on their large estates.

Some fifty files in the National Archives give abundant detail on the planning for both parts of the visit. The files, still with some redactions, were opened for public inspection on January 1, 2011, after 50 years of closure. In the files is an 18-page paper written by Major Dudley Spain, a Brigade of Gurkha's officer then serving in Nepal, which gives his account of each day that the royal party spent in the United Kingdom.

He was included in King Mahendra's official party and was described as 'his right hand man.' He was awarded the Order of Gorkha Dakshina Bahu and the Order of Tri Shakti Patta for his services during the visit. In early 1964 he transferred to the Diplomatic Service and was employed for some 14 years in the British Embassy Kathmandu. A Foreign Office file, very recently released after a Freedom of Information request, shows that a job was created for him in the embassy in late 1963 primarily to act as personal advisor to the Chief of Police, S. P. Lama, on countering communist subversion. He was a long-time resident in Nepal and a long-standing confidant of successive kings of Nepal. This article will draw on information in his personal account, as well as from other relevant files in the National Archives and in the Oxford University Archives, to outline points of interest. First, however, it is useful to give some background on the state of Nepal at the time of the visit.

King Mahendra had been a witness to, and participant in, the momentous changes that had taken place in Nepal in the years leading up to the ending of the Rana regime in 1950 and in the decade of rapid change that followed. Indeed, after the coup on January 15, 1961, the US ambassador reported Mahendra as saying to him 'that he himself had brought democracy to Nepal.' Mahendra was born on June 11, 1920. (His father, King Tribhuvan, was aged 13 at the time.) Chandra Shum Shere Rana died on November 26, 1929. Mahendra, therefore, would not just have remembered Chandra; he would have had clear and sharp memories of the endlessly humiliating ways in which Chandra and his Rana successors treated his father and his family. He would also have seen at first hand how the Rana regime remained brutally repressive to the end. Gobar Dhan Maskey was a civil servant in the 1930s and 1940s. He recalled the regime in these terms: 'The Ranas were so strict they viewed us, the people, as pauko dhulo, the dust of their feet. They viewed themselves as gods, and we respected them as gods,' (People, Politics & Ideology: Democracy and Social Change in Nepal, Hoftun, Raeper, and Whelpton).

In 1940, Mahendra had been active with his father in communicating with and encouraging the leaders of the anti-Rana movement, the Nepal Praja Parishad, and would have had full knowledge of the brutal way in which the ringleaders had been executed in January 1941. After this event, an attempt was made to force Tribhuvan to resign, but Mahendra indicated that he would not take the crown. Erika Leuchtag was a physiotherapist who was invited to Kathmandu

Gurkha King Escapes (1950)

A screenshot showing Tribhuvan being greeted personally by Nehru on arrival in Delhi.

in early 1949 by Maharaja Mohan Shumsher to treat one of the two wives of King Tribhuvan. In her book, *With a King in the Clouds*, she gives some revealing insights into the Kathmandu of the day, including how strictly the daily curfew was imposed, the arrogance of the ruling Rana elite, how pampered their children were, and their humiliating treatment of Tribhuvan and how much he deeply resented it. She also brings out how Mahendra was active in events that eventually led to Tribhuvan and most of his family seeking refuge in the Indian embassy on November 6, 1950. Five days later, as a result of Nehru's intercession, they were allowed to fly to Delhi.

Despite the Ranas depriving him of a formal education and strictly controlling his social life, Mahendra's anti-Rana fervor did not last long. Always a driven man, he could see that Ranas would continue to dominate the senior ranks of the army for many years to come, and that army support would be needed to implement any future plans he might have. He could also see that Rana influence through marriage with Indian political leaders from former princely states could be useful to him in relations with New Delhi. In 1940 he had married Indra, the daughter of a senior Rana general, and granddaughter of Maharaja Juddha, when marriages to well-connected Ranas were *de rigueur* for future Shah kings. After Indra died in 1950, he clearly had wider options but in 1952 he married her sister, Ratna, a marriage that was bitterly opposed by his father who had a deep distrust of Juddha's family. Tribhuvan refused to attend the marriage ceremony. At the request of Mahendra, B.P. Koirala tried to persuade him to relent, but Tribhuvan upbraided him for taking Mahendra's side and warned him of his eldest son's strong authoritarian streak by saying: '(Y)ou don't know my son. He will make you, he will make all of you weep' (*People, Politics & Ideology*).

An agreement brokered by India in Delhi on February 8, 1951, effectively ended Rana rule. King Tribhuvan and his family returned in triumph on February 15, 1951. In a historic proclamation three days later, King Tribhuvan, exercising the sovereign power which had been denied to his family for over a hundred years, charged the new interim government with responsibility for conducting a smooth transition to a new political order 'based on a democratic constitution framed by elected representatives of the people.' In his proclamation of November 16, 1951, he again expressed his determination to establish 'a fully democratic political system functioning in accordance with a constitution prepared by a Constituent Assembly.' No elections were held until February 1959, and then not for a Constituent Assembly as promised since 1950, but for a Parliament established under a constitution granted by Mahendra to the people. (After his father's death, Mahendra had become king on March 13, 1955.)

Sir Ivor Jennings, a leading constitutional authority from the United Kingdom, was brought in to guide a five-man committee of officials and politicians on how to prepare a constitution that would balance the demands of Mahendra to have a continuing influential role and the demands of the parliamentary government to make the popular will, democratically expressed, decisive. The 1959 Constitution in some crucial areas was not as written or as advised by Sir Ivor Jennings. A note from the British ambassador states that Mahendra rewrote parts of it himself to strengthen the position of the monarchy. It is a safe assumption that this information came from Sir Ivor Jennings. Mahendra reserved for the monarch a wide range of discretionary powers. The Constitution explicitly stated that if ever a question arose over whether any matter was one in which the king could act on his own discretion, his decision was to be regarded as final and the validity of any of his actions was not to be questioned. In essence, 'these constitutional provisions brought into being a dyarchical form of government with two loci of power, one in the royal palace, staffed by the Palace Secretariat and based on the King's personal discretionary, emergency and inherent sovereign powers, and the other in the civil secretariat led by elected representatives of the people but based on only limited authority formally delegated and tolerated by the royal palace' (Joshi and Rose in *Democratic Innovations in Nepal*). As later events were to prove, the constitution that was 'granted' was basically unworkable except under a prime minister who was willing to be a stooge of the monarch. To his eternal credit, B.P. Koirala was not prepared to be anyone's stooge.

The 1959 elections started on February 18 and were completed by April 3. The last result was declared on May 10. The result of the election was a sweeping victory for the Nepali Congress party, which won 74 of the 109 seats. As its leader, B.P. Koirala was asked to lead, in the first instance, an interim government, and took office as prime minister on May 27, 1959. Finally the new constitution was brought into force on June 17, 1959 and King Mahendra opened Parliament on July 24, 1959.

Constitutional limitations on the power of his office were not the only handicaps facing the new prime minister during his time in office. From the outset, everything he attempted to do was opposed by ultra conservative forces. This was particularly true for policies related to land and forest reform. These forces also sensed that Mahendra's heart was not in the new constitutional arrangements, and certainly not since the surprising and overwhelming election victory of Nepali Congress. On January 28, 1960, Mahendra made a speech in Nepalgunj exhorting all Nepalis to work together to eradicate evil, 'so that I may not be compelled to take some other measures.'

Another problem facing B.P. Koirala stemmed from the fact that many previously dominant political figures failed to win a seat. (Dr. K. I. Singh and Dr. Kesar Raymajhi both forfeited their deposits.) This left the group highly disgruntled and willing to align with anyone to thwart the government's policies. This quote from the 1959 annual report from the British embassy is worth repeating for its prescience and its reminder of enduring problems: 'The new government has not yet shaken off the long established customs of graft and nepotism, the Public Service Commission is still ineffective and the Civil Service is woefully inadequate to translate the administrative measures of Parliament into executive action. Much will depend on the personality of the Prime Minster who in the last eight years has matured from the idealist but volatile revolutionary into a man of able and sound judgement, and upon his relations with the King who still holds powers of dissolution.'

The political brief for Mahendra's UK visit from the British Foreign

Office was also very clear on the weight of expectation and responsibility resting on B.P. Koirala and his government. It stated, 'The government have shown a welcome determination to tackle the difficult problems with which they are faced in trying to create a modern system of administration and to bring about social and economic reforms in an extremely backward country. There is little doubt that this Government represents Nepal's best hope for the future.'

This is the political background to King Mahendra's visit. Letters in the file show that he was extremely keen to get an invitation for a state visit to the United Kingdom. One letter from a Conservative member of parliament, Lord John Hope, to the prime minister, Mr. Harold Macmillan, dated June 9, 1959, stated, 'I have it on good authority that the Nepalis are very hurt that the King of Nepal has not been approached with regard to a visit to England. My informant has been told personally by Field-Marshal Kayser, who is one of the ousted family of Ranas to have any influence, that the King would cherish such an invitation.' The files show that there was no need for the fuss. King Mahendra was slotted in for a state visit in late 1960 but protocol demanded that no invitation could be issued until after the visits of the French and US presidents.

Also in the files is a brief that gives highly personal biographical details of King Mahendra and his suite. The likely British conduit for some of the information is clear from the visit to Oxford University. An *Oxford Mail* report covering the visit states that King Mahendra and Queen Ratna 'both met an old friend, Mr. Thomas Stonor, who after leaving Eton, went to Kathmandu as tutor to the Crown Prince, who is now an Etonian. Mr. Stonor, son of the Hon. Sherman Stonor, has just received a copy of a book of poems written by the King. The King writes under the name of M.B.B Shah.' Thomas Stonor is now the present Lord Camoys. At the time he had just completed his first year at Balliol College but had taken a term out. The files show that he was very active as an advisor and lobbyist before and during the visit. One file records a note by a Foreign Office official saying that, 'Mr. Thomas Stonor called in to see me last Friday and gave me some very useful information about the suites.' The level of personal detail in the pen pictures suggests that some may well have come from Crown Prince Birendra himself. Slightly different versions of the pen pictures were issued to various groups who would be hosting the visitors, varying in their frankness.

The king's interests are described as being mainly chess, hunting, music, and literature. The note goes on to say, 'The King speaks good

English. He is liable to be taciturn in public and is somewhat difficult to talk to, particularly as he is shy and speaks in a very soft voice. He is said to have a great sense of humour in private.' On his daily routine at home, it stated, 'At home he lives a simple life with not too many servants. He normally likes to get up at about 10.30, eat at about 1.30 and have dinner from 11 o'clock to 2 am.' On personal habits, 'He smokes fairly heavily. He drinks whisky, and before dinner a gimlet – at meals a little white wine or ginger ale.'

Subarna Shamsher Rana, the deputy prime minister, was described as 'being inclined to sleep late and miss engagements but appears to take a sane and balanced view of things.' Major General Sher Bahadur Malla, the chief military secretary, was described as 'the efficient member of the party who is constantly at the King's side and always carries a firearm in a hip holster.' Pusparaj Raj Bhandary, the chief personal secretary was described as, 'a high caste Brahmin and very devout. He has worked in the Palace Secretariat for more than 40 years. He is an expert on the history of the monarchy. His interests include the study of religion and Sanskrit manuscripts. He tends to be old fashioned and stubborn and is not very reliable.' Rude things were also written about his belching and spitting habits and that 'during long meals he nods off to sleep but manages to sit upright.' Madhusudan Raj Bhandary, the private secretary was the son of the chief secretary. He was described as 'quiet and intelligent and not so oriental as his father and a less strict Brahmin.' (Note: Pusparaj Raj Bhandary and Madhusudan were not Brahmins; they were high caste Newars.) Nara Pratap Thapa, the foreign secretary, was described as 'a man who lived privately having inherited considerable money. He has a good knowledge of Sanskrit, is intelligent, able and cultured and has been helpful to Britain.'

Both the state and official parts of the visits, apart from some minor hitches, generally went smoothly and both sides judged the visits to be a great success. Two subsidiary facets of the visit did, however, give the host country a few headaches. Both concerned gifts for Mahendra. A thin separate file gives details of 'an awkward predicament' faced by the host nation over the official gift. The original intention was to present Mahendra with a sporting rifle but it was learned that he had already received such a gift from the Russians and Americans. The British ambassador in Kathmandu, Mr. L.A. Scopes, no doubt seizing on the information that Mahendra loved music, proposed 'a stereo-radio-gramophone.' A Foreign Office official relates the follow-up: 'The Palace were enchanted by this suggestion which seemed to them both novel and interesting. They asked Mr Antony Armstrong-Jones, who is much interested in sound reproduction, to take charge of the matter and he has caused to be built in the room destined for the King of Nepal at Buckingham Palace a stereophonic machine of such splendour that it excels anything hitherto seen in England. It plays not only records but also tapes and will allow the King to record his own court orchestra and his own compositions and then replay them to himself.'

Antony Armstrong-Jones was a photographer and filmmaker. In February 1960, he became engaged to the Queen's sister, Princess Margaret. He married the princess on May 6, 1960 at Westminster Abbey, thus becoming the first commoner in four centuries to marry an English king's daughter. He was created Earl of Snowdon on October 6, 1961. In the interim, he was given this opportunity to impress his new parents-in-law.

There can be little doubt that the future earl would have done the job well, but that did not solve 'the awkward predicament.' Lord Plunkett, Equerry to Queen Elizabeth II and Deputy Master of the Household of the Royal Household, conveyed the nature of the problem to the Foreign Office official who wrote the note quoted above. It concerned getting the money to pay for the gift. A separate note in the file written by a Foreign Office official records that 'no doubt the King of Nepal will be delighted but unfortunately it turns out that the cost will be £640. The maximum which the Crown pays on these occasions is £300 and Lord Plunkett was enquiring whether the Foreign Office would produce a further £350.' Other correspondence indicates that there was no point in approaching a hard-nosed Treasury. The money was eventually found 'out of funds that had been used in recent years for a project connected with Nepal.' After the Royal Air Force refused to fly the gift to Kathmandu, the Nepali embassy was invited to organize and pay for the delivery using commercial firms.

There is no record of the arrival in Kathmandu of this state-of-the-art 'stereo-radio-gramophone,' nor, if it did arrive, how it was installed and how it performed. There is, however, a record of the arrival of a second 'gift.' Doing justice to the full saga of this would require a long separate article. In brief, while visiting an agricultural center near Reading, Mahendra expressed a wish to buy a bull. In the end, over many months of argument and debate, this materialized into 'a gift' of a bull, two cows, three Shetland ponies and a charger from the Household Cavalry called

Killarney, army number 5238, 'a good looking black mare rising six years who was bought in Ireland in 1959 for £200 and has had over a year's training and been on several escorts and guards with the Household Cavalry.'

There is voluminous correspondence between the Treasury, the Foreign Office, and the War Office as to which department would pay for what. There was an agreement that the British would fund transporting the animals to Calcutta by ship and Nepal would be responsible for getting them to Kathmandu. However, the file records that the British paid for the hire of a specially equipped aircraft to fly the animals from Calcutta to Kathmandu. A letter from the Foreign Office dated June 12, 1961 reported their safe arrival in Kathmandu. A corporal from the Household Cavalry accompanied them throughout and by all accounts performed far beyond the call of duty.

The visit to Oxford University was judged to be one of the highlights of the whole trip but it was also tinged with disappointment because, despite raised expectations that King Mahendra would follow Maharaja Chandra Shum Shere Rana in having an honorary degree conferred on him, none was offered. The Foreign Office pushed the idea but their files say little on why the proposal failed. The proposal was discussed within the University and files in the University Archives reveal the full story, including how those very close to Mahendra, and perhaps even the king himself, felt about the way the Rana rulers had deliberately and severely curtailed his education.

King Mahendra arrived with his entourage in Oxford on the morning of October 28, having spent the night on the Royal Train in railway sidings nearby. The previous day, on the journey south from Scotland, he had caused some consternation to those running the rail network when he announced that he would like to visit Stratford-upon-Avon, the birthplace of William Shakespeare. After some quick planning, his request was accommodated and he was suitably received in Stratford and escorted to the major points of interest. The next morning he was received at Oxford station on behalf of the University by a pro-vice-chancellor, the Master of Pembroke College, Mr. R. B. McCullum.

The official visit to the university started with tours of parts of Christ Church, which the king particularly asked to visit, and Balliol College. At Balliol, the master, Sir David Lindsay Keir, introduced six undergraduate members of the College, including Thomas Stonor, already well known to the royal party; Crown Prince Harald of Norway; and the ninth and

Photo courtesy of *Oxford Mail/The Oxford Times* (Newsquest Oxfordshire)

From left, the Master of Balliol, Sir David Lindsay Keir; King Mahendra; Queen Ratna; Crown Prince Harald; Princess Shanti; and the Nawab of Pataudi.

last Nawab of Pataudi. The last named, who was studying French and Arabic, was the son of a legendary cricketer who played for both England and India. His son, nicknamed 'Tiger,' was also a hugely gifted cricketer who would probably have matched or even surpassed his father's achievements if he had not suffered severe impairment in the sight of one eye in a car accident on July 1, 1961. Even with the handicap he was named Wisden's cricketer of the year in 1968. An *Oxford Mail* group photograph taken in Balliol, shows the master with the king, queen and Princess Shanti and, unsmiling, the crown prince and the Nawab. Lunch was taken at the adjacent college of Trinity hosted by the president of the College and the then Vice-Chancellor, Mr. A. L. T Norrington. Thomas Stonor was included in the lunch party.

The afternoon program started with a visit to the Bodleian Library. The original intention was to display an exhibition of Chinese manuscripts, but, to quote from a letter from the librarian to the registrar, 'There is a modification in the nature of the programme we are putting on. We learnt from one Stonor of Balliol who has been a tutor to the Crown Prince that it might be thought tactless to concentrate on Chinese manuscripts and this view has been checked with the F.O. and confirmed by them. We

King Mahendra walking in Christ Church with the dean, Dr. C.A. Simpson.

are therefore making it a Sanskrit show.' This change meant exhibiting instead manuscripts from the Chandra Shum Shere Collection. Library staff must have been bemused by the party's recorded gloomy reactions to the display of such treasures. Dudley Spain's record of this part of the program states that the king 'had seen and no doubt taken note, as had members of his suite, of the articles presented to the University by a Rana Prime Minister of Nepal upon whom was conferred an honorary degree.'

The visitors next walked across the road to the Indian Institute to view a special exhibition of Nepali and Tibetan art, including, *The Oxford Times* reported, 'a number of ritual objects brought back by the Younghusband expedition to Tibet in 1903–1904.' The afternoon concluded with a visit to New College with the king and queen taking tea with the warden, Sir William Hayter, and his wife at the Lodgings. (The

Newspaper cutting: King Mahendra and Queen Ratna walking with Oxford University Vice-Chancellor A.L.P. Norrington.

Visit of King and Queen of Nepal

The King and Queen of Nepal with the Vice-Chancellor, Mr. A. L. P. Norrington, on their way to the Indian Institute from the Bodleian during their visit to Oxford on Friday.

Sam Cowan, from cuttings in file at the Oxford University Archives

warden's residence in College.) In the evening, a dinner was organized for the king at Worcester College and for the queen at Somerville, where there was a Nepali undergraduate. A letter in the files from the principal of Somerville College is full of praise for her: 'We have a most remarkable graduate from Nepal, Mrs Joshi. She is completing an excellent B.Litt on the Royal Household (of England). She chose this subject as she thought it would be so apposite to the problems of Nepal. Professor Beloff, her Supervisor, thinks this thesis should be published it is so good.' There is more in the same vein. Her husband was described as a physicist working in Glasgow. (Somerville was at the time one of five women's colleges in Oxford. Five all-male colleges – Brasenose, Jesus College, Wadham, Hertford and St. Catherine's – first admitted women in 1974. St Hilda's College, which was originally for women only, was the last of Oxford's single-sex colleges. All colleges have admitted both men and women since 2008.)

The warden of New College consulted the Foreign Office on the question of whether he could invite one of his undergraduates, Pashupati Shumsher Rana, the other Nepali student at Oxford at the time, to join the select party for tea. Part of the Foreign Office reply said, 'I am told that Mr. Rana is an excellent young man, a distant connection of the Queen, and a person whose presence would in every way be pleasing to His Majesty.' There is no record of how pleasing or otherwise Pashupati's presence was at this tea meeting, or indeed whether he was present at it, but Oxford almost certainly would not have been aware of sensitivities that could have led to some coldness. Pashupati was the great grandson of Maharaja Chandra Shum Shere Rana and was a beneficiary of the expensively funded formal education that his grandfather and Rana successors had denied Mahendra. The maharaja had an honorary degree conferred on him during his Oxford visit and he had funded the large Sanskrit collection associated with his name, some of which had been shown to Mahendra and his party earlier in the afternoon with the gloomy reactions described.

Pashupati was Queen Ratna's cousin, but she was the granddaughter of Maharaja Juddha, who became prime minister three years after Chandra's death. Grandchildren of Chandra have a reputation for looking down on grandchildren of Juddha. Forty years later, Devyani, the daughter of Pashupati and girlfriend of Crown Prince Dipendra, the grandson of Mahendra, received the last fateful telephone call from the crown prince as he sat in his bedroom a few minutes before he descended the stairs of his house in the Royal Palace grounds to start his murderous spree which killed his father King Birendra and all members of his immediate family, including Princess Shanti, among others. One of the many reasons quoted why Queen Aishwarya, Birendra's wife and Juddha's granddaughter, so strongly opposed her son's wedding to Devyani was that Devyani was of the Chandra lineage. All that lay in the future.

British Pathe

Crown Prince Birendra, Queen Ratna and King Mahendra with the Lord Mayor at the Guildhall.

On the subject of the honorary degree, the proposal was pushed hard by the Foreign Office but files in the University Archives indicate that, from the outset, doubts were raised within University circles. A letter dated August 18, 1960, from Lord Lansdowne, a Foreign Office minister, set the ball rolling. In asking the University to accept a visit by the royal party, he said that the king had particularly asked to visit Oxford and that the Nepali ambassador in London had hinted that he thinks that the king wants to make a gift to the University. He said that 'the King has a considerable literary reputation in Nepal and he is also something of a poet. It would add greatly to the success of the visit if the University felt able to award him an appropriate honorory degree. The Foreign Secretary has asked me to put this to you.'

In a reply dated August 24, 1960, the Vice-Chancellor pointed out that time was short to get all the mandatory approvals and that 'there has of recent times been some reluctance to use degrees in this way, but the fact he has a literary reputation in his own country will no doubt be of assistance.' Lord Lansdowne replied the next day expressing the hope that the Council could be persuaded to give the degree. The last sentence said: 'I understand that a Nepalese Prime Minister, Maharaja Chandra Shumsher, was given an Honorary Degree about 1906/7.'

In an internal note, dated September 7, the registrar, Sir Folliot Sandford, wrote that the proposal could only be considered at the next meeting of the Hebdomadal Council, the executive body of the university at the time, on September 19, if 16 or more members were present and agreed to the suspension of Standing Orders. He also said, 'bearing in mind, *inter alia*, that Cambridge did not confer a degree on the King of Thailand in July, I should myself doubt whether Council would, in fact, approve the proposal.' His assessment proved correct. In a letter to the Foreign Office dated September 20, he gave this account of the outcome of the meeting held the day before: 'Unfortunately it was not possible to reach a decision yesterday, but it would be possible to bring the matter before Council again on 3 October.

A note in the files indicates that Lord Lansdowne phoned the registrar on receipt of this letter and was told that there was no certainty as to the outcome of the October 3 meeting. At the conclusion of this meeting Lord Lansdowne was informed by telephone that a degree would not be conferred. This information was relayed immediately to the Nepali ambassador in London. Unfortunately he had raced ahead of the decision-making process to inform Kathmandu, including Mahendra, that the conferring of an honorary degree would be part of the program.

Papers in the University Archives give a fuller version of what transpired. One problem for Mahendra was that, unlike Chandra, he did not have a powerful friend such as Curzon as chancellor to fix matters whatever the rules. More crucially, again unlike Chandra, his visit did not coincide with Encaenia, which is the ceremonial high point of the Oxford academic year. It is the ceremony at which the University awards honorary degrees to distinguished men and women and commemorates its benefactors. It is held annually on the Wednesday of the ninth week during Trinity Term, which invariably falls toward the end of June. During his 1908 visit, Chandra Shum Shere Rana had the honorary degree of DCL (Doctor of Civil Law) conferred on him as Prime Minister of Nepal.

Degrees by diploma are conferred on heads of state and royalty. It was appropriate, therefore, to propose Mahendra for a Doctor of Letters (DLitt) degree but Standing Order 43 for the Hebdomadal Council laid down that 'proposals to confer Degrees by Diploma shall be subject to the same rules of procedure as proposals to confer Honorary Degrees on occasions other than the Encaenia.' The first paragraph of Standing Order 39 stated that when proposals are made for the conferring of degrees on occasions outside the Encaenia, 'the qualifications of the persons proposed shall be stated and may be discussed. Questions may be asked concerning the names proposed. Each name shall then be voted upon in writing, and a two-thirds majority of the votes of the members present shall be required for the conferment of an Honorary Degree.' Standing Order 42 stated, 'None of the foregoing Standing Orders respecting Honorary Degrees shall be dispensed with unless sixteen members of Council concur in the suspension.'

The minutes of the Council meeting on September 19 record that '(a) s fourteen members only were present, it was agreed to defer a decision until the 3 October.' A note in the file made clear the decision facing Council members at their next meeting. It stated, 'Under Standing Orders 42 and 43 the question of the conferment on the King of a degree of D.Litt by diploma could only be considered if sixteen members of the Council concurred in the suspension of the first paragraph of Standing Order 39.'

Although a quorum of members was not present, it is clear from other papers that there was discussion on the merits of the proposal at the September 19 meeting. Before the meeting, the Master of Balliol had submitted a letter supporting the proposal. In it he said, 'What I would like to mention is the King's interest in letters and learning – which he has cultivated himself and under many difficulties up to the age of thirty and his intention to ensure that a University is established in his Kingdom.' Presumably, the Master of Balliol had assumed the role of championing the proposal through the agency of Thomas Stonor. For his pains, he received a letter from the registrar informing him that the matter would be considered again at the next meeting on October 3, and that, 'it would help matters if you could supply a little more information about the King's interest in literature and his own prowess as a poet.'

For the next meeting, the master produced a letter that presented the case for Mahendra. Given the likely source of the information in it, it is worth quoting in full:

> Your second letter of 20th September dealt with the literary and educational interests of the King of Nepal, and my enquiries disclosed the following information.
>
> What he has done must be judged in the context of his earlier years when the Royal Family lived under the heavy restrictions imposed by the Rana regime, whose policy appears to have been to restrict the Royal Family to a life of idleness, removed from all political interests, and particularly to deny them the means of education. His boyhood reading was got through books which had to be smuggled into the Palace. They seem, however, to have had enough influence and to have been of the right kind to inspire him when he succeeded his father after the Ranas were overthrown to recognise how much could be gained by himself and his people from education and the spread of knowledge.
>
> The King's record since his succession includes the promotion of art and drama, the renovation of the ancient temples of Nepal, the establishment of an academy for the teaching and study of music, folk-lore and dances of the country; and, more lately, the scheme for the establishment of the first Nepalese University.
>
> I ought to add that his interest in education is sufficiently liberal to have induced him to get foreign bodies to extend their activities to Nepal, and that the revenues of the country are, under his influence, being applied to the educational and cultural sides of national life.
>
> As to his personal interest, he has, notwithstanding the restrictions

placed upon his education, become well-read, and he now fluently writes and speaks Hindi, Sanskrit Urdu and English, as well as Nepali. He has a gift for poetry, and I have seen an English translation of one of his poems which seems to show something of a lyrical gift.

You will understand that all of this is second-hand but I believe it to be accurate and the general picture it seems to disclose is that of an eastern potentate who realises that there are other means than military ones of exercising authority.

I hope that this information, rather hurriedly put together, will be of some use to Council in coming to its decision.

It was a gallant effort from the Master of Balliol, though possibly his 'faint praise' for the king's talent as a poet could have been omitted, but the proposal failed. The minutes of the Council meeting held on October 3, record that 'Mr. Vice-Chancellor having asked whether Council wished to suspend Standing Orders 42 and 43 in order that consideration should be given to the conferment of a degree by diploma on the King of Nepal, thirteen members only voted in favour, and the matter was not further pursued.' It was, in effect, a straightforward vote on whether to confer a degree by diploma on Mahendra, and it failed to muster the votes needed.

One can only speculate why the proposal failed. It is very possible that in the Oxford of the 1960s some academics resented the idea of ministers and senior Whitehall bureaucrats making demands at short notice, as well as making assumptions that what they proposed would automatically be accepted. Oxford had changed since Curzon's day, and no modern Chancellor could simply drive through what he wanted. Just 25 years later, amid huge publicity and controversy, Oxford voted down a proposal to confer an honorary degree on Prime Minister Margaret Thatcher, herself an Oxford graduate, mainly because of disagreement over her higher educational policies.

Foreign Office officials and Dudley Spain, in their write-ups of the visit, expressed the hope that there might be another occasion on which Oxford could confer a degree, but it is a reasonable assumption that the coup d'état King Mahendra launched shortly after he returned to Kathmandu scuppered his chances of it ever happening. His actions might even have given some quiet satisfaction to those who refused to support the proposal presented to them at the Hebdomadal Council meeting on October 3. Despite the disappointment expressed by members of King

Mahendra's party over the failure to confer a degree, it is clear that Oxford pulled out all the stops to make the visit a great success. Lord Home, then foreign secretary, in his letter of thanks to the University, wrote, 'The whole Royal visit seems to have been a great success, but I think that in a way the visit to Oxford was what most appealed to the King himself.' There is more evidence of this personal satisfaction in the report written by Dudley Spain. He records, 'It was hardly possible to do justice to the many interesting things and places shown to the King. He is not naturally demonstrative, and it may not have been appreciated by those conducting him, just how much he enjoyed this visit to what he called 'This great seat of learning with so many brilliant men'. The day culminated with dinner at Worcester College which can be considered one of the 'Highlights' of the whole tour.'

Photographs from the *Oxford Mail* show a smiling and relaxed King Mahendra and Queen Ratna. Given the warm reception he received, and his obvious genuine enjoyment of the visit, perhaps Mahendra regretted an action taken just before he left Kathmandu. In a letter dated October 10, 1960, Lord Lansdowne wrote to the University registrar: 'Some months ago, there was a rumour that the King wished to present an early Nepalese manuscript to the Bodleian, an admirable intention which I encouraged. I was disappointed to learn from the Nepalese Ambassador last Thursday that recent legislation has now virtually prohibited the export of such treasures.' The date of the 'last Thursday' mentioned in this letter was October 6, just three days after the ambassador was given the news that the conferring of an honorary degree would not be part of the program.

In the last week of the visit, King Mahendra and Queen Ratna attended the annual ceremony of the State Opening of Parliament as personal guests of Queen Elizabeth. This is an occasion full of historical and symbolic significance. Above all it is a demonstration of the monarch's nominal position as head of the Legislative, Executive, and Judicial branches of government and the separation of powers. Dudley Spain records that '(t)he King was impressed by the grandeur of the proceedings and conscious also that he was the first foreign monarch invited to attend. He said that the Queen's speech was the 'the usual sort of thing' and was gratified to hear himself mentioned.' On the penultimate day, the king and queen attended a lunch at 10 Downing Street presided over by Prime Minister Macmillan. The guest list consisted mainly of leading figures of the government and opposition. On the last morning of the visit, at the personal request of Queen Elizabeth, Mr. Macmillan called at the Nepali embassy to bid farewell.

There is no hint in the Foreign Office files of Mahendra telling anyone what he intended to do when he returned to Nepal. We know, however, from impeccable sources quoted in People, Politics & Ideology: Democracy and Social Change in Nepal, by Hoftun, Raeper and Whelpton, that before Mahendra left Kathmandu for the United Kingdom he had decided to remove the Koirala government. During his journey to the United Kingdom, he told Subarna Shamsher of his decision. While still in Bombay en route to Europe, he had summoned Rishikesh Shaha, Nepal's representative at the United Nations, to a meeting in Paris to reveal his intentions to him. In a later conversation, Rishikesh Shaha said that he warned Mahendra that he would get a bad name doing away with the democracy that his father had introduced into the county. '(B)ut,' he said, 'I found him hell-bent on assuming power.' On his return to Kathmandu, Subarna did not tell the prime minister. He was convinced that Mahendra would not act until late February so as not to jeopardize a planned state visit of Queen Elizabeth II. Rishikesh Shaha was convinced that Mahendra was in a hurry, and he was right. The actions he was soon precipitously to take would have profound negative consequences for the development of Nepal as a properly functioning democracy, and for the future of the Shah lineage as kings of Nepal.

On December 15, 1960, thirty-six days after leaving the United Kingdom, using the instrument of the Royal Nepal Army, King Mahendra launched his coup, which ultimately gave him absolute authority over the entire machinery of government. All members of the Nepali Congress cabinet who were in Kathmandu at the time were arrested, including the Prime Minister Koirala. Mahendra's reasons for acting as he did were complex, but Joshi and Rose are correct in asserting that a major motivation was Mahendra's dissatisfaction with the relegation of the crown to a comparatively minor role after the installation of the Nepali Congress government on May 27, 1959. Joshi and Rose also produce strong evidence for asserting that 'it is doubtful that King Mahendra's deep seated aversion to political parties and party politics would long permit him to play a purely constitutional role, as designated in the 1959 Constitution.' (From personal knowledge, this description perfectly fits King Gyanendra's attitude in 2002, both toward political parties and the 1990 Constitution.) Within a few weeks it was obvious that Mahendra planned no mere change of government. In typical style, many consultations took place and confusing statements were issued, but there was never any doubt about the end point: the restoration of the monarch's absolute authority.

The Foreign Office files from the time initially give few details or comments on Mahendra's seizure of power. A stunned silence would not be too strong a phrase to describe the reactions. There was a general sense of disbelief that he could have done such a thing. Up to this stage the British position was that B.P. Koirala's government represented Nepal's best hope for the future. Diplomats did quickly work out that Mahendra had not spoken the truth about his reasons for acting, but in the circumstances one official wrote, 'it is probably best to refrain from commenting as much as possible.' Reacting to reports of the forced closure of newspapers in Kathmandu, another Foreign Office official wrote on February 10, 1961, 'The King is finding that to maintain power in his own hands more and more repressive measures are necessary. There is seemingly no end to the process. The fact that the liberty of the press is being restricted shows that the King is becoming uncertain of his position, an ominous sign that he may have bitten off more than he can chew.' As events unfolded during 1961 and 1962, this looked to be an accurate assessment, but the official, like everyone else, could not have predicted China's invasion of India on October 20, 1962, coming to the rescue of an increasingly fearful Mahendra. Evidence from sources very close to him in the Foreign Office files indicates that he had mounting concerns about his personal safety and the survival of his Panchayat system. That is a story for another day.

Despite the doubts expressed by some officials, there is no record of public or private censure from the United Kingdom. One large inhibiting factor was that ten weeks and two days after the date of the coup, on February 26, 1961, Queen Elizabeth II and Prince Philip were due to arrive in Nepal for a four day state visit. The files indicate that there was never much doubt that the visit would go ahead. Two Labour Party members of Parliament did write to the prime minister proposing that the visit should be postponed. Their central point was that such a visit at the present time 'may be construed among members of the Commonwealth, and Asian countries generally, as implying endorsement of measures which are now in operation and which deny democratic rights and the human values of the Commonwealth.' After advice from the Foreign Office that what the king had done was legal under the constitution and that 'public reaction in Nepal to the recent measures seems at present to verge on indifference,' Macmillan's reply was magisterially dismissive. It pointed out that King Mahendra's action had not caused any deterioration in the security situation and that 'Her Majesty's visit is to King Mahendra as Head of the Nepalese state and conveys no implied commentary on the political arrangements currently in force in the country.'

It is worth saying at this point that the diplomatic records suggest that the Panchayat system that Mahendra introduced had no stronger supporter than Britain. Reading through the annual embassy reports written during the 1960s, concern about Gurkha recruiting appeared to be all that mattered: there is barely a word for the incarcerated B.P. Koirala, and of sympathy none. So much for the man on whom British diplomats lavished so much praise during his early tenure as prime minister, the man who 'led a government which showed a welcome determination to tackle the difficult problems it faced in trying to create a modern system of administration and to bring about social and economic reforms in an extremely backward country; and whose government represented Nepal's best hope for the future.' Within a few months, all these brave and accurate words were forgotten as Britain quickly adjusted to giving total support to an autocratic monarch who quickly established a political system that give him absolute power.

There was indeed remarkably little public reaction to the overthrow of a government elected by such a large majority just 18 months prior. As C.K. Lal graphically remarked in a recent article in *Republica*, 'Not a dog barked in Kathmandu when Prime Minister BP Koirala, commanding a two-third majority in the parliament, was whisked away by the military from a public program of the youth wing of his party in the center of the city.' The army was also the instrument, and long involved in the planning, of King Gyanendra's coup on February 1, 2005. To spell this point out bluntly, in both instances, the coup d'état was not carried out by the monarchs; they may have given the order, but those who carried it out, the putschists, were senior army officers who planned it with military precision and deployed their soldiers on the streets and in such places as media outlets to make it effective. Such actions puts into proper perspective the often loudly proclaimed assertion from some senior Nepal Army officers, and particularly vociferously voiced by retired army chief General Rukmangad Katawal, that the army in Nepal has always stood on the side of the people. Even the most cursory examination of Nepal's history shows this claim to be totally bogus.

During its long period of transition from a tiny and impoverished hill state to an established Himalayan empire, Gorkha was a formidably efficient and ruthless war machine. More revenue from conquered lands sustained a bigger army, which in turn needed more land and more conquests. In his book *The Rise of the House of Gorkha*, Ludwig F. Stiller brought out in convincing detail that the land-military nexus was fundamental to the successful growth of Gorkha. The nobility made up the bulk of the army leadership, and it was their loyalty to Gorkha and to the throne that ensured the throne of the loyalty of the army. In the most literal sense, Gorkha was a military state; political power rested on the army, and its loyalty had to be constantly cultivated. This was perfectly illustrated after the huge loss of conquered, revenue-producing land in 1816, which followed Gorkha's defeat in the Anglo-Nepal War. Instead of the army taking an appropriate cut in size, it continued to be indulged and pampered by Bhimsen Thapa to ensure that it supported him staying in power. Indeed, it increased in size, and with the loss of revenue from conquered lands, the ordinary peasant had to be squeezed even more – many to the point of total impoverishment – to produce the money needed. Their unheard, anguished appeal for some relief was 'the silent cry' of Ludwig Stiller's 1976 book.

The 104 years of Rana rule which followed the neutralization of the power of the Shah kings, and the likes of Bhimsen Thapa, was a period of undisguised military despotism. 'The Prime Minister's authority was absolute. It was personal rule, butressed by a strong army whose maintenance and efficiency was the first care of the Prime Minister himself' (*Political Relations between India and Nepal 1877-1923*, Kanchanmoy Mojumdar). Chandra Shum Shere, ever-paranoid about his personal safety, totally reorganized the Bijuli Garat, a unit of soldiers formed as personal guards by Rannodip Singh. As one of the leading conspirators in Rannodip's assassination, Chandra had seen how ineffective it was in protecting the prime minister from family members. He transformed the Bijuli Garat into an elite battalion of above-average sized soldiers armed with personal weapons. It remained active for the rest of the Rana period with the exclusive role of protecting the Rana prime minister. It was permanently stationed within Singha Durbar. Up to the 1950s it was the only battalion that had its own barracks; other soldiers were housed in rented rooms on the outskirts of Kathmandu. The name Bijuli (as in *lightning*) signified that the battalion was required to act at rapid speed in all situations. Without their clearance, the Rana prime minister never visited any place. They took orders directly from the prime minister and had the authority to frisk even his closest relatives.

The Bijuli Garat battalion featured in a seminal moment in the history of control of the army in Nepal when direct command of it passed to Tribhuvan in 1951. B.P. Koirala, who was then the home minister in the Rana–Nepali Congress interim cabinet, reminisced thus toward the end of his life: 'Soon Kiran Shamsher brought the entire battalion marching over. The next morning, without my knowledge and informing no one else, the king took the salute of the troops. It was as if the king were telling them; henceforth show me the loyalty you have shown to Mohan Shamsher. Looking out of my window, I saw the king receiving the salute. I was there as a guest (inside Narayanhiti Palace), and at the very least should have been informed, but he didn't see it fit to do that. From that day onwards, the king had an upper hand, and democracy lost a notch. . . . From that day, the king became powerful' (BP Koirala's Atmabrittanta: Late Life Recollections, translated by Kanak Mani Dixit). Shortly afterward, Mohan handed over the ceremonial baton of command of the army to the palace along with the keys of the Lal Mohar (the Royal Seal) box.

In 1959, Mahendra enshrined the monarch's absolute control over the army in his new constitution. He also became his own defence minister for an extended period. Rishikesh Shaha in his book *Nepali Politics Retrospect and Prospect*, published in 1975, well describes his actions and their consequences: 'King Mahendra's personal interest in the welfare and training of the officers and men of the army, and the bestowal by him of special favours on them in the form of royal grants of land and other concessions, have in recent years created bonds of a personal nature between the King and the army. The Royal Army thus regards the King as the sole personification of the state, with the result that to the army it appears as if there is no such thing as loyalty to the state and the people, as distinct from loyalty to the King as a person.'

Even with a more than two-thirds majority, B.P. Koirala was in no position to challenge Mahendra's absolute control over the army. His revolutionary fervor had long since been worn down against the rock of Mahendra's implacable intransigence, but, in any case, whatever the constitutional provision, officers of the army – almost all of them Ranas, Thapas, Basnyats, and Chhetris tracing their ancestry to the Gorkha court – would have never agreed to be directed by the new civilian government. The senior ranks of the army are still dominated by officers of these lineages, and, from personal knowledge, some of this anti-democratic culture lingers still. This was manifest in the zeal with which the army supported King Gyanendra's coup of February 1, 2005. The 1990 Constitution fudged the issue of command of the army, but this action showed that nothing had changed: the army acted as the monarch's willing and enthusiastic agent just as it had done for Mahendra 45 years previously. The situation today will be addressed in the concluding section of this article.

United States diplomatic records in the aftermath of Mahendra's coup show none of the British inhibition and are worth quoting for the insight they provide into the realities behind the coup. As with his British visit, Mahendra had been anxious to pay an official visit to the Untied States. He finally received the official invitation after he announced his intentions to hold elections. Fear of increasing Russian influence in Kathmandu was also a factor. The duration of the four-day official visit was April 26 to 30, 1960. As he was to do later in the United Kingdom, Mahendra stayed on to tour the United States until May 13, 1960 at the expense of the host country. Joshi and Rose record that Mahendra, addressing a joint meeting of Congress on April 28, 1960, 'spoke with pride of the shared democratic ideals and appealed for an expansion of Nepal-US economic and political ties on this basis.' During a meeting at the White House, President Eisenhower assured Mahendra that the United States wanted to do all in its power to assist Nepal in preserving and further developing its democratic institutions.

In a dispatch dated December 21, 1960, the ambassador, Henry E. Stebbins, gave an account of his meeting with Mahendra the previous day. There was clearly an awkward edge to the meeting. Stebbins had seen Mahendra on December 9, prior to going on leave, and the king has assured him that nothing would happen in his absence. It was at this meeting on December 20, as previously quoted, that Mahendra, 'professed a strong belief in democracy, which he claims he himself has brought to Nepal and will continue to work towards it.' The ambassador further reported that Mahendra said that 'he had planned this move for some time and knew of the approximate timing when the Ambassador last saw him on December 9.' The king also told him that 'he took the step on his own responsibility with no outside influence whatsoever brought to bear,' and that, 'he dismissed the Government and imprisoned its leaders because they were guilty of corruption and of aiding and abetting Communism.'

The ambassador in his comments gave Mahendra's explanation of why he had acted the short shrift it deserved. He wrote, 'In analyzing this coup d'état, for this is what we believe it to be, we feel that the King's motives in taking the precipitate action he did were guided less by the issues of corruption and Communism than by a growing fear that his own personal position and prestige were dwindling and that if he did not act soon, it might be too late . . . the real motive behind the move was the preservation of the monarchy and the Shah dynasty in its absolute form.' He continued, 'Although the King protests that the decision was his alone, we are convinced that it was aided and urged by the group around him, which may also have misled him. This group includes members of his and his wife's family, remaining Class A Ranas, hereditary Generals and reactionaries and 'feudal remnants' generally, who, themselves, are concerned over the survival of their privileged positions. Added to these forces are those land owners and others who stood to suffer financially from the enforcement of the recent tax and land reform laws.'

Two further comments from the ambassador are worth repeating. First: 'The King's method of seizing power is consistent with Nepalese history. Confident of the Army's complete loyalty (without which he would have failed and which he may not have in the next crisis), he acted with great secrecy and superb organization.' Second: 'The King has solved his immediate problem – that of disposing of B.P. Koirala and the Nepali Congress. However, by doing so he has created a new set of problems and it is characteristic that in solving the first one he seems to have failed to anticipate solutions to the consequent ones.'

In reading these comments, I was struck by the stark similarities with the coup that King Gyanendra initiated in 2005, not least the central role of the army and the same crowd of sycophants, with senior army officers in the van, urging him on and acting as cheerleaders. There is also a more important connection. With the clarity of hindsight, one can see that Mahendra's action in December 1960 started the long process that led to the end of the Shah monarchy in Nepal. His inability to see that preservation of the lineage lay in accommodating the monarchy to a constitutional position, which, for all its inadequacies, was sketched out in the 1959 Constitution, set the monarchy on a precipitous road. His choice of preserving the monarchy and the Shah dynasty in its absolute form was ultimately unsustainable in the modern world, short of Nepal reverting to a despotic military state, as in the Rana era. The 1990 Constitution, again for all its inadequacies and ambiguities, gave the monarchy another chance to move to a purely constitutional basis, but Gyanendra rejected it by his unconstitutional actions that started in October 2002 and ended by his assumption of absolute power on February 1, 2005.

From personal knowledge, King Gyanendra was motivated by a desire to emulate his immediate predecessors by granting his people a constitution that would restore his father's Panchayat system in a modern form and give him a central role in decision-making. Beyond this aspiration he had no plan worthy of the name, nor had he the people with the talent to implement an appropriate plan even if there had been one. It was a fiasco from the start but this did not prevent the same crowd, who had urged on Mahendra, from repeating the performance. From an early stage, those with eyes to see and a functioning brain understood that, in the circumstances of the time, it was bound to end in disaster for the monarchy.

The circumstances of that end were emblematic of the nexus between king and army that has dominated the history of Nepal since the time of Prithvi Narayan Shah. The day of denouement was April 22, 2006. Up to the day before, the army chief, General Pyar Jung Thapa, like his predecessors, had repeatedly told Gyanendra, as he had for the previous four years and beyond, that he had no need to conduct meaningful negotiations with the Maoists. Those around him regularly assured Gyanendra that the army was on the point of so weakening the Maoist military threat that their leaders would soon come on hands and knees begging for mercy and forgiveness. (From personal knowledge some senior serving and retired Nepal Army officers continue to propagate this myth.) By all accounts, Gyanendra fervently believed what he was told – it was clearly what he wanted to hear – and in doing so increasingly lost contact with reality on the ground.

The supreme example of his detachment was the television address he gave on the morning of February 1, 2006, to mark the anniversary of his first year as absolute ruler. In it he spoke of how terrorism in his country had now been reduced to the level of petty crime. As he spoke, the public buildings in the historic town of Tansen were still in flames as a result of a large Maoist attack the evening before, as the video at this link vividly shows.[1]

In a diplomatic dispatch, dated April 10, 2006, the US ambassador in Kathmandu, James Moriarty, succinctly summed up military reality on

---

1   https://bit.ly/2wXiF9r

the ground. Over the previous two years, the Royal Nepal Army (RNA) had no stronger supporter. In a dispatch headed 'Government losing control?' he reported a number of Maoist attacks over the previous two months, and ended it by starkly summarizing the strategic stalemate existing on the ground: 'The Maoists have not been able to remain in, or take control of, any of the places they have attacked. The RNA can only defend its own garrisons, and cannot provide security to the rest of the country or prevent Maoist attacks' (Wikileaks 06 Kathmandu 934 dated April 10, 2006).

Reality finally dawned for King Gyanendra on April 22, 2006, at a meeting at the Palace to discuss how to deal with a huge demonstration planned for April 25. Up to two million people were expected to take part. At this meeting, General Pyar Jung Thapa, prompted by a visiting Indian emissary, Shyam Saran, during a visit to Kathmandu on April 19, effectively told Gyanendra that the game was up: the army would not use the firepower that would be necessary to control the crowds expected.

For the record, it is worth setting down what, a few years later, Saran said he told the army chief on April 19, 2006. First, that it would be, 'a good idea to convey to His Majesty that the situation was more serious than he thought.' He also warned the army chief that the demonstrations were massive and told him, 'if there were orders to shoot and there was a big incident, it would be impossible to control and you should think about the effort required to tackle 250,000 people.' He also emphasized to the chief that there was no military solution to either the Janandolan or the Maoist insurgency. A similar message was passed to the RNA from the chief of the Indian Army. The Indian assessment was that the RNA had understood the gravity of the situation and had played 'a positive role' in communicating to the monarch that the status quo was not tenable. 'That is why Thapa is not too popular with the royalists anymore. But he took the correct decision which saved the army' (all from *Battles of the New Republic*, Prashant Jha).

Understanding and agreeing with the message was one thing, but for General Pyar Jung Thapa, the challenge was when and how to pass it on given the highly subordinate position he was in. For example, the convention of the time was that when the army chief offered the monarch a drink at a social function, he did so on bended knee. Much more critically, what he was now being asked to pass on was totally at variance with what he had been saying to Gyanendra over the previous four years. These were years of endlessly unfulfilled army promises about being on the verge of 'breaking the back of the Maoists.' (A much favoured metaphor at the time by both Gyanendra and senior army people.) Also, if the situation was more serious than Gyanendra thought, one of the main men responsible for his complacency was the army chief for failing to convey to him the reality of what was happening on the ground. At the meeting on April 22, General Pyar Jung Thapa finally conveyed the unpalatable news to Gyanendra that he could no longer rely on army support to enforce his will. Put crudely but accurately, and echoing Saran's point about saving the army, the army chose to preserve itself at the expense of the monarchy. At that point the Shah lineage as kings of Nepal was effectively on a downhill path to being consigned to history. With both India and the army withdrawing their support, Gyanendra had run out of options. In his historic proclamation of April 24, 2006, he finally conceded the fundamental point that had been in contention since his grandfather returned from Delhi on February 15, 1951: sovereignty rested not with a monarch, but with the people of Nepal.

Another crucial point must be made. However sound the advice from Shyam Saran, which was reinforced by the Indian Army chief, his intervention exemplifies what the historical record shows to be India's consistent highest priority in Nepal from the downfall of the Ranas to the present day: namely, the maintenance of direct political and military links to the army and the preservation of its institutional integrity. These priorities have effectively made it impossible to develop mechanisms in Kathmandu to achieve what is held to be inviolable in India: namely, the absolute control of the military by the elected government and keeping the military, and particularly its generals, out of all politics. In sum, what India holds to be sacrosanct in Delhi is apparently to be denied to Nepal permanently. The ramifications of this for the development of a properly functioning democracy in Nepal are profound.

Appropriately, it fell to an officer with singularly close links to the monarchy, General Rukmangad Katawal, to deliver the final blow to Palace hopes. His early education and rise through the ranks had benefited hugely from Palace patronage but his ultimate test of loyalty came on May 28, 2008, when the first Constituent Assembly declared Nepal a republic by 560 votes to 4. We know from his recent book that over the previous two years he had worked tirelessly to ensure that the monarchy would continue to exist and that a particular target of his effort was the prime minister, Girija Prasad Koirala. On the day, the vote was long delayed because of various disputes, notably the system for electing the president. Given his close contacts with the monarchy, it is certain that, as the moment of final decision loomed, the Palace would have been putting great pressure on the army chief to use all possible means to stop the vote. Despite what he describes as his deep regret, he states that he knew that the army could not stand against the popular will on the issue. On all previous form, it might not have been as simple as that. As in the days before Gyanendra's proclamation of April 24, 2006, 'advice' from Delhi could also have played a decisive part. As with his predecessor, assurances on the inviolability of the sanctity of the army in the new order would have been judged by General Katawal to be more important than loyalty to his long standing patrons in the Palace. Whatever the full story, Gyanendra must have regarded it as treachery, as something out of a Shakespearian tragedy, that someone who had benefited so much from the support of his family would turn his back on him at his hour of greatest need to throw his lot in with political leaders they both publicly so utterly despised.

However, ultimate responsibility for the loss of his kingdom must rest on King Gyanendra himself. He gambled his throne on a ludicrous and unachievable aim, and lost. But the seeds of destruction were planted by his father in December 1960, when, against a constitutional option, he chose to preserve the monarchy and the Shah dynasty in its absolute form. To do this he jailed a leader of a democratically elected government that did indeed, 'represent Nepal's best hope for the future.' Nepal continues to suffer the disastrous consequences of this action, which badly stunted the country's development toward being a mature, efficiently functioning democratic state. One highly significant hallmark of such a state is an effective means of controlling the army and making it accountable to a democratically elected government. No such mechanism exists in Nepal: hence we see the unhealthily dominant position of the army in the affairs of the state. A short historical review of how this came about is an appropriate way to conclude this article.

Learning from their Rana predecessors, the four Shah kings that followed kept the army under extremely tight control by running it directly from the Palace through the agency of the Military Secretariat based there. Army Headquarters was entirely subservient to it. In later years, to fool donors, some civil servants were installed in a few offices, perhaps with a dog, and called the Ministry of Defence. When it suited the army, it was occasionally used as a post box. With the downfall of the monarchy, this rigid Palace control passed to Army Headquarters where it has effectively stayed. Under a strong, highly conservative chief such as Rukmangad Katawal, all inhibitions about being seen to play politics were quickly shed. It is more discreet now, but its influence is just as strong. No one effectively holds it to account on anything, and certainly not for its present bloated size. All political party leaders are terrified of offending its leaders, with many journalists and media outlets in the same subservient state of mind. Nepal seems to have moved back to something akin to the world of Bhimsen Thapa when, 'political power rested on the army and its loyalty had to be constantly cultivated.' However active its large and ever-vigilant public relations organization works to deny it, or to silence and intimidate critics who assert it, the reality is that, whatever the Interim Constitution might say, the army is now the ultimate arbiter in Nepali politics. It is not possible to build a properly functioning democracy on such a basis.

A properly functioning democracy would, of course, require a state based on equal rights for all its citizens, whatever their gender, caste, or ethnic origins, not just in the theory of a written constitution but in the reality of everyday life. It would also be one in which all of Nepal's diverse people were properly and proportionately represented in the machinery of state administration and state security, including in the army. Nepal falls a long way short when measured against such universal standards. Sadly, too many influential people in Kathmandu, inside and outside politics, prefer things to stay as they are, and see the army as the means to ensure that end. And so it goes on, as in the days of Bhimsen Thapa.

I am most grateful to the staff of the Oxford University Archives for giving me access to some of the material I have drawn on in writing this article and for their most helpful guidance in finding it. I am also grateful to Oxford Mail/The Oxford Times *(Newsquest Oxfordshire) for providing and giving me permission to use the photographs taken in Balliol College.*

This article has been republished with permission from *The Record*.
The original can be found online at: https://www.recordnepal.com/
wire/maharaja-and-monarch-0/.

Addendum May 2018

On the comments made in the penultimate paragraph about control of the army, *Himal Khabarpatrika*, a Nepali language weekly news magazine, on 8 April 2018, published a long article on the subject, under the title of, 'Pampering the army'. On 19 April 2018, *The Record* published an abridged translation of it. The article describes how the army makes a mockery of the budgetary allocation system by constantly demanding and getting more money than the amount allocated to it in the annual budget, and how this makes it very difficult to maintain fiscal discipline at the national level. More significantly, and worryingly, it indicates how the army gets its way on this and other matters by cutting senior political leaders and bureaucrats in on the commissions it receives on projects it is involved in. I am confident that these extracts from the translation in *The Record* convey the main sense of the article.

Pampering the army: Rules breached, army appeased

Almost every government in recent years has short-circuited parliament to meet army demands for additional money. This trend makes it look as if governments in Nepal are competing to please the army. Since the government allocates resources to the army by throwing to the winds the established procedures and rules, and without any consideration about the state of the national coffers, the Ministry of Finance is obliged to fork up the amount requested. Demanding additional money above that allocated in the national budget, and approving it without any question, poses a serious challenge to fiscal discipline. Former chief secretary Bimal Koirala observes that the trend of arbitrarily spending money has alarmingly increased and this is fatal for the maintenance of fiscal discipline.

Government officials have failed to rein in the trend of high army officials visiting the Ministry of Finance whenever they are not satisfied with the budget allocated. Analysts argue that a weak civil administration has paved the way for the army to go beyond the bounds of established procedures. Former chief secretary Koirala speaks of the need for all government agencies to remain within budgetary parameters, saying that the practice of exceeding the budget allocated, while ignoring the agreed national budget, increases the risk of the amount being misused. For the current fiscal year, the government had allocated NPR 39.12 billion (USD 372,618,000) and NPR 5.6 billion (USD 53,340,000) for general and capital expenditures respectively for the army. Till April of this current fiscal year, an extra NPR 1 billion (USD 9,529,255) and NPR 3.72 billion (USD 35,448,828) have already been released for general and capital expenditures respectively. Because of the army, an additional liability of NPR 18 billion (USD 171,526,590) has already been created for the Finance Ministry this year.

As revealed by the Mid-Term Review of the budget, the army has demanded an additional NPR 33 billion (USD 314,465,415) till mid-January 2018.

Meanwhile, the army is buying more than 10 helicopters and planes, raising the question: if it were so indispensable to enhance the aviation capacity of the army, why was this not included in the annual budget itself? Why did the government feel obliged to equip the army with helicopters and planes by short-circuiting the process without waiting even for the next budget?

One Ministry of Finance official says the Army's interest in economic transactions is growing by the day, leading to a demand for ever more additional money. 'The army's particular interest lies with purchases and everyone knows what this is for,' he adds.

What the Finance Ministry official is referring to is the irregularities involved in procurement processes. High ranking army officials focus on big purchases as they receive hefty amounts in commission while buying helicopters, planes and other logistical goods. This is why both buyers and suppliers look enthused when it comes to purchases.

Pressure from the army is difficult to withstand. 'When a two-star general himself walks the office corridors supported by a retinue of armed body-guards, it automatically creates psychological pressure on officials. When army officers go to see an under-secretary or a joint-secretary with such followers their intention is to create such pressure,' says one official. A relatively old story continues to do the rounds in the ministry. According to officials, the then army chief Prajjwal Shumsher JBR had threatened the then finance secretary Bimal Koirala 'to throw him along with his chair into the Bagmati' if the budget request was not met.

Now, high-ranking army officials issue threats in a roundabout way. In the 2017/2018 annual budget, NPR 3.35 billion (USD 31,923,004) was earmarked for the army in capital expenditure, but the army had the Council of Ministers transfer an extra NPR 3.85 billion (USD 36,687,631) that year for capital expenditure. In the fiscal year 2014/2015, the army had 150 percent more non-budgetary amount than specified in the annual budget. An ex-official of the Ministry of Finance observes that political leaders never hesitate to release the required amount outside the annual budget because they fear being put on the spot.

The army is not as powerful as it was during the monarchy. Army officers now seek to achieve their aims by pleasing political leaders rather than by issuing threats. Why do political leaders want to make the army happy? One Finance Ministry official says: 'One of the reasons may be the hefty commissions received in procurement.' If the army's demands are spurned by the Finance Ministry, instructions come from the prime minister or the Council of Ministers to release the extra money. Ministry officials then have no choice but to release the amount. Army headquarters has bought helicopters and planes by taking the prime minister into confidence.

Let's take an example – when Dr. Baburam Bhattarai was the prime minister, the army demanded an additional budget of NPR 3 billion (USD 28,587,765) to buy two new MI-17 helicopters. But his cabinet sanctioned even more than what was asked by giving NPR 3.50 billion (USD 33,352,392). 'On the initiative of the commission agent, the prime minister himself becomes interested in such deals and there is no possibility of holding them back,' the official says.

The new Finance Minister, Dr Yubaraj Khatiwada, in his White Paper, said the treasury was almost empty, largely because of breaches of fiscal discipline. According to ex-finance minister Dr Devendra Raj Pandey, arbitrary spending going beyond the limits of determined budget represents the height of fiscal indiscipline. Tax cannot be collected nor can it be spent unless the budget is approved by the sovereign parliament. Pandey questions, 'If the Council of Minister continues to make decisions going beyond the bounds fixed by budget, why make a budget at all?'

Interest in profit

The Nepal Army seems to be more interested in areas of economic benefits in recent years. Its unnatural interest and involvement in infrastructure development and lucrative businesses, increases the risk of irregularities and opaqueness in its activities.

Unlike other government agencies, the Army has no fear of being subjected to investigation or scrutiny. Nor are its activities publicly debated. This is one reason why decision-makers become lenient when providing money to the army. The Commission for Investigation of Abuse of Authority (CIAA) does not have a mandate to question the army and this makes it easy for others associated with the army to take benefits from financial activities the army is involved in.

Every year, the Office of the Auditor General (OAG) criticizes the army for not following existing laws and regulations in its purchases and other activities. The 2017 OAG annual report questions the limited competition among venders, contracts not being given on time and reports not being submitted even after completion of the project. The army which hitherto was participating in non-profit making health and education activities in the name of doing welfare activities both for incumbent and retired army personnel and their families, has been involved in the operations of petrol pumps, medical colleges and real estate.

The Tri-Chandra Military Hospital of historical significance has been demolished and converted into a business complex, ready to be rented out. The army now seems to be more eager to do construction work. It has prepared proposals for hydropower projects and for bank operation. The Army has now bagged a contract for construction of the 76-kilometre Kathmandu-Tarai fast track, a project costing more than NPR 100 billion (USD 952,925,500). The army is also constructing the Kaligandaki corridor, the Karnali corridor and the Jajarkot-Dolpa road; projects which cost more than NPR 5.14 billion (USD 48,980,370).

The army has also bagged contracts for construction of 121 km stretch of the 183-km Benighat-Aarughat-Larkebhanjyang road and the Mailung-Syaphrubeshi road. The cost of these projects is yet to be divulged. The Army faces criticism for grabbing the Fast-track project without having the technical and professional capacity required for construction. Sher Bahadur Deuba's government handed over the project to the Army. A recent advertisement had been put out for hiring a consultant to prepare a detailed project report (DPR), an expertise the army lacks. The project has been handed over to the army without trusting the Department of Roads which has long experience in road-building, with hundreds of engineers.

The army plans to have the work done by others with relevant experience and expertise. When the DPR will be prepared and when the project will begin is still up in the air. Though the project has a period of four years to be completed, there is no doubt that it will share the fate of Melamchi Drinking Water Project and Chameliya Hydropower Project, the construction of which took years.

According to informed sources, the army's increased interest and direct involvement in large procurement transactions and construction only serves as a shot in the arm to boost the army's ambition. A former finance secretary says: 'To encourage the army to get involved in profit-making businesses and economic transactions in this way is risky not only from the viewpoint of having a competitive open-market policy but also, in the long run, from the angle of civilian supremacy over the army.'

https://www.recordnepal.com/wire/pampering-the-army/
http://himalkhabar.com/news/7305

Full details on the NA's actions at the Tri-Chandra Military Hospital, is given in a report published by the Centre for Investigative Journalism, Nepal, on Jan 18, 2018, under the eye-catching title of, 'Military Inc : Nepal Army demolishes a historic building to make way for a business complex.'[2] It is claimed to be, 'an expose of how the military is driven by profit-making.'

This short extract from the opening paragraphs sums up the alleged wrongdoing:

> The business complex area had previously been occupied by Tri-Chandra Military Hospital. Around 3 years ago, Nepal Army demolished the 89-year-old building and replaced it with a modern complex with amenities. Three years ago, when the Army demolished the building, it said it was going to retain its name and build a modern hospital for treatment of current and former soldiers, their families and civilians. It also claimed that the hospital will not be for profit and will provide medical care to those in need.
>
> But as soon as the construction was completed, the Army decided to rent out the complex. Why did the army demolish a historic building and make way for a commercial complex? An investigation into this case has revealed that the Army is after money and is openly disregarding provisions to meet its goal.

---

2 http://cijnepal.org.np/military-inc-nepal-army-demolishes-historic-building-make-way-business-complex/

Who Will Guard the Guards Themselves?

What the earthquake revealed about the state of civil-military relations in Nepal. Attitudes to foreign assistance from leading personalities are examined with an example of how civil-military relations worked extremely well at the local level

Karl Marx's book, *The Eastern Question,* was first published in 1897. It is, to quote from the sub-title, 'A Reprint of Letters Written 1853–1856 Dealing with the Events of the Crimean War.' Marx could be a dull, even tedious writer, and we know that a lot of his more memorable lines were written for him by his long-time friend, partner, and financial supporter, Friedrich Engels, starting with the famous opening words of the 1848 *Communist Manifesto*, which they co-authored, 'A spectre is haunting Europe – the spectre of communism. All the powers of old Europe have entered into a holy alliance to exorcise this spectre: Pope and Tsar, Metternich and Guizot, French Radicals and German police-spies.' Engels also had a formidable intellect to go with a gift for dramatic expression, which he put at Marx's disposal. They made a formidable duo.

The contribution by Engels to books attributed only to Marx is well illustrated in the most interesting chapters of *The Eastern Question*. In the introduction, the editors of the compilation state, '(W)e have included certain military articles bearing very directly on the war. Most, if not all of these were written by Engels, or grew out of letters written to him by Marx.' These chapters cover England's preparation for the war and some of the military engagements fought. In both areas, examples of monumental incompetence and petty back-stabbing abounded, and gave Marx and Engels a rich canvas on which to display their full range of expressive talent. The British Army had not fought a battle since Waterloo, nearly 40 years previously. Logistically and operationally, it was ill-prepared for the task it was asked to perform. Even the pride of the nation, the Royal Navy, performed poorly when deployed against Russian positions in the Baltic.

This is the wider context in which Marx wrote the few lines that are now about the only reference one ever finds to 'the Eastern Question.' Since the quote has been much debated, and misunderstood, it is worth giving the narrower context in which the words were written. Writing about the way Admiral Sir Charles Napier, who had been removed from command for the poor performance of his fleet in the Baltic, was able to get letters published which showed that responsibility for the debacle should properly rest with Sir James Graham, the First Lord of the Admiralty, Marx wrote that this correspondence 'had revealed to the English people that their navy was as rotten as their army. When the Crimean campaign stripped from the British Army its time-honoured reputation, the defenders of the ancient regime pleaded not guilty on the plausible ground that England had never pretended to be a first-rate military power. However, they will not dare to assert that Great Britain has laid no claim to be the first naval power of the world. Such is the redeeming feature of war; it puts a nation to the test. As exposure to the atmosphere reduces all mummies to instant dissolution, so war passes supreme judgement upon social organisations that have outlived their vitality.'

The much quoted and debated words are in the last two sentences. All can recoil in horror about war having redeeming features but there can be little debate about it putting armies, which are social organizations par excellence, to the test. Bombastic but ill-founded claims about preparation and the certainly of victory can be exposed as baseless very quickly, as can the reasons for failure, which usually stem from ossified thinking built on the comfort of previous victories.

By reasonable extension, the same thinking can be applied to great and sudden natural disasters putting a state to the test. How did the state mechanisms in Kathmandu measure up to coping with the destruction caused by the earthquake on April 25? The massive scale of the disaster would have tested even a well-functioning state. Even allowing for the fact that Nepal falls well short of that mark, an earthquake of the strength that hit had long been predicted. What preparedness that had been done, was shown to be seriously inadequate. Vitality, the state of being strong and active, was notably missing. Others have written at length on the general failings that emerged but few have addressed how civil-military relations stood up to the test.

We have an excellent source on how the army acted and interacted locally in one particular area but assessment is more difficult at the national level for various reasons. The media appear reluctant to say anything about the Nepal Army (NA) unless it can do so in the most laudatory terms. There is also the great gap between theory and practice when it comes to control of the army. Up until the downfall of the monarchy and the establishment of a republic, the king kept the army under extremely tight control by running it direct from the palace through the agency of the military secretariat based there. Army headquarters was entirely subservient to it. With the downfall of the monarchy, this rigid palace control passed to army headquarters where it has effectively stayed, whatever the Interim Constitution might say. All political party leaders appear to be terrified of offending its leaders, with many journalists and media outlets in the same subservient state of mind. The outcome is, to put it mildly, that the army is strongly influential when it comes to promoting its interests and in asserting its views on how things should be run.

To see how this influence has worked in practice over the last six weeks I have had to rely on a few media reports which, perhaps unintentionally, pull back the curtains just a little to allow us to see into this normally secretive and protected world.

This article from *eKantipur*, 'Mess due to absence of central mechanism,'[1] from May 1, 2015, is an excellent place to start as it goes to the heart of civil-military relations in Nepal.

These sentences from the article could not be clearer or more disturbing: 'The absence of a powerful central disaster response mechanism adversely impacted the coordination of rescue and relief operations ... Led by a joint-secretary, a Disaster Management Department under the Home Ministry is mandated to respond to natural disasters at the central level .... The joint-secretary-led department has been unable to provide instructions to the Nepal Police, the Armed Police Force, and the Nepal Army due to issues of protocol.'

The question that springs out is, what issues of protocol? The statutory framework for disaster response in Nepal could not be clearer: it gives the leadership role to the Ministry of Home Affairs (under the Natural Calamity (Relief) Act, 2039 (1982 A.D.)). The mechanism through which the Home Ministry is meant to work is the CNCRC (the

---

1   http://bit.ly/2uR1WQG

Central Natural Calamity Relief Committee). The Nepal Army, Nepal Police, National Planning Commission, volunteer organizations, and others, are members of the CNCRC. If there are issues of 'protocol,' the Home Ministry has had over 30 years to resolve them. Since the Nepal Police and Armed Police Force work under the Home Minister, there cannot be a problem of 'providing instructions' to them. By a process of elimination, the problem must therefore lie in 'providing instructions' to the Nepal Army. So in responding to a disaster, who does the army take orders from if 'issues of protocol' prevent the Home Minister from discharging his responsibilities under the law for coordinating rescue and relief? Quoting the role of the National Security Council hardly helps. It has the narrow mandate of advising the Council of Ministers on the mobilization, operation, and use of the Nepal Army, and seldom meets. In any case, the provision of 'formally mobilising' the NA was surely not intended to cover the need to respond urgently to a natural disaster. A new national strategy on dealing with disasters was 'approved' in 2009 after a long and expensive process of consultation, but appears never to have been implemented.

The lessons from 'the mess' described in *The Kathmandu Post* article are that, however great the sensitivities, there is a need to align what the law and the constitution say about control of the army and, to put it bluntly, what is acceptable to the army in practice. Organizational structures built on separating responsibility and authority are doomed to fail. The indications are that the 1982 Act is soon to be replaced. A key test of the new act will be whether it addresses these issues head on and clarifies them once and for all. The 2009 approved strategy for dealing with disasters should be dusted off and reviewed to incorporate lessons from the ongoing tragedy into the new act.

The army chief, General Gaurav Rana, is a strong and influential man. It is worth examining his public statements carefully, starting with these words from his widely distributed address to the army[2] on May 17:

> The nation, residents of the nation and the national army – bearing the glorious history of the Nepali people who joined their hands together and, without any foreign assistance, were able to undertake such sacred tasks as building the nation during Nepal's unification, reaching from Tista in the East to Kangra in the west, and during

2   http://www.nepalarmy.mil.np/coas/coas-speech-20720203.pdf

the great earthquake of CE 1934 – remain capable and committed
to face any challenges and to shoulder obligations like the national
campaign for rehabilitation and reconstruction.

These few lines merit more detailed deconstruction than I can give in
this article. The reference to conquering Sikkim and the more distant
parts of what is now Uttarakhand as part of a campaign of 'unification'
is eye-catching to say the least. On a point of detail, it is not strictly
accurate to say that the Nepali people received no foreign assistance
in the aftermath of the 1934 earthquake. Given that a major plank of
Rana foreign policy was to keep all foreigners out, there was no chance
that Maharaja Juddha would allow direct help or even indirect help
from foreign governments. He made that clear in a speech he gave on
March 1, 1934, during which he announced an 'earthquake victim relief
organization' and an accompanying 'fund.' Collections for the fund
began immediately. The British, Indian, and Japanese governments
wrote to offer donations as assistance for the earthquake victims, but he
forcefully refused to accept their donations. He accepted only donations
from foreign organizations and personal donations. Lakhs of funds were
collected from these foreign organizations and from personal donations
(*Sri 3 Haruko Tathya Brittanta, Part 2,* by Purushottam Shamsher JBR;
published by Bidyarthi Pustak Bhandar, Bhotahiti, Kathmandu; 2062
(third edition)). In the English translation of his book *The Great Earthquake
in Nepal (1934),* Major General Brahma Shumsher JBR lists these foreign
donations in detail, most from India and England, and a few from Japan.
The largest donation listed from England was from 'Lt Col CT Dax British
Envoy 500.00 Indian note.' The donations also included one of £10 from
a small parish church in rural England.

In his address the army chief does make generous reference to the
help which foreign armies gave but the suggestion that essentially
'if necessary we can do this alone,' is striking. This attitude has
manifested itself in the desire of some supporters of the army to praise
its contribution by playing down the role of foreign help. The attitude
reached its nadir in remarks attributed to K. P. Oli, the leader of UML in
an *eKantipur* article on May 25, 'Will take initiatives to raise cash relief
to Rs 300,000: Oli.'[3]

---

3   http://kathmandupost.ekantipur.com/news/2015-05-25/will-take-initiatives-
to-raise-cash-relief-to-rs-300000-oli.html

Oli also repeatedly praised the efforts of Nepal Army and other securities agencies during this national crisis.

Praising Nepal Army for their unceasing vitality in relief and rescue efforts for earthquake victims, leader Oli criticized the foreign countries for their show-off attitude in the name of assistance.

'Foreign dogs ate foods worth Rs 100,000 daily and also digested equal amount of allowance,' said Oli, 'But they did nothing more than sniffing some holes.'

Oli went on to say that the assistance provided by foreign countries was normal. 'China might have pulled two bodies, US might have pulled four,' said Oli, 'But most of the works were done by ourselves.'

It is shocking that a man who could be prime minister within a few weeks could use such derogatory and disparaging language when referring to the contribution of foreign armies and organizations. It was reasonable to expect it to be publicly condemned in the strongest terms, but I searched the Kathmandu media in vain to find even one further reference to it. Such silence by the media is deeply worrying. 'Our government right or wrong' is disturbing enough but 'our politicians right or wrong' is even more dangerous. Very sadly, this most astute of politicians would not have used such language without assessing that it would find some measure of resonance, even ingratiation, with people he was anxious to impress.

Enough has probably been said about the barring of the British Chinooks from entering Nepal, but in this context, of the use of foreign military resources, it is worth recording that this was a decision made entirely by the army and, although there are indications that at least one senior minister had doubts, none dare question what the army insisted on. There was little comment on the subject in the Kathmandu-based English language media but one tweet from senior journalist Kanak Mani Dixit is worth repeating: 'My conclusion on return of British Chinooks – inability of Nepal Army & Min of Foreign Affairs to play designated roles, plus sluggish PMO.' The clear message in that underlines what was said earlier. If an assertive army led by a strong chief does not play its designated role, there is not much chance of weak politicians or bureaucrats standing their ground to discharge their designated roles under the law.

Another eye-catching decision came to light on May 25 in this article, 'Chinese rescuers return from Rasuwa as deadline expires[4].'

---

4 http://bit.ly/2zUbErD

The short report is worth reading in full. It explains how a Chinese rescue team, deployed to reopen the heavily damaged new road between Rasuwa Gadhi and Syabrubesi was asked to leave as 'the Nepal government's deadline' had expired before they could complete their task. The road was still not fully operational and sources said that the rescuers wanted to return home only after completing their task. Whether connected with this 'deadline' decision or not, it is worth recording in this context that one week later, on June 1, China arbitrarily shut all border points between Nepal and Tibet saying that landslides on the Nepal side made travel too dangerous. The decision and its implications were extensively covered in the Indian media. See this article[5] from Business Standard.

Since I know the area well, I followed the story closely. The destruction near Rasuwa Gadhi was massive, and the extent of it has not yet been fully reported. On the Nepal side of the new bridge, a landslide buried the Immigration Office, Customs Office, and China-Kerung Business Association office, among other buildings. Photographs available on social media show that the Chinese Armed Police committed a lot of heavy earth-moving equipment to a task that was a considerable engineering challenge. Why not give them a few more days to finish the work the Nepal government had specifically invited them in to do – to open the road? Who laid down an arbitrary deadline? Why the unseemly haste? One reason could be the desire to show that Nepal and its army can do the job without outside help. Linked to that could be the motivation to clear the decks so that the NA would be put in the best position to show that it is fit and ready 'to shoulder obligations like the national campaign for rehabilitation and reconstruction.' Did this desire also lie behind the premature declaration, that confused so many donors keen to help, that the relief phase was over at the same time as reports were emerging that many villages had yet to receive any help from anyone? The questions are necessarily rhetorical, but given the NA's strongly declared interest, it is legitimate to at least raise them.

The determination to go it alone is coming through in the message, wittingly or unwittingly, which Nepal increasingly appears to want to give to the world about future foreign assistance: in essence, that the country has all the capacity needed to do what has to be done; all that is needed is money, and lots of it. Most countries do not hand over

---

5   http://bit.ly/2uBLnsI

vast sums of cash on such a basis, and particularly not to countries so poorly placed in the global corruption index as Nepal. National pride can be a powerful driver, and must always be respected by outsiders, but surely it should be moderated by practical considerations and the imperative of doing what has to be done to alleviate distress and suffering with all speed? The full cost and scale of the rebuilding that will be necessary is just starting to emerge. The latest data reveals that 370,580 'infrastructures' have been damaged, including 3,552 schools. Add to that the need to repair roads, and to keep them open however many landslides occur during the monsoon, and the task of resettling permanently the large number of internally displaced people. A more open mind to receiving practical help from abroad, which would work in support and alongside Nepal's own efforts, would seem to be more appropriate.

On reconstruction, the chief secretary has recently put forward proposals that reject calls to install an apolitical and technocrat-led high-powered reconstruction body in favor of setting up such a panel to be headed by the prime minister. An outline of what is proposed is given in this article, 'PM-headed body proposed[6].'

No doubt the peculiarities of high level civil-military dynamics in Kathmandu will manifest themselves in the consultation now initiated. We must await events.

How civil-military relations worked at the local level in one particular location is the subject of a long article published in *Kantipur* on May 30, 'Leader during the disaster, the great hero of Melamchi' available in Nepali here.[7]

It is a graphic and utterly engaging article which at times reads like a dramatic screenplay except that it is a real life story of how Major Prem Hamal, the commander of Bhim Kali Company, acted with his officers and soldiers during the early rescue and relief stages following the earthquake. The sub heading, 'From rescue to relief, a model Major,' correctly indicates that Major Hamal is the hero of the piece, and, for his energetic leadership and commendable initiative, deservedly so. Echoing back to *The Eastern Question*, he certainly did not fail to discharge what Sir James Graham in a letter to Admiral Sir Charles Napier memorably described as 'the noblest of

---

6   http://bit.ly/2zSkFS0
7   http://kantipur.ekantipur.com/news/2015-05-30/409921.html

duties – which is the moral courage to do what you know to be right, at the risk of being accused of having done wrong.' On that point, Major Hamal's judgment on when to follow what he describes as 'an internal chain of command' cannot be faulted. The same can be said for his rebuke to Lokman Singh Karki, the head of the Commission for the Investigation of Abuse of Authority, when he was on his way 'to the place where his own guru was living to provide relief supplies.'

It is a long article. Below is a translation of extended extracts from it which record, through a journalist, Major Hamal's thoughts and insights about what motivated him, what failed and what worked, and his ideas for how things should be organized as the exercise of recovery and reconstruction moves forward. The words speak for themselves. They deserve to be widely read and critically reflected on.

I believe that the extracts retain enough of the sense of breathless action from the original and in a way which pays proper tribute to the bravery and general conduct of the officers and soldiers of Bhim Kali Company, and what they achieved under pressing and extreme circumstances. It is easy to say that this is what soldiers are trained and paid to do. It is, but that cannot be used to take away anything from how this particular company reacted to being put to this test. All too clearly, in contrast to what was happening in Kathmandu and with other agencies at local level, these officers and soldiers displayed vitality in abundance. There can be no doubt that their quick action saved many lives. In the absence of any mechanism previously agreed on how the distribution of aid and the response in general would be managed at the local level, Major Hamal was also correct to seize the initiative to get a fair system going. I have no visibility of how other NA units scattered round the country reacted in the initial stages of rescue and recovery. In such situations, as exemplified in this account, decisive, energetic, and brave leadership is all-important. Without that, things can be very different.

The extracts should come with a warning. Security forces are deployed locally and are therefore best placed to respond quickly, but, as this extract from a very recent article in *The Kathmandu Post* shows, 'Remembering to forget[8],' just being in position and ready to act is not sufficient.

The security agencies – the Nepal Army, Armed Police Force and the Nepal Police – did arrive at the sites of disasters within hours. But they

---

8   http://bit.ly/2LlbnT1

did so without any stock of critical information about the 'zone'. They did not have household level topography maps; they had no idea about crucial entries, exits, or arteries; and they had no tools to handle fire or cut concrete and lift columns. After they reached the sites, they were seen asking about the location of the damage. Confused and poorly equipped, they appeared expendable to the community and thus, were pushed by locals to take extreme risks.

However praiseworthy the army's actions at Melamchi, they should not blind us to the need, at every level, for making and rehearsing appropriate contingency plans so that more coordinated action can be initiated immediately. The state and civilian authorities cannot be allowed to opt out of their responsibilities. 'Let's just leave it to the army' is not acceptable as a policy. The absence of the chief district officer during the early critical days is deplorable and inexcusable. In the translated extracts reference is specifically made to '(w)hile internal disputes were heating up in the capital over whether the government or the army was in command after the earthquake, good will was evident in this section of Sindhupalchowk.' There is a need for caution in thinking that what worked at the microcosm of Melamchi can be scaled up to work nationally by simply allowing the army to lead on. For multiple reasons, it would not work, and would be wrong. The state has an obligation to protect and support its citizens in every way possible by utilizing all the agencies available to it.

A bigger warning to end. Deserved praise for the NA, particularly across social media, has contrasted its speedy response at the local level with the snail-like reactions of all other agencies of the state. Invariably hefty blows are landed on what are perceived to be out-of-touch, self-serving, and endlessly bickering political parties. From there it is but a small step to cry out for a strong man or a strong body to be given unlimited powers for some fixed period to oversee not just the reconstruction of infrastructure but a complete reform of the state that would speedily solve all the multiple ills that beset Nepal, politically, culturally and in every other way. Here be dragons! There is no possibility of wiping the slate clean and starting again as one might do with some failing business. However unpalatable it may sound at this juncture, the only way forward is the long slow slog of not just rebuilding infrastructure but reforming the basis on which Nepal functions as a state with inclusion at its heart; a country where all its citizens have equal rights, whatever their gender, caste, or ethnic origins, not just in the theory of a written constitution but in the reality of everyday life. To that can be added decent and safe houses, jobs for young people, breaking the feudal and extractive mindsets of political leaders and the monopolistic powers of the syndicates and cartels that hold the country back economically, and so much more. All of this is possible. Thanks to their own heroic struggles, the people of Nepal are now sovereign, and they should use this potent power and the new opportunities now open to refuse to go back to business as usual. Within such a context, civil-military relations will function as they should: the army will be proud to keep out of politics, the Ministry of Foreign Affairs will play its designated role, and the Prime Minister's Office will ooze vitality.

Translated extracts of the article published on eKantipur on May 30, 2015[9]:

Leader during the disaster, the great hero of Melamchi
From rescue to relief, a model Major

Basant Basnet

Melamchi (Sindhupalchowk), May 30 – Major Prem Hamal had been watching TV. The way the ground shook called to mind some terrible battle. He ran out from the barracks. It was Saturday, April 25. Because it was a holiday, apart from the soldiers who were on duty, mostly everyone was dressed casually. Adjoining the barracks were houses where nine troops lived along with their families. All of the houses around shook and fell like fallen playing cards. Dust began to rise up everywhere. Gas containers exploded and spilled fuel began to catch fire here and there. Not even a minute had passed since the great earthquake and the land and sky of Melamchi, this lovely bazaar in the hills, had already filled with thick smoke.

Private First Class Pushpa Basnet of Bhim Kali Company was on duty at the checkpost. And when right in front of him he saw the house where he lived begin to lean, with his family inside, it fell immediately.

Company Commander Hamal of Bhim Kali Company, Lieutenant Human Singh Kunwar and the troops on duty were successful in getting the entire family out of the fallen house alive, one by one. All of this work was successfully completed within five minutes. Witnesses say

---

9   http://kantipur.ekantipur.com/news/2015-05-30/409921.html

the house had fallen in such a way that no one would have survived if there had been a delay of even one minute more.

Hamal shouted out to the five hundred troops who had assembled immediately and were awaiting orders: 'Everyone, no matter how you're dressed, run toward the bazaar right away. You don't need to carry a gun today. Put on your helmets and go, go quickly.'

In the blink of an eye, three teams had split off in three directions. The first team deployed down below, toward the bazaar. The second team was deployed to Sarkigaun, up above the barracks. The third team ran toward the upper section of the bazaar. Hamal himself was the leader of the third team. Right there from the road he was giving the message to the commanders that they should form support teams of 10–11 troops and divide into small groups for the rescue efforts.

Those who had survived were confused about whether they should flee or what they should do.

But how could anyone flee when their family had been buried right in front of them? The army came, shouting and urging them on, 'Those who died are dead and gone.

Flee to an open area.' Only then did the locals begin to run.

A common principle for rescue teams says – don't start rescue work under tall buildings while an earthquake is still shaking. Go only when the tremors have stopped.

A fundamental value of the army says one shouldn't deviate from the 'chain of command' – everything else is written down. One should follow orders without question.

On that day the army in Melamchi violated both 'principles.'

'People who were pinned down inside were asking for help, saying 'Save me, save me.' And you could see some who had been completely buried, except for an arm,' says Hamal, providing a terrifying account of that day. 'At a time like that how can you hold back your heart? So we went inside even while the earthquake was still shaking and began to get people out.'

There had been more than a hundred landslides, large and small, on the road between the village and the bazaar. The army worked to open up one track after another with help from local drivers and youth. They asked for an excavator to open the road.

And to monitor this a 'dozer mobilization committee' was immediately formed under the leadership of local business people.

A helicopter was sent to remote areas that could not be reached by vehicle. Some political leaders were trying to have the helicopter sent according to their own priorities. The army did not accept this. They worked with locals to assess the damage. The helicopter went to areas that had greater numbers of injured. The locals themselves built a helipad. They boarded the army helicopter and then showed them the way.

Melamchi bazaar has a small group of Armed Police and Nepal Police. Bhim Kali Company immediately mobilized them as well to come along with them. Regional treasurer for the Nepali Congress Prakash Shrestha said, 'The ones who died immediately, well, they were gone, but if there hadn't been rescue operations – so far in this area we haven't heard of anyone who was injured and then died afterwards. This area benefitted from the presence of the barracks.'

In the army, the chain of command is like this: the company looks to the brigade. The brigade looks to the division. The division looks to headquarters. This principle is very strictly followed. But when disaster strikes, there's no 'chain of command' path to follow. And in addition, the earthquake disrupted most communications. In such a situation, there's no alternative but to follow an internal chain of command.

Melamchi has Nepal's first night-vision helipad. Two more helicopters can land inside the barracks simultaneously. The army immediately built a fourth helipad, in a field on the far side of the Indrawati River. Local youth helped the army to clear the area.

Hamal added, 'Even though they thought they were almost certainly going to die, the boys took the risk; they weren't the only ones deployed, even locals who survived were also immediately brought into the rescue work.'

Even up until the third day the army's communication set wasn't working properly.

And as for mobile phones, there was no hope at all. On the third day, on the evening of April 27, Hamal made contact with the brigade commander at Bhakundebesi in Kavre, Ashwin Kumar Thapa, by mobile. The phone kept cutting in and out.

Thapa managed to say, 'Focus on humanitarian rescue work to the degree your judgment and manpower allow. It's not the case that you must follow the chain of command. Given the condition of the phones.'

The army, police, and armed police transported the ill, even making use of villagers who had come to ask them to transport the injured. Residents of Melamchi themselves say that Hamal and Kunwar, who understood that the resources of the state were limited, were able to get extraordinary results by making use of even the locals.

On the evening of April 26, the parliamentarian for the area, Sher Bahadur Tamang, was found at the Melamchi Health Post. Lieutenant Kunwar recognized him right away. He took him with him to the barracks. He brought him to meet Major Hamal.

Tamang said that miraculous rescue work was taking place and thanked Hamal and Kunwar. Hamal said that the political parties would have to be proactive in relief and rehabilitation. While internal disputes were heating up in the capital over whether the government or the army was in command after the earthquake, good will was evident in this section of Sindhupalchowk. Tamang began to gather information from locals.

And based on this the army was deployed in rescue efforts. Speaking with *Kantipur* on Thursday, Congress treasurer Shrestha praised the active involvement of UML parliamentarian Tamang.

Constituency number three has 23 VDCs, including Melamchi, under the army's command. They went from village to village transporting the injured. They had divided this work into two phases. After rescue work ended during the first phase, distribution of relief materials intensified. As far as the rescue work, this was absolutely work for the army. But as for relief, all of the parties and civil society had to have a role. In this as well, the ones with the greatest experience were the very same two, Hamal and Kunwar.

Hamal, who had been deployed to Sudan during its political crisis, had done research on the earthquake in Haiti. He had that as an example of how foreign assistance, in the name of aid, had deepened the political crisis there. As for Kunwar, he had been deployed to Haiti itself at that time. By the time the district natural disaster rescue committee sent DEO Dilnath Puri to Melamchi as its chief representative on the evening of April 30, the sixth day after the earthquake, the army had already managed to create three mechanisms composed of political parties and prominent locals.

The army called representatives from the local parties, including Congress, UML, and the UCPN-M; traders; teachers; journalists; and social activists to the barracks on April 27. Up until the disaster it had been natural for the army not to interact with the locals. Hamal got help from police officials.

At the gathering, Hamal presented the example of how disasters were dealt with in Haiti and Sudan. He said that this could be carried out in a way that is in accordance with the lives of local people, and told them that they would be the ones responsible for relief and rehabilitation. He went so far as to say that even though rescue operations were a task for the army, without social mobilization in the distribution of relief it would be pointless for the army to try to do it alone.

At that very meeting a regional-level disaster management committee was formed. Up until that point it hadn't been possible to coordinate with CDO Gyawali. Even though the army hadn't been able to maintain the chain of command, Major Hamal had not given up the command of his judgment.

Though 1,438 had died and 2,954 had been injured, the army was able to save the lives of more than two hundred in this area.

Would this have been possible if they had sat waiting for an order from the chain of command? It wouldn't have been – the answer is right there in the question itself.

Hamal reasons that during a disaster things are like this all over the world. 'During a major disaster everything happens of its own accord. If we had tried to say we need an authorization letter from up above for us to be mobilized, everyone who was buried would have died,' he says. 'Six hundred injured people would have died.'

Local journalist from Melamchi, Balaram Sapkota, says 'Puri created a one-window system for relief. Records were kept of everything. Donors weren't allowed to do just anything they liked. Whatever was received, they didn't accept food supplies.'

He noted that the army's coordination in this had been dependable. Talking with *Kantipur* in Chautara, the district headquarters, Puri turned this around and gave the praise to the army in Melamchi.

DEO Puri arrived and began coordinating with the CDO. VDC secretaries were summoned. On the morning of May 1, three committees were formed under leadership that included DEO Puri and parliamentarian Tamang. The first, an area disaster management committee under Hamal's leadership. The second, an area-level monitoring committee under parliamentarian Tamang's leadership. The third, a village-level relief collection and distribution committee under DEO Puri's leadership.

The responsibilities which the army had been taking up to this point were now divided and taken up by local bodies.

Hamal began to hold a coordination meeting at the barracks every morning at 9:00.

There was an interesting issue in the relief distribution when the chief commissioner for the Commission for the Investigation of Abuse of Authority, Lokman Singh Karki, went to the place where his own guru was living to provide relief supplies.

When he said he had come to provide relief supplies as he liked, without coordinating with the local relief distribution committee, the civilians themselves were the ones who halted his relief efforts. The army had divided the relief supplies in Melamchi (because if) individuals go about distributing relief as they like, relief won't even reach some places while in other places Haiti's experience will be repeated.

CDO Gyawali visited the barracks on Thursday for the first time since the earthquake just as the *Kantipur* team arrived at the barracks. Major Hamal said, 'Chief Commissioner Karki tried to distribute relief on his own. When we appealed to him that this should be distributed through the one-window policy, he didn't agree.

I maintained the position that even if relief came from the president himself, there would be no going outside of the one-window system.' CDO Gyawali, who had been criticized for not being able to provide 'delivery' immediately, said to Major Hamal, 'We had heard about your work. We give you many, many thanks.'

UCPN-Maoist parliamentarian Rekha Sharma told *Kantipur,* 'We haven't seen the distribution of relief carried out in such an organized manner anywhere else. Others should learn from the army in Melamchi.' Representative of the local people UML parliamentarian Sher Bahadur Tamang added, 'The army got extraordinary results in the rescue work by coordinating with locals; if this is how rescue teams were deployed everywhere, there wouldn't be a need for foreign armies no matter how big the disaster.'

No irregularities have been found in the distribution of relief in Melamchi. Whatever is available, it's being divided and shared while giving priority to the injured, Dalits, and the underprivileged. Substandard relief supplies have been sent back. It's the army that has been monitoring all of this.

I am most grateful to Mark Flummerfelt for his unstinting work to provide the translations which made this article possible.

This article has been republished with permission from *The Record*. The original can be found online at: https://www.recordnepal.com/ perspective/who-will-guard-guards-themselves/

The Indian Checkposts, Lipu Lekh, and Kalapani

How Indian security personnel came to be deployed on Nepal's northern border in 1952, and of the history of two of the most emotive and contentious border disputes between Nepal and India

In his book *Border Management of Nepal*, Buddhi Narayan Shrestha states that 'Indian Armed military-men of the Indian Military Check-posts, deputed on 9 June 1952 in the northern frontier of Nepal, were put away and sent back to India by the Government of Nepal on 20 April 1969' (259). This article examines the political and security contexts that led to the deployment of these foreign soldiers and police officers on Nepali soil. It will include detail about the checkposts given in the accounts of early foreign travelers who encountered them in various remote places. The vexed disputes between Nepal and India over Lipu Lekh and Kalapani will also be examined. The great scoop comes at the end.

Buddhi Narayan Shrestha's dates for the deployment and withdrawal of the checkposts need treating with care. We can be more certain about the withdrawal timescale because of detail given in Rishikesh Shaha's book *Nepali Politics: Retrospect and Prospect*. It gives extracts of an exclusive interview that Nepal's then prime minister, Kirti Nidhi Bista, gave to the official English language daily, *The Rising Nepal*, on June 25, 1969. In it he stated, no doubt at the behest of King Mahendra, that since India had not consulted Nepal either at the time of the 1962 Sino-Indian armed conflict or during the 1965 Indo-Pakistani War, the commitments with regard to mutual security based on the 1950 Treaty of Peace and Friendship had fallen into disuse and by the same token were no longer binding on either party (Shaha, 130). He expressed Nepal's resentment of the term 'special relationship' and stressed that 'Nepal could not compromise its sovereignty for India's so called security.' A specific demand was made for 'the immediate withdrawal both of the Indian 'wireless operators' from the checkposts on the Nepal-China border and of the Indian Military Liaison Group.' The Indian Ministry of External Affairs initially pretended not to take notice of this interview, with a spokesman inviting a formal communication from the Government of Nepal on the subject. Eventually after much diplomatic sparring, during which India threatened to close the border, an agreement was reached in September 1969 to withdraw the checkposts by August 1970. Significantly, Nepal did not insist on scrapping the 1950 treaty.

A well-sourced and widely carried Associated Press report[1] from Delhi, dated December 29, 1969, confirms that that the agreement to withdraw the checkposts was generally adhered to. The report states correctly that the Indians were stunned to get the request to remove the 17 checkposts, but that seven posts were evacuated in December 1969 and that 'the evacuation of nine remaining border watchposts' would take place during 1970. (One checkpost may have been withdrawn earlier and although most sources refer to 18 checkposts, it is possible that one initially planned was not deployed, though there are some indications that at one stage the number might have gone up to 20.)

The deployment dates of the checkposts are more problematic. Buddhi Narayan Shrestha states, 'This happened during the premiership of Matrika Prasad Koirala, beginning 9 June 1952, at 18 checkposts of the Nepalese frontier. In each of these checkposts, 20 to 40 Indian army personnel equipped with arms and communication equipment were deployed, together with a few Nepali army and civilian officials. The Indian army deployment was completed in two trips to Nepal' (51). Buddhi Narayan Shrestha gives no reference to support his statement on the composition of the checkposts or the June 9, 1952 deployment date. He is also vague about the specific authorization for the deployment of the checkposts, linking it simply to the well-known letter of Sardar Patel to Nehru of November 7, 1950. Patel was the Indian home minister at the time. He was a charismatic and powerful character who played a leading role in the fight for Indian independence. In 1946, at the request of Gandhi, he stood aside to allow Nehru to be elected Congress president and hence, on August 15, 1947, to become the first prime minister of an independent India. He died on December 15, 1950 and knew that he was terminally ill when he wrote his impressive and comprehensive letter. It was aimed at alerting Nehru to the new military threat facing India following the Chinese Army's incursion into Tibet and to stress to him

---

1   http://bit.ly/2LvcTCc

the need for India to take immediate wide-ranging actions to counter it, including in Nepal.

No separate secret protocol authorized the deployment of the checkposts, but Clause 1 of the secret exchange of letters attached to the 1950 treaty (made public in 1959) did state that 'neither government shall tolerate any threat to the security of the other by a foreign aggressor. To deal with any such threat, the two governments shall consult with each other and advise effective counter-measures.' That was a convenient cover, retrospectively applied I believe, for India's actions. Many years ago I asked a retired senior Royal Nepal Army officer about the subject. He simply said that the Indians just did it and there was nothing Nepal could do about it. Research indicates that this was an accurate assessment. The prevailing political and security contexts help to explain how such a state of affairs existed.

In the area of politics, an agreement brokered by India in Delhi on February 8, 1951 effectively ended 104 years of Rana rule. King Tribhuvan and his family returned in triumph from their three-month exile on February 15, 1951. The last Rana maharaja, Mohan Shumsher, remained as prime minister of an interim administration until November 12, 1951. Matrika Prasad Koirala of the Nepal Congress party was prime minster from November 16, 1951 until August 14, 1952, after which King Tribhuvan introduced a period of direct rule, which lasted until June 15, 1953 when M. P. Koirala again took over as prime minister. It is well documented that in the build-up to this historic change, and through the years that followed, India's influence over those running Nepal was very strong. One respected source says: 'So marked was the growth of Indian influence during this period that at times it came close to total political and economic domination.' (From *People Politics and Ideology, Democracy and Social Change in Nepal*, Hoftun, Raeper and Whelpton, 27.)

The Indian ambassador from 1949 to 1952, C. P. N. Singh, played a key part in the 1950 revolution, and his meddling in the affairs of the Nepali Congress party and in the shaping of Nepali government policy was notorious. Stories about his activities abound, but during a recent visit to the National Archives in London I unearthed this, new to me, account of how he saw his role and justified his actions. In a dispatch to London dated March 1, 1951, the British ambassador reported that the previous evening he had held a reception for the new Council of Ministers during which Prime Minister Mohan Shumsher had told a guest that he recently told C. P. N Singh that he had information that

Singh had obtained direct telephone connections to King Tribhuvan and B.P. Koirala, the leader of the Nepali Congress party. He had asked him if he thought that such direct contact was consistent with normal relations of a foreign representative. C. P. N. Singh had replied that it was not consistent with normal relations of a foreign representative, but his position as India's representative in Nepal was not normal. The last sentence in the dispatch stated: 'An Indian on friendly terms with the Congress leaders told me yesterday that it was they who asked Nehru to appoint C. P. N. Singh as Ambassador to Nepal in August 1949 and it was through him that funds were sent to Congress followers in Kathmandu.'

King Tribhuvan himself was very active in seeking Indian guidance. In his annual report for 1952, the British ambassador wrote that 'the King of Nepal was in India when the year opened and again at its close. As also on four other occasions in between, and this was an indication of his dependence there.' Later in the report, referring to a dip in Tribhuvan's popularity, which had peaked when the Rana regime ended, he wrote: 'There is also a wide suspicion that he has no deep patriotism and his frequent trips to India for rather undignified relaxation do not help.'

In *Nepal: Strategy for Survival*, Leo Rose sums up Nepal's willingness to accede to India's demands in an appropriately stark way: 'New Delhi's concept of Nepal's interests was accepted almost automatically in Kathmandu, at least at the official level. Indeed, it is probable that some Nepali leaders tended to be over-responsive in this respect, interpreting even casual suggestions by the Indians as advice to be acted on. . . . On a number of occasions, the Nepal government not only tamely followed New Delhi's guidance but actually took the initiative in seeking it. That the Indians began to take Kathmandu too much for granted and tended to act in a rather cavalier and condescending fashion with regard to their own prerogatives, is therefore hardly surprising' (195).

This political reality was directly linked to India's perceived security needs. In a speech to the Indian Parliament on December 6, 1950, Nehru made the position very clear: 'Now we have had from immemorial times a magnificent frontier, that is to say the Himalayas. . . . Now so far as the Himalayas are concerned, they lie on the other side of Nepal. . . . Therefore as much as we appreciate the independence of Nepal, we cannot risk our own security by anything going wrong in Nepal which either permits that barrier to be crossed or otherwise weakens our frontier.' Nehru's feelings about the Himalayas, bordering on the romantic, played a significant role in shaping Indian policy, right up to the start of the Sino-Indian 1962 War. These phrases, extracted from the opening lines of a speech he gave in Kathmandu on June 16, 1951, at the conclusion of his first visit, exemplify this: 'Mountain-girt Nepal, daughter of the Himalayas, young sister of India, I have come here at last. . . . I am a child of the mountains myself, the mountains of the far north. . . . The Himalayas are the guardians and sentinels of India and Nepal . . . the fate of India and Nepal is linked closely together . . . it is particularly necessary that we hold together.'

How these political and security conditions directly led to India's decision to deploy the checkposts on the northern frontier of Nepal is well explained in a book written by B.N. Mullik, the all-powerful head of India's Intelligence Bureau (IB), called *My Years with Nehru: The Chinese Betrayal*. Early in Chapter 6, under the heading 'New Security Problems,' Mullik writes that that the IB had no doubts about Chinese intentions: that it would soon militarily overrun the whole of Tibet and close up to the borders of India. In August 1950, the IB submitted a detailed proposal recommending the establishment of twenty-one checkposts to guard the passes on the Indo-Tibetan frontier 'from Ladakh in the north-western extremity to the Lohit Division in the north-east.' On November 3, 1950, the IB produced a long note describing the new problems of frontier security that would result, and making comprehensive recommendations. This is a prelude to Mullik asserting that Sardar Patel accepted these suggestions and acted quickly by producing his long letter of November 7, 1950 to Nehru. The letter referred to the IB note and made a number of other recommendations. Mullik reproduces the Sardar Patel letter in full, which tells Nehru that 'we have to consider what new situation now faces us as a result of the disappearance of Tibet, as we know it, and the expansion of China almost up to our gates.' Key extracts from Sardar Patel's letter pertinent to this article are:

> 4. Let me consider the political consideration on this potentially troublesome frontier. Our north-eastern approaches consist of Nepal, Bhutan, Sikkim, Darjeeling and the tribal areas of Assam. From the point of view of communications they are weak spots. Continuous defensive lines do not exist. There is almost unlimited scope for infiltration. . . . Nepal has a weak oligarchic regime based almost entirely on force; it is in conflict with a turbulent element of the population as well as with enlightened ideas of the modern

age. . . . In my judgment, therefore, the situation is one in which we cannot afford either to be complacent or to be vacillating. We must have a clear idea of what we wish to achieve and also the methods by which we would achieve it. Any faltering or lack of decisiveness in formulating our objectives or in pursuing our policy to attain these objectives is bound to weaken us and increase the threats which are so evident.

6. It is, of course, impossible for me to be exhaustive in setting out all these problems. I am, however, giving below some of the problems, which, in my opinion, require early solution and round which we have to build our administrative or military policies and measures to implement them:

(f) The political and administrative steps which we should take to strengthen our northern and north-eastern frontiers. This would include the whole of the border, i.e. Nepal, Bhutan, Sikkim, Darjeeling and the Tribal Territory in Assam.

(h) Improvement of our communications, road, rail, air and wireless in these areas, and with our frontier outposts.

(i) Policing and intelligence of frontier posts.

Mullik writes that as result of this letter and the IB note, among other measures, a high-powered committee presided over by Major-General Himmat Singhji was formed to make recommendations 'about measures that should be taken to improve administration, defence, communications, etc. of all the frontier areas.' The relevant lines for checkposts in Nepal appear in the last paragraph of the chapter: 'Earlier when the scheme for frontier checkposts had been accepted, we had also impressed on the Government that no security measures for northern India could be anything near perfect unless the passes between Tibet on one side and Bhutan and Nepal on the other were properly guarded. The working out of a scheme, so far as Bhutan was concerned, was left to the Political Officer, Gangtok, but for one reason or the other this did not materialise for nearly a decade. But, after consulting our Ambassador in Nepal, a Deputy Director from the IB, Warriam Singh, was sent to Nepal and he had a very fruitful discussion with the Maharajah, who was then the Prime Minister. The Maharajah took some time to consider the offer made by us to assist Nepal to open checkposts on the Nepal-Tibet frontier. These checkposts were subsequently opened and manned jointly by Indian and Nepali staff. *The number of posts was further increased and the staff expanded at the time of the Koirala Government.'* (Emphasis added.)

Further helpful indications are given in Chapter 7 of Mullik's book, 'The Quest for Security.' The Himmat Singhji committee (also called the North and North-East Border Defence Committee) reported in two parts with the second part containing recommendations on Ladakh and the frontier regions of Himal Pradesh, Punjab, Uttar Pradesh, and Nepal being submitted in September 1951. Mullik writes, 'Actually the second part was held up to receive the recommendations of another committee headed by Major-General Thorat, which had been set up to assess the security needs of Nepal and its requirements for Indian assistance – and this latter committee submitted its report in August, 1951.' Two pages later, this committee is given another mention: 'With regard to Nepal, on the basis of the Thorat Committee's recommendations, this Committee also recommended that the Nepal government should be persuaded to survey the frontier and passes, establish checkposts where necessary, extend effective control to the remote areas, improve the road system and reorganise the Nepalese army on modern lines.' Mullik published his book in 1971 and his reference to 'persuading' the Nepali government may have been an attempt to avoid touching on Nepali sensitivities. Starting with the tone of the Sardar Patel letter, India's assertiveness and determination is clear, as is the mass of evidence pointing to Kathmandu's willingness to respond with alacrity to any suggestion from Delhi. The point is made because another source states that Thorat recommended that the Government of India should carry out the land reconnaissance of 16 passes as a high priority (*Mutual Security: The Case of India-Nepal*, Sangeeta Thapliyal, 50).

This résumé of Indian decision-making puts a question mark over Buddhi Narayan Shrestha's claim that the checkposts were deployed 'during the premiership of Matrika Prasad Koirala, beginning 9 June 1952.' As maharaja, Mohan Shumsher was prime minister up to February 18, 1951, and, following Tribhuvan's return from Delhi, he retained the appointment as head of the interim Rana and Nepali Congress government up to November 16, 1951, when he was succeeded by M. P. Koirala. Other evidence suggests that the first deployments could have taken place as early as late 1951, and subsequent deployments took place, as Buddhi Narayan Shrestha indicates, over a number of years.

In his book, Buddhi Narayan Shrestha gives the location of the checkposts by name and district as follows:

Indian Military Check-posts on the Northern Frontier of Nepal
(Deployed from 1952 to 1969)

Check-post	District
1. Tinkar Pass	Darchula
2. Taklakot	Bajhang
3. Muchu	Humla
4. Mugugaon	Mugu
5. Chharkabhot	Dolpa
6. Kaisang (Chhusang)	Mustang
7. Thorang	Manang
8. Larkay Pass	Gorkha
9. Atharasaya Khola	Gorkha
10. Somdang	Rasuwa
11. Rasuwagadhi	Rasuwa
12. Tatopani (Kodari)	Sindhupalchok
13. Lambagar	Dolakha
14. Namche (Chyalsa)	Solukhumbu
15. Chepuwa Pass	Sankhuwasabha
16. Olangchungola	Taplejung
17. Thaychammu	Taplejung
18. Chyangthapu	Panchthar

(Shrestha, 259)

The name given to some of the checkposts is confusing. The one in Bajhang was located north of Chainpur to cover the historic trade route to Taklakot over the pass at Urai Lekh. The checkpoints were located from one to five days' walk from the frontier. Given that they were in position throughout the year, survival was a major determinant of the exact place chosen. For example, the Larkye Pass was covered by a detachment at Setibas, some five days walk from the frontier. The accounts of the foreign travelers who encountered these checkposts indicate that at different times the checkpoints were occupied by Indian Army soldiers or Indian police officers or a mix of both. Perhaps early on it was more army with police taking over in the later stages. A Royal Nepal Army security presence was invariably located close by. The detachments reported by radio to a base station in the Indian embassy in Kathmandu, which had a small police presence dedicated to the task of command and control. Initially the police section in the embassy was headed by a superintendent of police. Over time this was upgraded first to deputy inspector and later to inspector general rank. Most of the checkposts were engaged in asking locals who crossed into Tibet for trade or for work to gather information on troop deployments, road construction, and the economic state of the local population. They also attempted to recruit locals from across the border to act as informers. No doubt China was in the same game.

Given that India was making all the decisions on these checkposts and the passes they should cover, Lipu Lekh's absence from the list is striking and revealing. Before plunging into such deep waters, it is useful to follow the military principle of first assessing the ground or geography before anything else. Google Earth is a useful guide, but so also are the blogs and photographs of the Indian pilgrims who have followed the officially approved route (by India and China) over Lipu Lekh to travel to Manasarovar and Kailash. This account[2] offers a good example.

Kalapani is first mentioned on Day 11 (or Page 8) of the blog when the pilgrims stop briefly for a meal on their way to Nabhidhang, which is the last camp before they cross the Lipu Lekh Pass early the next day. On

@DKay/bcmtouring.com

From one pilgrim's account: 'Nabhidhang, the overnight stop before crossing Lipu Lekh early the next day.'

---

2   http://bit.ly/2O2OSAE

Kalapani, I quote, 'Also this is the first and the only time when we cross River Kali and go on the other side. Apparently this part of land has been taken from Nepal on lease by the Govt. At Kalapani we go through Indian emigration and while we have breakfast our passports are stamped and returned back to us.' Note also the traveler's remark, to be elaborated on later, that 'Kalapani . . . is supposed to be the origin of River Kali.' The pilgrims have to get close to Lipu Lekh shortly after first light as they cannot enter Tibet until the previous cohort of pilgrims exits, and this is complicated by Chinese time being two and half hours ahead. On the Chinese side, four-wheel-drive vehicles can now reach very close to the pass and busses can be driven to within a few kilometres of it. Pilgrims therefore only have a short distance to walk before traveling in comfort to Taklakot. The photos and the images from Google Earth on this and other blogs are helpful in showing the trail and geographical layout. It is worth noting, and this is particularly clear from Google Earth, that from Nabhidhang, as the valley narrows and becomes steeper, the trail goes higher above the west side of the river to approach Lipu Lekh. A ground reconnaissance would be needed to confirm the exact place of the source of the river. From Nepal's point of view, this should be done jointly with India. But to quote from a recent article[3] by Buddhi Narayan Shrestha, 'Even the Joint Technical Level Nepal-India Boundary Committee, which worked for 26 years up to the end of 2007, never ventured into delineating the source of the river Kalee, because it needs a political decision.' A necessary prelude to any 'political decision' would be a decision by China and India to start demarcating their long border, and this remains a distant prospect.

The latest public airing of the dispute over Lipu Lekh came on June 9 this year when Nepal's parliament raised serious objections to the twenty-eighth point of a joint communiqué issued after the Indian prime minister's visit to China. It stated that the two sides agreed to hold negotiation on augmenting the list of trade and commodities, and expanding the border trade, at the Lipu Lekh Pass. It is worth noting just how limited and restricted this trade is. The commodities are limited to what can be carried on pack animals and, for 2015, the period stipulated is from June 1 to October 31. For the rest of the year the pass is covered by deep snow.

Equal status with India and China over Lipu Lekh, and even for its

---

3   http://nepalforeignaffairs.com/authenticity-of-lipulekh-border-pass

recognition as a tri-junction, is now a difficult case for Nepal to make for a number of reasons. In contrast to official silence from Kathmandu, India, from the date of its independence, has assumed and acted on the basis that the trail to Lipu Lekh fell exclusively within its territory and that control and ownership of the pass was a matter exclusively between it and China. There is ample proof that China accepted this last premise. A copy of an extract of 'The Sino-Indian Trade Agreement over Tibetan Border (1954),' dated April 29, 1954, can be found here.[4] Article IV states: 'Traders and pilgrims of both countries may travel by the following passes and route: (1) Shipki La pass . . . (6) Lipu Lekh pass.' China initially insisted that the wording should be 'the Chinese Government agrees to open the following passes' and India claimed that the final wording indicated Chinese acceptance that 'the use of these six passes did not involve ownership because they were border passes.'

The 1962 Sino-India War ended trading, and much else, but during Rajiv Gandhi's visit to Beijing in 1988 both countries agreed to resume border trade and to sign fresh agreements to make this possible. A memorandum of understanding (MoU) on 'Resumption of Border Trade' was signed in December 1991 during Premier Li Peng's visit to New Delhi. In an effort to strengthen border trade through the mutually agreed trading routes, India and China further signed a 'Protocol of Entry and Exit Procedure' for border trade in July 1992. Lipu Lekh Pass was mentioned in both these agreements as a mutually recognized border trading point. Subsequently, both countries agreed to expand border

The cover of the May 15, 2005 issue of *Nepal* magazine.

trade in 2003 but to add the Nathu La as an additional entry and exit point to those agreed in the December 1991 MoU. Again, on April 11, 2005, the Chinese premier, Wen Jiabao, and his Indian counterpart,

---

4   http://bit.ly/2uOJsAt

Manmohan Singh, signed an agreement[5] aimed at confidence-building along the Line of Actual Control, Article V of which stated: 'Both sides agree in principle to expand the mechanism of border meeting points to include Kibithu-Damai in the Eastern Sector and Lipulekh Pass/Qiang La in the Middle Sector. The precise locations of these border meeting points will be decided through mutual consultations.'

The signing of this last agreement prompted the redoubtable Sudheer Sharma to write a long article in Nepal, dated May 15, 2005, with the eye-catching and significant title of 'Kalapani: China's gift to India.' The article argued that the new agreement had effectively stamped China's endorsement of the Indian occupation of the Kalapani area and that this was linked to China recognizing Sikkim as part of India. An image of the front cover of this issue of Nepal can be seen above. The image shows Kalapani camp as it was some years ago, the valley leading north to Lipu Lekh and the title of Sudheer Sharma's feature article. The text in the bottom right hand corner is a short extract from the April 11, 2005 agreement. This article was published during the absolute rule of King Gyanendra, but there is no record of him or his ministers uttering a single word of protest about the agreement at the time, or later. Part of India's case, which puts the spotlight on China's role, is that if China saw Lipu Lekh as a tri-junction or as part of Nepal, it would not have signed these exclusive MoUs and agreements with India.

Tri-junctions of international borders cannot be fixed when, as in this case, two of the three countries, China and India, have not demarcated their border, nor have even agreed to do so. What divides the two countries at present is what is called a Line of Actual Control (LAC) of 4,057 kilometres in length. The term is a misnomer. Despite the two sides having signed three much-lauded border-related accords in 1993, 1996, and 2005, there is no mutually agreed line of control, never mind an actual line of control. The line that exists is disputed at numerous points. Prospects for resolution are well summed up in these lines from a recently published book, Beijing's Power and China's Borders: 'In recent years the broadening of the Sino-Indian border talks into an all-encompassing strategic dialogue has been an unmistakable reminder that negotiations stand deadlocked. Yet neither side wants to abandon the apparently fruitless process.' (Brahma Chellaney, 'Sino-Indian Border Dispute,' in Beijing's Power and China's Borders, Elleman,

---

5   http://bit.ly/2LlHT7j

Kotkin, and Schofield). Until this deadlock is broken, there can be no progress in fixing the western tri-junction of India-Nepal-China nor the eastern tri-junction of Nepal-China-Sikkim. By way of another example, the exact location of the China-Myanmar-India tri-junction also remains in dispute, despite the signing of a Sino-Burmese Boundary Treaty on October 1, 1960. China supports Myanmar's case, but there is general recognition between the parties that a settlement of the dispute must await a final settlement of the Sino-Indian boundary.

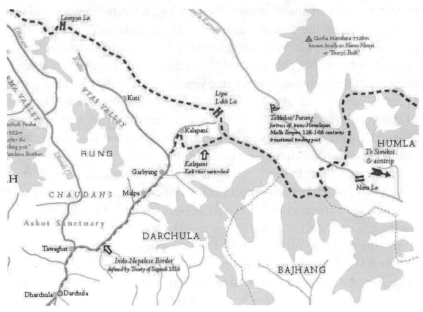

Detail of a map of Uttarkhand, India showing Lipu Lekh Pass.
©Rajiv Rawat/uttarkhand.org

How is Kalapani linked to the argument over Lipu Lekh? At the heart of the dispute over both Lipu Lekh and Kalapani is the origin of the headwaters of the Mahakali River, as the Kali River is known in its lower reaches. Though there was no map attached to it, there is general agreement that the 1816 Sugauli Treaty between the British Raj and Nepal stipulated that 'the Kali river' would mark Nepal's western border. A glance at the map above, which shows a river flowing down from Limpiya Dhura (below Lampya La), makes clear that with such a delineation, Nepal's case for control of Lipu Lekh and all the territory immediately south of the pass was indisputable. Maps originating after the treaty was signed confirm the acceptance of this river as the Kali and as the international border. Nepal's claim to the Lipu Lekh pass remains unflinchingly based on the Sugauli Treaty. It maintains that it has never concluded any treaty with British-India or with independent India that supersedes the Sugauli Treaty. Strictly speaking, this is correct, but successive rulers of Nepal – Rana maharajas, Shah monarchs, and political leaders – have by their actions and inactions weakened Nepal's case. After 1860, most British maps show the border to be the line of the river that flows down from Lipu Lekh. There is also an 1879 map that shows the frontier further to the east, following a ridge that runs down from near the Tinker Pass. Trade was a great obsession in the British colonial mind, and presumably Britain realigned the border to gain exclusive control over trade across the Lipu Lekh Pass and the traders using it.

As part of this shifting of the border, and to give legitimacy to it, the river flowing from Lipu Lekh, which previously did not have a name, was designated by the British as the Kali and the river that formerly had that name became the Kuti Yangti, as it flows down near Kuti village. This change meant that Nepal lost some thousands of hectares of territory north of the river running down from Limpiya Dhura. It also meant that the historic trail to Lipu Lekh now fell exclusively on the west or British-India side of the river. One Nepal source has called this shifting of the border and renaming of rivers as 'cartographic manipulation with a sinister motive' (*Nepal-India Boundary Issue: River Kali as International Boundary*, Mangal Siddhi Manandhar and Hriday Lal Koirala). Britain at the height of its colonial power was certainly capable of such actions, and worse. See as one example the action of Sir Henry McMahon at the Simla Conference of 1914, the record of which shows 'responsible officials of British India to have acted to the injury of China in conscious violation of their instructions; deliberately misinforming their superiors in London of their actions; altering documents whose publication had been ordered by Parliament; lying at an international conference table and deliberately breaking a treaty between the United Kingdom and Russia' (Dr. A. P. Rubin quoted in *India's China War*, Neville Maxwell, 42). Integral to all the actions listed was the attempt by McMahon, secretly and by sleight of hand, to shift a historic international boundary by the stroke of a pen on a map, 'by the judicious use of a little extra red ink' (*The McMahon Line*, vol. 2, Alastair Lamb, 530). McMahon explained to London that his objective had been to secure a strategic watershed boundary and with it access to the shortest trade route to Tibet.

The Rana usurpation of the power of the Shah kings started on September 14, 1846, when Jung Bahadur Kunwar (later to change his name to Rana) massacred his rivals and quickly moved to establish the political system that bore his adopted name. It is unclear whether this change in the frontier was made with or without the agreement of the Rana maharaja. Addressing an audience[6] in Kathmandu on August 13, 2015, a retired Indian Army Major General, Ashok Mehta, asserted that the Lipu Lekh issue was resolved by Maharaja Chandra Shumsher Rana, and that he had in his possession the map which the maharaja handed over to the British. Chandra was the maharaja and ruling prime minister with absolute power from June 27, 1901 until his death on November 26, 1929. Even by Rana standards, his rule was notably repressive but he was notorious for working assiduously and obsequiously to gain British support for his position. The map, therefore, that Ashok Mehta claims 'the Maharaja handed over' could be based on a case of British force majeure which Chandra was, as ever, given sufficient inducement, ready to accept. Nepal has asked the Indian authorities to produce any reliable documents pertaining to the disputed claims, but nothing has yet been handed over.

Whatever the sequence that led to this new border being imposed or agreed, or whatever date it occurred, maps prepared in Nepal during the Panchayat regime are identical to the post-1860 maps in showing the border as following the line of the river that flows down from below Lipu Lekh. Again, this indicated an acceptance, whether consciously or not, that the traditional trail to the pass fell exclusively on the Indian side and that the border agreed as part of the Sugauli Treaty was no longer valid. Also unhelpful to Nepal's case is that the China-Nepal Boundary Treaty, formally signed by King Mahendra in Beijing on October 5, 1961 makes no reference at all to Lipu Lekh. The opening lines of Article 1 state: 'The Chinese-Nepalese boundary line starts from the point where the watershed between the Kali River and the Tinkar River meet the watershed between the tributaries of the Mapchu (Karnali) River on the one hand and the Tinkar River on the other hand.' (Emphasis added.) This roughly corresponds to the border shown on the 1879 map and the one claimed by India today. Article 3 of the China-Nepal Boundary

---

6   http://bit.ly/2LnHVvD

Agreement of March 21, 1960, required the two countries to exchange maps and to set up a joint committee to start the process of delineation and demarcation. The map Nepal submitted has not been published.

Nepali sources point to continuing strong Indian influence in Nepal's affairs during this period of the early 1960s and resolutely maintain that no treaty or agreements have been concluded between Nepal and India or British-India that supersedes the Sugauli Treaty as regards Nepal's western border. However, all western and eastern borders must end at some point, north and south. King Mahendra's signing of the 1961 treaty seems to indicate, at the very least, an acceptance of a northwestern junction point to the east of Lipu Lekh. Since the stated purpose of King Mahendra's visit to China was to sign this treaty, one must assume he knew what he was doing, and, in particular, that the boundary proposed was the outcome of the work of the joint committee and took account of the map submitted by Nepal. The China-Nepal Boundary Protocol of January 20, 1963 reported that the permanent boundary markers had been established by the two parties 'as numbered 1 to 79 in serial order from west to east.' The protocol had 'detailed maps' attached to it, but to my knowledge these have not been published.

A further major complication for Nepal is that India rejects the claim that the river from Lipu Lekh is the renamed Kali River. It asserts, and claims that it has maps and diagrams to prove it, presumably based on the 1879 map, that the river Kali begins from the junction of the river that flows from Lipu Lekh and a stream that flows from springs in Kalapani. Hence, the earlier quote from the Indian pilgrim that 'Kalapani . . . is supposed to be the origin of River Kali.' Nepali sources are united in claiming that the stream from within Kalapani camp originates from a manmade pond and that the channel connecting it to the river from Lipu Lekh has been artificially created. Sudheer Sharma strongly and very graphically spelled out this argument in an article in a July 1998 issue of Mulyankan, which was reproduced in the June 8, 2015 issue of Esamata. The translated title is: 'Kalapani: Why and how has India encroached upon the border?'

A working translation of the relevant lines is: 'India dug an artificial spring for the Kali (river) at the artificial Kalapani to give 'legitimacy' to its encroachment. There they collected the water which flows from the mountains into a small pond; a channel connects this to the Lipukhola (Lipu river). They have made the laughable claim that this very pond is the source of the Kali.'

Subhak Mahato

Pillar No 1 at Tinker Pass, seen from the Nepal side looking north into Tibet.

The date on which this Kalapani stream first appeared on maps is disputed, but, whatever the maps show or do not show, the ground reality is that Indian security forces occupy the area of Kalapani to the east of the river, which traditionally has been regarded as the Nepali side. What is the value of doing so? There is evidence that the Indians first used Kalapani simply because it was the only piece of flat land in the area to establish a rudimentary camp to cover the approach to Lipu Lekh. At a later stage they must have come to realize that under the complexities of Riparian water rights their claim to control the headwaters of the Mahakali River would be strengthened by their occupation of Kalapani. At the military and security level, answers can only be speculative, but presumably the thinking is that an Indian security presence there helps to balance the Chinese security force presence in Taklakot just a short distance away over Lipu Lekh. There may also be an intelligence advantage. It is clear from the photos of the Indian pilgrims that they are under strict orders not to take photos of the main buildings and installations on the site.

There is one other significant consequence of India's occupation of Kalapani. As the map shows, India has used its argument on the origin of the Kali river, and its occupation of the site, to claim a frontier line which corresponds to the 1879 map in following a ridge line ('Kali river watershed' on map) that runs from just south of Kalapani to a point slightly to the west of Tinker Pass, which is about 5 kilometres east, southeast of Lipu Lekh. Tinker Pass is the location of Pillar Number 1 of 79 marking the Sino-Nepal Border. Nepal maintains that the tri-junction should be at Lipu Lekh, where Pillar Number 0 should be placed. However, for the present, the reality is that the India-Nepal-China tri-junction is

The top line, which follows the river up from Kalapani to Nabhidhang toward Lipu Lekh, shows the border that appeared in maps after the 1860s and in the Panchayat era. The lower line, which follows a watershed from Kalapani to a tri-junction on the main ridge to the north, indicates India's view of where the border runs. An 1879 map produced by the British shows this border.

This shows in more detail where India considers the India-Nepal-China tri-junction should be, just to the west of the Tinker Pass. Lipu Lekh is 5 kilometres further west along the ridge.

de facto just to the west of Border Pillar Number 1. The following two screenshots from Google Earth should make this clear.

Nepal's case for Kalapani has been badly undermined by long years of silence on the issue by the country's leaders. Some key related questions make that clear. When did India first occupy Kalapani? Who in Kathmandu knew what, and when? What did they do about it? Received wisdom on the start of Indian occupation stems from the views of Bhuddi Narayan Shrestha, which have been endlessly repeated in just about every article written on the subject. His June 27, 2015 article, referred to earlier, restates his view:

> If we have a look on the history of Sino-Indian border dispute, there was a brief but fierce fighting border war from October 20 to November 21, 1962. During the border war, in the Western sector, the Chinese forces marched up to the borderline shown in the Chinese maps dating back to the Manchu Dynasty. India's option was to defend on the McMahon Line as its northern boundary-line. After the Chinese carried out an all-out counter-attack along the entire Sino-Indian border. So Indian forces were compelled to retard back after a heavy attack of the Chinese army. The Indian military, when pulling back, came to realize that the Lipulekh Pass could be a potential strategic point, given that it is located at 5,029 metres in the Nepali frontier. They established a camp at Kalapani area. The camp, which is outfitted with underground bunkers, is near about ten kilometers west of the Lipulekh Pass.

No reference has ever been given to support the contention of Kalapani first being occupied by the Indians in November 1962, and for the reasons described. However, we know emphatically that the Chinese did not conduct 'an all-out counter-attack along the entire Sino-Indian border.' The fighting was confined to the western and eastern sectors (Aksai Chin and Arunachal Pradesh) with the central sector, including north of Lipu Lekh, seeing very little action. Soldiers from both sides would have been deployed near the border in this sector but very few shots, if any, were fired. Toward the end of November, snow would have been falling on Lipu Lekh and any Indian Army soldiers in observation posts there would have pulled back a short distance down the valley, almost certainly to prepared winter accommodation in Kalapani as there is a weight of evidence that Indian security force personnel occupied this flat and sheltered spot well before 1962. For example: 'Official sources in India claim that the administrative and revenue records dating back to 1830s (available with the UP state government), show that Kalapani area has traditionally been administered as part of Pithoragarh district. A State Police post was established by the state government at the now disputed site in 1956 and operated from here till 1979. Since 1979, the Indo-Tibetan Border Police (ITBP) have been manning a post for surveillance over the area.' More information here.[7]

An earlier date than November 1962 is also confirmed by Nepali sources. An article in the *Annapurna Post* dated August 5, 2015, written by the journalist Syam Bhatta, stated that 'though it is commonly accepted that the Indian Army encroached upon Kalapani in 1962 at the time of the India-China war, an elected member of the National Panchayat from Byas, Bahadur Singh Aitwal, says that Indian security forces were present in Kalapani from 1959. Aitawal also says that he formally informed the government about this border encroachment in 1974/1975 (BS 2031).' (Note: Byas is a Village Development Committee in Northern Darchula. Bahadur Singh Aitwal was appointed as assistant minister on July 16, 1973, in the wake of Kirti Nidhi Bista's resignation as prime minister.)

Sudheer Sharma's *Nepal* article from May 15, 2005, referred to earlier, states: 'While conducting the border survey with China four decades ago the Nepalese side had already found out about the presence of an Indian platoon in Kalapani. In Asar month of 2056 B.S (June–July 1999), Retired Major Shambhu Sumshere Jung Bahadur Rana of the Royal Nepalese Army, who had also worked under the Border Commission, revealed in public that, 'In the year 2018 B.S (1961/1962) itself, the Indian army were stationed in Kalapani.'' (Note: 2018 B.S. ended on April 12, 1962, which is seven months before the 1962 war started.) The article also addresses the key question:

'Why was the Indian army's presence in Kalapani so grossly overlooked? When *Budhabar* (Shrawan 13, 2055 – 1998), a weekly newspaper, posed this question to Rishikesh Shah, he said, 'During that time King Mahendra was there. Yes, I was in the Council of Ministers, but I was not the foreign minister. I asked the King about this, but he told me that this was not a matter concerning me or my ministry, so I should shut

---

7   http://bit.ly/2O5H9Sf

up. As far as I understand, during that time King Mahendra's thinking was that India should not be annoyed in any way.'. . . After the Border Administration Office had been set up below Kalapani at Changru in the year 2034 BS (1977), the office used to send reports and information about it to Kathmandu every year. The District Administration Office used to inform the Home Ministry about it in a timely way but people at the top did not show much interest in it. This issue remained a topic not to be discussed during the entire Panchayat era.' (Note: Rishikesh Shah was finance minister from December 1960 to August 1962 at which point, for just two months, he became foreign minister. He retained a status equivalent to ministerial rank for another year.)

Sudheer Sharma's July 1998 article in *Mulyankan* dates Rishikesh Shah's interaction with Mahendra to very shortly after the monarch's coup on December 15, 1960. A working translation of the relevant lines is: 'It has been said that King Mahendra received information about the encroachment at Kalapani right when it happened. Rishikesh Shah, who was Finance Minister in the government which came after the 1960 coup, said: 'We had known a long time back that the army had been staying in Kalapani. And in my status as a minister, I reported this matter to King Mahendra. His Majesty said in fact – India is quite angry with me, let's not anger them further right now. Let them stay in Kalapani for now.'

In his book, Buddhi Narayan Shrestha makes the same point on why Mahendra refused to act on information received about Kalapani: 'Nepalese officials, especially the Chief District Officers of Darchula have reported to the center time and again mentioning that the Nepalese territory of Kalapani has been encroached on by the Indian army men who have erected some constructions there. But it was ignored during the Panchayat era to sustain the Panchayat system in Nepal. At that time Nepal was not in a position to protest and oppose India for the sake of Panchayat regime.'

King Mahendra's coup against the democratically elected government of B.P. Koirala on December 15, 1960 showed that what ultimately mattered to him was the preservation of the monarchy and the Shah dynasty in its absolute form. This was also demonstrated when he authorized the signing in New Delhi of the secret Arms Supply Accord on January 30, 1965, the details of which were finally made public in 1989. For Mahendra, national interest was always placed below what for him was the vital interest of preserving his regime.

The historic trading pass of Urai Lekh looking east, with Nepal and the Seti gorge on the right and the trail into Tibet on the left. It is the site of Border Pillar Number 2. Wignall and his companions used this pass when illegally entering Tibet in the late autumn of 1955. They were forced to return by the same route in winter.

His inaction over Kalapani exemplifies the same order of priority despite all the talk throughout the Panchayat period of nationalism and protecting territorial integrity. The same can be said about his successor King Birendra who, during his period of absolute rule, never allowed his ministers to utter a word on the subject. It was not until 1996, six years after the collapse of the Panchayat system, that Nepal officially for the first time raised the issue of Kalapani with India at the time of signing the Mahakali Treaty. A joint technical committee was eventually formed in 2002 to address the issue. It would take another article to elaborate on all the bureaucratic and political maneuvering that has gone on subsequently, all to achieve little progress. Nepali politicians of all shades have been reluctant to press India strongly on the issue; like their Rana and Shah predecessors, despite much talk, their actions have shown that they also placed getting Delhi's personal recognition and support ahead of other considerations. An article[8] in *The Kathmandu Post* of January 6, 2015 had a heading of 'Nepal aims to settle boundary dispute with India in 4 years.' In the course of a few lines it said that a new field survey with India would not include Kalapani but doing so was 'now under consideration at the top bureaucratic level.' We must await developments, which are likely to be long drawn out. Any meaningful process to resolve the issue must await India and China agreeing to start the demarcation of their long border – and that day still looks some way ahead. Until then, India can only stall, as they have adroitly been doing, with Nepal's covert connivance, for many years.

8   http://bit.ly/2LaHQfz

Foreign travellers and the checkposts

Sydney Wignall, 1955

The last part of this article returns to the subject of the checkposts and the accounts given by some notable foreign travelers who stumbled upon them in various remote locations. These throw interesting light on the checkposts and none more so than Sydney Wignall's account of meeting a detachment of the Indian Army in Dhuli village, north of Chainpur in Bajhang district, in December 1955. In 1996, Wignall published the story of how this came about in his excellent book, *Spy on the Roof of the World*. The title gives the clue to the adventure. During the planning for a small expedition to climb Nalkankar in northwest Nepal, he was approached by an intelligence officer based in the Indian High Commission in London. This operative persuaded Wignall to cross the border into Tibet to climb Gurla Mandhata, from the slopes of which he would have a good view of Chinese military activity in the Taklakot area. On October 21, 1955, Wignall, his friend John Harrop, and a young Nepali liaison officer entered Tibet having climbed through the Seti Gorge and crossed the Urai Lekh Pass. Shortly afterwards they were arrested by the Chinese and imprisoned in Taklakot, during which Wignall and Harrop were subjected to some harsh interrogation. In December they were released by the Chinese after international concern had been expressed about their disappearance. By far the most convenient and safest way back to safety was to cross the Lipu Lekh Pass into India, but the Chinese, with the intention that they would not survive to tell the story of their imprisonment, insisted that they go back over the Urai Lekh Pass and descend the Seti Gorge, something that locals considered impossible to do in winter. The gripping chapter describing how they managed this descent is worth the price of Wignall's book alone. A good summary of the book is given in this *Nepali Times* article.[9]

In the opening chapter of his book, Wignall describes how in 1936 the Austrian mountaineer Herbert Tichy made an attempt to climb Gaurla Mandhata having ridden from Austria to India on a Puch motorcycle and crossed the Lipu Lekh into Tibet dressed as an Indian religious mendicant. This underlines the earlier point that sometime after 1860 the British had shifted the border to the river that flows down from Lipu Lekh. The briefings Wignall received from two Indian intelligence officers before

---

9 http://nepalitimes.com/news.php?id=7071#.Wipgt0qWbGh

departing on his adventure indicate that after independence the new rulers in Delhi had no doubts on the matter. In London he was advised to return over the Lipu Lekh Pass into India as the Urai Lekh Pass would be difficult after October and the Seti Gorge was far from safe even in summer. He was told, 'Whatever happens we will have men stationed on the Indian side of the Lipu Lekh.' He was also told that moves were afoot for India to participate in forming Nepal's foreign policy and to place Indian Army detachments at key strategic places close to the Nepal-Tibet border. In Delhi he was told that India was getting intelligence from an agent in Taklakot 'who is posing as an Indian trader, and continually crosses and recrosses the Lipu Lekh between India and Tibet.' He was again warned about the dangers of getting trapped on the Tibetan side when the winter snows set in, 'but India was now sending army patrols into Nepal and with luck we might have a military post established in your area before you come out of Tibet. If we do, then that detachment will be equipped with a radio transmitter and any intelligence you can bring out of Tibet will be sent to our HQ here in Delhi very quickly.'

After surviving the descent of the gorge on his return into Nepal, Wignall describes how the first locals they met passed on the news that since they last passed through Dhuli village on their way into Tibet, a checkpoint with a radio had been set up staffed by two Indian Army officers and a number of Indian Army Gorkha soldiers. Shortly afterward, the two officers came to see them and expressed surprise that they had not returned to safety by crossing the Lipu Lekh Pass into India. Later the three survivors arrived at the accommodation that housed the detachment. The Indian and Nepali flags flew above the house, and, as they approached, the Gorkha soldiers formed up and presented arms to greet them. Wignall had managed to gather some vital intelligence, but the commanding officer told him that the detachment's radio had 'packed up.'

Malcolm Meerendonk, 1963
It is striking that David Snellgrove, who passed through Dunai and Jomsom in 1956 on his epic journey across a number of the Tibetan-speaking areas on the northern border (memorably recounted in his *Himalayan Pilgrimage*) makes no reference in his writings to Indian checkposts. However, there are indications that he was being discreet, presumably because the first edition of his book was published as early as 1961 when there were still considerable national sensitivities about the existence of

these foreign-manned outposts on Nepali soil. When in Dunai he refers to having a farewell meal with 'officers of the Frontier check-post,' but his silence about the checkpost in Jomsom is more revealing. He remarks that 'the people were very friendly and Professor Tucci who was here before me was very well remembered.' Tucci's second visit to Jomsom was in October 1954 when he commented specifically: 'Here there was another involuntary stop. At the guard house Indian soldiers and Nepalese officials were stationed to keep watch on the caravans descending from the north. They came to meet us, shook hands with us and invited us to take tea with them. . . . The controls are very strict on both sides of the frontier; Indian soldiers to the south and Chinese soldiers to the north keep watch.' (*Nepal: The Discovery of the Malla*.) Tucci had also passed through Jomsom in 1952, and in his book *Journey to Mustang* made no reference to Indian soldiers.

The Mustang checkpost played a significant role in an incident that caused a major diplomatic rift between Nepal and China. British Foreign Office files in the National Archives give exhaustive detail on it. They record that on June 26, 1960, the radio at the checkpoint was used to transmit a request from the raja of Mustang for 500 army reinforcements to deal with the sudden appearance of over 1,000 Chinese troops on the border. It was not clear if an incursion had taken place. An order was passed the next day to the Nepal Army commander attached to the checkpost to send out an unarmed party to verify the raja's report. (The boundary agreement signed on March 21, 1960, stipulated that no armed personnel were permitted to operate within 20 kilometres of the border.) On the evening of June 28 information was transmitted to Kathmandu that one member of the unarmed group sent to act on the order had been killed and another wounded after Chinese troops opened fire on the party 300 metres inside Nepali territory. Others in the group were taken prisoner. The incident generated a number of tough diplomatic exchanges. The two prime ministers, Chou En-lai and B.P. Koirala, sent personal letters to each other: the former's exuding his famous charm; the latter's polite but impressively robust. Some details are disputed, and both sides never budged from where they said the firing occurred, but B.P. Koirala, under pressure from all sides, emerged as the hero of the hour, forcing the Chinese to make a qualified apology and pay the demanded 50,000 rupees as compensation. A future article[10] will give a full account of the incident and its diplomatic aftermath, but this extract of a statement by the home

---

10 See 'The Curious Case of the Mustang Incident', pp. 262-298.

Malcolm Meerendonk, left, with Dor Bahadur Bista and Captain Krishna Raj Pant, the householder, in Bijeshwari, Kathmandu in 1963, prior to departing on his secret mission to Dolpo.

minister, S.P. Upadhyaya, to the Nepal Senate on July 1, 1960 exemplifies Nepali sensitivity on the checkposts:

> He refuted the propaganda that the reports of the Chinese attack had come from 'Indian check-posts.' He made it 'absolutely clear once more' that there were no Indian check-posts in Nepal; all the check-posts were Nepalese and reports of the incident came from Nepalese check-posts in Nepalese code. There might be Indian technicians working on the radio-communication system at the check-posts just as there were foreign technicians and experts in other departments of the Government of Nepal.' (*China–South Asian Relations, 1947–1980*, vol. 2, ed. Ravindra K. Jain.)

The best detail on checkposts at Dunai and at Jomsom, and the best from any foreign traveler for any checkpost, comes from an unlikely source. In early 1963 Major Malcolm Meerendonk was the senior education officer at the Training Depot, the Brigade of Gurkhas, at Sungei Patani in northwest Malaya. He was responsible, along with other work, for Nepali language training of British officers joining the brigade. Apart from Nepali, he had a practical working knowledge of both Chinese and

Tibetan, and had been attached to a Nepal Army unit during his war service in India. In 1949, he wrote a 'Basic Gurkhali Grammar' (in Roman script), and in 1959 he published a pocket book, *Basic Gurkhali Dictionary*, described in 2013 by James F. Fisher, an anthropologist renowned for his work in Nepal, as 'the best pocket dictionary of Nepali.'

In the summer of 1963, Meerendonk did an epic 50-day trek from Pokhara to Dolpo and back. He published an account of this in two parts in *Torch*, the journal of the Royal Army Educational Corps Association: Part 1 in the May 1964 issue and Part 2 in the November 1964 issue. He took 30 days to get from Pokhara to Shey Gompa following the route that Peter Matthiessen describes so graphically in his book *The Snow Leopard*. Matthiessen did the journey with George Schaller in 1973, so by ten years Malcolm Meerendonk was the first foreigner to reach the heart of Dolpo by the very difficult route they followed. From Shey he went on to Saldang, Tarap, Chharka, Jomsom, and back to Pokhara. It was clearly not done for the good of his health, particularly as the army had already medically downgraded him. The only clue he gave in his 1964 articles was that on his way to Saldang he met a messenger saying that Nyima Tshering was expecting him. Meerendonk remarks that he had business with Nyima Tshering and later recounts that he had many audiences with him in Saldang. It is clear from the text that Meerendonk had read Snellgrove's book before going on this trek, and would have greatly benefitted from doing so. Indeed it would have been essential reading for him. The significance of Nyima Tsering as 'the big man of Dolpo' who was the key informant on all that had recently happened in the district and all that was currently going on, comes out very clearly in Snellgrove. Meerendonk knew, therefore, that Nyima Tshering was the man in Dolpo he needed to contact to get the intelligence he sought. But what information was he seeking? An officer serving with Meerendonk at the time told me recently that on his return to Sungei Patani, 'He would only say that he had been to a very remote area, gathering intelligence, but would not elaborate on the location or the task.'

In 2011, while searching through Foreign Office files in the National Archives in London for information on Khampas, I came across references not just to a secret report written by Major Meerendonk as a result of his trek in 1963, but direct quotations from it. However, of the actual report there was no sign and various Freedom of Information requests failed to locate it. Fortunately, this secret report is now available for all to read thanks to Lieutenant Colonel Gerry Birch, a retired Brigade of Gurkha's officer and long-time stalwart of the Britain-Nepal Society, and currently the editor of its journal. The secret report was published in the 2012 issue[11].

The report is at Pages 7 to 18 and Gerry Birch's introduction to it, and the opening paragraph of his introduction on Page 2, gives its provenance. What he does not say is that what was handed over to him by Malcolm Meerendonk's widow was a flimsy, barely legible carbon copy that required many hours of work to decipher and type into the form we can now read. It is clear that the trek had high-level approval from some Nepali authorities in Kathmandu, and most certainly from the top ranks of the Nepal Army. His mission was to find out if there had been any Chinese Army activity in this part of the northern border following the 1962 Sino-Indian War. It is also clear that a subsidiary task was to find out what information he could about Khampa activity in Dolpo and Mustang. Based on what we know now, Meerendonk was a little mixed up about 'the Dalai Lama's soldiers' and the Khampas in lower Mustang, but in the circumstances of the time this was understandable. It is a very interesting report, even though it covers just the Dunai to Jomsom part of his 50-day walk.

From his conversations with Nyima Tsering and his grandson we learn that the checkpost at Dunai had originally been located near Saldang, 'with a company of Nepalese soldiers to deal with Khamba bands who were making a nuisance of themselves, but that due to the intense cold winter and to the impossibility of obtaining food in Dolpo, the post had been withdrawn to Dunai on Nyima Tsering's offer to undertake to deal with the Khamba nuisance himself and to render reports if necessary.' Meerendonk writes: 'As the acknowledged unofficial link between the people of Dolpo and the central government, a source of info and influence for good, Nyima Tsering is a man of unusual importance in a region where powerful foreign influence and disturbing elements are so close at hand, while the central government is far away and its authority or influence for the good of the people as yet nowhere apparent.'

The report gives revealing detail about the checkpost at Dunai and what life was like in these lonely outposts. Much of it is worth repeating:

(a) The establishment was for five Indian police officers, of whom one was on leave in India and one in India sick. Met the OSP, an elderly

11 http://himalaya.socanth.cam.ac.uk/collections/journals/bnsj/pdf/bnsj_36.pdf

Sikh who was to retire in 6 weeks time and had been four years in check posts. He was most amiable, and did all he could to make me welcome: he was assisted by a ASP (a Brahmin) somewhat younger with similar service in check posts, and a Brahmin wireless operator.

(b) They appeared to have nothing whatsoever to do and were entirely concerned with minor domestic economy and efforts to provide for day to day needs, including various hobbies to pass the time such as running a tiny school for the local children, in a place where there were no amenities, no rations supplied, and very little obtainable locally to supplement the meagre stores of rice and flour brought from India by members of the post returning from leave. They did some arrangement whereby reports of any unusual movements or events reached them from Dolpo, where the check post used to be but was proved untenable. They sent or received Sitreps from the Indian embassy by radio about twice per week. They received a course in Gurkhali and Tibetan in Delhi, before they were posted to check posts.

(c) Describing themselves as there purely for the protection of the Indian officers were a Nepalese Army naik and a section of H. R. Company. There was also a section still there whom they had relieved, with orders from the C-in-C to remain till I had gone and to detach men to accompany me to Dolpo should I require it. I politely declined the offer.

(d) The relations between the Indians, Nepalese soldiers and local people were the most amicable and intimate. Nothing and no-one passed without their coming to hear of it. Significant of this 'intelligence' system was that the OSP and officers were all waiting to greet me a quarter of a mile from the check post when I arrived unexpectedly along the path over which there was no observation possible from the post, and that they knew of my arrival in Tarakot the day before. . .

(e) Owing to the unexpected number of signals from Army HQ about me before my arrival (six days late) all were intensely intrigued about my mission and personal importance. They turned out the Guard for my inspection on arrival. They did not however bother me with pointed questions, though they were particularly interested to know if I was looking for Khambas. They appeared to know nothing about Khambas themselves which was not surprising, as it turned out, for I met none myself in the part of Dolpo with which they were concerned.

On the morning of my departure the ASP left before daybreak to meet the Nepalese liaison officer with the Austrian Dhaulagiri Expedition; Lt Krishna Bom Rana, somewhere in the Tarakot direction.'

Much of Meerendonk's detail on the checkpost at Jomsom is also worth repeating:

(1) The post was manned by a complete company (No. 4 H. K. Company) under Capt Lalita SJB Rana, an amiable simple type who slept when he had nothing better to do. His sentries had their rifles chained to their waists. He greeted me warmly, was not in the least inquisitive but having received advance notice from the C-in-C of my arrival took me for granted. He arranged rations, accommodation, detailed a L/Cpl to guide me to Kaji Govindra Sher Chan's house in Tukcha next day, and gave me dinner in his quarter. He did not take me to meet the Indian officers who lived in separate quarters, but we all met up by chance in the evening and chatted about nothing in particular. He told me that he had been stationed with a platoon in Mustang last year but that there was now no-one there. He had also been detailed to take a section and register the numbers and needs of Khamba refugees in the mountains on the way to Tsarka off the main route, but had found the way blocked by snow and the Khambas not co-operative. While investigating reports of Khamba raiders north of Tukcha a few months back they had been fired on while returning to camp by Khambas armed with machine guns. They had no further trouble and were confined to barracks pending any need for operations against marauding Khamba gangs. Their job was to prevent the unauthorised use of the main road by gangs going south or north. This was apparently the Nepalese Government's effort to control Khamba activities, but as somebody was supplying them with arms and ammo it was difficult to do more, since they were elusive and untraceable in the mountains. He had no idea who supplied the arms or how, but thought it was easy enough to accomplish.

(2) The Indian police officers of the post were on the same establishment of five as in the case of Duniahi, with two on leave; they were inquisitive to the point of suspiciousness, and their OSP, a Rajput, asked me point-blank if I had been looking for Khambas, and what I had seen, and did I know where they got their arms from? It

is possible that they quite honestly did not know, and were trying to find out if it could possibly be the British who were behind it. I was able to tell them no more than they could see with their own eyes. No-one knew anything about air-drops. (Note: There had been two CIA airdrops by this stage, both just north of the border. The weapons and supplies were brought back into Mustang by prepositioned Khampas.)

(3) The relationship between the Nepalese, the Indians and the local people was obviously friendly though by no means as cordial and intimate as at Duniahi. The only apparent reasons were:
    (a) The Nepalese troops had their own officer and refused to introduce me to the Indian OSP on my arrival. They kept me waiting half an hour until their own OC was available.
    (b) The local people are not Nepali but Lo-pa, Thak-pa and mutually suspicious Tibetan groups.'

George Patterson, 1964

In 1964, George Patterson and a small film crew arrived in Kathmandu intent on getting to Mustang. His aim was to persuade some Khampas to carry out an armed raid into Tibet so that he could film it to prove to the outside world that Tibetans were still resisting the Chinese armed invasion of their country. He was told that it was impossible for him to go to Mustang, but by chance he heard about a small Khampa band in the remote area of Tsum. He managed to obtain a trek permit to travel from Kathmandu to Pokhara. On reaching Arughat he headed north up the Budhi Gandaki on the trail that leads toward Nubri and the Tibetan border. After passing through the small village of Setibas he knew that the way to Tsum broke away from the river to head northeast up a long and steep trail. In his book *A Fool at Forty*, Patterson reveals that he knew there was an Indian checkpost in Setibas and that there was no way to avoid it. He wrote: 'This was our most critical test since leaving Kathmandu. We not only had to be unsuspected here, we had to be so lily-white that they would not think of radioing news of our presence to Kathmandu.' In the event all went well. He states: 'The officer in charge was a friendly Indian with two junior officers – one a Nepali – and a few soldiers. We stopped at the post for an hour, drinking tea and exchanging items of information. The officer-in-charge had spent twelve years in the Himalayas in various check posts, and we gathered that there had been an increase in the number of refugees crossing the border – thousands in this area alone, according to reports reaching the check post.' Characteristically, Patterson could not resist giving his views on the utility of deploying such checkposts: 'While the idea of wireless communications from the remote snows to the capital of Kathmandu was excellent in principle, in practice it was a feeble, almost completely useless, precaution. There were only ten of these remote check posts in less than 800 miles of gigantic mountain, valley and forested frontiers. What went on in the next valley was unknown to them, let alone what was taking place five days' journey northward to the border.'

Patterson did manage to persuade the small Khampa band to carry out an ambush across the border and it was with some trepidation that he passed through Setibas again on his way back to Kathmandu carrying the precious film of the ambush. Fortunately for him, he reached the checkpost during a storm with torrential rain falling and was able to report that those in the checkpost were 'as unsuspicious and friendly as before.' He reported that they spent some time in the Officers' Mess 'drinking tea, and we gave to the Mess a welcome gift of several packets of cocoa. After we had signed the Registration Book we said that we must get further down the trail that night – and the friendly officers even offered us the services of a guide.' (For a full account of Patterson's activities at this time, read my article 'Raid into Tibet.'[12])

Duncan Forbes, 1956
In his book *The Heart of Nepal*, Duncan Forbes, an officer in Britain's Brigade of Gurkhas, describes a trek he made in 1956 to the border post at Rasuwa Gadhi during a visit to Nepal to attend King Mahendra's coronation. When he arrived at the village of Timure, which lies a few kilometres from the frontier, he found 'a small body of Indian police who were maintaining a signal station, and we accepted their hospitality for the night.' On returning from visiting the frontier post he stopped overnight at Timure and had what was clearly a jovial evening with the Indian detachment. He said: 'They seemed to be very much a group of exiles in this foreign land, being at the extremity of a long, thin line down to Kathmandu, and then to Delhi. They said they had been long periods out of touch with their families, and without leave. In fact the Inspector, who was shortly to be relieved, could almost have been described in

---

12 See 'Raid into Tibet', pp. 128-135.

Air Force parlance as 'round the bend'. He sought to forget his exile by flying kites and saying his prayers, and it was to the accompaniment of an incantation 'Hari-Ram-Sita-Ram-Hanuman-Vishnu-Narayanji' that we dozed away.'

Everest Story, 1953

Another group of foreigners who encountered an Indian checkpost were members of the 1953 British Everest Expedition under the leadership of Colonel John Hunt. In his book *The Ascent of Everest*, he writes that when the team arrived in Namche, 'We were surprised to find a small wireless station manned by Indian Government officials. Characteristic of the kindness of the Indian Ambassador in Kathmandu were his instructions to Mr. Tiwari, who was in charge of the post, that he should assist us by handling urgent messages. We had reason to be most grateful for this concession on several occasions during our stay.'

The Times newspaper was a major sponsor of the expedition, and, to the anger of many other journalists deployed to Nepal to cover the story, it laid down very strict conditions to ensure that it had exclusive rights to all news from Colonel Hunt and his team. A journalist from *The Times*, James Morris, was embedded with the expedition as a Special Correspondent. In 1972, she changed from living as male to living as female and became Jan Morris. She has earned a well-deserved reputation as an outstanding travel writer and historian of the British Empire. In 1958 she published *Coronation Everest*, a very well reviewed account of her time on Everest. It is an excellent read. This part of my article draws heavily on many details from it.

Another journalist from *The Times*, Don Hutchinson, was based in Kathmandu. His job was to receive Morris's dispatches, interpret them and add to them where necessary, and to get them safely and quickly transmitted to London from the cable office. The messages were delivered to him by runner from the expedition's base camp. There was no shortage of foreign journalists in Nepal who wanted to break the monopoly of *The Times* by using any means necessary. It was obvious that news of a successful ascent would be the ultimate prize for any journalist. Morris and Hutchinson gave considerable thought to how they would protect the privileged position of *The Times*. It was impossible to encode complete descriptive passages, but code words were drawn up to cover personal names, key events, places, and altitude. The particular words selected meant that a message would read as nonsense, and obviously coded to cover something important. The trustworthiness of the runners was achieved by paying them well with an attractive bonus based on the number of days they took to get from base camp to Kathmandu: typically, from six to eight. The British ambassador, Mr. Summerhayes, readily agreed that Foreign Office secure communications to London could be used to transmit the message announcing success or failure of the expedition.

Morris traveled with the Rear Party some ten days behind the climbing group. Major Jimmy Roberts was in charge. The party's main job was to bring further supplies of oxygen that would be needed higher on the mountain. On the evening of the first day's walk out of Kathmandu, the British defence attaché drove up in a large station wagon and told Roberts that John Hunt had sent a radio message from Namche asking him to check all the oxygen cylinders because tests on some with the main party indicated that there might be a problem. There was not, but this was the first time that Morris heard that there was a radio so comparatively close to base camp. Later Roberts went ahead of the rear party to meet John Hunt, so Morris entered Namche to be greeted by: 'Good day, Mr. Morris, Major Roberts told us to expect you, said the voice. I looked around to see an enormous bearded Sikh, in some sort of uniform topped by a fur-lined jacket. 'Please! Come this way, Mr. Tiwari would like to see you'. . . . We entered and climbed a flight of stairs, and there in the dark recesses of an upstairs room was a wireless transmitter. It looked quite a powerful one, and near it was a contraption like a stationary bicycle used to generate its electric power.' Mr. Tiwari was the Indian police officer in charge of the detachment. He explained that he had been given instructions by the Indian embassy to transmit any urgent messages for the expedition. He communicated with Kathmandu twice a day and invited Morris to send a short message there and then. He explained that it would be received by the Indian embassy and would be delivered to Mr. Summerhayes. Morris obliged but he noted that Tiwari inspected it carefully before asking the operator to transmit it. Morris explains that the detachment was there to cover people coming and going over the Nangpa La, the principal gateway from Tibet into this part of Nepal, with a special responsibility to be alert to Chinese infiltrators. That night, reflecting on Tiwari's actions and general demeanor, Morris drew up a new code system that would simply communicate that Everest had been climbed and by which members of the team. He knew that if he sent the message 'in clear,' the whole world would know its contents long before it reached London. He also knew that Tiwari would be reluctant to pass a message that he could not understand. What was needed was a system of designation that would allow Morris to convey the news in a way that looked intelligible but would mean something different from what was written to the person who held the code. The new code was dispatched to Kathmandu by runner the next morning.

Hillary and Tenzing summited Everest on May 29, 1953. They arrived back at advanced base camp, well above the icefall, in the early afternoon of May 30 to give the news of their successful summit to John Hunt and most of the rest of the climbing team. By chance, Morris had come up to the camp that morning and was able to hear the news at first hand and join in the celebrations. Later that afternoon, along with a member of the team, Mike Westmacott, he left to descend through the icefall to return to base camp. Morris had done little climbing before the expedition, and, as the light faded, he found it increasingly hard going. At one stage he asked Westmacott to go ahead as he needed to rest. He was pulled back to his senses by the sharpest of retorts from Westmacott: 'Don't be so ridiculous!' Morris arrived back in his tent at base camp worn out. He took some time to recover from his exertions before he typed out in code the most important message of his life: 'snow conditions bad stop advanced base abandoned on May 29 stop awaiting improvement stop all well.' The next morning, May 31, he gave the message to one of his runners with instructions to make best speed back to Namche. It was handed to Mr. Tiwari at the checkpost on the morning of June 1 for transmission by Morse code to the base station in the Indian embassy in Kathmandu on the afternoon radio schedule. Late that afternoon a message was delivered to the British embassy, signed by the vice consul at the Indian embassy, Mr. G. R. Joshi. The heading said: 'Copy of a Message received from COL HUNT, NAMCHE BAZAR on June 1, 1953.' The message read: 'snow conditions bad **hence expedition** abandoned advance base **camp** on 29th **and** awaiting improvement **being** all well.' (The Indians, either at Namche or in the embassy, added the bolded words presumably to make, as they thought, the message clearer.)

In the British embassy, Ambassador Summerhayes deciphered the message using the code, which had been handwritten by Morris on *The Times*–headed notepaper at the camp above Namche after he had first met Mr. Tiwari. The ten words transmitted to the Foreign Office in London by secure telegraph are given in italics with the code in capitals: *Mt*

Everest climbed (SNOW CONDITIONS BAD) *29 May by Hillary* (ADVANCED BASE ABANDONED) *and Tenzing* (AWAITING IMPROVEMENT) *All well.* The information arrived in The Times newsroom in time for the afternoon news conference. The layout of the next day's paper was suitably planned. That evening the news was delivered to the Queen and Prince Philip at Buckingham Palace. The final midnight news bulletin of the BBC Home Service reported the news and every newspaper in the United Kingdom immediately changed its front page to carry the story.

Thus, on the morning of June 2, 1953, the day of Queen Elizabeth's coronation at Westminster Abbey, the news was on the streets to much rejoicing. That same morning, having breakfast at a rest stop below Namche, as he headed back to Kathmandu as fast as he could, James Morris caught a BBC news bulletin that declared that Everest had been

Image: AP

Hillary ('Advanced base abandoned') and Tenzing ('Awaiting improvement') on Everest, 1953.

climbed and that 'the news had been first announced in a copyright dispatch in The Times.' John Hunt and most of the team arrived back at base camp during the afternoon of June 2. That evening in the mess tent the youngest member of the team, George Band, who two years later with Joe Brown was to make the first ascent of Kanchenjunga, tuned in to All India Radio to hear that the news had been announced the previous evening and that the Queen and prime minister had sent telegrams to the team via the ambassador in Kathmandu. There was much rejoicing that the news had indeed reached London in time for the coronation. In his book, John Hunt, with typical understatement, wrote: 'Another jar of rum was called for'!

In their early days the Indian checkposts were probably reasonably effective in gathering low level intelligence, but between 1950 and 1970 much changed in the field of intelligence acquisition and particularly in the technique of aerial surveillance. Over the last few years of their existence they became an embarrassment to Nepal and of increasingly limited use to India, of more political and psychological value than anything else. In sum, they had served their time. In stark contrast, unlike in 1969 when a peremptory demand from the prime minister, Kirti Nidhi Bista, gave Nepal what it was seeking on the checkposts, no such direct approach is likely to work to Nepal's advantage on Lipu Lekh and Kalapani. Nor will engaging China prove to be of much help. Whatever it might say now, China's position on Lipu Lekh is badly compromised by all the MoUs and agreements it has signed unilaterally over many years with India, and not just on trade, with no regard to Nepal's interests or sensitivities. On Kalapani, China's consistent position has been that it is a matter for Nepal and India to resolve.

India must know that no Nepali government is ever likely to accept what is perceived to be India's arbitrarily established border east of Lipu Lekh, but presumably it considers Nepali rancor and continuing protests on this as a price to be paid to secure its position on Kalapani. Given the history and the evidence from the maps, Lipu Lekh does look a difficult case for Nepal to sustain, but even a concession on this is unlikely to improve Nepal's chances of regaining Kalapani. In India's mind, both issues are indissolubly linked and intimately tied to its larger unresolved border dispute with China. Therefore, for India, the relative strength of Nepal's case on both issues is of no consequence. This is what makes the disputes so complex and intractable. The prospect is for a long drawn-out process that is unlikely to give Nepal what it seeks, though some form of palliative words may be agreed at a future stage of negotiation.

On a lighter note, the final word goes to the man, now a woman, who achieved one of the greatest scoops any journalist could ever aspire to. Sitting in his tent at base camp, recovering from his exertions through the icefall, as the words formed in his head, James Morris was well aware that the series of dots and dashes the wireless operator at the Indian checkpost at Namche was shortly to transmit to his embassy in Kathmandu would resonate round the world: 'I extracted my typewriter from a pile of clothing and propped it on my knees to write a message. This was that brief dispatch of victory I had dreamed about through the months. Oh, Mr. Tiwari at Namche and Mr. Summerhayes at Kathmandu! Oh, you watchful radio men in Whitehall! Oh, telephone operators, typists and sub-editors, readers, listeners, statesmen, generals, Presidents, Kings, Queens and Archbishops! I have a message for you!'

I am most grateful to Subhak Mahato for permission to use his photo of the Tinker Pass and to Jamie McGuinness for permission to use his photo of the Urai Lekh Pass. My thanks also to Jim Fisher for permitting me to use his photo of Malcolm Meerendonk and Dor Bahadur Bista.

This article has been republished with permission from *The Record*. The original can be found online at: http://www.recordnepal.com/wire/indian-checkposts-lipu-lekh-and-kalapani/

The Curious Case of the Mustang Incident

On June 28, 1960, Chinese troops fired on an unarmed party of Nepalis in northern Mustang, killing one, wounding one, and capturing others. The Chinese subsequently apologised but maintained that the shooting had taken place inside Chinese territory

Boundary Marker Pillar Number 24 of 79 on the Sino-Nepal border in northern Mustang, looking south into Nepal. The location of this post, as with the 78 others, was formally established by the China-Nepal Boundary Protocol, January 20, 1963. It is a distance of 2.7 kilometres to the Kora La and 4.2 kilometres to the point that was previously recognized as the traditional border.

On November 3, 2015, the opening lines of an article[1] in *The Indian Express* caught my eye:

---

1   http://bit.ly/2mx1XWA

In the summer of 1960, a thousand People's Liberation Army troops crossed into Nepal and advanced towards Bu Ba La. Ever since the Tibetan rebellion began the previous summer, Bu Ba La had become a base for insurgents who, aided by the CIA, were staging strikes against Chinese troops. Nepal's King Mahendra had given China permission to strike deep inside his territory, even arranging for police to arrest the insurgents as they fled.

The central claim astonished me, as did most of the rest of the detail. A quick check for the source of this information revealed that it was from a paragraph of the book *Protracted Contest: Sino-Indian Rivalry in the Twentieth Century* by John W. Garver, published by University of Washington Press in 2001 (148). Garver is professor emeritus in the Sam Nunn School of International Affairs at the Georgia Institute of Technology, and the author of eleven books and over one hundred articles dealing with China's foreign relations. It is worth quoting the paragraph in full:

Almost as troubling to New Delhi as the Kathmandu-Lhasa road was the beginning of secret military cooperation between China and Nepal. As rebellion spread across Tibet in 1959, many refugees fled into Nepal. Several of the camps where those refugees assembled became centers of support activity for the insurgents inside Tibet. Men were recruited and trained, supplies and food assembled, and operations planned from these camps. One of the largest refugee camps was in the Bu Ba La (transliterated from Chinese) area of western Nepal, a region not effectively administered by the Kathmandu government but controlled by a local tribe in cooperation with the Tibetan refugees. In 1960 the Chinese government explained to Nepal's leaders the serious, hostile nature of the activities emanating from this camp, and the Nepali government invited China to send PLA forces into Nepal to expel the insurgents cum refugees. In a highly secret operation about a thousand PLA soldiers advanced quickly on the rebel base/ refugee camp. No artillery was used so as to lessen chances of outside detection. Nepali liaison officers accompanied Chinese forces, and the Chinese advance was coordinated with deployments of Nepali police. The Chinese advance pushed the Tibetans into a Nepali police net, where they were detained for deportation. The entire operation lasted only a week or so and from the Chinese point of view was highly

successful. It was a highly secret operation so as not to to disturb
India. Indian intelligence assets within Nepal nonetheless learned of
the operation and informed New Delhi. (Footnote 20)'

As indicated, the source for all that is claimed is contained in a
footnote. Another footnote in the same chapter gives the full details:
'Yang Gongsu, 'Xin zhongguo duiwai yu wai zhengce yu waijiao shilu
(1949–1982)' (New China's foreign policy and diplomatic practice
(1949–1982)), MS' (Footnote 14). In the acknowledgements we learn the
specific provenance of the manuscript: 'Thanks are due especially to
Ambassador Yang Gungsu, who shared with me a manuscript on China's
diplomacy.' In the book, the reader is informed that Yang Gungsu was
'the young foreign affairs assistant of the central government team
dispatched to Lhasa in 1951.' He later became a senior diplomat as he
headed up the Chinese team in crucial talks with India on the border
dispute in 1960–61.

Very little of the information that stems from this shared manuscript
is corroborated in any other account of the history of the period. No
other authority that I have seen supports the claim that in the summer
of 1960, or at any other time, the Nepal government invited a 1,000-man
PLA force into Nepal 'to expel insurgents cum refugees,' with Nepali
liaison officers accompanying the Chinese forces, and with the advance
coordinated with deployments of the Nepal Police. There is, however,
a mass of evidence that convincingly refutes it. It must be a matter of
conjecture why the location of this claimed major military operation
is given an unrecognized name 'transliterated from the Chinese.' We
are told that it is an 'area of western Nepal, a region not effectively
administered by the Kathmandu government but controlled by a local
tribe in cooperation with the Tibetan refugees.'

This can only relate to Mustang, and there might be a clue in the use
of the obscure term 'Bu Ba La.' 'La' designates a pass in Tibetan, and
in a map associated with the 1961 Boundary Treaty, the Kora La Pass,
close to the Nepal-Tibet border in northern Mustang, appears in Nepali
as the Kuku-la. The pinyin transliteration of the Chinese characters that
designate the same pass on the same map is 'Peng Peng la.' The term
'Peng' rhymes with 'sung,' so is pronounced 'Pung Pung la.' Possibly this
is the origin of Garver's mysterious Bu Ba La. Only he and his Chinese
source can properly explain why a Himalayan pass at a height of 4,600
metres is designated as the spot housing 'one of the largest refugee

camps,' and why he deliberately avoided using the area designation of Mustang.

What we do know for certain is that the buildup in Mustang of the 2,000-strong CIA-backed Tibetan armed force did not start until September 1960, following a seven-man reconnaissance party which arrived in June. All were recruited in India, mostly from the Darjeeling-Kalimpong area, but also from the Bomdila and Misamari refugee camps, and from Mussoorie and elsewhere. Many had been part of the Chushi Gangdrug (Four Rivers, Six Ranges) army inside Tibet, which had been formed in 1958 to bring together all the Tibetan resistance groups fighting the Chinese army, the PLA. Many had been working in road-building gangs, mostly in Sikkim. None of the 2,000 who quickly assembled in Mustang came directly from Tibet into Mustang, though later some refugees from across the border were conscripted into the group.

There is only one record of a group of CIA-trained fighters being in Mustang for a short period in late 1959. They were a nine-man group who had trained in Colorado for nearly a year before being parachuted into Tibet near the Nam Tso, Tibet's second largest saltwater lake, 190 kilometres north of Lhasa. Their mission was to meet up with a resistance group who were reportedly operating in this area. They were dropped near a PLA encampment and, frightened of detection, they fled the scene without pausing to recover any of the supply bundles that had been dropped with them. These bundles contained their radio and would also have had the reserve ammunition in them. They then found that the resistance group they were to meet had departed six months previously. Their lack of equipment and shortage of ammunition meant that they were in no state to take offensive action against anyone. They had no option but to abort the mission.

With the exception of this one drop near Nam Tso, all the agents parachuted into Tibet were inserted well to the east of Lhasa. When the Chinese started to get the upper hand over the resistance groups, following the rapid and massive deployment of the PLA, the escape route for the agents and other fighters was directly south to India. This was not an option open to this nine-man group. If they had gone directly south to India they would have bumped into major PLA concentrations south of Lhasa. Hence their decision to exit Tibet by taking a circuitous southwest route to Mustang, a distance of over 500 kilometres. The arrival of this group would have made a deep impression on all who met them. A few of them might have stayed in Mustang but, for the reasons already given, they were in no position to take any offensive action. Most returned to India to convey the message to the resistance leaders living there that 'their ethnic kin in Mustang were generally supportive.' This was one of a number of factors that led the leaders to approach the United States in February 1960 to seek support for setting up a base in Mustang. (See Conboy and Morrison, *The CIA's Secret War in Tibet*, 119 and 146.) Key to the case was Mustang's remoteness, which made it an area where Nepali central government control was weak. Knowledge that a 1,000-man PLA invasion had just taken place would have forced a fundamental reassessment.

I am grateful to Carole McGranahan (author of *Arrested Histories: Tibet, the CIA, and Memories of a Forgotten War*), for pointing out to me that it is her understanding that Mustang was not necessarily the preferred location of the Tibetans, rather it was the U.S. government that forced King Mahendra to station them there. As the Tibetans saw it, Mustang was too far away from the action for it to truly be useful as a military base. As the Americans saw it, Mustang was available due to the weakness of the Nepali monarch to say no, and was potentially useful as an intelligence base rather than a military one. Carole McGranahan has also pointed out to me that the men in Mustang referred to themselves as soldiers in the Chushi Gangdrug army – many but not all of the soldiers came from the eastern Tibetan province of Kham – and that they should not be denied the right to be referred to by the designation they rightly claimed: soldiers in Chushi Gangdrug.

The first of three CIA airdrops of weapons to the Chushi Gangdrug in Mustang took place on the evening of April 2, 1961. The drop zone was 10 kilometres inside Tibet. The first cross-border raid from Mustang took place in September 1961. There is no record of any other raids from Nepali territory before this date. It follows that Garver's assertion, that 'in 1960 the Chinese government explained to Nepal's leaders the serious, hostile nature of the activities emanating from this camp,' does not make sense, to put it mildly. No such hostile camp existed in Mustang or anywhere else in Nepal in the summer of 1960.

Just as incredible is the assertion that King Mahendra gave permission to the Chinese to move deep inside Nepali territory, and even arranged for police to arrest the insurgents as they fled. King Mahendra was shocked by the margin of the Congress Party victory in Nepal's first general election on February 18, 1959. After B.P. Koirala became prime minister, the king intensified his foreign visits. On April 10, 1960, he left for a trip to Japan and the United States and did not come back to Kathmandu until July 28, 1960. He was not, therefore, in the country to give permission to any Chinese military to move deep into Nepal in the summer of 1960, and, given the constitutional arrangements at the time, there would have been political mayhem in Kathmandu if he had attempted to do so.

Most telling of all, there is the indubitable fact of history that on June 28, 1960 Chinese troops fired on an unarmed party of Nepal Police in the area of the Kora La in northern Mustang, killing one, wounding one, and capturing others. By any standards this was an important story that generated a considerable number of tough diplomatic exchanges between the governments of Nepal and China. It was quickly reported by the international media and generated stories in many western capitals, as this headline from *The New York Times* of June 30, 1960 exemplifies.

Unsurprisingly, the claims in the Garver book find their way into other academic literature as accepted truth. One example is M. Taylor

CHINESE TROOPS KILL A NEPALESE

18 Captured in Reds' Raid Across Border—'Urgent' Protest Sent to Peiping

Special to The New York Times.

NEW DELHI, India, June 29 —Chinese Communist troops clashed with a Nepalese border patrol Monday in the territory of Nepal, according to an official report received today by the Nepalese Government. One Nepalese soldier was killed and eighteen persons were reported to have been taken prisoner.

The incident took place at Mustang, a small trading center about 140 miles northwest of Katmandu, Nepal's capital.

The New York Times   June 30, 1930

CLASH IN HIMALAYAS: Nepal's border policemen fought Chinese Communist troops at Mustang (cross).

Story from *The New York Times,* June 30, 1960.

Fravel's, *Strong Borders, Secure Nations: Cooperation and Conflict in China's Territorial Disputes*, acclaimed in a review in *Pacific Affairs* as a 'tour de force work of scholarship.' On page 91, supported by a footnote to page 148 of the Garver book, Fravel writes, 'Subsequently, sometime in 1960, Nepal allowed China to conduct military operations against rebel groups stationed in Nepal . . .' Then on page 93, quoting from another source, and seemingly unaware of the incongruity of it, he writes, 'On June 28, 1960, Chinese and Nepalese forces clashed in the Mustang region of Nepal. At the time, PLA units were pursuing Tibetan rebel groups near the border, violating the terms of the March 1960 agreement. Chinese troops killed a Nepali border patrol officer and captured fifteen others, which threatened to become a cause for Nepal to jettison the boundary agreement.'

Fravel does at least include some details of the June 28 incident. Garver's book has a 30-page chapter on 'Indian-Chinese rivalry in Nepal.' Within this there is a lengthy section detailing the period of the late 1950s and early 1960s. It is striking that there is not a single mention of the June 28 border incident, its significant diplomatic aftermath, and the bad publicity it generated for China internationally. Instead, we are offered what is essentially a piece of fiction, culled from a manuscript of a retired Chinese diplomat, which seems to be an attempt to turn what all published sources, and all known historical scholarship, portray as a major Chinese blunder into a great Chinese triumph. The silence is all the more surprising as Garver in his text makes numerous references to Leo Rose's book, *Nepal: Strategy for Survival*, and there are other references too: 'based on a personal conversation with Leo Rose.' In the acknowledgements he thanks Rose for having read and commented on some selected sections of the draft. In his book, Rose devotes three full pages to describe the June 28 border shooting, under the heading of 'The Mustang Incident.' It is worth giving his assessment of it as a prelude to the rest of this article:

'The behaviour of both the Nepali and Chinese governments in the Mt Everest and Mustang incidents is curious indeed, and it is difficult to avoid the impression that much more lay behind these events than was apparent on the surface. Is it really possible that the Chinese expedition to Everest and the assault on an unarmed Nepali police party were unintentional infringements of Nepal's rights and sensitivities? It seems most unlikely. It is far more reasonable to presume that these were deliberate provocations carried out in such a way as to constitute a subdued but pointed reprimand to the B.P. Koirala government, and a reminder of the ease with which China could create difficulties all along the border' (229–231).

So what is the truth? Some details are still disputed, but a 1960 British Foreign Office file in the National Archives in London (FO 152554 'Political Relations China') has over 100 pages of information containing contemporaneous reports from the British ambassador and other officials. These are based on personal observations and conversations with B.P. Koirala and other political leaders and senior bureaucrats. This essay draws directly on details in the file, and also on statements and documents in *China–South Asian Relations, 1947–1980*, vol. 2, edited by Ravindra K. Jain, to describe what happened close to the Kora La Pass in northern Mustang on June 28, 1960 and to detail its diplomatic consequences. Particular reference will be made to two long reports about the incident from the British ambassador: Kathmandu Dispatch No. 28 of July 13, 1960 and Kathmandu Dispatch No. 31 of August 4, 1960.

The diplomatic build up to the incident

Three months before the incident, in March 1960, B.P. Koirala had visited China. The Chinese appeared not to be upset with him for continuing to resist their proposals to build a road from Lhasa to Kathmandu or for his criticism of China's policy in Tibet. The Chinese were receptive to his concerns about the border, and on March 21, 1960 a boundary agreement was signed that set in motion the formal process of delineation and demarcation. Article 4 of this agreement stated: 'The Contracting Parties have decided that in order to ensure tranquility and friendliness on the border, each side will no longer dispatch armed personnel to patrol the area on its side within 20 kilometres of the border, but only maintain its administrative and personnel and civil police there.' China's claim to control all of Everest had already led to anti-China demonstrations in Nepal. After the visit it was not clear if this claim had been abandoned, but on April 26, during a short visit to Kathmandu, the Chinese prime minister, Chou En-lai, announced that Mao Tse-Tung had told B.P. Koirala during a private meeting that China could follow the Nepali delineation, which showed the mountain on the boundary line, and that this was now the Chinese government's official position. Not all in Kathmandu were happy with this news as many saw it as a surrender of Nepal's claim to the whole mountain. Presumably this is why B.P. Koirala did not disclose what Mao said to him on the issue when he returned to Kathmandu. Keeping anti-China feeling simmering strengthened his hand in dealing with other Chinese demands. The papers in the embassy file speak of 'Chou En-lai being received in Kathmandu with correctness, but without enthusiasm.'

The program for the Chinese party included a visit to Pokhara. On arrival, 'the Chinese noted a group of Khampa refugees who either by accident or design were collected on the airfield, and Chou had to be hurried away, trepidation, to the King's bungalow on the shores of the lake.' His short visit included what is described as 'typical Nepalese Army entertainment during which Chou En-lai applauded the performance of one Subedar (Officer) Bam Prasad.' No one there could have imagined that just two months later the officer would be killed by Chinese bullets on the Tibetan frontier in Mustang. The Chinese pressed for the signing of a 'Treaty of Friendship and Non-Aggression,' but B.P. Koirala resisted, arguing 'it would imply some differentiation between the Chinese and others which accorded ill with Nepal's position of complete neutrality.' The Chinese had to be content with the signing of a treaty of 'Peace and Friendship.'

On the evening prior to the Chinese party's departure, a reception was held at which 'Chou En-lai turned on the charm and walked among the guests carrying a bottle of Chinese liqueur and calling on one after the other to drink, and manfully drinking glass after glass of the fire water without any apparent outward effect.' Unfortunately, all the good will achieved evaporated a few weeks later when news reached Kathmandu that a Chinese party had begun an attempt on the Everest summit on May 17 and had succeeded ten days later. The authorities in Kathmandu were upset by China's failure to seek consent to make the climb or even to inform them that it was taking place. Public opinion was inflamed and Rose has a footnote that states: 'BP Koirala told newsmen on May 28 that China was under no obligation to inform Nepal about the expedition but maintained that this did not affect his government's claim that Everest belonged to Nepal and to Nepal alone' (41, page 227). One can imagine that, given all that had gone before, this would not have been well received in Beijing.

This was the politico-strategic background to the shooting near the Kora La Pass in northern Mustang on the morning of June 28, 1960. The British embassy passed to London details of the incident as they emerged, including the ambassador's two long personal dispatches referred to earlier. The file contains details of the messages and personal letters exchanged between B.P. Koirala and Chou En-lai, beyond those that I have seen published. Some of the information came from personal briefings to the ambassador from B.P. Koirala. A major complication in handling the diplomatic aftermath was that until July 10, 1960, there was no direct diplomatic representation of Nepal in Beijing or of China in Kathmandu. All the exchanges, some oral and some written, took place in Delhi between the Chinese ambassador, Mr. Pan Tzu-li, and the Nepali ambassador, General Daman Shamsher Rana, who received his instructions from Kathmandu partly by telegraph and partly by air courier.

Details of the incident and the diplomatic aftermath

The first indication the Nepal government received of impending trouble on the frontier came from the Indian embassy on the evening of June 26. Earlier that day a message from the raja of Mustang had been transmitted by radio from the Indian checkpost in Mustang, one of eighteen that had been established in the early 1950s to cover the main passes on Nepal's northern frontier. (For details of these checkposts, see my article here.[2]) The message was a request for 500 army reinforcements to deal with the sudden appearance of a large number of Chinese troops on the border. It was not clear if an incursion had taken place. On the same day in Delhi, the Chinese ambassador verbally briefed General Daman Shamsher Rana that Chinese troops had entered the 20 kilometre zone north of the frontier because of '(a) batch of rebel bandits who are making harassment within our territory close to the Sino-Nepalese border. This not only affects local public security, but also hampers the implementation of the Sino-Nepalese Agreement on the Boundary Question. We have decided to send troops to suppress them so as to ensure tranquility on the border between the two countries and so that Sino-Nepalese friendly relations will not be affected thereby' (Jain 328). Assurances were given that the border would not be crossed in pursuit and that Chinese troops would retire beyond the 20 kilometre zone as soon as the rebels were dealt with. The Chinese Foreign Ministry on June 30 issued a long statement on the incident that included full details of this briefing. When General Daman Shamsher passed this information to Kathmandu he was instructed to protest immediately in the strongest possible terms about the violation of the demilitarized zone.

---

2   http://bit.ly/2JDnvd8

On June 27, the day after Chinese troops appeared at the border, an order was passed to the Nepal Army commander attached to the Indian checkpost for security purposes to send out a party to verify the raja's report. On the morning of June 28, the assembled group of 17 set out on horseback. Among the party were Nepal army soldiers from the checkpost security detachment, a customs officer, and some local residents, including a village headman who was familiar with the position of the traditional frontier. All were in civilian clothes and, in accordance with the border agreement with China, unarmed. On approaching the frontier they saw what they claimed were up to 2,000 Chinese soldiers. Three hundred yards short of the border, they came under fire. Subedar Bam Prasad was killed and another man wounded. The rest of the party dismounted and took what cover they could. Ten men, including the wounded man, and the horses were taken into Tibet under PLA control, as was the body of the Subedar. Six members of the party fled the scene and were able to bring the news to the outside world. By that evening full details of what had occurred had been sent to Kathmandu via the checkpost radio.

This speedy action gave the initiative to Nepal as it is clear from later events that Beijing first learned of the incident from foreign press reports. On the morning of June 29, a special air courier was sent to the Nepali embassy in Delhi with a message from B.P. Koirala to Chou En-lai. General Daman Shamsher Rana passed it to the Chinese ambassador for onward transmission to Beijing. It gave details of the incident and demanded an apology and the immediate release of all those captured. Chou En-lai's response to B.P. Koirala of June 30, is worth giving in full:

> Your Excellency's letter of June 29, 1960 reached me at 10a.m. on June 30. Before I received Your Excellency's letter, we had already learnt from foreign despatches the news that there had occurred on Sino-Nepalese border the killing of a Nepalese national by Chinese troops.
>
> The Chinese Government is much concerned about this and has immediately contacted the local authorities for finding out the truth of this matter.
>
> The Government of Nepal will be immediately informed as soon as a report is received.
>
> If the unfortunate incident of the killing of a Nepalese national referred to in Your Excellency's letter is true, the Chinese Government will express its deep regret. If it has actually happened

that any Nepalese nationals have been detained, they will of course be released expeditiously. (Jain 350)

The details and tone of this letter were reflected in the official statement issued on June 30 by the Chinese Foreign Ministry. The statement said, 'According to foreign news agency reports of June 29, an incident took place on the Sino-Nepalese border on June 28, in which Chinese troops killed and captured personnel of the Nepalese side. The Chinese government is deeply surprised at the news and extremely concerned over it.' The statement also repeated details from both B.P. Koirala's message and Chou En-lai's letter.

These were the opening salvos, and more exchanges were soon to follow. The first was a long letter from Chou En-lai on July 2:

I suppose Your Excellency has received my reply of June 30. The Chinese Government has now received a report from the frontier guards in the ARI district of China's Tibet Region on the recent incident on the Sino-Nepal border. The course of the incident was as follows:

At 16.45 hour on June 28 a unit of the Chinese People's Liberation Army suppressing Tibetan rebel bandits within our territory near the Sino-Nepal boundary discovered, at about one kilometer north of the Kore Pass, a group of men with horses advancing towards it. Mistaking them for Tibetan rebel bandits, the Chinese troops fired, killing one man, and captured ten (one of whom was wounded). It was then found that they were not Tibet's rebel bandits but were Nepalese. It can be seen from the above factual account that was an unfortunate incident resulting entirely from misunderstanding.

This incident occurred at the point north of the Kore Pass, but not in the Mustang Area. According to the maps, exchanged between the Chinese and Nepal side in March this year, the Kore Pass lies to the north of the Sino-Nepal traditional boundary line. Therefore, the place of the incident is clearly within Chinese territory, and Chinese troops have not entered territory of the Kingdom of Nepal. Nevertheless this unexpected unfortunate incident was due to carelessness on the part of certain low ranking personnel of Chinese troops. The Chinese Government expresses deep regret at this, apologizes to His Majesty's Government of Nepal and condoles on the unfortunate death. The Chinese

Government has already instructed the troops in the locality to look at once into responsibility for the incident and to escort the 10 Nepalese personnel detained and send the dead body, together with the horses of these Nepalese personnel and all the articles taken along by them to Manipuri, 150 metres south-east of the Kore Pass at 1200 hours, Peking time on July 4. It is requested that the Nepalese side will send responsible personnel there at that time to take them back. The Chinese Government is also willing to accept compensation demand made by the Nepalese side. (Jain 331–333)

On July 4, immediately after this letter was released publicly, The Guardian newspaper carried a story titled 'A Chinese apology,' which began: 'An apology from the Chinese Government is almost as rare and splendid as the phoenix, and Mr. Chou En-lai, in his letter to the Prime Minister of Nepal, has turned his hand to this unaccustomed literary form with exquisite art. We are profoundly sorry, he says in effect, and it is such a pity that it is all your fault.' As will become clear, this characterization is a reasonably accurate summation of the position maintained by the Chinese in the aftermath of the shooting.

Another letter from Chou En-lai reached Kathmandu on July 4 carrying the message that there were no longer any Chinese troops within 10 kilometres of the border. B.P. Koirala replied to both letters on July 7. This is a summary of what he wrote:

In his reply to Mr. Chou En-lai, Mr. Koirala strongly protested against Chinese violation of the Sino-Nepal Border Agreement concluded in March 1960 and demanded that Chinese troops should immediately withdraw from the demilitarized zone. The letter referred to the Nepal Government's serious concern over the reported Chinese military build-up in the demilitarized zone in contravention of the Border Agreement, where it was clearly laid down that no armed forces would be deployed within 20 kilometres of the Nepal-Tibet frontier and that no military patrols would be undertaken. While appreciating the tone of the letters from Mr. Chou En-lai offering apologies for the Mustang incident, the letter said that there was absolutely no justification for the Chinese entry into the demilitarized zone without prior consent. It re-affirmed Nepal's strict adherence to the Border Agreement and asked China also to scrupulously comply with its terms. It rejected once again China's contention that the incident of June 28 resulting in the death of one Nepali and capture of ten others, took place within Chinese territory. This, it said, happened well within Nepal territory (Jain 333).

Details of a further communication from B.P. Koirala are given in Dispatch 28 of July 13, 1960, which states:

> On the 11th of July, yet another Nepalese note complained that Chinese troops were still at Rasuwa, Riu and Larkya, all within a short distance of the frontier, and that Chinese troops had actually crossed the frontier at the Namja Pass and Mala Kharka, in which areas, the Nepalese claim there has been no Khampa activity. B.P. Koirala took time to compose a formal reply to this letter. The captured men were duly returned on July 4, and the body of Subedar Bam Prasad was cremated in Mustang on the 5th with military honours.

In Dispatch 31 of August 4, 1960, the ambassador comments further on the context and content of this letter. He writes that the information of what was in this note had been given to him by the foreign secretary and that the exchange of these particular letters had not been published, 'in the interest of keeping the temperature down and of not exacerbating the Chinese unduly.' The dispatch said that in the note B.P. Koirala had also asked 'why the ten prisoners taken at Mustang had been interrogated and been forced to sign statements and what these statements contained. Mr Chou's reply, dated 26th of July which is at present before the Nepalese cabinet, asserts that the men seen on the frontier were civilians, apologizes for 'the mistake' of interrogating the prisoners and gives a somewhat curious assurance that the signed statements (the contents of which were not explained) will never be used against His Majesty's Nepalese Government.' (Presumably the information about the interrogations and statements came from the released prisoners who would have told the Nepali authorities exactly what they had been forced to sign.)

It is not surprising, given the anger against China that was prevalent in Kathmandu at the time, that the details of these two exchanges, notably the interrogation of the prisoners and the fact that they were forced to sign statements, were not generally known. It is a reasonable assumption that what the Chinese would have wanted in the statements was a confession that the incident had taken place on Chinese territory, hence the ambassador's reference to 'the curious assurance.' He could well have been hinting, with some justification, that it read like a veiled threat.

Chou En-lai replied to B.P. Koirala's letter of July 7 in a long letter dated July 12, 1960. The key paragraphs follow:

> Your Excellency's two messages dated July 7 have been received. In your message, Your Excellency made a demand for compensation to the value of Rs. 50,000 for the losses incurred by the Nepalese side in the recent incident on the Sino-Nepalese border. The Chinese Government accepts this demand, and will remit the sum to His Majesty's Government of Nepal in the immediate future. . . .
>
> Your Excellency has in your message once again referred to the question of the place where this unfortunate incident occurred. I would like to reiterate to Your Excellency that the Chinese Government has confirmed, through repeated investigations, including on-the-spot investigations, that the Chinese troops engaged in suppressing rebel bandits operated in Chinese territory north of the Sino-Nepalese boundary and that this unfortunate incident in fact occurred at a place about one kilometre north of the Kore Pass within Chinese territory. Now, since the matter has concluded and Chinese Government has borne its due responsibility for the incident, I believe Your Excellency will surely agree that it would be meaningless and unprofitable for the two sides to continue to argue over the place of the incident.
>
> As regards the entry of Chinese in areas close to the Sino-Nepalese boundary to suppress Tibetan rebel bandits, it was notified to His Majesty's Government of Nepal beforehand on June 26 by the Chinese Government. In the notification, the Chinese Government specially emphasized that the Chinese troops would by no means cross the boundary to pursue the rebel bandits and that as soon as the task of suppressing them was completed, the Chinese troops would withdraw from the areas within twenty kilometres on the Chinese side of the boundary. This fully shows that the Chinese Government respects the Agreement on the Boundary Question and attaches great importance to Sino-Nepalese friendship. His Majesty's Government of Nepal announced on June 28 that it had received the above-mentioned notification of the Chinese Government which was given rather late, only one day remove from the day the Chinese troops began their suppressing operations. His Majesty's Government of Nepal was faced

with difficulties and could not in time issue orders to make necessary arrangements in the areas on the Nepalese side of the boundary. This should be deemed a shortcoming. . . . (Jain 333–334)

In Dispatch 31 of August 4, the British ambassador records:

The existence of this letter became generally known in Kathmandu from about 16th of July, but the Government were strangely reticent about it for a week, although indications of the rough tenor of its contents leaked out. Its ultimate publication in the press revealed no compelling reason for this reticence, but I can only assume that the Prime Minister thought that the problem of replying to it raised questions of policy sufficiently serious to require careful deliberation with his ministers unaffected by the clamour of public comment. The problem lay in striking the right balance between conciliation and firmness, between the danger of offending China, against which Nepal is materially defenceless, and that of appearing too weak in the eyes of an excited public, of a watchful India only too prone to intervene and indeed, once again, of a China only too likely to take advantage of any obvious sign of weakness.

In his reply, sent on the 24th of July and revealed to Parliament on the following day, I think that Mr. Koirala has continued wisely, as before, *fortiter in re, suaviter in modo. (Firm in action, gentle in manner.)* In the light of the compensation paid and the Chinese admission of carelessness among low-ranking troops he is willing to agree that further argument about the location of the incident would be fruitless, but he maintains the claim that the incident occurred in Nepal and that incursion into the 20 Km. demilitarized zone was a violation of China's agreement with Nepal and an action that should not be repeated without prior Nepalese agreement. He reciprocates Mr. Chou's views on Sino-Nepalese friendship, with the added barb that this is vital for the peace of Asia and for the peace of the world.

The tone is that of equal speaking to equal and this can hardly be very acceptable to the Chinese. This tone does not in my view reflect undue confidence in interpreting Chinese policy.

Below are some verbatim extracts from B.P. Koirala's letter of July 24:

It gives me much pleasure to acknowledge receipt of Your

Excellency's letter of July 12 1960, the contents of which have had my thorough and careful perusal.

In the first place I want to express my thanks for the promptitude of the Chinese Government in remitting a sum of Rs. 50,000 which we demanded as a token compensation for the material damages caused by the border accident (sic) in the Mustang Area. His Majesty's Government of Nepal appreciates this readiness in paying reparation as evidence of your desire to maintain and further consolidate the friendship between our two countries.

As regards the place of incident it appears that the view of our two sides are at variance. But when I consider that the Chinese Government have stated that the incident has taken place on account of the carelessness of low ranking personnel of the Chinese Army and that Chinese Government have borne their responsibility, I agree with your view that it would not serve any gainful purpose to continue arguing over the incident. I want to place on record however that nothing has given His Majesty's Government reason to change their stand that the incident took place on Nepalese territory.

In Your Excellency's letter reference is made to the notification to His Majesty's Government of June 26th concerning the entry of Chinese troops within an area of 20 kilometres from the border.

Your Excellency has admitted as a shortcoming that the notification took place only one day before the military actions started. In this connection I would recall that immediately upon the receipt of the notification of June 26 His Majesty's Government have expressed the view that this unilateral decision on the part of the Chinese Government amounted to the violation of the Agreement on Boundary Question. While, therefore appreciating your frank admission of the shortcoming of the Chinese Government in regard to the short notice at which the action was taken, I would also emphasize that the unilateral action has in itself been a shortcoming on the part of the Chinese Government. Your Excellency will certainly agree with me that any unilateral action from either Government is definitely against not only the words but also the spirit of the Agreement. (Jain 336–337)

Dispatch 28 of July 13, 1960 also gave some interesting insights into B.P. Koirala's thinking at the time and the relevant paragraph is worth quoting in full:

The Prime Minister has been meticulously careful to brief his small diplomatic corps about the uncertain development of events and has received all four resident ambassadors at Kathmandu successively on two separate occasions. His own view is that the incident was genuinely the result of a misunderstanding. He argues that if it were part of a deliberate policy of probing partly to find weak spots and test reactions, and partly to create and nourish a continual ferment of unease in this part of the world, the Chinese would have played a more procrastinating game. Subject to the apology which he has now received, and the compensation of which he has the promise, he was prepared to regard the incident as closed. He agrees that it might be unwise to press the Chinese to the point of their losing face more than they had already done by admitting error and tendering apology. Nevertheless, he is strongly pressing the point about the location of the incident, Chinese insistence on which has probably caused them more damage than any other aspect of the whole affair.

Where was Subedar Bam Prasad killed?

The last point made by B.P. Koirala to the ambassadors was loudly echoed by other prominent people in Kathmandu and in the local media. It is clear that China's sustained and vehement insistence that Subedar Bam Prasad had been killed on Chinese territory is what irked the Nepalis most during this whole affair. Looking at the evidence, even over this distance of time, this was understandable. A local village headman, who was familiar with the position of the traditional frontier, had been included in the unarmed party sent to investigate the sudden arrival of the mass of Chinese troops. The small group who were able to escape capture reported within hours of the killing that they were fired on as they approached the Chinese troops on the frontier. They estimated the distance as 300 metres inside Nepali territory. On the other hand, all of Kathmandu knew that the Chinese government had first learned of the incident from the international media more than 24 hours after it happened and that for subsequent information it had to rely on local PLA commanders who in addition to being unfamiliar with the precise position of the frontier also knew their men had made a serious mistake that was very likely to lead to them being severely chastised for landing their government in a diplomatic mess. In sum, these were hardly men who could be trusted to give an independent and objective assessment.

So where was the Subedar killed? In answering this, I have been greatly helped by Galen Murton who has generously allowed me to use his photos of the area of the Kora La, and has shared his local knowledge with me. I am most grateful to him for his unstinting help though, clearly, responsibility for all judgments offered rests with me alone.

The Nepali case is clear-cut. What of the Chinese claim? A summation of it, based on what Chou En-lai wrote in his letters to B.P. Koirala, is as follows:

> At 16.45 hour on June 28 a unit of the Chinese People's Liberation Army suppressing Tibetan rebel bandits within our territory near the Sino-Nepal boundary discovered, at about one kilometer north of the Kore Pass, a group of men with horses advancing towards it. Mistaki 1 ng them for Tibetan rebel bandits, the Chinese troops fired . . .
>
> This incident occurred at the point north of the Kore Pass, but not in the Mustang Area. According to the maps, exchanged between the Chinese and Nepal side in March this year, the Kore Pass lies to the north of the Sino-Nepal traditional boundary line. Therefore, the place of the incident is clearly within Chinese territory . . .
>
> I would like to reiterate to Your Excellency that the Chinese Government has confirmed, through repeated investigations, including on-the-spot investigations, that the Chinese troops engaged in suppressing rebel bandits operated in Chinese territory north of the Sino-Nepalese boundary and that this unfortunate incident in fact occurred at a place about one kilometer north of the Kore Pass within Chinese territory.

The Nepalis also agreed that the maps exchanged in March 1960 showed that the Kora Pass lay to the north of the Sino-Nepal traditional boundary line. There was no dispute on this point. That said, Chou En-lai's references to the maps do not appear to help the Chinese case in any way. Article III of the Nepal-China Border Treaty, signed on March 21, 1960, begins: 'Having studied the delineation of the boundary line between the two countries as shown on the maps mutually exchanged (for the maps submitted by the Chinese side, see attached Map 1; for the map submitted by the Nepalese side, see attached Map 2) and the information furnished by each side about the actual jurisdiction over the area bordering on the other country, the Contracting Parties deem that, except for discrepancies in certain sections, their understanding of the traditional customary line is basically the same.'

I doubt if the precision claimed by Chou En-lai was possible with either of these two single maps. If 'one map' covered the entire frontier, it must have been on a very large scale. The 1961 maps, associated with the China-Nepal Treaty of October 5, 1961, but not referred to in the text of the treaty, had a scale of 1:500,000. Seven such maps were needed to cover the frontier. The detail on them is still hard to define with straight lines drawn between many features, rather than, for example, following ridges. This was understandable as, at this stage, the border had not been demarcated. It is only with the 1:50,000 scale maps that were integral to the China-Nepal Boundary Protocol of January 20, 1963 that more precise definition becomes possible. This protocol fixed the exact location of all 79 concrete border markers, including Number 24, at a distance of 2.7 kilometres north of the Kora La.

In sum, the Chinese, like the Nepalis, probably had to rely on a local man, perhaps a trader or herder, to show them the traditional border which fell south of the Kora La. But precisely where? This Google Earth screenshot below is a helpful introduction to the local terrain.

The 'Kora la large chorten' is on the pass itself, at a distance of 2.77 kilometres south of where the 1963 Protocol placed Border Pillar Number 24. According to Galen Murton, the Kora La is not a pass in the typical sense of there being a steep approach from either side, but rather

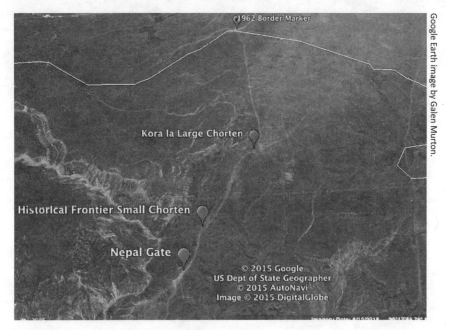

a general space at which the climb from the Mustang Valley (which runs from Lo Manthang up through Choser and Nyechung) reaches the Tibetan Plateau and levels off. What is labeled as 'Historical Frontier Small Chorten' is most likely, according to the maps exchanged between China and Nepal in March 1960, to have been the point that marked the traditional frontier. The distance between the two chortens is 1.5 kilometres. (The screenshot aspect is deceptive.) The 'Nepal Gate' was built nine years ago by the Nepal government, in a meaningless position historically, against the wishes of the local people, but no doubt at some great cost. It is located 600 metres south of the small chorten. It is a very steep climb from the gate to the chorten. (A Mustang source indicates that locals may have recently 'dismantled' the monument with a view to building another one in a more significant position.)

The following photographs help support my estimate of where Bam Prasad was killed. They also show how weak and inconsistent the Chinese claim was.

The photo below, looking northwest to north, shows the main chorten on the Kora La. North therefore is to the right. From this point it is a distance of 2.7 kilometres to the present border marker. To the south it is a distance of 1.5 kilometres to the small chorten that marked the traditional boundary.

Galen Murton

Galen Murton

The photograph above, taken from the Kora La, looking north to northwest, more than any other, demolishes the repeated Chinese claims that Subedar Bam Prasad was shot 1 kilometre north of the Kora La; in other words, from where this photograph was taken. A number of questions highlight this. The unarmed Nepali party knew the line of the traditional boundary at the small chorten. They would have known that the PLA soldiers were first seen at that point, and they would have expected to meet them in the same area. The reports of thousands of PLA soldiers being present had already engendered considerable fear among the local residents. Why would this small unarmed group have ridden past the small chorten that they knew marked the traditional frontier and then past the large chorten on the Kora La into this totally featureless terrain? Common sense dictates that they would not have done so. On the PLA side, why would they have been in a defensive position in this terrain from where, looking south, they could see nothing at all of the frontier which they were supposed to be guarding? There is surely only one place where they would have been: on the frontier by the small chorten where they could at least see the approaches to the border from the Nepali side. The photograph shows Chou En-lai's impressive sounding words that the Chinese government has confirmed through 'repeated investigations, including on-the-spot investigations' that the Subedar was killed 1 kilometre north from where this photo

Galen Murton

was taken, are, in terms of both good military practice and common sense, to be no more than bombast.

The above photograph, looking south, shows the view from Kora La toward the small chorten that marked the traditional frontier, 1.5 kilometres away. Its location is round to the left beyond the bend of the gentle descent seen in the photo.

Galen Murton

The photograph in the preceding page, looking south toward the Annapurna and Dhaulagiri ranges, shows the small chorten that marked the traditional frontier. It is located at the point where the climb from the Mustang Valley (from the right) begins to level out. The steep descent toward Lo Manthang starts from the end of the short stretch of level snow-covered road on the right, which is better seen in the photograph above.

Any PLA force deployed to the border for observation or guarding would have had to position a proportion of the force on the steep slopes forward of this point to see the trail from Nepali territory and to offer an effective defense. It is likely, therefore, that it was on these forward slopes, just ahead of where the photo above was taken, that the PLA soldiers were first seen by the raja of Mustang's men and, two days later, by the small party led by Subedar Bam Prasad. From this small chorten it is a very gentle climb to the large chorten marking what is generally accepted to be the historical Kora La.

The photograph on the following page, looking north, shows the 'Nepal Gate.' The small chorten lies about 600 metres to the north. It is along this trail that the unarmed party sent to investigate the arrival of PLA soldiers on the frontier would have traveled. After they rode round the bend to the right, they would have hit the steep ascent toward the traditional frontier marked by the chorten. It is most likely, at a point 300

Galen Murton

meters from the top, probably just as they saw the PLA soldiers massed on the forward slopes in front of the point that marked the frontier, that they were fired on. Subedar Bam Prasad was killed instantly and another member of the party was wounded. The party would have dismounted rapidly, but the PLA soldiers must have moved quickly down the slope to capture ten of them. Fortunately for Nepal, six members of the party reacted even more speedily and made their escape on their horses down this track to give the news of what had happened to Kathmandu, and ultimately to the outside world, before anyone in Beijing was alerted to the incident. That detail raises yet another question. Why was the information relayed back to Beijing so slowly? Why did it require a prompt from the Chinese authorities to elicit the detail required? This reluctance to report is not, to say the least, what you would expect from military commanders who were confident that they had acted properly and had nothing to fear.

Is it possible that this incident influenced China to be more generous to Nepal when it came to settling the 1963 border demarcation? As map on the following page shows, Border Pillar Number 24 is 4.2 kilometres north of where the maps exchanged by Nepal and China as part of March 1960 Boundary Agreement showed the border to be, and 2 kilometres north of where China falsely, in my view, said that that Subedar Bam Prasad was shot. As can be seen, seven of the 79 border markers

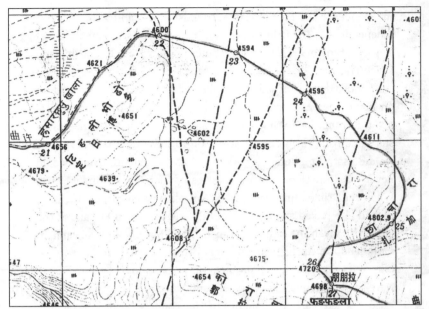

Map showing Border Pillars 21 to 27 in northern Mustang.

demarcate this short stretch of the border, which, at the very least, suggests a determination that there should be no more 'carelessness on the part of certain low ranking personnel of Chinese troops' on this part of the frontier.

The impact of the killing within Nepal

Any account of this incident would be deficient unless it included details of its impact on the people of Mustang and on the political debate in Kathmandu. Great anger was expressed about the killing on the streets of Kathmandu, exacerbated by the repeated Chinese claims that the killing had taken place on Chinese territory. The local media gave full vent to this. The tone was set by a statement in the Nepalese Senate on July 1 by Home Minister S. P. Upadhyaya, extracts of which are given here:

> The Government had received a report that the Chief of Mustang had fled the territory after the Chinese attack on June 28 and that the people, in panic, were fleeing to the south.
> He said that the Government had decided to strengthen the border defences as it felt that no friendship was greater than 'our

independence and for the sake of friendship we cannot sacrifice our independence'. The firing on and killing of Nepalese and violation of Nepalese territory had been the Chinese reply to 'our Friendship and Peace Treaty'.

He added that Nepal had known about the Chinese military build-up on her border and near it. The Government had received reports about it from time to time and was all the time taking the necessary steps and had drawn China's attention to these reports. 'Every time we did that, the Chinese assured us that the Chinese troops would never cross into Nepal and always stressed their friendship for Nepal. When the Prime Minister, Mr. B.P. Koirala, visited earlier this year, he had also talked about this build-up with Mr Chou En-lai and the latter had given the same assurance. Then, Mr. Chou En-lai came to Kathmandu in April, 1960, and again this issue was discussed with him, and again the same assurance was given. And so, foreign bullets were fired upon unarmed Nepalese and killed one of them.'

He warned 'certain elements in the country' against acts 'that might be treason'. There might be some elements in the country who would under-rate the incident but he would warn them that his Government would not tolerate such 'treason'.

He declared that Nepal demanded every satisfaction and reserved the right to claim compensation, the return of the body of the Nepalese official killed and those captured by Chinese.

He said that his report was that the 17 captured Nepalese and their horses had been taken to the Brahmaputra Headquarters of the Chinese Army. The body of the Subedar (officer) killed had been dragged to the Tibetan side of the border.' (Jain 330–331)

Media reaction to the incident and the political turmoil it generated are well covered in the two long personal dispatches from the ambassador, as illustrated by these verbatim extracts from Dispatch 28 of July 13:

The local Nepalese newspapers have been uninhibited in their nationalistic sentiments. The change that has come over the tone of the press is remarkable and might indeed have gone further but for the obvious tendency of Indian journalists to egg their Nepalese colleagues on even further by an annoying post-facto assumption of greater knowledge of the true nature of Chinese aggressiveness. In Parliament too, where the opposition forced a debate, feeling against the Chinese ran high. The leader of the Opposition, Bharat Shamsher, claimed that the violation of the border was deliberate and demanded stronger military precautions and the cancellation of the frontier agreement with China. Some leading members of the ruling Nepali Congress have been much more outspoken than their leader and this has given rise once again to the suggestion that there is a difference of opinion in the party. It may be, however, that Mr. Koirala is quite happy to have his men cry halloo while he himself assumes an Olympian air of comparative detachment and calm consideration.

The Communists have naturally been calling for a more measured approach to the incident and have been making what excuses they could for the Chinese but, for once, they appear to have been silenced by a fairly general flood of execration. Some Communists, including even one Senator, were in fact arrested by the police after public speeches on the subject and, except for the Senator, remain in jail.

Meanwhile, the border area remains disturbed. The population of Mustang apparently showed a tendency to move south, the Raja himself having reportedly set the example. This might give rise to a difficult situation in view of the doctrine of effective administration rashly included in the border agreement. Troops from Pokhara have, however, been moved into the Mustang salient to reassure the people and a three day air-lift (of some 18 Dakota sorties) has taken place thus depleting the Pokhara garrison. The delicate economic balance of the frontier area, already seriously disturbed by Chinese measures in Tibet, must have suffered further deterioration and it is significant that the government are already seeking new sources of supply of salt. Refugees too, about whose existence the Nepalese Government has hitherto been very reticent, have been coming into Nepal from the north in increasing numbers. Official reticence has been largely ascribable to the lack of suitable land, not already occupied by Nepalese, for the settlement of refugees and to the obvious difficulties of caring actively for the refugees when the Government can do so little for its own citizens.

At the moment of going to press, the latest atmosphere regarding the Mustang incident is given in a report of yesterday's debate in the senate in which Mr. Subba Shamsher of the Gorkha Parishad, the main opposition party, deplored the incident, described it as an aggression and an offence to the sovereignty of Nepal, stated that apology alone was not enough, demanded the surrender to Nepal of the guilty person and tabled a motion on military security provisions for the northern frontier. Mr. Lakshman Jang Bahadur, a nominated senator, asked the government to say whether or not the Chinese action constituted an act of aggression. If so, he went on to say 'We must fight it to the last drop of our blood'. This view was widely supported. Mr. Shambu Ram Shrestha, the Communist Senator who was arrested for a few hours after the incident, deplored the happenings in Mustang but pointed out that the Chinese had already apologized. If the Khampas had been carrying out military activity from Nepalese soil action should be taken against them. Replying, the Prime Minister said that there was no reason why the Mustang incident should embitter relations with China. The Chinese Government had apologized. Their assertion that the events took place in Chinese territory seemed to have been based on an incorrect report. There would be no rupture of relations between China and Nepal. He was satisfied with his correspondence with Mr. Chou. The motion was defeated.

Mr. Koirala appears to me to be handling this matter with much skill and a nicely calculated balance of conciliation and firmness, both applied in exactly the right places.

Further insight on media comments is given in Dispatch 31 of August 4:

The press, unconstrained by the responsibility which weighs upon the Prime Minister continues to be heavily critical of China. The compensation paid has been described as 'smacking of the arrogance of an unrepentant big brother'. Faith in Chinese assurances, in spite of honeyed Chinese words, remains generally shaken. The right-wing newspaper Rastrabandi, taking its cue from Bharat Shamsher the leader of the opposition, demands that Nepal should revoke the broken frontier agreement, defend her borders and join other countries in South East Asia to face Chinese expansion. The opposition are making the most of reports of further Chinese incursions, removal of boundary stones and tales by refugee Tibetans, to all of which the Prime Minister presents a stolid defence of lack of confirmation. I have not, however, seen any attempt to deny reports of increasing Chinese military concentrations at such places as Tingri, Rongbuk, Kyirang and Khojarnath.

The many instances of high praise for B.P. Koirala stand out in all the ambassador's dispatches. King Mahendra is never mentioned, so what of him during the period? He had left Kathmandu for a visit to Japan and the United States on April 10, 1960. He returned to Kathmandu on July 28. There is no record of him expressing any views on how B.P. Koirala handled this affair, but on all previous form he was unlikely to have enjoyed the praise lavished on him. Before departing for a state visit to the United Kingdom on October 6, 1960, he had already decided to seize absolute power by means of a coup using the instrument of the army. The political brief for his visit from the British Foreign Office stated that the B.P. Koirala–led government 'has shown a welcome determination to tackle the difficult problems with which they are faced in trying to create a modern system of administration and to bring about social and economic reforms in an extremely backward country. There is little doubt that this Government represents Nepal's best hope for the future.' Thirty-six days after his return on December 15, 1960, Mahendra launched his coup, which ultimately gave him absolute authority over the entire machinery of government. B.P. Koirala and most of his ministers were arrested and jailed; in the deposed prime minister's case, indefinitely. Reading through the annual British embassy reports written during the 1960s, concern about Gurkha recruiting appeared to be all that mattered: there is barely a word for the incarcerated B.P. Koirala, and of sympathy, none. So much for the man whom British diplomats lavished so much praise on for his handling of the Mustang incident and whose government they judged to represent Nepal's best hope for the future. So much for *fortiter in re, suaviter in modo*! (See my article here[3] for details of Mahendra's U.K. visit and coup.)

The assessment of Leo Rose?
In the light of all of the above, how do we assess the views of Leo Rose (given earlier but repeated here for ease of reference)?

> The behaviour of both the Nepali and Chinese governments in the Mt Everest and Mustang incidents is curious indeed, and it is difficult to avoid the impression that much more lay behind these events than was apparent on the surface. Is it really possible that the Chinese expedition to Everest and the assault on an unarmed Nepali police party were unintentional infringements of Nepal's rights and

---

3   https://www.recordnepal.com/wire/maharaja-and-monarch-0/

sensitivities? It seems most unlikely. It is far more reasonable to presume that these were deliberate provocations carried out in such a way as to constitute a subdued but pointed reprimand to the BP Koirala government, and a reminder of the ease with which China could create difficulties all along the border.

In his meeting with the Kathmandu ambassadors, reported in Dispatch 28 of July 13, 1960, B.P. Koirala entertained no such thoughts or doubts about Chinese motivations. His view was that 'the incident was genuinely the result of a misunderstanding. He argues that if it were part of a deliberate policy of probing partly to find weak spots and test reactions, and partly to create and nourish a continual ferment of unease in this part of the world, the Chinese would have played a more procrastinating game.'

Perhaps he was correct but, having looked at all the evidence, it is hard to dismiss Rose's view as being entirely without foundation. As outlined in the introduction to this essay, B.P. Koirala had given the Chinese plenty of cause to believe that their interests in Nepal would be better served by a prime minister or head of state who was more responsive to their needs rather than, as they saw it, to India's. We can assume that the killing of the Subedar was a mistake and not part of any plan. As Chou En-lai wrote in his letter of July 2, 'this unexpected unfortunate incident was due to carelessness on the part of certain low ranking personnel of Chinese troops.'

Doubt stems from two questions. First, what was the real reason for the Chinese deploying large numbers of troops across such a wide stretch of the Nepali frontier in June 1960? Second, where is the evidence for all these 'Tibetan rebel bandits' that Chou En-lai makes so much of in his letters, who allegedly were operating just north of Mustang and in adjacent areas?

Resistance to the Chinese invasion of Tibet was at its strongest in Kham in eastern Tibet, and gradually spread west toward Lhasa. CIA support to the resistance started in the mid 1950s with the recruitment of some Tibetan refugees in India for training in Colorado prior to inserting them back into Tibet by parachute to make contact with local resistance groups and assess their armament needs. This was followed by numerous airdrops of weapons and other military supplies, mostly well to the east of Lhasa. However, by mid 1960, in the face of a fierce and highly effective Chinese military reaction, based on the deployment of large numbers of highly trained combat troops and a rapid road building program, resistance within Tibet had mostly come to an end, and the CIA-inserted agents were either killed or had withdrawn to India. Other guerrillas also made their way back into India. It was a very long way to reach west Nepal from the main centers of the resistance. Escape through India offered a much shorter route. Refugees had started to come from Tibet into places like Mustang and Dolpo after the flight of the Dalai Lama to India on March 31, 1959, and armed bands of brigands had been a problem in the areas north of both districts for many years and may well have been among them. Some isolated groups of the Chushi Gangdrug, like the Nam Tso group, may have escaped this way but very few, and by mid 1960 they would have been in no state, either in terms of morale or firepower, to take offensive action against PLA soldiers, nor make any raids from Nepali territory. As stated earlier, there is no record of any such raids before 1961.

How did the situation portrayed justify the deployment of thousands of troops to the Mustang border in June 1960, and to other adjacent areas as highlighted in B.P. Koirala's letters? And how do we explain the great fuss that Chou En-lai made about it in his letters to the Nepali prime minister? By this stage, the Chinese knew that the center of Tibetan resistance outside Tibet was in the Darjeeling-Kalimpong area of India. Nepal was not involved in any way. What is most striking is the stark contrast on the one hand between this loud public protestation when the threat from Nepali territory was minimal, and on the other the prolonged public silence during King Mahendra's period as an absolute ruler when the Chinese knew that from 1961 Mustang was being used as a base for raids against PLA targets in Tibet, and that from April 1964 Tibetan agents trained by the CIA were being infiltrated into Tibet from northeast Nepal.

It is possible that the primary aim of this large deployment of troops was to secure and close the border areas as a means of signaling and establishing Chinese control. From the earliest stages of its military occupation of Tibet, China's cutting off of Tibet's traditional commercial links with Nepali traders in the areas of the northern border was a high priority. By doing this, China achieved another of its main objectives: establishing total control over Tibet's nomadic population. However, Article IV of the China-Nepal Boundary Agreement specifically banned armed personnel from operating within 20 kilometres of the border. This would have left the main passes clear for cross-border trade to continue on the same basis as before, something that China was determined to stop. Even though there was an assurance that Chinese troops would withdraw after 'the suppression of the rebel bandits,' this would again leave the passes open. Perhaps, therefore, the repeated stress in Chou En-lai's letters on the threat posed by these 'Tibetan rebel bandits making harassment within our territory' was intended to provide a cover to circumvent the 20 kilometre border restriction zone. It also had the additional advantages of distracting attention from the killing of the unarmed Subedar and of weakening and embarrassing B.P. Koirala. From what is published, no definitive judgment can be made on any of these issues, but, in the circumstances described, Leo Rose's word 'curious' does seem to be particularly apt.

I am most grateful to Galen Murton for allowing me to use his excellent photos of the area of the Kora La, and for so generously sharing his local knowledge with me.

This article has been republished with permission from *The Record*. The original can be found online at: https://www.recordnepal.com/ wire/curious-case-mustang-incident/

Addendum May 2018

As highlighted, M. Taylor Fravel, in his book, *Strong Borders, Secure Nations: Cooperation and Conflict in China's Territorial Disputes*, repeats Garver's claim about China's large scale incursion into Nepal in 1960 and gives details of the 28 June 1960 Mustang incident. (p. 91) He also records that, 'According to a Chinese Diplomat, the PLA conducted additional operations against Tibetan rebels in Nepal in June 1964.' His source for this information is pages 324 and 325 of a book written by Yang Gongsu: '*Zhongguo fandui waiguo qinlue ganshe Xizang difang douzheng shi* (History of China's Struggle against Foreign Aggression and Intervention in Tibet) which was published in Beijing by Zangxue chubanshe in 1992.' Yang Gongsu is the diplomat who Garver says shared with him the manuscript which contained the allegation about the 1000-man PLA incursion in 1960. It is worth noting that Garver's book was published in 2001, nine years after the publication of Yang Gongbu's book, yet I can find no reference to it in Garver's book. Note also that by saying, 'additional operations..... in Nepal', Taylor Flavel is again taking Garver's account of the large

1960 PLA incursion into Nepal as a given, and is indicating that a similar incursion took place inside Nepal in 1964.

To get more details of these alleged additional PLA operations in Nepal in 1964, I had the relevant chapter of Yang Gongsu's book professionally translated. The chapter is headed, 'New relationships develop between Tibet Autonomous Region of China and Nepal.' The major part of the chapter is devoted to describing how China and Nepal collaborated to resolve their border differences, work which led to the signing in January 1963 of the China-Nepal Boundary Treaty. Pages 324 and 325 fall under a short final section headed, 'China and Nepal coordinate to eradicate rebels in Nepal territory.' The first part describes the build-up, 'aided by American and Indian reactionaries', of an armed Tibetan rebel force in Mustang and the trouble caused by the cross-border raids they carried out. It is worth giving the final part of the translation in full:

'From 1963, this group of insurgents often invaded the Houzang area of Tibet, blockading highways and killing civilians. In June of the same year, they mounted a sneak attack against a PLA truck, killed several officers and raided several thousand cows and sheep. Simultaneously, they also committed robbery and even killed some Nepalese army officers and merchants. These insurgents lorded over the territory. Not only were the Nepal army and police unable to control them, even the local lord of Mustang had to submit to them. They would even disguise themselves as Nepalese civilians or army officers and cross the borders at the Kodari Mountain Pass into Tibet to kill and raid, disrupting security and sowing discord between both nations. While the PLA stationed in Tibet was patrolling the Kodari Mountain Pass, they attacked some Tibetan insurgents and mistakenly killed a Nepalese officer and twelve soldiers. The China Government investigated the situation and immediately sent an apology and a compensation of 50,000 rupees to the Nepal Government. The Nepal Government expressed their understanding and satisfaction. Since then, the China Government commanded the PLA to refrain from attacking insurgents in China within 10 kilometres from the China-Nepal border. The escaped Tibet insurgents grew even more outrageous. From 1963 onwards, they even occupied the area around Mustang, evicted the Nepalese civilians, set up their own blockade, collected taxes and declared themselves an independent kingdom. Under such circumstances, in 1964, China and Nepal negotiated on ways to collaborate to eradicate the insurgents. Nepal continued to provide intel about the insurgents' activities, and distributed a large number of recruitment pamphlets printed by the Chinese Government to the Tibetan 'refugees' living within the borders of Nepal. These pamphlets had some segregation effect and isolated the stubborn rebels. The Nepal Government also restricted the activities of the rebels, stopping them from transporting food and ammunition. The PLA stationed along the border launched an attack against these insurgents in coordination with Nepal's own army units. Through this, in June 1964, the Tibet guerrillas in the Mustang region were finally eradicated.'

As a reliable source, this is a mixed bag. No mention is made of a large-scale incursion into Nepal in 1960, yet Garver quotes Yang as the source for this claim. In addition, the prominence given to 1963 as the start of the Tibetan force's control over Mustang and of their raids into Tibet is dubious. The force was firmly established in Mustang with weapons and equipment supplied by CIA by mid 1961. A successful attack against a small PLA outpost in Tibet was carried out in September of that year. In October 1961, there was a successful ambush of a jeep carrying a PLA regimental commander, which yielded a treasure trove of secret documents. There is no record of any such raid in June 1963, as claimed by Yang. However, the incident in Mustang on 28 June 1960 is described by Yang. The Chinese apology and offer of compensation is accurately recorded but the incident took place in Mustang itself, not near the Kodari pass, and only one Nepalese was killed. Perhaps significantly, no date is given for this incident but the context wrongly suggests that it happened in 1963. It is correctly recorded that the Tibetan force was outside the control of the Nepal army and police.

The reference to 'recruitment pamphlets' printed by the Chinese government and distributed by the Nepalese to 'refugees' does not make sense. More likely, this is a reference to a pamphlet dated, 10 Dec 1963, issued in Tibetan and Chinese under the official seals of 'The Preparatory Commission for the Tibet Autonomous Region' and 'The Tibetan Military Region of the People's Liberation Army.' I have a copy culled from a British Foreign Office file. It was attached to a letter the British ambassador sent to London, on August 10, 1964. He wrote: 'The Chief of Intelligence told me that the Chinese embassy had complained to him once or twice about Khampa activities in the north – specifically, Khampa raiding – and had even, I understood, offered to send in Chinese troops to deal with the Khampas. He also said that the Chinese had appealed directly to the Khampas, and more recently they had printed this appeal in pamphlet form and given him a lot of copies for distribution to the Khampas. He had not been able to do this. I enclose two copies of the pamphlet he gave me.' The pamphlet is headed, 'Policy towards those Tibetan compatriots who took part in rebellion and fled abroad, and who wish to return to their former allegiance.' The pamphlet is clearly designed to encourage desertion. The opening paragraph reads, 'No questions will be asked of those returning to their former allegiance about the magnitude of their past evil deeds, nor will there be discussion of what their positions were; it is laid down once for all that that what is past is past.' Other paragraphs promise freedom of religious belief and rewards to those who bring back weapons and documents.

Yang is strikingly vague and brief about how the alleged eradication of the Tibetan force was achieved. No detail is given. All we have are two short sentences: *The PLA stationed along the border launched an attack against these insurgents in coordination with Nepal's own army units. Through this, in June 1964, the Tibet guerrillas in the Mustang region were finally eradicated.* In analysing these, it is pertinent to note that in Chinese no distinction is made between singular and plural nouns unless specifically indicated. Further advice from a native Chinese speaker is that in the original, no such specific indication is given. Therefore, my professional translator has erred by saying, 'an attack'. It could be one attack, or one offensive operation, or many. Yang simply does not say. Much more significantly, nowhere in the original does it say, 'in Nepal.' All Yang says is that the PLA stationed *along the border*, or *on the border*, launched an offensive operation or operations against these insurgents. This could be taken to mean, for example, an ambush or a series of ambushes carried out on the Tibetan side of the border based on good intelligence from spies. Again, Yang is not specific. Perhaps the ambiguity is deliberate, and that extends to his vagueness on timing. Is he saying that such an attack or attacks actually took place in June 1964? Or did an earlier attack or attacks lead to a situation in which the Tibetan guerrillas in the Mustang region were finally eradicated? The answer does not matter. As with the Garver claim of the attack into Nepal in 1960, there is no corroboration in any other account of the history of the period of such PLA attacks into Nepal taking place at any time, with or without Nepalese government approval, in coordination with the Nepal army or without it. It can also be stated with confidence that in the early 1960s, the Royal Nepal Army was in no position to take any action against the heavily armed guerrilla force in Mustang.

Furthermore, the claim that the Tibetan force was eradicated in June

1964 is far-fetched in the extreme. A mass of evidence indicates that the guerrillas remained a well-trained, well-armed and well-disciplined force until the late 1960s. It is true that by mid 1964 the Chinese had made it more difficult for raids to be carried out from Mustang by increasing their surveillance efforts north of the Nara la pass and by their use of spies in Mustang itself. Demonstrably, none of this required large-scale or even small-scale PLA incursions into Nepal. As a reflection of this, the CIA shifted their main point of effort in early 1964 to infiltrating small groups of Tibetan fighters into Tibet on intelligence missions from north east Nepal and India. This was run from a new joint operations centre with the Indians in New Delhi

In conclusion, first, only Garver can say why he made no reference to the 28 June 1960 incident despite its significant diplomatic aftermath or the bad'publicity it generated for China internationally. Likewise, only he can explain why he made no reference to the highly significant detail given above from Yang Gongsu's book which was published nine years before the publication of *Protracted Contest*. We can only speculate on whether this is related to Yang avoiding any specific mention of a large PLA incursion taking place into Nepal. Secondly, on M Taylor Fravel, for the reasons given above, his sentence summarizing what Yang Gangsu wrote in his book is inadequate and misleading. Only he can say why he chose to repeat without question Garver's piece of historical fiction about the PLA incursion into Mustang in 1960, and to indicate wrongly, and without justification from the source he quotes, that a similar incursion took place in an unspecified part of Nepal in 1964.

Corruption in World Football and the Fall of Ganesh Thapa

A detailed examination of how Ganesh Thapa, who had been President of the All Nepal Football Association for 20 years, was suspended by FIFA for 10 years from all football activity on multiple charges relating to corruption

nepalsportsphoto.com

Ganesh Thapa with Mohammed Bin Hammam at the opening of the Chyasal Technical Center in Kathmandu on May 14, 2005.

Ganesh Thapa was the strong man of football in Nepal for two decades. On October 24, 2013, he was re-elected as the president of the All Nepal Football Association (ANFA) for a further four-year tenure, a position he had held since 1995. In the latter part of his 20 years as president, he faced several challenges to his position by colleagues dissatisfied with his performance, but his strong grip on all levels of the organization down to district level, aided by a core of loyal officials in key positions, enabled him to thwart all efforts to unseat him.

The Mohammed Bin Hammam link

Thapa was an Executive Committee Member of the Asian Football Confederation (AFC) from 1995 to 2010 when he became a vice president of the organization. He developed a close friendship with the most powerful man in Asian football, the Qatar-born Mohammed Bin Hammam, who became the president of AFC on August 1, 2002. AFC is a 47-member organization covering a swathe of the globe from Syria to Australia. Bin Hammam was an influential figure in the International Federation of Association Football (FIFA) through being a member of its powerful 24-man Executive Committee (EXCO, now called the FIFA Council) since 1996. He is a business magnate who made his fortune in the construction industry and property.

On May 29, 2011, FIFA suspended Mohammed Bin Hammam from all positions in world football, news which should have given Ganesh Thapa some cause for concern. Bin Hammam's fall from power started when, late in the electoral process, on March 18, 2011, he declared his intention to stand against Sepp Blatter as FIFA president. The sequence of events which then led to him being banned for life is complex but the summary below is taken from an unimpeachable source: the media release of July 19, 2012 giving the decision, by a majority of 2 to 1, of the Court of Arbitration for Sport (CAS)[1] to uphold Bin Hammam's appeal against the life suspension imposed by FIFA:

> During his campaign for the FIFA presidential election, Mr. Bin Hammam attended a meeting of the Caribbean Football Union ('CFU') in Trinidad and Tobago on 10 and 11 May 2011. On 10 May 2011, he made a speech about his candidacy. Following the speech and Mr. Bin Hammam's departure from the conference room, Mr. Jack Warner, who was at the time a member of the FIFA Executive Committee, announced that there were 'gifts' for representatives of the attending associations. In the afternoon of 10 May 2011, the CFU General Secretary collected from Mr. Warner's office a locked suitcase, containing a number of unmarked envelopes, each containing USD 40,000, which were distributed to the CFU delegates on the same day.

---

1   http://www.tas-cas.org/fileadmin/user_upload/Media20Release202625.pdf

On 11 May 2011, after Mr. Bin Hammam had already left Trinidad and Tobago, Mr. Warner called an unexpected meeting during which he declared that Mr. Bin Hammam had provided money to the CFU in lieu of traditional 'gifts'. On 15 May 2011, Mr. Chuck Blazer, also a member of the FIFA Executive Committee, hired an attorney to investigate these events, who later issued a report concluding that Mr. Bin Hammam had offered bribes in order to buy votes. On 29 May 2011, the FIFA Ethics Committee announced its decision to provisionally suspend Mr. Bin Hammam from all football-related activities. Beforehand, Mr. Bin Hammam had withdrawn his candidacy for the FIFA Presidency. On 18 August 2011, the FIFA Ethics Committee informed Mr. Bin Hammam that he was banned for life further to several violations of the FIFA Code of Ethics. By decision of 15 September 2011, the FIFA Appeal Committee confirmed the sanction.

On 9 November 2011, Mr. Bin Hammam appealed the decision to the CAS.

In its full judgement giving the reasons for upholding Bin Hammam's appeal, the CAS, at Paragraph 204,[2] stated,

The Panel wishes to make clear that this conclusion should not be taken to diminish the significance of its finding that it is more likely than not that Mr. Bin Hammam was the source of the monies that were brought into Trinidad and Tobago and eventually distributed at the meeting by Mr. Warner. . . . The Panel therefore wishes to make clear that in applying the law, as it is required to do under the CAS Code, it is not making any sort of affirmative finding of innocence in relation to Mr. Bin Hammam. The Panel is doing no more than concluding that the evidence is insufficient in that it does not permit the majority of the Panel to reach the standard of comfortable satisfaction in relation to the matters on which the Appellant was charged. It is a situation of 'case not proven', coupled with concern on the part of the Panel that the FIFA investigation was not complete or comprehensive enough to fill the gaps in the record.

Immediately after the CAS decision was made public, Bin Hammam announced his resignation from all football activities but, five months

---

2   http://bit.ly/2O3EiJN

later, on Dec 17, 2012, FIFA handed him a second life ban[3] for 'repeated violations of Article 19 (Conflict of Interest) of the FIFA Code of Ethics, edition 2012, during his terms as AFC President and as member of the FIFA Executive Committee in the years 2008 to 2011.'

The audit of AFC's accounts

On **July 13, 2012,** the accountancy firm PricewaterhouseCoopers (PWC) completed an audit on AFC's finances which had clearly been initiated shortly after Bin Hammam's suspension. Its details were quickly leaked to The Associated Press (AP) and seven days later its account of what the audit revealed was widely reported. The article from Hello Khabar headed, 'ANFA president Ganesh Thapa's son received $100,000 from AFC's corruption accused prez'[4] gives details of what AP reported. The first three paragraphs state:

> Gaurav Thapa, the son of All Nepal Football Federation (ANFA) President Ganesh Thapa received $100,000 (Rs 88 lakhs) from the suspended President of Asian Football Confederation (AFC) Mohamed bin Hammam as the latter used the AFC bank accounts to enrich himself, pay for the lavish expenses of his family and hand out tens of thousands of dollars in cash to federation presidents and their relatives.
>
> The cash handed out to federation presidents and their relatives went to their personal bank accounts and none of it was for football related expenses, according to the Associated Press.
>
> In one of the biggest corruption cases to rock the football world, Hammam, the 63-year-old Qatari who was once a candidate to oust FIFA President Sepp Blatter as the sport's worldwide leader, is accused of using the AFC bank accounts to hand out hundreds of thousands of dollars to friends and relatives, according to an audit obtained by the AP.

We know that the detail in this AP report is accurate because the full PWC report was subsequently made available online.

Before examining parts of it, it is worth recording Ganesh Thapa's reported reaction:[5]

---

3 http://bit.ly/2LrIeFA
4 http://bit.ly/2zWXh5I
5 http://bit.ly/2LvHtrU

The head of the Nepal's football federation said Sunday his son had taken a loan of $100,000 from Mohamed bin Hammam but denied the money came from an Asian Football Confederation bank account.

Ganesh Thapa, the president of All Nepal Football Association, told The Associated Press his son had taken a personal loan from suspended AFC chief bin Hammam in 2009 and has already paid it back.

'It was a personal loan for a personal reason from a personal friend and it has nothing to do with football or AFC,' Thapa said Sunday, arguing it should not be scrutinized by football officials.

The son, Gaurav Thapa, has been working with AFC since 2007 and has been sent to Newcastle, England, on Olympic duty working as assistant manager of a football venue.

This explanation needs careful scrutinizing against the detail given in the full PWC report. Even a cursory scan through the audit report indicates that Mohammed Bin Hammam was not in the loans business. There are many examples given of money and gifts being distributed to numerous individuals, AFC member organizations, unnamed third parties, and to Bin Hammam himself and family members; and the distinction between AFC funds and his personal money was blurred in the extreme. The following extracts from the audit make this last point clear:

Para 18. From an analysis of activity in the Sundry Debtors account 1-3230, it appears that Mr. Hammam routinely instructed a significant number of purportedly personal receipts and payments to and from the AFC's bank accounts. These receipts and payments, along with his AFC entitlements, have been processed through the AFC's general ledger to the effect that at any point in time, the AFC was either in debt or credit to its President.

Para 22. A number of payments of significant value were also made on Mr. Hammam's behalf from AFC bank accounts, notably:

    a.   Payments of significant value to Jack Warner (CONCACAF) and an individual named Ellias Zaccour. These individuals also received benefits in kind from the AFC.

    b.   Payments to, or to the benefit of, a number of AFC Member Associations and associated individuals.

    c.   Payments to, or to the benefit of, other third party individuals, including FIFA, EXCO and other AFC Standing committee members, possibly lobbyists, media and AFC staff and contractors.

  d. Payments which appeared to be for the personal benefit of Mr. Hammam and his family including transfers to his personal or company bank accounts, cash advances and other expenditure such as significant flight and hotel expenditure, chartered flights and the purchase of assets.

The detail of the amount of money involved in each gift or transfer is given in the audit report but some examples include: transfers to Mr. Hammam's personal and company accounts ($11.6 million); to the benefit of Mr. Hammam and his family ($1.2 million, split between $492,660 for his family and $220,937 for Mr. Hammam personally, including $12,395 to Lord's Tailor for suits); and payments to third parties ($2.0 million, including $1,983 for 13 shirts from Lord's Tailor for Sepp Blatter and $4,366 for the purchase of air tickets for Ganesh Thapa's wife and son). On the 'President's Personal Bank Accounts,' the audit report states:

Para 23. In the course of our work, we located a file maintained at the AFC titled '*President's Personal Account*' which contains documents relating to two personal bank accounts in Mr. Hammam's name.

Para 24. Until April 2011, all monies in these personal accounts originated from AFC bank accounts, comprising purportedly personal transfers by Mr. Hammam recorded in the sundry debtors account referred to above in the AFC's general ledger.

| 31.01.2011 | $4,366 | Ganesh Thapa | Purchase of air tickets for Ganesh Thapa's wife and son. The claims form attached states that this was in relation to the Asian Cup 2011 held in Doha. |
| | | | Ganesh Thapa is the President of the All Nepal Football Association and is an AFC Vice-President. |

SCREENSHOT A: Air Tickets – Paragraph 183 of PWC audit report.

This point is forcefully expressed again in Paragraph 223, which states, 'Although apparently for personal transaction, this file appears to have been maintained at the AFC and evidences transfers of cash to and from AFC bank accounts' and, in Paragraph 232, 'In summary . . . all monies in these accounts originated from the AFC.'

Para 26. Five payments totalling $210,000 were made directly to three individuals associated with Member Associations in the period July 2009 to October 2010 as follows: $100,000 to Gaurav Thapa (Nepal), $50,000 to Franciso Kalbuadi Lay (Timor Leste), and $60,000 to Jose Mari C. Martinez (Philippines). Payments were also made directly to five Member Associations from these accounts.

The screenshot below gives the detail of the payments made to Gaurav Thapa from the 'President's personal bank accounts.' No payment description is given for the first $50,000 but the second is clearly described as 'gift exp.'

Payments to individuals

236. Five payments totalling $210,000 were made directly to three individuals, the details of which are as follows:

Payee	Date: Value	Description
Gaurav Thapa	9.7.2009: RM177,250 ($50,000) 13.8.2009: RM177,000 ($50,000)	Two payments totalling RM354,250 ($100,000) were made to Gaurav Thapa as follows: - RM177,250 ($50,000) on 9 July 2009. Supporting documentation comprised a remittance application form detailing his bank transfer information – there was no payment description noted on this form and no TT confirmation was included in the file. - RM177,000 ($50,000) on 13 August 2009 described as "gift exp".

SCREENSHOT B: Payment to Gaurav Thapa – Paragraph 236 of PWC audit report.

The descriptions given below for the other two payments listed to Mr. Lay from Timor-Leste and Mr. Martinez from the Philippines, again from the 'President's personal bank accounts,' make it clear that they are not loans to be repaid.

The screenshot on the following page gives the detail of the $430,000

SCREENSHOT C: Payment to two other individuals – Paragraph 236 of PWC audit report.

Payee	Date: Value	Description
		Gaurav Thapa is a current AFC staff member in the National Team Competitions department. We understand he is also the son of Ganesh Thapa, the President of the All Nepal Football Association and an AFC Vice-President.
Francisco Kalbuadi Lay	8.10.2009: $50,000	Paid to Francisco Kalbuadi Lay's bank account in Indonesia. The payment description on the TT confirmation is stated as "personal expenses". Francisco Kalbuadi Lay is the President of the Timor Leste Football Association, as well as a member of the AFC Finance Committee.
Jose Mari C. Martinez	16.10.2009: $50,000 21.10.2010: RM31,522 ($10,000)	Two payments were made to Jose Mari C. Martinez's bank account in Philippines as follows: - $50,000 on 16 October 2009 described as "payment on behalf"; and - RM31,522 ($10,000) on 21 October 2010 described as "fund for friend". Jose Mari C. Martinez was the President of the Philippines Football Federation until November 2010, when he was removed amid allegations of mis-use of Football Association funds.

paid directly to four member associations, again from the 'President's personal bank accounts.'

Payments to member associations

238. Five payments totalling $430,253 were made directly to five member associations, the details which are as follows:

Date	Value	Description
18.6.2009	$250,000	Paid to Cambodia Football Federation. The purpose of this payment was not stated.
22.10.2009	$100,283	Paid to Lao Football Federation, purportedly as a contribution towards the installation of furniture, air-conditioning and floodlights at their training centre.
30.11.2009	$29,970	Two payments totalling $29,970 were transferred to the Pakistan Football Federation ($15,000) and the Uzbekistan Football Federation ($14,970) on 30 November 2009. The telegraphic transfer confirmations state the payments were for the U19 Championship 2010 Qualifiers.
28.6.2011	$50,000	Paid to the Philippine Football Federation. The telegraphic transfer confirmation states the payment details as being *"payment on behalf"*.

239. We do not know why the AFC President would be making personal payments (of some signifi

Payment to four member associations – Paragraph 238 of PWC audit report.

There are numerous other extracts that could be given to highlight the fact that the money in the personal accounts came from AFC accounts and, to quote from Paragraph 133, 'Mr. Hammam appears to have routinely used the AFC's company bank accounts to facilitate personal transactions as if they were his personal bank accounts.' Among all the examples given of money and gifts handed out, there are no indications that 'loans' were ever involved.

In view of later revelations, it is worth highlighting these two screenshots which show that Kemco Group was owned by Bin Hammam and how its accounts fitted into the AFC picture. Here is a summation of how the system worked:

When Bin Hammam wanted to slip someone in world football a sweetener, he had a system. Often it was merely a matter of

Deposits by Kemco Creditors

165. A sum of $250,000 was received from Kemco Creditors on 27 September 2010. The cash re journal to this transaction states that this was *"received from President's account"*.

166. Background searches indicate that Mr Hammam owns Kemco Group and his immediate fai plays a significant role in its senior management.

SCREENSHOT E: Kemco 1 – Paragraphs 165 and 166 of PWC audit report.

Company bank accounts

178. Three transfers totalling $4.9 million were made to Kemco Real Estate, referred to in supporting documentation as *"Hammam real estate"*, on 19 September 2005 ($112,000), 26 March 2008 ($800,000) and 2 May 2008 ($4 million). As stated above, background searches indicate that Mr Hammam owns Kemco Group.

SCREENSHOT F: Kemco 2 – Paragraph 178 of PWC audit report.

instructing Gan (AFC finance secretary) to wire the money from his sundry account at the AFC under some flimsy football-related pretext, but there were times when a less traceable route was prudent. Thankfully over in Doha his accounts staff at Kemco operated a network of ten funds which provided the perfect cover for clandestine transactions. The accounts were generally marked for commercial mundanities such as 'real estate', 'transport', 'retention' and 'overheads'. Bin Hammam's personal bank account, and another in the name of his adult daughter, Aisha, were also operated by the Kemco staff to make payments to football bosses. (p 71–2 of The Ugly Game: The Great Qatari Plot to Buy the World Cup, by Heidi Blake and Jonathan Calvert)

Given the lack of follow-up in the Kathmandu media, Ganesh Thapa probably had good reason to believe that he had weathered with some ease the publicity generated by the payments to his son, but much darker and threatening clouds were gathering. We now know, thanks to a FIFA media release published in October 2014, that ANFA was 'selected by FIFA to undergo a KPMG Central programme audit for the year 2012 which proved unsatisfactory and unappropriated cash movements were identified. As a consequence, a Forensic Audit (Project 'Play') has been initiated by FIFA for the years 2011/2012. Findings of this audit were transmitted to the Ethics Committee secretariat.' (See below for reference.) As FIFA was considering follow-up action, a series of articles in The Sunday Times, published on three successive Sundays in June 2014, generated a storm of publicity across the world of football. They disclosed payments made to Ganesh Thapa from Mohammed Bin Hammam, and revealed the close links between the two men.

The *Sunday Times* revelations

Note: (1) The two *Sunday Times* journalists responsible for all the articles, Heidi Blake and Jonathon Calvert, subsequently wrote a book, quoted from above, which repeated and elaborated on what was in the original articles: *The Ugly Game: The Qatari Plot to Buy the World Cup*. Though the articles are behind a paywall, the links given will show the headlines and the first few paragraphs of each article. (2) For context, the FIFA decision to award Qatar the 2022 World Cup was announced on December 2, 2010.

June 1, 2014

In the issue of June 1, 2014, under a heading 'Plot to buy the World Cup,'[6] the paper claimed:

> The secret payments that helped Qatar to win the World Cup bid are revealed for the first time this weekend in a bombshell cache of millions of documents leaked to *The Sunday Times*.
>
> The files expose how Qatar's astonishing victory in the race to secure the right to host the 2022 tournament was sealed by a covert campaign by Mohamed bin Hammam, the country's top football official.
>
> The Qatari vice-president of Fifa, the governing body of world football, used secret slush funds to make dozens of payments totalling more than $5m to senior football officials to create a groundswell of support for Qatar's plan to take world football by storm.

A separate article on the same day, headed 'Slush funds and hospitality: the masterminding of a dirty game,'[7] claimed that Bin Hammam 'used 10 slush funds controlled by his private company and cash handouts to make dozens of payments of up to $200,000 into accounts controlled by the presidents of 30 African football associations who held sway over how the continent's four executive committee (Exco) members would vote.'

While acknowledging that Qatar maintains that Bin Hammam played no part in securing its winning bid for the 2022 World Cup, *The Sunday Times* claimed that it had 'a mountain of proof' to support its claims, namely:

> The Fifa files contain hundreds of millions of secret documents leaked from the heart of world football by a senior figure inside the sport's governing body who decided to blow the whistle.

---

6   https://www.thetimes.co.uk/article/plot-to-buy-the-world-cup-lvxdg2v7l7w
7   http://bit.ly/2L9Wy6o

They include emails, faxes, phone records, flight logs, documents and accounts that chart the activities of Mohamed bin Hammam, the Qatari Fifa vice-president, before and after his country's 2022 World Cup bid.

The documents originate from several organisations including Bin Hammam's private office in Doha, his private construction company Kemco, Fifa itself, the Asian Football Confederation, the Qatar FA and the offices of the Qatar 2022 bid team.

June 8, 2014

On June 8, a further series of articles were published. One headed 'Secret deals turn heat on World Cup'[8] and subheaded, 'Qatari fixer's $1.7m for key Asian votes' claimed that the 'cache of hundreds of millions of documents leaked from the heart of world football today reveals that Bin Hammam shored up his own seat on Exco by using secret slush funds to make payments totalling $1.7m to football officials across Asia.' It went on to claim, 'The $1.7m he paid from the funds, controlled by his private company Kemco, often into the bank accounts of officials whose support he was seeking across Asia.

The glut of Asian payments came as Bin Hammam was campaigning for both the Qatar World Cup bid and for his own re-election to the post of president of the Asian Football Confederation.'

Another article headed 'Pact with enemy sealed Bin Hammam victory,'[9] stated, 'Our second tranche of Fifa files show that masterful diplomacy, extravagant largesse and Machiavellian strategy played a crucial part in securing Asia's votes. Bank transfer slips and emails also reveal that Bin Hammam made payments totalling $1.7m to football bosses across Asia from the same secret slush funds he used in Africa.'

This article alleges that to help defeat a challenge to his appointment as president of AFC, Bin Hammam 'used the services of Manilal Fernando, a rotund, Sri Lankan hustler and long-standing ally, who was employed by Fifa as its South Asian regional development officer. . . . The documents show that Fernando also received a payment of $23,000 from Bin Hammam's slush fund as reimbursement for a cash gift he said he had given to Alberto Colaco, the general secretary of the Indian football association – after winning a guarantee of his support.'

---

8   http://bit.ly/2JDoiL8
9   http://bit.ly/2JE3xi9

The article continued:

> With his presidency secure, Bin Hammam had a new project to attend to: Qatar's bid for the 2022 World Cup.
>
> Strategy documents show that as early as June 2008, the Qatari had concluded that buying up support in Asia and Africa was crucial to winning the right to host a World Cup.
>
> The files show that in 2009 he made a string of unexplained payments from accounts held by his private company, Kemco, to football bosses across Asia. Among them was Mari Martinez, president of the Philippines football association. An unknown sum was paid into his wife's bank account, and he went on to receive $12,500 in his own.

Bin Hammam's 'loyal electoral fixer,' Fernando, demanded his pay-off and Ganesh Thapa, 'another loyal ally,' was also rewarded. From the same article:

> (T)he Sri Lankan sought large rewards for the countries he had locked down.
>
> Fernando had an official role with the Goal Programme, the Fifa fund for football development in poor countries chaired by Bin Hammam. He sent Bin Hammam a list of Goal Programme payments of $400,000 each to countries in his group – Pakistan, Afghanistan, Nepal, Bhutan, Kyrgyzstan, Uzbekistan and Sri Lanka, asking the Qatari to use his position to obtain approval from the Goal Bureau.
>
> Fernando was also keen that another source of football development money was generously lavished on key voters, writing to Bin Hammam in August to recommend loosening the purse strings of the AFC's Aid 27 budget. 'Until elections are over we must see that all funds due from Aid (27) to countries are paid without making it difficult for them with too many questions asked,' he suggested.
>
> Bin Hammam continued to lavish football bosses with direct payments from the network of slush funds operated by Kemco. Asatulloev Zarifjon, president of the Tajikistan football federation, received $50,000 in June 2010. The next month, Fernando's ally, Nidal Hadid of the Jordan FA, received $50,000 into his personal bank account from the account of Bin Hammam's daughter, Aisha.
>
> Another loyal ally of Fernando was handsomely rewarded for backing Bin Hammam. Ganesh Thapa, president of the Nepalese FA,

was paid a total of £115,000 from two separate Kemco accounts in March and August 2010. He said last week that the money was paid as part of a business arrangement he had with Kemco.

(Note: With Bin Hammam's help, Manilal Fernando was elected as a FIFA executive committee member in January 2011 following the 24th Asian Football Confederation Congress in Doha. On October 9, 2013, FIFA imposed a lifetime ban on him[10] based on four breaches of the FIFA code of ethics, including, 'offering and accepting gifts and other benefits' and 'bribery and corruption.')

June 15, 2014

Ganesh Thapa featured again in an article published by The Sunday Times on June 15, 2014, headed 'Mr. Fixer's bid for Fifa's crown.'[11] The opening paragraphs allege that after the success of the winning World Cup bid on December 2, 2010, Qatar set out to topple Sepp Blatter from the position as president of FIFA and replace him with Mohamed Bin Hammam. On March 10, 2011, just 10 weeks before the ballot, in which Sepp Blatter was expecting to be re-elected as president to extend his 13-year reign by another four years, Bin Hammam announced his candidacy for the post. The Sunday Times states that 'this surprise announcement started a frenzied ballot-buying campaign. The Fifa files lay bare the full story of Bin Hammam's corrupt operation to propel himself to the top of Fifa. . . . Bin Hammam's methods were familiar – he hosted a junket in Doha, flew football chiefs in business class to secret summits at five-star hotels, dished out cash and used the same slush funds that had shored up support for Qatar's World Cup bid.'

The article further states:

Southeast Asia was a key constituency for Bin Hammam, as he was president of the Asian Football Confederation, and the documents reveal he was typically generous with the region's football leaders.

Account ledgers show he had already withdrawn $20,000 as 'cash advance for Al Musabbir Sadi', president of the Bangladesh Football Federation, in March and a further $40,000 in cash for unspecified purposes the same day.

Emails and bank records show that those who were willing to pledge their support were rewarded handsomely.

10 http://bit.ly/2O1l8nX
11 http://bit.ly/2zVdd8C

On April 1, Bin Hammam received an email in which Viphet Sihachakr, president of the Lao Football Federation, provided his personal bank details with the promise: 'Any support from me please call any time Brother.'

Sihachakr had $100,000 paid into his personal bank account. (Note: On November 16, 2014 he was banned by FIFA for two years from all football related activity.)

Another old acolyte of Bin Hammam, the Nepalese FA president, Ganesh Thapa, also secured a handsome cash injection through Qatari contacts.

A total of $115,000 had been paid into his personal bank accounts in 2010 from Bin Hammam's slush funds in the run-up to the World Cup vote.

Now in the days before Bin Hammam announced his presidential campaign, Thapa set up a meeting with Sheikh Hamad Bin Khalifa bin Ahmed Al Thani, president of the Qatar Football Association and a member of the ruling family. On March 8, Thapa emailed Bin Hammam's assistant to report back on the meeting.

'He agreed with my proposal for paying US$2,00,000 (sic) ... for 4 years. On this regard he had told me to send you a confidential letter for releasing our 1st year's payment which amounts US$ 2,00,000,' Thapa reported.

The money, he said, was for Nepal's national league, the 'total estimated budget' for which was $800,000, and Qatar had agreed to pick up the whole bill. Thapa followed up with another email on March 12 providing the bank details of the Nepalese FA.

Thapa said last week that the total amount paid had been $200,000 not $800,000. It had been 'financial support' for a developing country and had 'no connection whatsoever with the voting process for Mohamed bin Hammam'.

In their book,[12] Blake and Calvert give a further mention of Ganesh Thapa in the above context. It concerns a letter written by one of Bin Hammam's fixers, Manila Fernando, of Sri Lanka, to Dr Chung Mong-joon, the president of the Korea Football Association who also happened to be the major shareholder in Hyundai:

The Sri Lankan wrote to Chung on 9 March asking him whether he

---

12 http://bit.ly/2LnWJKI

would support Bin Hammam and suggesting a private chat to reassess his own future in football. He also asked whether Chung intended to continue 'the development programme and assistance you promised (sic) for persons in my region' and whether it would be possible to help Bin Hammam's ally Ganesh Thapa 'secure a percentage from the Hyundai Car Agency in Nepal'. History does not relate Chung's reply (p 371).

Mounting pressure on Ganesh Thapa from within Nepal

ANFA vice president calls for Ganesh Thapa to be ousted

The Sunday Times revelations were widely reported internationally and in Nepal. Despite his power and influence, Ganesh Thapa soon began to feel the heat. Leading the campaign for action to be taken against him was the ANFA vice president, Karma Tsering Sherpa. On June 12, 2014, an article in *The Kathmandu Post* stated:[13]

> As Sepp Blatter faces calls at the general convention in Brazil to step down as Fifa boss over corruption surrounding the Qatar's successful but controversial World Cup bid, voices against Thapa's excesses in Nepal are picking up a decibel.
>
> ANFA Vice-president Karma Chhiring Sherpa calls for Thapa's immediate ouster to clean up the mess in Nepali football. The fresh scandal comes at a time when Sherpa and a few other senior Anfa office bearers are at loggerheads over the dictatorship and the autocratic rule of Thapa.
>
> 'If such misdeeds are not immediately stopped, the Nepali football will continue to suffer and fall further behind,' said Sherpa.

Ganesh Thapa nominated to the Constituent Assembly

On **August 29, 2014,** as controversy mounted, the cabinet nominated Ganesh Thapa as a Constituent Assembly member to take one of the 26 seats reserved for political parties. He took the single seat that was reserved for Rastriya Prajatantra Party-Nepal (RPP-N), whose chairman, and dominating personality, is Kamal Thapa, a former deputy prime minister and foreign minister. Ganesh Thapa is Kamal Thapa's younger

---

13 http://bit.ly/2uOX92k

brother. (Note: After a recent amalgamation, the RRP-N is now the Rastriya Prajatantra Party. Kamal Thapa is the executive chairman of the new party.)

Public Accounts Committee calls for suspension of Ganesh Thapa

On **September 28, 2014**, the PAC called for the suspension of Ganesh Thapa and other ANFA officers for an initial period of two months. An AP report stated:[14]

> Nepal's powerful parliamentary committee accused the long-time chief of the national football association of embezzling millions and ordered government agencies to investigate, file a case in court, and suspend him.
>
> Ramhari Khatiwada of parliament's public accounts committee (PAC) said on Tuesday they have ordered the government to immediately begin the investigation and suspend Ganesh Thapa as president of the All Nepal Football Association.
>
> Thapa has been accused by the committee of embezzling 582 million rupees (about US$6 million or Dh22m) during his 19-year tenure in the office.
>
> 'There are no proper records or audit reports of where much of the funds received from Fifa or AFC for development of football in Nepal have gone. We believe that all these funds have been misused by Ganesh Thapa and people in the association close to him,' Khatiwada said.
>
> The committee has ordered the government's sports ministry to suspend Thapa, and the Commission for Investigation of Abuse of Authority (CIAA) to investigate him, Khatiwada said.

On the following day, **September 29, 2014**, Ganesh Thapa appeared at a press conference at ANFA headquarters to reject all PAC complaints against him.[15] The report quotes him as saying, 'We have proper evidences with us. We are ready to go anywhere and we are confident that the issue will be sorted out soon. He added that ANFA was a transparent association and nobody has done anything wrong in the governing body.' He made no reference to accepting the suspension.

On **October 13, 2014**, with still no action having been taken against

---

14 http://bit.ly/2zTOktM
15 https://www.goalnepal.com/index.php?id=21961

him, the PAC again 'directed the government' to suspend Thapa and three other named ANFA office bearers,[16] including General Secretary Dhirendra Pradhan and Treasurer Birat Jung Shahi.

ANFA vice presidents call on FIFA to investigate Ganesh Thapa

Ganesh Thapa continued to defy all calls for his suspension but events were now moving rapidly against him. On **October 18, 2014**, Reuters published a well-sourced report with the dramatic heading, 'Exclusive: Nepal FA chiefs ask FIFA to investigate own president':[17]

Senior officials at Nepal's football association (ANFA) have asked FIFA's ethics chief Michael Garcia to launch an investigation into their own president Ganesh Thapa.

In the e-mailed letter dated Oct. 15, addressed to Garcia and also sent to FIFA General Secretary Jerome Valcke and the AFC, two ANFA vice presidents ask the investigator to look into Thapa and how funds to Nepal from FIFA and the AFC were used.

'We write to you to request that you open an immediate investigation into potential breaches of the FIFA Code of Ethics and All Nepal Football Association (ANFA) Statutes by ANFA President Ganesh Thapa and Vice President Lalit Krishna Shreshtha,' it said.

'With the ANFA mired in unresolved allegations of impropriety and scandal, we respectfully request that an investigation be immediately launched by the FIFA Ethics Committee Investigatory Chamber to resolve these many concerns and questions.'

'We have witnessed conduct that causes us concern, and based on our observations, and allegations of impropriety that have appeared in the media, we have reason to believe that Mr. Thapa and Shrestha may have violated the FIFA Code of Ethics and the ANFA Statutes.'

The e-mail is signed by ANFA vice presidents Karma Tsering Sherpa and Bijay Narayan Manandhar.

Thapa said he would cooperate with any investigation, but insisted there had been no wrongdoing and he was continuing as head of ANFA.

'Of course I continue as ANFA head, I am the head of the football

---

16 http://bit.ly/2zWdKqI
17 https://reut.rs/2LBBCkL

association here. From my side I can tell you, no allegation has been made from ANFA. This is only propaganda.'

The secret FIFA investigation of ANFA in 2012

On **October 20, 2014**, Reuters published another well-sourced article[18] which stated:

> Nepal's football association (ANFA) is implementing 'corrective measures' amid allegations from its own senior officials about embezzlement of funds, soccer's governing body FIFA said on Monday.
>
> FIFA said the Nepalese FA had been the subject of an 'unsatisfactory' external audit in 2012, when 'unappropriated cash movements' were identified, and was also targeted by an ethics committee investigation in 2013.
>
> In a statement sent to Reuters on Monday, FIFA said it was 'aware of the matter and exchanged correspondence in this regard with ANFA.'
>
> ANFA had been examined by international auditors KPMG, working in partnership with soccer's governing body two years ago, FIFA said.
>
> 'ANFA was selected by FIFA to undergo a KPMG Central programme audit for the year 2012 which proved unsatisfactory and unappropriated cash movements were identified,' it said.
>
> 'As a consequence, a Forensic Audit (Project 'Play') has been initiated by FIFA for the years 2011/2012. Findings of this audit were transmitted to the Ethics Committee (secretariat).'
>
> FIFA said that 'considering these findings, Nepal was also targeted the following year by an ethics committee investigation.'
>
> 'Known as "project Orange", the investigation was concerned with "Tsunami funds" and the "Goal" (development) projects managed by the former development officer Manilal Fernando between 2005 and 2012 in the south Asia region,' FIFA said.

Ganesh Thapa finally accepts suspension

On the same day that FIFA released this information, *The Kathmandu Post* carried an article stating that Thapa had finally agreed to accept the suspension[19] that PAC had ordered on September 20, 2014:

---

18 https://reut.rs/2L9Z7Fn
19 http://bit.ly/2zV8lQD

Adhering to the Public Accounts Committee's (PAC) directive, Ganesh Thapa on Monday (October 20, 2014) stepped down as the president of All Nepal Football Association (Anfa), paving the way for an investigation into the alleged misappropriation of funds in the football governing body.

Along with Thapa, Anfa Treasurer Birat Jung Shahi has also stepped aside from the office.

The PAC on September 28 directed the Ministry of Youth and Sports to suspend the Anfa office bearers for two months over alleged embezzlement of funds. Thapa, along with General Secretary Dhirendra Pradhan, Treasurer Birat Jung Shahi and an Anfa Academy building construction supervisor, faces the charge of misappropriating Rs 580 million of association's funds.

'I decided to step aside for the sake of Nepali football. Fifa would have certainly suspended Nepal from all footballing activities if I didn't take the step,' Thapa said at a press meet on Monday.

ANFA vice presidents denied knowledge of FIFA audit

On **October 24, 2014**, another Reuters article headed 'Nepal officials deny knowledge of FIFA-ordered audits,'[20] made it clear that Ganesh Thapa kept the FIFA-initiated investigation to a tight circle within ANFA. The article states:

> Senior officials at the All Nepal Football Association (ANFA) say they have no knowledge of a string of past financial audits carried out by world soccer's governing body FIFA into potential irregularities at ANFA.
>
> ANFA Vice Presidents Karma Tsering Sherpa and Bijay Narayan Manandhar have asked for details regarding the audits in a letter dated Oct. 22 to FIFA Secretary General Jerome Valcke and Ethics chief Michael Garcia, seen by Reuters.
>
> 'As Vice Presidents and Executive Committee members of ANFA . . . we are surprised and deeply concerned to learn of these allegations,' the ANFA Vice Presidents said in the letter to Valcke and Garcia.
>
> 'If these allegations are true, they are not only new information to us but also contradicted what we were led to believe by ANFA President Ganesh Thapa,' they said.

---

20 https://reut.rs/2O2H2Hf

'As leaders of the ANFA, the very least we deserve is to know of any alleged impropriety or wrongdoing that may have occurred within our football association.'

FIFA, contacted by Reuters, said it had received the letter from the Nepalese officials.

'FIFA has received a letter sent by two ANFA Vice-Presidents. For the time being we have no further comments to make,' an official told Reuters.

Calls from within RPP-N to recall Ganesh Thapa from the Constituent Assembly

On **November 24, 2014**, Setopati carried a report[21] which stated that 'an assembly of a dissatisfaction faction of Rastriya Prajatantra Party-Nepal (RPP-N) led by Padma Sundar Lawati has demanded that the party recall Ganesh Thapa from the post of Constituent Assembly (CA) member. The assembly also demanded to replace Thapa by a capable personality. The assembly, which the group claims was attended by 1000 party cadres from around the country, has given an ultimatum of 21 days to call back Thapa from the post of CA.'

Nothing more was heard of this protest. Presumably Kamal Thapa ignored it. Of note, in passing, is the fact that the Rayamajhi Commission, formed to probe the suppression of Jana Andolan II, recommended the prosecution of Kamal Thapa, the then Home Minister, on corruption charges.[22]

CIAA puts Ganesh Thapa case 'on hold'

On **February 18, 2015**, despite all the new information released by FIFA and *The Sunday Times*, *The Kathmandu Post* published a short article[23] giving the news that the CIAA, under its now thoroughly discredited chairman, Lokman Singh Karki, had decided to put the case against Ganesh Thapa 'on hold.' Given very recent publicity about the CIAA, these sections of the article are worth quoting in full:

The Commission for Investigation of Abuse of Authority (CIAA) on Wednesday put on hold the corruption case concerning the All Nepal

---

21 http://archive.setopati.net/politics/4267/
22 http://bit.ly/2LmjEpz
23 http://bit.ly/2uAUJVI

Football Association (Anfa) President Ganesh Thapa after failing to gather enough evidences.

Thapa along with Anfa General Secretary Dhirendra Pradhan and Treasurer Birat Jung Shahi faced the charges of misappropriation of fund amounting to Rs 580 million. A CIAA board meeting on Wednesday dismissed Thapa's case which was recommendation by Parliamentary Account Committee (PAC) to investigate with higher priority. 'The Commission has decided to put his (Thapa) case on hold for now,' said CIAA Spokesperson Begendra Raj Poudel without elaborating in details.

The PAC has expressed serious concern over anti-graft body's failure to deal the corruption cases involving high-profile people. Parliamentarians say the CIAA decision has raised a serious ethical question whether the anti-graft body is truly committed to eliminate corruption. 'The CIAA has been protecting its cronies and dragging its adversaries to the court,' said Ramhari Khatiwada, one of the PAC member.

Khatiwada said PAC is planning to summon anti-graft chief and officials before the parliamentary committee to grill over their decision to acquit high profile individuals involved in corruption. 'It's not only our conclusion that corruption is rampant in Anfa. The world football governing itself is investigating the matter,' said Khatiwada.

Thapa said the CIAA decision came as a huge relief to him. 'I have been repeatedly saying that all the charges against me was brought to taint my image.'

AFNA vice presidents appeal again to FIFA

On **February 20, 2015,** shortly after hearing the CIAA judgement, and presumably driven by a sense of despair, ANFA vice presidents Karma Tsering Sherpa and Bijay Narayan Manandhar wrote a letter to FIFA, urging it to launch a full investigation into Ganesh Thapa and his leadership of ANFA. This news was also quickly leaked to AP. Its report stated:[24]

In a letter to FIFA, ANFA vice presidents said the ruling body now needed to launch a full investigation and not a mere review of claims, listing a number of issues that require closer scrutiny.

We would kindly request a full investigation of Mr. Thapa and his

24 https://dailym.ai/2LbzdRR

leadership of the ANFA by the FIFA Ethics Committee Investigatory Chamber ahead of his return in the upcoming weeks.'

The chaos in the administration of ANFA that has persisted for years under the leadership of Mr. Thapa must be brought to an end. We urgently request your kind assistance,' they added.

The letter was addressed to Robert Torres, a member of the FIFA Ethics Committee's investigatory chamber, who was in charge of looking into the claims back in November.

Thapa, who has repeatedly denied any wrongdoing, did not want to comment when contacted by Reuters on Friday.

'Right now I don't want to talk about the issue,' Thapa said before refusing to say whether he would return to ANFA.

FIFA refused to comment on the letter, the state of its claims review or even if the review led by Torres was completed, instead referring to their four-month old press release.

'More information will follow in due course,' a FIFA official said. The official also refused to say whether Thapa was eligible to return to office or not.

Ganesh Thapa resumes ANFA's presidency

On **June 25, 2015** Nepali media outlets carried the news[25] that Ganesh Thapa was now back as president of ANFA:

All Nepal Football Association (ANFA) President Ganesh Thapa, who had voluntarily stepped down from his chair last year to comply with the investigation by Public Account Committee (PAC) on corruption allegations against him, joined office from Thursday.

Thapa was welcomed by General Secretary Dhirendra Pradhan, CEO Indra Man Tuladhar and other members of ANFA's executive committee upon his return to office on Thursday afternoon.

Thapa's voluntary three-month suspension from all football related activities had ended on June 19, but his return to office was delayed for a few days as the association remained closed for 13 days to mourn the untimely passing away of its acting president Lalit Krishna Shrestha on June 12.

Although Thapa's first four month period out of presidency ended on March 19, he extended it to further 3 months.

---

25 http://archive.setopati.net/sports/7360/

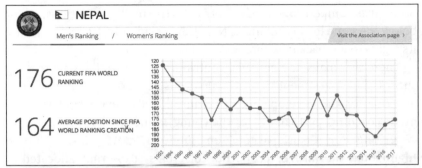

SCREENSHOT G: Nepal's FIFA rankings.

Ganesh Thapa's performance as president of ANFA

FIFA ranking

Ganesh Thapa's return as president coincided with continued mounting criticism within Nepal and in the international media of his management of ANFA. These highlighted serious failures in its internal administration and in its management of FIFA funds.

One measure of how competently football is run in any country is its position, commensurate to its population, on FIFA's world rankings. As can be seen above, in February 1994, Nepal stood at 124. In 2015 it had sunk to 192, three places above Macau with a population of 566,000. Before the recent Solidarity Cup, Nepal's ranking had recovered a little to 186. After winning the competition, Nepal moved up to 175, but this is still a woefully low ranking given its population and the great enthusiasm for the game within the country. Timor-Leste with a population of 1.1 million is now at 191, Bhutan (population 750,000) at 176, and Brunei (population 400, 000) at 190. Afghanistan, Myanmar, and Malaysia, with similar sized populations to Nepal, are at 151, 159, and 161 respectively. Maldives with a population of 345,000 is at 145.

This should put the recent highly acclaimed victory in the Solidarity Cup, while very welcome, in perspective. The competition replaced the AFC Challenge Cup, last played for in 2014. Six teams were eligible to compete after losing in the first round of the 2018 FIFA World Cup/2019 AFC Asian Cup qualification competition, and three teams were eligible to compete after losing in the play-off round two of the 2019 AFC Asian Cup qualification competition. After Pakistan and Bangladesh withdrew, seven teams were left in the tournament. Laos, with a population of 6.7 million was, at the time of the tournament, on a ranking of 177, but the other five competitors were countries with small populations, on or below the same lowly ranking as Nepal. Self-evidently, Nepal must raise its sights to get back to where it should be.

There are many factors that contribute to a country's footballing success, but investment in infrastructure is key. Good playing surfaces are vital for the development of technical skills. Investment in high-grade coaching, particularly for the young, is another key factor.

Writing for GoalNepal.com on June 21, 2015, Sakar Prasain highlighted the meager proportion of FIFA's 2015-grant allocated to infrastructure[26]. Of the $1,050,000 ANFA received from FIFA, it spent $545,000 on men's competitions, $237,696 on event management, $112,500 on women's football, $54,000 on youth football, $46,000 on planning and administration, $26,500 on infrastructure, and $28,000 on 'other.' To quote him directly:

> In Nepal there is just one proper football pitch. The field at the national stadium in the country isn't even completely filled up with grass. This sector is one of the biggest issues in Nepal football. Yet ANFA spent just 2% of the money they received on infrastructure. Comparatively, Afghanistan and Maldives, arguably the two best countries in the SAFF region spent $250,000 and $81,000 respectively on this sector.

Sakar Prasain is also highly critical of the comparatively small sums spent on women's football and the mere 5 percent spent on youth football. He finishes the article by stating, 'These numbers prove exactly why the development of Nepali football is moving at a snail's pace. They prove that ANFA is in dire need of a new leader and reform. Ganesh Thapa has shown that he is not the right man to fulfil Nepal's potential in football. After the untimely death of late Vice President Lalit Krishna Shrestha, I feel there is no one within ANFA who has the quality to lead.'

Reuters investigative report

An even more graphic description of maladministration within ANFA, highlighting the way Ganesh Thapa used his absolute powers to make arbitrary decisions on FIFA-allocated grants, is given in an investigative report produced by Reuters on September 7, 2015 under the heading,

---

26 https://www.goalnepal.com/index.php?id=24338

Dharan Technical Center in 2015 with the photos of Sepp Blatter and Ganesh Thapa supermiposed on it.

The Kathmandu Post

'Blatter's corroded legacy on South Asian football fields.'[27] These extended extracts speak volumes and need no elaboration:

> There are no recognisable football fields, no players, and just a rusting goalpost at Pakistan's Hawksbay training centre, built with a $500,000 FIFA grant on a windswept plot by the Arabian Sea near Karachi, and officially completed two years ago.
>
> In Nepal, goats graze on a rutted playing field near decrepit facilities at the Dharan soccer academy built with FIFA cash in the Himalayan foothills. The sole member of staff, a watchman, says he hasn't been paid for a year.
>
> A Reuters review of football development projects in these two South Asian countries shows they are littered with half-built and under-used facilities, despite receiving more than $2 million from the sport's world governing body this year alone.
>
> In recent weeks, Reuters reporters visited seven projects in Pakistan and Nepal that received FIFA money under its 'Goal' programme – which funds football fields for youth academies, known as technical centres, and playing surfaces in stadiums. They found that just one had an active full-time training programme. Three had no proper playing fields.
>
> The Dharan technical centre was built in 2002, but was mainly used by drug addicts and then Maoist rebels for the next six years, said Deepak Rai, the academy's director.

27 https://reut.rs/2JFB6AC

Local clubs occasionally trained there, but it was never professionally turfed, nearby residents say, and when the centre was due to be inaugurated in 2008, local people dug clods of grass from their fields to make the pitch presentable, said Rai.

A plaque at Dharan marks the centre's inauguration by FIFA's then South Asia director of development, Manilal Fernando, and Thapa, the ANFA president.

FIFA banned Fernando for life in 2013 after an investigation into bribery and corruption related to a 2009 election within the Asian Football Confederation. Fernando, a Sri Lankan who had been a member of FIFA's executive committee, was in charge of distributing 'Goal' project funds in South Asia.

In interviews with Reuters, Thapa acknowledged that the Dharan centre was not functioning. He blamed uncooperative local officials and the association's weak finances. 'We are facing a very big financial problem. We do not have the money to run the centre at the minute,' he said.

Since 2000, FIFA has given ANFA $6.9 million for football development, including $1,050,000 this year. In 2010, under 'Goal', FIFA donated $400,000 'for financing of three existing football academies,' including Dharan. But that year, ANFA provided just $13,000 for the centre's costs. In 2009-12, it granted between $13,000 and $21,370 each year for a full-time training programme for 25 youths – the only time the centre has been used for its intended purpose in 13 years, according to Thapa and ANFA audits.

Thapa said ANFA had stopped funding the Dharan centre because of a dispute with local officials over treatment of the boys. 'I went to visit them, they were crying and saying 'we're not being treated well, we're not learning anything',' he said.

Two graduates of the programme denied this. Mohan Katwal, now 18 and a professional player with local club Morang, described his training at Dharan as good and said he enjoyed his time there. Sushant Chaudhary, now a commerce student, also said the training had been good.

Thapa said he had decided to spend the 'Goal' training money on the running costs of an academy in Kathmandu instead. He declined to elaborate, saying this was an 'internal matter.'

His focus on Kathmandu has limits. A second 'Goal' technical centre in the capital, the Chyasal academy, lies semi-abandoned.

Rooms are locked, corridors are filled with trash and a large part of its grass field is worn down to dirt. It has never hosted a full-time training programme because, Thapa says, it's too dangerous. 'It's not a suitable location. There are drug users around there,' he said.

Thapa said ANFA was still deciding how to spend this year's FIFA grant.

In Dharan, watchman Arjun Budathoki, 45, keeps an eye on the mostly derelict centre. He says he was last paid his ANFA salary in August 2014. For the two tournaments organised locally each year, the centre borrows a lawnmower.

'For the rest of the year we let the goats do it,' said Digmar Puri, who owns the animals and was an assistant manager when the centre was running.

The match-fixing bombshell

On **October 14, 2015,** came the shattering news of the arrest of key international players over allegations of match fixing. Those detained included the captain and vice captain of the national team, Sagar Thapa and Sandip Rai, and the goalkeeper, Ritesh Thapa. Former national players, Bikash Singh Chhetri and Anjan KC were also arrested. Sagar Thapa and Ritesh Thapa had made their debuts for the national team in 2003, Anjan KC in 2005, and Rai and Chettri in 2008.

This Agence France-Presse (AFP) report gives the most detail[28] of many media reports, not least about the active engagement of the Nepal police in collecting evidence against the players concerned:

> The captain of Nepal's football team was among five current and former internationals who have been arrested over allegations of match-fixing, including during qualifiers for the last World Cup, police said Thursday.
>
> Skipper Sagar Thapa was detained in Kathmandu on Wednesday as part of a coordinated series of arrests in the capital which also saw four current or former team-mates on the national side taken into custody. Detectives said the arrests came after investigations found significant sums of money had been deposited in the players' bank accounts from suspected match-fixers based in Southeast Asia.
>
> 'We've recorded banking transactions ... between them and

---

28 https://dailym.ai/2LqSU7r

international match-fixers, including in Malaysia and Singapore,' Sarbendra Khanal, chief of the Metropolitan Police Crime Division in Kathmandu, told AFP. 'Our investigations will continue and we are discussing what charges they will face.'

Khanal said that several matches played in 2011 as part of Nepal's unsuccessful bid to qualify for the 2014 World Cup in Brazil were under the scanner, including a match against Jordan that they lost 9-0.

'We suspect that there was fixing in several competitive matches and also in some friendly matches which Nepal lost,' he said.

Khanal said matches involving Bangladesh and Afghanistan, played as part of a regional competition, were also being investigated.

Bishwa Raj Pokharel, Kathmandu police's chief spokesman, told AFP that sums ranging from $1,000 to $1,500 had been deposited in the players' accounts courtesy of the alleged overseas betting syndicates.

Nepal's football association said that all of the accused would be suspended pending the outcome of the police investigation, and expressed sadness at the allegations.'

This report in *The Himalayan Times* gave further detail[29], including an assertion from the police that more people are likely to be dragged into the case:

'SSP Sarbendra Khanal, the chief of MPCD, said that the arrests were made after receiving complaints and tip-offs that the five were involved in match-fixing of national and international games.

'They are accused of making quick bucks through match-fixing in cahoots with national and international bookies and fixers, and hurting the faith of fans and fellow countrymen,' SSP Khanal said.

'We were keeping tab on the suspects for some time,' SSP Khanal said. 'We had been monitoring their Facebook activities and international banking transactions.'

It has been learned that police were alarmed at Nepali national team's dismal performance in international matches since 2011.

Police said at least one of the suspects has allegedly made investment in a casino in Sikkim of neighbouring India.

Police are looking into the allegations and are also trying to ascertain which laws would be applicable against their alleged offences, which, according to SSP Khanal, were tantamount to organised crimes against the state.

---

29 http://bit.ly/2JElxsS

Sandip Rai, Ritesh Thapa, Bikash Singh Chhetri, Anjan KC, and Sagar Thapa leave the Special Court on December 3, 2015, having been released on bail.

Udip Singh Chetry

'More people are likely to be dragged into the case as investigation progresses,' SSP Khanal said.

The AFC statement about the arrests and investigation stated:

'On the back of long-term collaboration between the AFC, Sportradar Security Services and Nepal Police, the Kathmandu Metropolitan Police Crime Division arrested five Nepali players, former and current, linked to match-fixing this week,' the AFC said in a release.

'The process leading to the arrests began when suspicious betting patterns were detected on a number of matches played by the Nepali national team. A year-long investigation followed, involving matches stretching back to 2008, further intelligence gathering revealing suspicious financial transactions linked to Nepali nationals,' the release added. 'The intelligence gathered was shared with Nepali Police and a formal investigation began which has so far resulted in five arrests.'

The five footballers were presented before the Special Court on October 27, 2015. On November 8, 2015, an AFP report quoted the registrar, Bhadrakali Pokharel, as saying that the government had charged them with treason and had sought a life sentence as punishment.[30] He added that the players were charged under a 1989 act, which says that anyone 'causing or attempting to cause disorder with the intention of jeopardising Nepal's sovereignty, integrity or national unity, shall be liable for life imprisonment.'

On **August 26, 2016**, the AFC published its verdict rejecting the

---

30 https://dailym.ai/2myQ1n4

appeals made against the suspensions. (Details of the matches fixed are listed at the link given at the end of this AFC statement.) Five games are listed over a four-year period, starting with fixtures against Afghanistan on October 17, 2008 and December 9, 2009, followed by matches against the Philippines on October 11, 2011, Malaysia U-23 on October 15, 2011 and Cameroon on August 26, 2012. Sagar Thapa, the captain, and Ritesh Thapa, the goalkeeper, played in all five games, and Sandip Rai, the vice captain, played in the last four listed fixtures. Anjan KC played in the first two listed fixtures and Bikash Singh Chettri in the first and fourth. In all cases, the two charges faced were corruption and unlawfully influencing match results contrary to Articles 62 and 69 of the AFC Disciplinary Code.

On November 8, 2015, the Nepali-language magazine, *Himal Khabarpatrika*, published a long and wide-ranging article on the match fixing allegations[31]. The front cover of the issue carrying the article had a portrait photograph of a pensive-looking Ganesh Thapa. The heading, emblazoned in red, translates as, 'Planned 'treason,'' and the pertinent question as: 'The AFC vice chairman and ANFA chairman Ganesh Thapa had information that Nepali footballers were 'match fixing' against the country in 2008 but stayed silent, why?'

These short translated extracts are intended to give details in the article not covered previously, and to highlight again how many aspects of this sordid affair have apparently been left hanging in the air:

> ANFA's apathy, even when the players, including the captain and five players, are found to be engaged in a 'treasonous' campaign to defeat the country, is suspect. Apart from issuing a press release about the accused players, ANFA has not said a word. ANFA president Thapa has not begun internal investigations, nor has he resigned on moral grounds. Instead, police officials say he is not really helping the investigation. But Thapa says he is. He says, 'I am giving the information requested by the police.'
>
> According to ANFA vice chairman Karma Tsering Sherpa, AFC had asked ANFA to investigate the match fixing repeatedly since 2008, but ANFA chair Thapa gathered the players and made them swear. (The apparent implication: to keep things secret.) In their statements to the police, the players have accepted their crime. The statement says

---

31 http://nepalihimal.com/article/5470

Himal Khabarpatrika cover.

the players received up to $5,000 (520,000 rupees) for match fixing in different games.

The police say Anjan used the illegal match fixing money to invest in casinos together with gangster Dinesh Adhikari (Chari). Anjan himself invested in casinos in Kathmandu and Sikkim. Anjan has invested the money in a restaurant owned by Gaurav Thapa, the son of parliamentarian Ganesh Thapa nominated to the parliament by the RPP.

People knowledgeable about Nepali football say the five players arrested for match fixing are only the 'faces.' One official from ANFA says, 'Nobody believes that the players, who considered Ganesh Thapa god, raised this much money without his orders and consent.' ANFA vice chair Karma Tsering Sherpa says it is not only the players but the officials of ANFA who should be investigated. He claims that the five thousand dollars the players took per game to lose was only token money, and the real planning could have been done by others.

Thapa is being investigated by both the CIAA and the Department of Money Laundering Investigations. Because he is a man of 'access,' his case has been put on hold by the CIAA, and the Department of Money Laundering Investigation also says 'the investigation is ongoing.' The

Department chair Kebal Bhandari says the relevant bodies are not helping enough with the investigations. He says, 'We have asked for Thapa's property details, FIFA's investments, and banking details.' He claims since questions have also risen about Thapa's son Gaurav, they are handling it as a single case. The next investigation will also pay attention to the match fixing aspect, Bhandari says.

Knowledgeable people say match fixing is tied to the reason former coach Graham Roberts' contract was not extended. The source says that Graham had repeatedly raised the issue of match fixing with chair Thapa. Graham became suspicious after the incident at the October 11, 2011 game against the Philippines in the Rizal Stadium in Manila. Nepal conceded the first goal after 17 minutes because of weak defending. Captain Sagar was the leader of the defence and Graham took him off. According to the source, a bookie told Graham that Nepal was going to lose 4–0, and his players were involved. 'He didn't believe it but he was suspicious of the captain and sent Bhola Silwal on to the pitch,' the source says. When Nepal lost 4–0 just as the bookie said, the hard-mannered Graham came down firmly on the players.

On links between the match fixing and Ganesh Thapa's son, Gaurav, investigations show that he might have arranged the deals between the match fixers and players. The source claims that the investigations show that Gaurav, who has an officer level job in the AFC, organized many games on his own initiative, and those games were fixed. The 2011 friendlies with Malaysia and the Philippines were organized for fixing. Such fixing is called 'sporting fixing.' The fixings done to win money are called 'beating fixing.'

There are suspicions that Gaurav, the ANFA chair's son, who had received the role of match commissioner from AFC, had organized

FIFA president, Sepp Blatter, with Ganesh Thapa in Kathmandu on March 8, 2012.

Binod Joshi

the friendlies to raise the FIFA rankings of the other countries. In such games, the organizing country pays for all travel and lodging for the visiting country, and pays up to $50,000 per game to the visiting country. The police are also suspicious why Gaurav went to Malaysia immediately after the players were arrested for match fixing.

The arrested players are not only intimate with Gaurav, but also have business partnerships. Gaurav, Anjan and Sandip are the products of the first batch of ANFA academy. According to vice chair Sherpa, AFC had repeatedly asked ANFA to recruit an integrity officer to investigate match fixing. Thapa unilaterally appointed former DIG Madhab Thapa as integrity officer. Chair Thapa chose to overlook his lack of knowledge of the issues.

Whatever Ganesh Thapa did or did not know or do, these disgraceful and criminal actions happened on his watch as president, and over an extended period when Nepal's position on FIFA's world rankings was plummeting. One is left wondering just how many games might have been fixed and who knew what and when. The Nepal police gave many hints that more games were fixed than the five listed on the AFC charge sheet, and that other people not named had been placed under surveillance. The Himal Khabarpatrika article highlights other related issues, such as the role of Gaurav Thapa, which cry out for investigation. What has happened to the Department of Money Laundering Investigation? The guilty players must have stories to tell and the proper place to tell them is in the criminal courts. There are strong indications that powerful people have large vested interests in them staying silent. It will be interesting to see what emerges at their trial. It is surely unthinkable that criminal charges of such a serious nature should be quietly dropped.

Why was FIFA slow to act?

It was not just ANFA's vice presidents who expressed increasing despair at the length of time it was taking FIFA to announce the outcome of its investigation of Ganesh Thapa. By the beginning of October 2015, this had dragged on for over three years. Why was it taking so long? Bin Hammam was suspended in May 2011. FIFA had access to the audit report of AFC, with its revelatory details, in July 2012. In the same year, FIFA initiated its investigation of ANFA. The Sunday Times articles appeared in June 2014. On the morning after the first article was published, the two journalists had contacted FIFA offering to share all their material.

In addition to Bin Hammam, many senior AFC football figures had been suspended, including one of his key fixers, the Sri Lankan, Manilal Fernando.

The longer FIFA remained silent on Ganesh Thapa, the more speculation grew that he enjoyed special protection because of his long-standing links to Sepp Blatter who had become FIFA president on June 8, 1998. Despite being dogged by persistent claims of corruption and financial mismanagement within FIFA, he was re-elected in 2002, 2007, 2011, and 2015. In an article published on February 19, 2015, Sushil Thapa wrote[32]: 'What baffles me the most is why it is taking so long for FIFA to review the case and give their verdict? I can only think of one thing that would explain it. Taking into account the upcoming FIFA presidential elections, Mr. Thapa is very important to FIFA boss Mr. Blatter. It is obvious that he has a vested interest in keeping Mr. Thapa afloat. On the other hand, Mr. Thapa's last hope is Mr. Blatter.'

On **October 8, 2015**, a FIFA media release broke the news[33] that: 'The adjudicatory chamber of the Ethics Committee chaired by Hans Joachim Eckert has provisionally banned FIFA President Joseph S. Blatter, UEFA President and FIFA Vice-President Michel Platini, and FIFA Secretary General Jérôme Valcke (who has already been put on leave by his employer FIFA) for a duration of 90 days. The duration of the bans may be extended for an additional period not exceeding 45 days. The former FIFA Vice-President Chung Mong-joon has been banned for six years and fined CHF 100,000. During this time, the above individuals are banned from all football activities on a national and international level. The bans come into force immediately.'

Two weeks previously, the Office of the Attorney General of Switzerland announced that 'criminal proceedings against the President of FIFA, Mr. Joseph Blatter, have been opened[34] on 24 September 2015 on suspicion of criminal mismanagement (Article 158 Swiss Criminal Code/SCC) and – alternatively – misappropriation (Article 138 Swiss Criminal Code/SCC).'

FIFA suspends Ganesh Thapa for ten years
On **November 16, 2015**, whether connected to Blatter's suspension or not, FIFA's independent Ethics Committee banned Ganesh Thapa for ten

32 http://bit.ly/2mvH39Z
33 http://bit.ly/2JCGoNm
34 http://bit.ly/2LybiYK

years from all football activities at both the national and international level.[35] The published judgement stated:

> Mr. Thapa, in the context of the 2009 and 2011 elections for the FIFA Executive Committee at the Asian Football Confederation (AFC) congress, committed various acts of misconduct over several years, including the solicitation and acceptance of cash payments from another football official, for both personal and family gain. Specifically, he was found guilty of infringing article 13 (General rules of conduct), article 15 (Loyalty), article 18 (Duty of disclosure, cooperation and reporting), article 19 (Conflicts of interest), article 20 (Offering and accepting gifts and other benefits) and article 21 (Bribery and corruption) of the FIFA Code of Ethics (FCE). Mr. Thapa has therefore been banned for ten years from all football-related activities and fined CHF 20,000.

Republica's first report of the ban included quotes from unnamed parliamentary officials calling for Thapa to resign immediately from his parliamentary seat since he had been given one of the 26 seats reserved for those who had given outstanding service to the nation. They said that FIFA's decision to ban Thapa made his holding one of those seats morally untenable. Within a few hours, these quotes were removed. I uploaded a long post to Facebook drawing attention to these words on November 17, 2015.[36]

The FIFA statement resulted in a very strong editorial in The Kathmandu Post,[37] the opening three sentences of which were: 'For as long as one can remember, Ganesh Thapa has been synonymous with corruption in Nepali football. Yet, even after being embroiled in a string of scandals, the former national team striker has always been able to escape justice by using his political connections. Not this time.' The final three paragraphs are worth giving in full:

> In 2012, an audit report of the Asian Football Confederation revealed that Gaurav Thapa, Ganesh Thapa's son, had received $100,000 in his account from Mohamed bin Hammam, former president of the Asian Football Confederation. Fifa has since banned Hammam from

---

35 http://bit.ly/2mtkrXE
36 http://bit.ly/2O7GPmi
37 http://kathmandupost.ekantipur.com/news/2015-11-18/stained-striker.html

all football-related activities for life. Thapa, however, shamelessly defended himself by saying that he had 'borrowed' money from Hammam for personal use. Thapa has also been accused of doctoring audit reports of Anfa, i.e., completely omitting the mention of the Goal Project through which it received $180,000 from Fifa in four phases from 2001 to 2012. An auditor also found that the company 'involved' in the construction of the Satdobato Sports Complex does not even exist.

By all accounts, remaining at the helm of Nepali football for over two decades only seems to have emboldened Thapa to scale new heights of corruption. His political clout is partly to blame. Despite his tainted image, he was nominated as a Constituent Assembly member by the Rastriya Prajatantra Party-Nepal led by his brother, incumbent Deputy Prime Minister Kamal Thapa. And now, Ganesh Thapa is a Member of Parliament.

The Fifa ban on Thapa, therefore, comes as a respite to many who have long been frustrated at successive governments' hesitation to take action against him. Against this backdrop, the PAC should now question the CIAA and demand that its officials clarify the grounds on which they dropped the case against Thapa. It should also direct other concerned authorities to thoroughly investigate all the accusations against him. It would also do well for Thapa and his toadies to cooperate, as all the skeletons have now stumbled out of the closet. Hiding is not an option.

Apart from the failure to call for Ganesh Thapa's removal from the CA, given that he had demonstrably sullied Nepal's name internationally, this article is as strong as one could have wished. But what did it achieve? There was no further action from the government, the PAC, or the CIAA and, as will become clear later, his toadies are still running ANFA.

It is also worth recording what was said in this short article from *The Kathmandu Post* on November 17, 2015:[38] 'Minister for Youth and Sports, Satyanarayan Mandal, has said that misconducts and irregularities surfaced in the country's football sector have inflicted pain upon nation's sovereignty. The disciplinary action taken by the Federation of International Football Association (FIFA) against All Nepal Football Association President Ganesh Thapa has drawn the serious attention of government, he said, adding that he has already proposed government

---

38 http://bit.ly/2LefwsM

to form a probe committee to find out the facts surrounding allegations on Thapa.'

Nothing more was heard of the probe committee. Nor was there any strong, sustained follow-up in the media calling for renewed action by the CIAA and highlighting how morally reprehensible it was for Ganesh Thapa to remain as a CA member. Why this reluctance to call for his immediate suspension? Several reasons spring to mind. The most generous is that there may have been confusion about his stated intention to appeal. *Republica* gave this quote[39] from his media release: 'I am very disappointed and I don't believe that justice has been served. I have fully cooperated with FIFA during their investigations since last four years. I shall demand a full statement regarding the decision. I intend to follow the necessary steps at FIFA and if necessary CAS (Court of Arbitration of Sports) to establish my innocence.'

On **April 22, 2016**, the FIFA Appeal Committee rejected the appeal but with the very minor concession[40] that the ten-year suspension should begin from April 16, 2015 to take account of 'the 210 days during which Mr. Thapa refrained from taking part in any football-related activity during the ethics proceedings.'

Following FIFA's emphatic rejection of his appeal, it is again hard to find any articles in the media calling for Ganesh Thapa's suspension from the Constituent Assembly, or even any which drew attention to the fact that he had been given a seat reserved for those who had given outstanding service to the nation, and that the FIFA decision made his holding of one of those seats 'morally untenable.' Again, a generous explanation might be that the media wrongly thought that the matter was somehow sub judice because of his immediately stated and loudly proclaimed intention to take his case to the CAS. The Kathmandu Post recorded his response to the rejection thus:[41] 'My hope and expectation, following recent FIFA reforms, was that the Appeal Committee would correct the earlier findings. Unfortunately, it failed to do so. I will now be taking my case to Court of Arbitration for Sport. This will be the first independent judicial body who will review the case.'

Elsewhere he was widely quoted as saying that he had every expectation that the CAS would reverse the FIFA decisions.

---

39 http://bit.ly/2JEoSrO
40 http://bit.ly/2LvO9d3
41 http://bit.ly/2NrYggb

The Court of Arbitration for Sport

CAS's procedural rules are clearly set down on its website[42]. Rule 48 details what must be in the content of the statement of appeal and Rule 49 states that the time limit for appeal 'shall be twenty-one days from the receipt of the decision appealed against.'

It can be seen from this link[43] that CAS publishes the date on which an appeal has been filed: for example, in the case of appeals against the decision of the FIFA Appeals Committee by Michael Platini and Sepp Blatter on March 2, 2016 and March 17, 2016 respectively, both submitted within the 21 days mandated by CAS. (On May 9, 2016, the CAS reduced Platini's six-year ban to four years. On December 5, 2016, the CAS confirmed Blatter's six-year ban.)

There is no record on the website of Ganesh Thapa submitting a statement of appeal for the simple reason that the Court Office of the CAS have no knowledge of him submitting a case to its jurisdiction. (Personal communication to author.)

The future

Mohammed Bin Hammam

In an epilogue to their book, *The Sunday Times'* journalists portray a sympathetic picture of a forlorn Mohammed Bin Hammam, still living the life of luxury in his large mansion in Doha, but with few friends, and now apparently ostracized by the Qatari authorities who are angry and embarrassed by the negative publicity his activities generated. They write:

> From time to time, some of his friends in the footballing world still get in touch. Not often, but it is pleasant to hear from them when they find time. His brothers in Africa and Asia still need a bit of financial assistance on occasion. A little help in funding their national leagues, or their children's school fees, or this new artificial pitch or that new car. Sometimes, rarely, they will still come to dinner – if he arranges the jets and hotels to get them here (p 454).

Bin Hammam made his fortune in the construction business so he is one of many to benefit from the large contracts let to build from scratch the

---

42 http://www.tas-cas.org/en/arbitration/code-procedural-rules.html
43 http://www.tas-cas.org/en/media/media-releases.html

nine stadiums needed to hold the 2022 World Cup, and the new urban areas surrounding them. But a consequential heavy price is being paid, and, in the same evocative epilogue, Blake and Calvert make it clear who is paying:

> Night is falling, the migrant workers who have toiled away all day building the World Cup city are retreating to their grim camps on the outskirts of Doha. They have flocked there in the thousands from India and Nepal but their dreams of joining a land of opportunity were soon dashed. They often go unpaid for months and the desert heat is harsh. They must labour all day under the scorching sun, often with no drinking water or food. Their employers have taken their passports so there is no escape, except in a coffin. In the summer, the migrant workers in Qatar die at the rate of one a day, mostly of heart attacks in the fierce temperatures. More than 1000 fell in just two years. There have been warnings that thousands more will perish before the World Cup arrives in Doha (p 455–6).

Ganesh Thapa

For Bin Hammam's friend, Ganesh Thapa, the outlook is much brighter. He gave a long interview to OnlineKhabar, which was published on April 26, 2016.[44] The image that comes across is of a man confident about his future – and in a contented state of denial. There is no hint of remorse for the serious wrongdoings highlighted in the FIFA ethics committee judgements, nor is there any indication that he has any moral scruples about occupying a seat parliament.

In the interview, he speaks about his political ambitions and declares himself to be a monarchist and a believer in Nepal as a Hindu state. When tackled on the source of his funds, his response is: 'I spend my own money for small things. In addition to that I am using my reach and influence to get resources. The AFC's former President Bin Hamam and I have a close relationship. He is a billionaire. He has shown interest in the work that I do, and helped me. We will soon sign an agreement with Bin Hamam for the development of Makwanpur.'

Two other answers are particularly revealing. First, when asked about the comments people make about him on social media, he says: 'The criticism that I have faced was of such a low grade one, that it has taken

---

44 http://english.onlinekhabar.com/2016/04/29/376104.html

me past criticism. I am waiting for my time to come. I know that those who are resorting to slander now will come to my defence in the future. For now, I don't have any answers to them.' Second, when asked about corruption his reply is: 'As regards the corruption case, I have already received clean chit in Nepal. No one can point a finger of suspicion at me. As regards the cases outside of Nepal, I would not prefer to speak at the moment. But I am assured that time will prove that I was innocent.'

Clearly he has no worries about the CIAA re-examining the serious charges against him which it put 'on hold,' though that would be an excellent test of what sort of chief emerges as Lokman Singh Karki's successor. Finally, instead of establishing his proclaimed innocence before the independent CAS, he declares that he is relying on the abstraction of 'time.'

Football in Nepal

Whatever Ganesh Thapa thinks, there will be no shortage of people who will continue to point the finger of suspicion at him. There will also be many who doubt his will, or even his inclination, to turn his back completely on the affairs of ANFA. Questioned on the subject in the interview, his answers were both ambiguous and evasive. 'I am waiting for my time will come,' with its hint of menace, is a case in point.

The election for the post of president and leading office bearers of ANFA was held on October 24, 2016. In the build-up, there were serious allegations that the ANFA leadership had manipulated the election list[45] to suit the candidates that they were backing.

The elections resulted in Ganesh Thapa's minions being elected to all the key positions. One of his closest confidants was elected as the new president and his brother-in-law emerged as a vice president. Shockingly, two of the key senior officials from Ganesh Thapa's time as president, General Secretary Dhirendra Pradhan and Treasurer Birat Jung Shahi, remain in post. The PAC had called for their suspension because of their alleged misappropriation, along with Ganesh Thapa, of 580 million rupees of ANFA funds. The CIAA, when they 'dealt with' the Ganesh Thapa case, had also put the case against Birat Jung Shahi 'on hold.'

Predictably, and ignoring the worldwide disgrace that his predecessor brought to football in Nepal, the new president paid a generous tribute

---

45 http://bit.ly/2uyYHhO

to Ganesh Thapa, reported *Republica*:[46] 'He had a big role in leading football to this stage. Our duty will be to give continuity to what he did by bringing new policies.' Karma Tsering Sherpa, who had led the opposition to Ganesh Thapa, lost by just 5 votes out of 67 cast. He is quoted as saying that lots of money had been used to influence the outcome of the election though he would accept the result.

A frank exposure of what Karma Tsering Sherpa only hinted at can be found in this article in goalnepal.com, headed, 'ANFA Election Outcome Is Defeat for Nepali Football.'[47] This brief extract gives the essence of what is alleged: 'No one disputes the fact that Mr. Thapa was the major force behind Mr. Shrestha's electoral success. With so much at stake, he was determined to get his candidates win the election by hook or by crook. Mr. Thapa's thirst for revenge against Mr. Sherpa, the man largely responsible for his humiliating disgraceful ouster from ANFA, was hell bent on doing whatever it took for him to foil his presidential aspirations. Mr. Thapa wanted to prove that he far from finished and still wields tremendous influence in ANFA. Ultimately he accomplished his mission with the help of his legion of cronies.'

The new president is quoted in the *Republica* article as saying that 'football has got back on track recently' and that he would give continuity to it. What is the hard evidence for such an optimistic assessment? Again, the recent welcome success in the Solidarity Cup needs to be kept in perspective. If ANFA had been run properly over the last two decades, Nepal would not have been reduced to playing in a competition against six small countries which are, in FIFA terms, footballing minnows.

As Sakar Prasain has written, any success of the national team is down to the willpower of the team and the coaches who are starting to deliver better results despite the woeful inadequacies of ANFA. He has also highlighted that major reforms in every area are needed to realize the full potential of the footballing talent that exists in Nepal, and to get the country back to where it should be on FIFA world rankings. The first requirement is to produce properly audited accounts to show how every dollar from FIFA and AFC is spent. Investment in new infrastructure is of paramount importance, as is an appropriate increase in the spending on youth development. Women's football is one of the fastest growing sports in the world. It would be a refreshing sign of progress to see a

---

46 http://www.myrepublica.com/news/7947/
47 https://www.goalnepal.com/index.php?id=28779

substantial increase in the money allocated to the women's game in Nepal.

At the most fundamental level, what is needed in ANFA is a total change of culture. The men who backed Ganesh Thapa all the way, and who have never uttered a word of criticism against him despite all his manifest failings, do not look up to the task. Expect more of the same, though it looks likely that there will be lot less money to throw about because of the tighter controls now promised by FIFA and AFC.

This article has been republished with permiss-ion from *The Record*. The original can be found online at: https://www.recordnepal.com/ wire/corruption-in-world-football-and-the-fall-of-ganesh-thapa

Addendum
On 5 May 2018, Ganesh Thapa's adversary, Karma Tsering Sherpa was elected President of ANFA, and his supporters swept the board in the central committee elections. In reporting the results, an article in the Kathmandu Post reported that football in Nepal was still said to have been run under the influence of Thapa and in a public programme a few months previously he had campaigned against Sherpa. The article concluded that the results, 'could be an end to the stranglehold disgraced former president Ganesh Thapa has had in the country's football governing body.' On 7 Jun 2018, the Special Court dismissed the treason charges brought against the five footballers. This does not impact on the AFC-awarded life suspensions.

A Secret Nepal File and the Battle for Information

An account of a long battle on a Freedom of Information matter with the British Foreign Office which was finally resolved by a judgement from the UK independent Information Commissioner

Over the years, quite a few foreigners have been dubbed as old Nepal hands, but few merit the designation more than Major Dudley Spain, who lived and worked in Nepal from 1957 to 1983. During this long period, he became a confidant of the Nepali royal family and well known in Kathmandu society. He was a serving officer in the Brigade of Gurkhas for the first seven years of his time in Nepal, after which, on retirement from the army in 1964, he worked in the British Embassy for 14 years. For five years starting in 1978, he was the Nepal Director for Save The Children Fund (UK). After his return to the UK in 1983, he was a frequent visitor to Nepal, with regular access to the palace, up until his death in 2006, aged 88.

Dudley Spain's first appointment in Kathmandu came in 1958, as the British Embassy Liaison Officer for the British Gurkha Recruiting Depot at Dharan and the Jogbani-to-Dharan road. In 1960, he accompanied King Mahendra during his state visit to Britain. On his return to Nepal he wrote a detailed account of the visit, which he rated as a great success. The report currently lies buried in a thick Foreign Office file, one of at least forty in the National Archives which cover the visit. After he left the army in early 1964, Dudley Spain was appointed to the post of Information Officer in the British Embassy. Research on a totally different subject unexpectedly shed interesting light on the specific nature of his responsibilities.

Khampas in Mustang

My research interest at the time was Khampas in Mustang in the early 1960s and, as they feature in this story, it is worth giving the background on how they came to this remote area of northern Nepal. The Chushi Gangdrug (Four Rivers, Six Ranges) army had been formed in 1958 to bring together all the Tibetan resistance groups fighting the Chinese army, the PLA. Supported by air-delivered arms from the CIA, they fought bravely and well, but by mid-1960, having taken heavy casualties from a fully mobilized PLA that was supported by artillery and fighter ground attack aircraft, they had been forced to withdraw into northern India. A large number found work in road-building gangs in Sikkim. After much discussion between their leaders and the CIA, the latter gave approval to continue the armed resistance using Mustang as a base area.

The agreed plan was to move to Mustang in increments of three hundred. This first group would then move across the border into Tibet to find a safe area to establish a base where they could receive shipments of arms and operate as guerrillas. Only after doing so, would the next increment be sent, first to Mustang and then into Tibet. This exercise would be repeated until there were seven independently operating bases. This plan went awry almost immediately as large numbers of former Chushi Gangdrug fighters started to make their way independently to Mustang. Over the winter of 1960/61, more than two thousand were jammed into makeshift camps in Mustang, creating serious political and logistical problems for the US government support. (For details, see article by John Kenneth Knaus, 'Official Policies and Covert Programs: The U.S. State Department, the CIA, and the Tibetan Resistance'1, published in the Journal of War Studies in 2003.)

The arrival of 2000 outsiders in the middle of winter must have caused severe hardship for local residents as well as for the new arrivals. It took some time for the CIA to set up the major logistic effort that was necessary to sustain such a large group in an area as difficult to get to as Mustang.

The first CIA air-drop of weapons took place in April 1961, with a second following in December 1961. In each case, two Hercules aircraft delivered the weapons to a drop zone 10 kilometres inside Tibet, just across the border from Mustang. The weapons were mainly of Second World War vintage.

The Indians were not officially notified of any of this CIA support.

---

1   http://bit.ly/2Lz1duJ

The first raid from Mustang into Tibet took place in September 1961. A second major raid into Tibet in October 1961 led to the ambush of a jeep carrying a PLA regimental commander. The many secret papers in his satchel proved to be a rich source of intelligence.

From the outset, keeping the operation secret was difficult. The exodus from India and the reported destination as Mustang were widely reported in the Indian press. On February 3, 1962, an article in *The New York Times* quoted a Nepali foreign ministry spokesman as saying that unidentified aircraft had been dropping arms to about 4,000 Khampas in Mustang. The same article noted that official Indian sources were expressing apprehension that 'an anti-Chinese military build-up' on Nepal's northern border could lead to China sending troops into Nepal.

The New York Times, 3 February, 1962

File FO 371/170877

While scanning through the list of Foreign Office files in the UK's National Archives for information on Khampas in Nepal, I spotted a file: FO 371/170877. It was dated 1963 but, unusually, there was no title to indicate its contents. The relevant entry simply said: 'This record is closed and retained by the FCO (Foreign and Commonwealth Office) under Section 3.4 of the Public Records Act.' This meant that the file had been retained by the FCO rather than transferred to the National Archives. This part of the Public Records Act was not repealed or altered by the Freedom of Information Act (FOIA) which came into force in 2005 but I knew that under FOIA I had a right to ask the FCO to consider releasing it to the National Archives as an open file. I submitted my request on September 19, 2013 saying, 'I clearly have no idea what is in the file since the National Archives states that 'This record has no title'. There may have been 'a special reason' (to quote from the Public Records Act) for its original retention but it is very hard to imagine that the sensitivities which originally dictated that decision could be relevant now over fifty years after the material in the file was first produced.'

On Oct 11, 2013, the FCO responded as follows:

> Thank you for your email of the 19 September requesting access under the Freedom of Information Act (FOIA), for information from the following file on Nepal retained by Foreign and Commonwealth Office (FCO) FO 371/170877.
>
> I am pleased to be able to tell you that the review of the file FO 371/170877 has determined that most of the material can now be released. A copy of the releasable information will be sent to you through the post. However, there are a number of redactions that have been made under Section 27 (2) of the FOIA.
>
> (Note: Section 27(2) of the FOIA states that 'Information is also exempt information if it is confidential information obtained from a State other than the United Kingdom or from an international organization or international court.')

The FCO subsequently sent me a copy of the file. This image below shows the top of the front page to which the other documents in the file were attached. Note for later reference, FN 1691/2G, at the top right hand corner. The file consisted of six documents which will be elaborated on shortly.

As can be seen, the file was entitled, 'Conversation with Inspector General of Police about Intelligence requirements and Counter subversion.' The FCO covering letter stated:

> Section 27 is a qualified exemption and is subject to the balance of the public interest. This means that a public interest test must be carried out to determine whether the public interest in maintaining the exemption outweighs the public interest in disclosing the information, as set out below.
>
> In favour of release: we acknowledge that disclosure of information relating to UK relations with the country concerned would add to the understanding and knowledge of this subject. There is a public interest in a greater understanding of the UK's foreign relations and the information could also aid the public to a better historical understanding of the UK's conduct overseas.
>
> In favour of withholding: release of the redacted material would prejudice relations between the UK and the countries concerned. (Emphasis mine)
>
> Our conclusion is that in this case, release would be prejudicial to the UK's relations with the countries concerned and would therefore not be in the public interest.

The letter indicated that if I was not satisfied, I could ask for an internal review. So, what information was in the six documents?

Document 1
Document 1 is a set of minutes dated November 22, 1963, by J D Laughton, an FCO official. It consisted of comments by FCO officials on information provided by the Inspector General of Police (IGP) P S Lama, which were available in the version of Document 3 provided to me. Six minor redactions had been made and, judging from context, I could not see how any of them could possibly be interpreted as falling under section 27(2) of the FOIA.

Document 2
Document 2 is a covering letter dated October 17, 1963, to Document 3 from P C Petrie, the Charge d'Affaires in the British Embassy, Kathmandu, to C M MacLehose, Head of the Far Eastern Department at the FCO. The first two paragraphs read:

> I enclose a record of a recent conversation with the Nepalese Inspector-General of Police. I believe that it may contain some new, or at least up-to-date, information about communist subversion here and Nepalese attempts to deal with it.
>
> To me the most interesting points were (one line redacted) and P S Lama's own request for British assistance. The latter coincides very neatly with our intention, which I do not think that P S Lama knows about, to establish an Information Officer here; and I would be most grateful if you would consider passing a copy of this letter and enclosure to John Drinkall in IRD (Information Research Department).

The fourth paragraph of this letter brought in the Dudley Spain connection:

> But when we do have an Information Officer with an IRD slant the Inspector General of Police would be one of his most useful contacts; and at that point we could no doubt imply that that we are responding to S P Lama's request for assistance. This conversation therefore seems to strengthen even further the case for having an Information Officer here before long, and I hope that the rather sketchy indications I have so far sent IPD (Information Policy Department) and IRD have been sufficient for them to allocate funds for the next financial year. At present I am waiting for a chance to make an offer to Major Dudley

Spain, who has been unable to come to Kathmandu since I arrived but is expected next week.

Some elaboration at this stage might be useful. The UK clearly planned to establish an Information Officer 'with an IRD slant' and therefore found it very convenient when IGP Lama made his request. Information Officers in British embassies work overtly, under the direction of the Information Policy Department (IPD) of the Foreign Office, to try to ensure that UK policy is properly understood and is reflected in the local media of the country they are based in. The Information Research Department (IRD), founded in 1948, was a covert anti-communist propaganda unit within the FCO, and was funded from the clandestine budget of the Secret Intelligence Service, MI6. It was closed by the then Foreign Secretary, David Owen, in 1977.

Correspondence in another file (FO 1110/1670) indicated that the need for an IRD officer was judged to be compelling and that Dudley Spain was the ideal man for the job. He was appointed as Information Officer in early 1964, after he retired from the army. His salary and allowances were paid by IRD. It is not clear how long this arrangement lasted. A minute in the file, signed by John Drinkall, the head of IRD, commented that, 'the sooner Major Spain gets to Nepal the better'.

Document 3

Document 3 is a two and half page record of a conversation P C Petrie had with IGP P S Lama, on October 12, 1963, during a private dinner party hosted by him. The other person present was Brigadier Gordon Richardson, Commander of the British Gurkhas Depot, Dharan. Petrie described the evening's conversation as 'the most interesting I have had in Kathmandu.' He continues:

Before dinner the IGP spoke about his troubles with the Khampas in the Mustang area, whose numbers he gave as 6-8000. It had been expected that these Khampas would spend their time raiding across the border into Tibet: PS Lama hinted that (two and half lines redacted) But during the last six months these Khampas had turned to looting and robbing on the Nepalese side: the Nepalese government did not have the security forces to deal with them and the situation was becoming difficult.

The 6000-8000 figure given by Lama raises doubts about the quality of the intelligence he had about what was going on in Mustang at this time. A British officer, Malcolm Meerendonk, visited Jomsom in the summer of 1963 and reported that the movement of Nepal Police was very restricted because of the dominance of Khampas in the area. In a dispatch dated Febraury 13, 1962, L A Scopes, the then British ambassador, stated that the Chinese ambassador, Mr Chang Shih-chieh, had told him, quite accurately, that there were 2000 armed Khampas in Mustang. (FO 371/166568) In the same dispatch, Scopes wrote, 'Mr. Chang denies warmly that any pressure has been on the Nepalese government, whose difficulties he understands perfectly. Far from admitting that Peking is pressing Nepal to end the menace or to allow Chinese troops to enter the Mustang area for this purpose, he states that he has had not even had any conversation or correspondence with the Nepalese Ministry of Defence on the subject'. It may be of interest, therefore, to record when the first official protest by the Chinese to the Nepal government was made. In a dispatch dated September 11, 1963, the British ambassador reported that, 'the Acting Secretary of the Nepalese Ministry of Foreign Affairs told me last week that he had just received, 'for the first time', a sharp protest from the Chinese Embassy about some Khampa raids in the Mustang area across the Tibetan border.'

After dinner, Lama gave his assessment of the danger to Nepal from communist subversion and elaborated on his request for UK assistance:

> P S Lama said that what he really needed was somebody in the British Embassy who could advise him about known Communist agents who entered Nepal from Hong Kong or Singapore and Malaya. He suggested that an officer should be appointed to the embassy who would ostensibly have other functions, but who would 'work with' P S Lama 'for two or three hours a week' on the above lines. He said that such an arrangement would only be known to the IGP, to the King, and to his Principal Military Secretary.

Petrie adds, 'P S Lama then said....(seven and half lines redacted) He implied that British collaboration would be more welcome to him.'

The next paragraph read:

> I asked PS Lama from whom his request came – had he consulted

the King about it? P S Lama said that he had not consulted the King before he made his arrangement (*one and half lines redacted*) The King had replied 'you are the Inspector General of Police, and you must do what you consider best for your department and the country'. He expected that he would get the same answer if he consulted the King again: I did not encourage him to do so.

Document 4

Document 4 is a five-paragraph letter from T J O'Brien, an official at the British High Commission in New Delhi, to E J Emery, an official at the Commonwealth Relations Office in London, dated November 18, 1963. This was written in response to comments attributed to P S Lama in Document 3. O'Brien's main concern was with the envisaged scope of the Information Officer's appointment in the Kathmandu embassy. He warned that what had been approved was 'a discreet and limited brief covering information work' and that it must not expand to take in work 'which could satisfactorily be carried out only by a representative of the friends' – embassy speak for a Secret Intelligence Service/MI6 officer.

Significant redactions appear in the third paragraph of the letter: 'On details, Lama is reported as having hinted he knew... (*Ten lines redacted*)

Document 5

Document 5 is a short two-paragraph letter from E J Emery to T J O'Brien dated February 13, 1964, commenting on Document 4.

Emery writes, 'Your letter of 18th November mentions you having reported recently a categoric denial (two lines redacted) The only such denial I can find on our files is John Bank's letter of 20th July, and the 'denial' mentioned thereon cannot really be described as categoric. Had you anything else in mind?'

Document 6

Document 6 is a short two-paragraph letter from T J O'Brien to E J Emery dated March 2, 1964, in response to the letter that is Document 5.

The first paragraph of the letter reads, 'Thank you for your letter of SEA 55/56/2 of February 13th about. (One line redacted)

Request for an internal review

So, what did Lama 'hint' at the dinner party? It was obvious from context, and from material in other open FCO files, that most of the redactions related to Khampas in Mustang, and specifically about whether the US or India were supporting them. I knew it had to be the US and I assumed that Lama would know that.

As I was interested in the subject, I sent an eight-page submission to the FCO on October 16, 2013, asking for an internal review of the decision to withhold the redacted material. I made a supporting submission on October 23, 2013. In both submissions I highlighted the amount of material that was now in the public domain about Khampas in Mustang and US support for them.

I also submitted a copy of a Minute (taken from File FO 371/176120) from our ambassador in Kathmandu dated August 10, 1964, in which the same P S Lama, whose utterances on the same subject were redacted in FO 371/170877, speaks openly about United States support for Khampas. This included naming a CIA officer who handed over sophisticated equipment to Khampas who were on their way into Tibet via Kathmandu, after their return from training in Colorado. I gave other examples, from open FCO files in the National Archives, of P S Lama privately passing other sensitive information on Khampas to British embassy officials in Kathmandu.

I also sent the FCO a link to a US State Department memorandum2 dated January 9, 1964, which was released in 1998. This memorandum gave budget figures to cover 'the cost of the Tibetan Program for FY 1964'. It specified, among other items, $500,000 allocated for 'Support of 2100 Tibetan guerrillas based in Nepal;' $400,000 allocated for 'Expenses of covert training site in Colorado;' $185,000 for 'Black air transportation of Tibetan trainees from Colorado to India;' and $125,000 for the operating expenses of 'equipment and supplies to reconnaissance teams, caching program, air resupply.'

I particularly highlighted the following extract:

> The Special Group approved the continuation of CIA controlled Tibetan Operations (one line of text redacted) Previous operations had gone to support isolated Tibetan resistance groups within Tibet and to the creation of a paramilitary force on the Nepal/Tibet border

---

2   http://bit.ly/2LrGgF6

of approximately 2,000 men, 800 of whom were armed by (less than one line of text redacted) airdrop in January 1961.

I pointed out to the FCO that it would be harder to get a more emphatic public acknowledgment of US support for Khampas in Mustang. However, the main argument in the submission was based on what I believed to be the FCO's wrong interpretation of section 27 (2) of the FOIA, which clearly refers to 'confidential information obtained from a state.' I specifically asked the FCO to explain how such a clear statement could be used to cover what some foreign national, acting in a private capacity, 'hints' about what he thinks another state might or might not be doing? Such an interpretation of section 27 (2) of the FOIA, I argued, must fall outside both the letter and spirit of this section of the FOIA.

On February 6, 2014, the FCO informed me that the internal review had concluded that some of the withheld material could now be disclosed. I was provided with a new copy of FO 371/170877. A quick check revealed that 'the withheld material now disclosed' amounted to 30 additional, mostly unconnected, words. The FCO again confirmed that the material which remained redacted was exempt from disclosure on the basis of Section 27(2) of FOIA.

Complaint to the Information Commissioner

In sum, all that I submitted, including my questions concerning the applicability of section 27(2), were ignored. On May 8, 2014, I wrote to the Information Commissioner – an independent public body responsible for upholding information rights and data privacy – to complain about the FCO's decision to withhold the remaining information contained in file 371/170877 on the basis of section 27(2) of FOIA. I also complained about the FCO's tardy handling of my request for an internal review. I subsequently complained about the amount of time it took the FCO to engage with the Commissioner's investigation of my complaint.

To back up the complaint, I included the eight pages I had submitted to the FCO as part of my request for an internal review. I also enclosed a list of further references to other open files in the National Archives where PS Lama is quoted as privately passing additional highly sensitive information about Khampas to British officials.

A month later, I was contacted by the Case Officer at the ICO. His letter concluded:

I have now contacted the FCO in relation to your complaint and have asked it to provide me with unredacted copies of the six documents in the file. I have also asked the FCO to provide me with submissions to support its application of section 27(2), particularly in light of your various points of complaint. Once I have received a response from the FCO I will contact you again and provide you with an update on the progress of my investigation.

As the process went on, FCO officials kept changing their arguments and, quite properly, the Case Officer kept passing them to me with an invitation to respond, which I did, most willingly and in full measure.

I sensed that the investigation was going in the right direction when the FCO refused to send the papers to the Case Officer on the grounds that they were so sensitive that they had to be viewed in situ. This introduced a long delay. I told the Case Officer that I was familiar with such stringent security considerations relating to, for example, very sensitive information concerning the UK's independent nuclear deterrent but I doubted very much if we were remotely near such territory.

My confidence in the outcome of my complaint increased considerably when I was informed that the FCO had shifted its defence to claiming that because the information was given at a private dinner party it enjoyed some special protection. In my comments to the Case Officer, I disputed, as a point of principle, the contention that information provided at a private venue and private function should be considered to be confidential forever. Many open files at the National Archives, I suggested, must be littered with examples of such discussions. I also pointed to a number of examples of discussions contained in the related files which, although not occurring at a private dinner party, were nevertheless clearly confidential. Finally, I highlighted the inconsistency of the FCO in redacting ten lines of what was discussed at the dinner party while leaving untouched two pages containing what appeared to be equally sensitive information.

The Information Commissioner's decision notice

On January 20, 2015, nine months after the submission of my complaint, the Information Commissioner published his Decision Notice on the case. It held that except for a few lines which hid the names of two CIA officers, all other redactions should be removed. This screenshot from the ICO website gives the summary of the Decision Notice:

Foreign and Commonwealth Office

20 January 2015, Central government

The complainant submitted a request to the FCO for a copy of a file dating from 1963 concerning Nepal, namely 371/170877 which is entitled 'Conversation with Inspector General of Police about Intelligence Requirements and Counter Subversion'. The FCO provided the complainant with a copy of the file but made redactions to six documents on the basis of section 27(2). The complainant sought to dispute these redactions (with the exception of a name that was redacted from document 3). The Commissioner has concluded that the disputed information, with a number of small exceptions, is not exempt from disclosure on the basis of section 27(2) of FOIA. The Commissioner requires the public authority to provide the complainant with unredacted copies of the documents numbered 1 to 6 in paragraph 9 of this notice. The only redactions which can be made are to certain parts of paragraphs 2 and 6 in document 3. The exact nature of these redactions is identified in the confidential annex, a copy of which will be given to the FCO only. The public authority must take these steps within 35 calendar days of the date of this decision notice. Failure to comply may result in the Commissioner making written certification of this fact to the High Court pursuant to section 54 of the Act and may be dealt with as a contempt of court.

FOI 27: Partly upheld

Decision notice FS50540559

PDF

Screenshot, decision notice.

The full text[3] of the Decision Notice makes for interesting reading. It shows both the increasingly spurious reasons the FCO advanced for maintaining the redactions, and the rigor with which the Information Commissioner exposes them as, essentially, not worth the paper they are written on. The Commissioner clearly paid close attention to my arguments, and impressively turned the FCO's own arguments against itself. This section of the article highlights some key points from the Decision Notice.

Most revealing is that the FCO never once quoted the correct section of the Freedom of Information Act in support of their assertion that release of the information would jeopardize the UK's relations with another country. To quote from the Decision Notice:

> However, section 27(2) exemption cannot be engaged simply on the basis that disclosure would prejudice relations with another State. Rather it is section 27(1)(a) of FOIA that provides an exemption for information if its disclosure would, or would be likely, to prejudice

---

3   http://bit.ly/2O4VU8b. If the link given does not work type in the case reference, FS50540559, on the ICO webpage.

relations with another State. The FCO has not cited this exemption.'
(Para 27)

The redactions made in Document 1 were given short shrift:

(In) the Commissioner's opinion the information redacted from
document 1 consists simply of the comments of UK officials about
information provided by PS Lama at the dinner party in question.
However, the information in question which the officials are
commenting on does not form part of the information that has
been redacted from document 3. Rather it consists of comments by
UK officials on information provided by PS Lama that has already
disclosed in the version document 3 that has been provided to the
complaint. Therefore, in the Commissioner's opinion it cannot
be argued that the information redacted from document 1 is
information which is confidential for the purpose of section 27(2)'.
(Para 31)

The Decision Notice had the following to say on the FCO's request to
examine the file in situ:

In its response the FCO explained that it required a representative
of the Commissioner's office to view the withheld information at it
offices given its sensitivity. In response the Commissioner explained
that he would prefer to be provided with a copy of the information
and in an exchange of emails, culminating on 25 September 2014, he
provided the FCO with details of the process he had in place for the
secure storage and viewing of such information. In an email of the
same date, the FCO confirmed that it would now send the withheld
information to the Commissioner. The Commissioner received a copy
of the withheld information on 31 October 2014. (Para 43)

The FCO's delay in responding to the request for the file led to the
following censure:

The Commissioner aims to conclude 90% of the complaints he
receives within 6 months of receipt. The delay in the FCO providing
him with a response to his letter of 3 July, and then its delay in
providing him with a copy of the withheld information, impaired

the Commissioner's ability to conclude this complaint within that timeframe. (Para 44)

The Commissioner also dismissed FCO's contention that special protection should be given to the information because it was shared at a private dinner party:

> The Commissioner agrees with the complainant that the disclosure of document 3 in a redacted form undermines the FCO's application of section 27(2) to withhold the remaining information... (He) notes that the FCO has only redacted a relatively small amount of information from document 3. In other words, it has disclosed the majority of the information provided to the UK officials by PS Lama during the course of the dinner party... Furthermore, the FCO's submissions to the Commissioner do not comment on the difference, or potential difference, between the content of the disclosed information and the redacted information.' (Para 32)

The ICO's guideline for carrying out internal reviews is 20 working days for most reviews and 40 days for complex cases. The time the FCO took in this case led the Information Commissioner to make the following criticism:

> It therefore took the FCO 78 working days to complete its internal review. The Commissioner considers this to be unsatisfactory. In the future he expects the FCO to ensure that internal reviews are completed within the timeframes set out within his guidance. (Para 41)

What information was redacted?

Within the time limit stipulated of 35 calendar days from the date of the decision notice, the FCO sent me the file again, following the ICO's order to remove the specified redactions. These are highlighted below in italics.

Document 1

The six minor redactions had been removed, all of which referred to the intelligence support the US was giving to Nepal, and the need for the UK to consult with the US before responding to any separate request.

Document 2

Paragraph 2: 'To me the most interesting points *were the details about American intelligence relations with the Nepalese* and PS Lama's own request for British assistance.'

Document 3

Paragraph 2: 'Before dinner the IGP spoke about his troubles with the Khampas in the Mustang area, whose numbers he gave as 6-8000. It had been expected that these Khampas would spend their time raiding across the border into Tibet: PS Lama hinted *that he knew the Indians were supplying them for this purpose* (one line still redacted).'

Paragraph 6: 'P S Lama then said *that he already had an arrangement with the Americans* (Two and half lines still redacted) *P S Lama thought that they were both from the CIA, but did not seem very definite about this.* He implied that British collaboration would be more welcome to him.

Paragraph 7: 'I asked PS Lama from whom his request came – had he consulted the King about it? P S Lama said that he had not consulted the King before he made his arrangement *with the Americans. (He did not say from which side the initiative for this came, but I imagine from the Americans)* The King had replied 'you are the Inspector General of Police, and you must do what you consider best for your department and the country'. He expected that he would get the same answer if he consulted the King again: I did not encourage him to do so.

Document 4

Paragraph 3: 'On details, Lama is reported as having 'hinted he knew that *the Indians were supplying the Khampas in the Mustang area for raids in Tibet'; we have reported recently a categoric denial from External Affairs that the Indians were doing so, and, even if this cannot be taken at its face value, we are at a loss to think why the Indians should waste resources in paying Khampas to needle the Chinese, a proceeding likely to provoke the Nepalese also and hardly consistent with their military policy towards China on the Sino-Indian border. It seems a good deal more likely to us that this is a story devised by the Chinese to embarrass the Indians vis-à-vis the Nepalese; it seems that they succeed.*

Document 5

Paragraph 2: Your letter of 18th November mentions your having reported recently a categoric denial *from the Indian External Affairs*

Department that the Indians were supplying the Khampas. The only such denial I can find on our files is John Banks' letter of 20th July, and the 'denial' mentioned therein cannot really be described as categoric. Had you something else in mind?

Document 6
Paragraph 1: Thank you for your letter SEA 55/56/2 of February 13 *about the Indian connection with the Khampas.*

Assessment of information released
Fifty-three years on from the events described, the information revealed by these previous redactions is unremarkable and, from the point of view of my research interest, rather disappointing. So much for the FCO's claim that 'it required a representative of the Commissioner's office to view the withheld information at it offices given its sensitivity.'

However, there is one glaring revelation. All the redactions which the FCO fought so tenaciously to protect are linked to IGP Lama telling the two people at the dinner party that it was the Indians who were supporting the Khampas in Mustang. This was incorrect. From start to finish, the Khampas in Mustang were supported exclusively by the CIA, as I highlighted to the FCO in my request for an internal review.

Before the Indo-China War of 1962 (October 20 – November 21), India had not been officially informed of the CIA support to the Mustang force, although the Indian military checkpost at Jomsom must have had some idea of what was going on. During the war, India started to recruit Tibetan refugees in India to form a guerrilla force of 5,000 to operate behind Chinese lines. (Later known as 'Establishment 22' and later still as the 'Special Frontier Force.') After the war, during a meeting was held in Delhi on November 21, 1962, with a US delegation led by Averell Harriman, it was agreed that the Indians, with CIA support, would work together to develop the new 5000-strong tactical guerrilla force. The Mustang force would remain under the CIA's unilateral control and, in addition, the CIA would unilaterally create a strategic long-range resistance force to operate inside Tibet.

This required bringing more Tibetans to Colorado for training. The aim was to produce self-sufficient three or four-man radio teams that would infiltrate overland into Tibet to report intelligence and organize underground groups that would resist Chinese rule. The plan would also create two 'road-watch teams' to report possible Chinese Communist build-ups and another six 'border watch communications teams' to take up positions along the frontier. In September 1963, the CIA obtained India's agreement to open a joint operations centre in New Delhi that would direct the dispatch of agents into Tibet and monitor their activities. Some of these teams were inserted through northeast Nepal, but they were separate from the Mustang force, which remained, as it had from the outset, exclusively under CIA control for operations and logistical support.

Where is File FO 371/170877 now?

Following the publication of the Information Commissioner's Decision Notice, dated 20 January 2015, the FCO should have released FO 371/170877 to the National Archives. But, as I was to find out, a researcher trying to locate it on the National Archives Discovery webpage could easily be misled. Typing in FO 371/1708774 on the National Archive's search engine takes one to this page.

FO 371/170877

Foreign Office: Political Departments: General Correspondence from 1906-1966. FAR EASTERN (F): Nepal (FN).

Held by:	The National Archives - Foreign Office
Date:	1963
Reference:	FO 371/170877
Subjects:	Indian Subcontinent | International

Closed extract: Jacket FN 1691/2G: record of conversation on 12/10/1963

Foreign Office: Political Departments: General Correspondence from 1906-1966. FAR EASTERN (F): Nepal (FN). Closed extract: Jacket FN 1691/2G: record of conversation on 12/10/1963.

Held by:	The National Archives - Foreign Office
Date:	1963
Reference:	FO 371/170877/1
Subjects:	Indian Subcontinent | International

Screenshot of the page.

The first The first instinct is to look at what it says about, 'Closed extract: Jacket FN 1691/2G; record of a conversation on 12/10/1963.' FN 1691/2/G should be familiar: it is the reference at the top right hand corner of the first page of the six documents the FCO originally sent to me. The 'record of conversation on 12/10/1963' must, therefore,

Reference:	FO 371/170877/1
Description:	Closed extract: Jacket FN 1691/2G: record of conversation on 12/10/1963
Date:	1963
Held by:	The National Archives, Kew
Legal status:	Public Record(s)
Closure status:	Closed Or Retained Document, Open Description
Access conditions:	Closed For 60 years
Review date:	2014
Exemption 1:	International Relations - prejudice
Exemption 2:	International Relations - Information Provided in Confidence
Record opening date:	01 January 2024

Screenshot of the page.

relate to the same conversation with Inspector General of Police about Intelligence requirements and Counter-subversion which took place on October 12, 1963. It appears, therefore, that what the FCO previously designated as File FO 371/170877, with its six documents, has somehow metamorphosed into Jacket FN 1691/2G, though now given the reference of FO/371/170877/1. This view is reinforced by clicking on 'Closed extract: Jacket FN 1691/2/G[4],' which brings one to the following page. Again, this looks like the original FO 371/170877 file which, apparently, despite the judgements given in the Information Commissioner's Decision Notice, the FCO has determined must be kept closed until January 1, 2024. The same two exemptions which the Information Commissioner so comprehensively dismissed are apparently retained. However, common sense dictates that, after the publication of the Information Commissioner's Decision Notice, the FCO must have released to the National Archives the six-document file originally designated as FO 371/170877, despite this web page suggesting otherwise. So, where is it? Clicking on FO 371/170877[5] on the original search result takes one to the page below.

---

4 http://bit.ly/2LBWsjZ
5 http://bit.ly/2O06zRk

Reference:	FO 371/170877
Description:	Intelligence and counter-subversion
Date:	1963-1964
Held by:	The National Archives, Kew
Former reference in its original department:	File 1691
Legal status:	Public Record(s)
Closure status:	Open Document, Open Description
Access conditions:	Retained Until 2016
Record opening date:	07 December 2016

Screenshot of the page.

The original File FO 371/170877 had the meaningful and helpful description of, 'Conversation with Inspector General of Police about Intelligence Requirements and Counter Subversion'. The file with the same designation is now given the abstract general description of 'Intelligence and counter-subversion' which is far too vague to be helpful. The page states that it was retained by the FCO until 07 December 2016, when it was released to the National Archives, some 10 months after the ICO's Decision Notice was published. But what documents does it contain? What new information might be in it?

There was only one way to find out. Early on the morning of June 27, 2017, I left our house in Oxford and left for the National Archives at Kew. I arrived some time after noon – a little agitated after having taken the Reading to Waterloo line to Richmond which rightly lived up to its reputation for being one of the slowest and most unreliable lines in England – but consoling myself that this was duty, in the battle for information.

After going through the usual security checks, I collected FO 371/170877 and walked to my reserved place in the reading room to study the file, noting immediately that it was particularly thin and in a newish-looking folder. When I opened the folder, this familiar page appeared but this time not a photo copy (see facing page).

A quick check showed that the file contained the same six documents which have been the subject of this article, with redactions removed as directed in the Decision Notice – and nothing else. The only material which had not been sent to me were very short handwritten comments on two 'With Compliments' slips.

Photo of page.

Having undergone this elaborate exercise, the first question which springs to mind is why the FCO, on the National Archives website, did not give the same description to FO 371/170877, as it had given in all previous correspondence with both me and the ICO; namely, 'Conversation with Inspector General of Police about Intelligence Requirements and Counter Subversion'? Why the deliberate opaqueness? Why the apparent obfuscation? The same two questions apply to its apparent double, FO 371/170877/1 or 'Jacket FN 1691/2G: record of conversation on 12/10/1963'. Record of a conversation about what and with whom? It is worth noting that the FN 1691/2G reference links it to the same conversation discussed at length in this article.

Some answers suggest themselves, none of which reflect well on the FCO; but they are of no consequence. All that matters is that an information battle was won, and FO 371/170877 is in the National Archives, and open for inspection.

As for Dudley Spain, doyen of old Nepal hands, he left his collection of extensive papers to the Gurkha Museum in Winchester. As yet, no reference has been found to what being an 'Information Officer with an IRD slant' entailed. However, all those who knew him in Nepal at the time, when broached on the subject, voiced the same suspicion: there was more to what Dudley did than any of his mere job titles suggested.

References

Knaus, John Kenneth. 'Official Policies and Covert Programs: The U.S. State Department, the CIA, and the Tibetan Resistance'. *Journal of War Studies*, 2003.

United States of America. 'China Memorandum for the Special Group', *Foreign Relations of the United States, 1964–1968*, Volume XXX. Office of the Historian.

United Kingdom, Decision Notice FS50540559 regarding Freedom of Information Act 2000 (FOIA) dated January 20, 2015. Information Commissioner's Office.

United Kingdom. 'Intelligence and counter-subversion'. The National Archives.

United Kingdom. 'Closed extract: Jacket FN 1691/2G: record of conversation on 12/10/1963'. The National Archives.

This article has been republished with permission from *The Record*. The original can be found online at: https://www.recordnepal.com/ wire/features/secret-nepal-file-foreign-commonwealth-office- nepal-information-khampa

Addendum May 2017

Given the Addendum added to 'Prisoners of War' earlier (pp. 136-147), it is pertinent to point out that that although this file (371/170877) was released to me with redactions on 11 Oct 2013, following my Freedom of Information request, it was not subsequently released to the National Archives, as it should have been. This was done, albeit under a changed name, in 7 Dec 2016, some 10 months after the ICO's Decision Notice was published, and more than three years after the file was first released to me.

It is wrong that the FCO should treat a FOI request as a personal plea to read a file. In such cases, release of a file to the National Archives should be automatic and immediate. In sum, it should follow the rules.